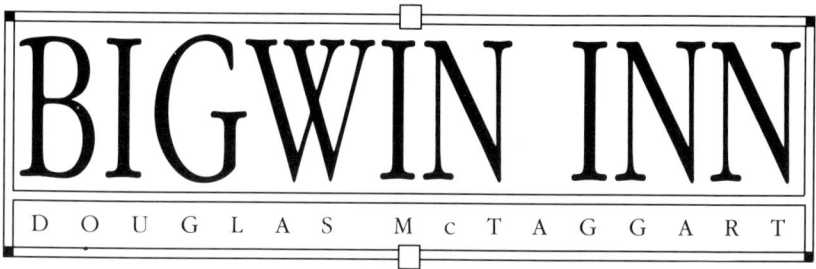

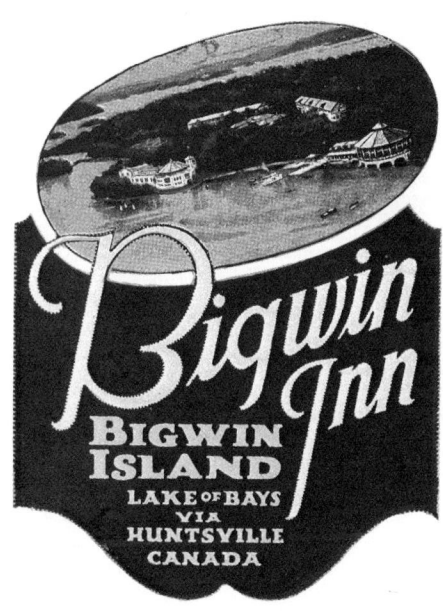

To holiday in Muskoka meant packing a full summer wardrobe. A steamer trunk label ensured proper delivery of guests' belongings to Canada's largest and finest summer resort, Bigwin Inn. Once received, luggage was quickly and conveniently unpacked by a battalion of housekeeping staff.
- *DGM*

BIGWIN INN

DOUGLAS McTAGGART

Stoddart — A BOSTON MILLS PRESS BOOK

Canadian Cataloguing in Publication Data

McTaggart, Douglas
  Bigwin Inn

ISBN 1-55046-035-8

1. Bigwin Inn – History. 2. Hotels, taverns, etc. – Ontario – Bigwin Islands – History. 3. Resorts – Ontario – Bigwin Island – History. I. Title.

TX941.B44M33 1992   647.94713′1601   C92-093910-4

© 1992 Douglas McTaggart

Cover Design by Gillian Stead
Design and Typography by Lexigraf, Tottenham
Printed in Canada

First published in 1992 by:
Stoddart Publishing Co. Ltd.
34 Lesmill Road
Toronto, Ontario Canada M3B 2T6
(416) 445-3333 Fax: (416) 445-5967

A BOSTON MILLS PRESS BOOK
132 Main Street
Erin, Ontario N0B 1T0
(519) 833-2407 Fax: (519) 833-2195

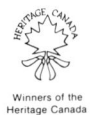
Winners of the Heritage Canada Communications Award

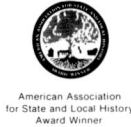
American Association for State and Local History Award Winner

The publisher wishes to acknowledge the support of the Canada Council, the Ontario Arts Council and the Ontario Publishing Centre in the development of writing and publishing in Canada.

Front cover photo:
Lady Eaton's private yacht, the 95-foot steamer *Wanda III,* was added to Bigwin's flotilla for the 1931 season. Pictured are Captain Elder and Allan Thaxter Shaw. An edition of the *Bigwin Banter* dated Saturday, August 26, 1939, noted: "Tea on the *Wanda III* was a delightful part of the cruise over Lake of Bays to which Mrs. C.O. Shaw invited thirty ladies, guests at Bigwin Inn. During the cruise Miss Amy Fleming, Toronto, and Mrs. Olive Barlow Blakely, Hamilton, sang for them from the deck of the *Wanda.* On the return trip a presentation was made to Mrs. Shaw on behalf of the Bigwin Ladies' Friendship Club by the president, Mrs. Graham Lackner."

This book is dedicated with love to the late M.E.H.H. and E.E.J., my dear friend P.J.T. and to my family: my sisters, father and, in particular, to my mother, who has been instrumental in the writing of this book.

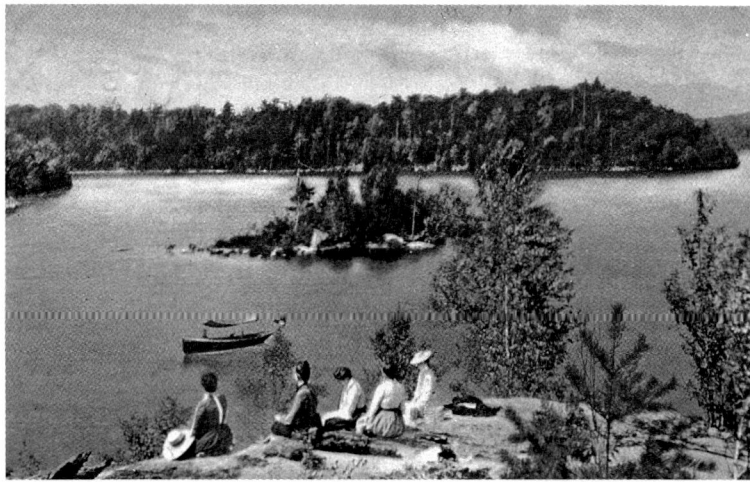
In August 1907, tourists from Baysville travelled to Burnt Island for an afternoon picnic. One of the earliest motor boats on the Lake of Bays, the *Monitor,* cuts the channel between the island and the mainland.   - *DGM*

Opposite: Many of the monolithic buildings of Bigwin Inn were arranged along the natural curve of the island's shoreline. One advertisement read: "Bigwin Inn, one of America's finest summer resorts, is as an architectural jewel amid spacious lawns and shady trees on historic Bigwin Island, 1,100 feet above sea-level, in the beautiful Lake of Bays, the most delightful section of the famed Muskoka District in the Highlands of Ontario."   - *Ontario Archives AO127*

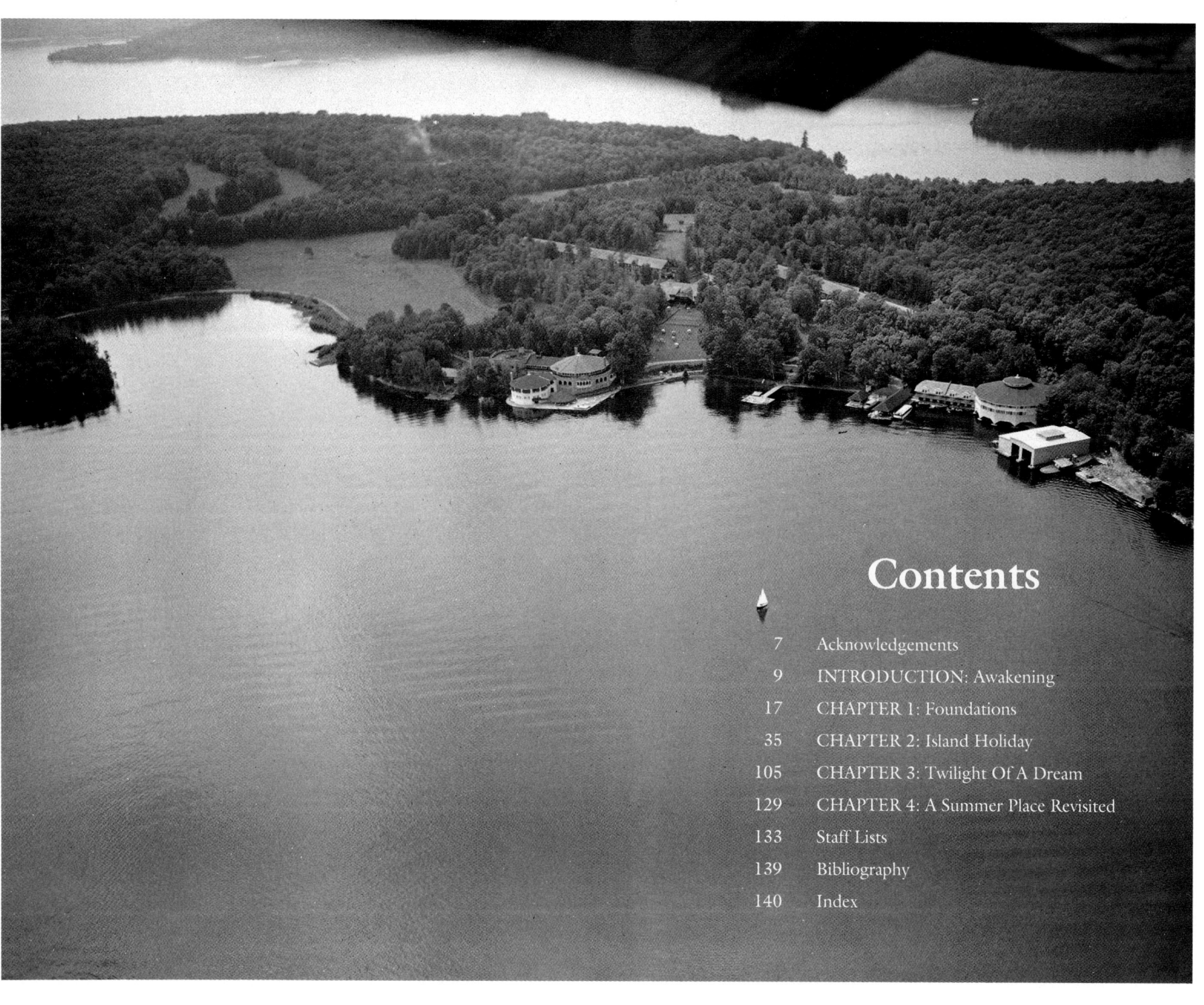

Contents

7	Acknowledgements
9	INTRODUCTION: Awakening
17	CHAPTER 1: Foundations
35	CHAPTER 2: Island Holiday
105	CHAPTER 3: Twilight Of A Dream
129	CHAPTER 4: A Summer Place Revisited
133	Staff Lists
139	Bibliography
140	Index

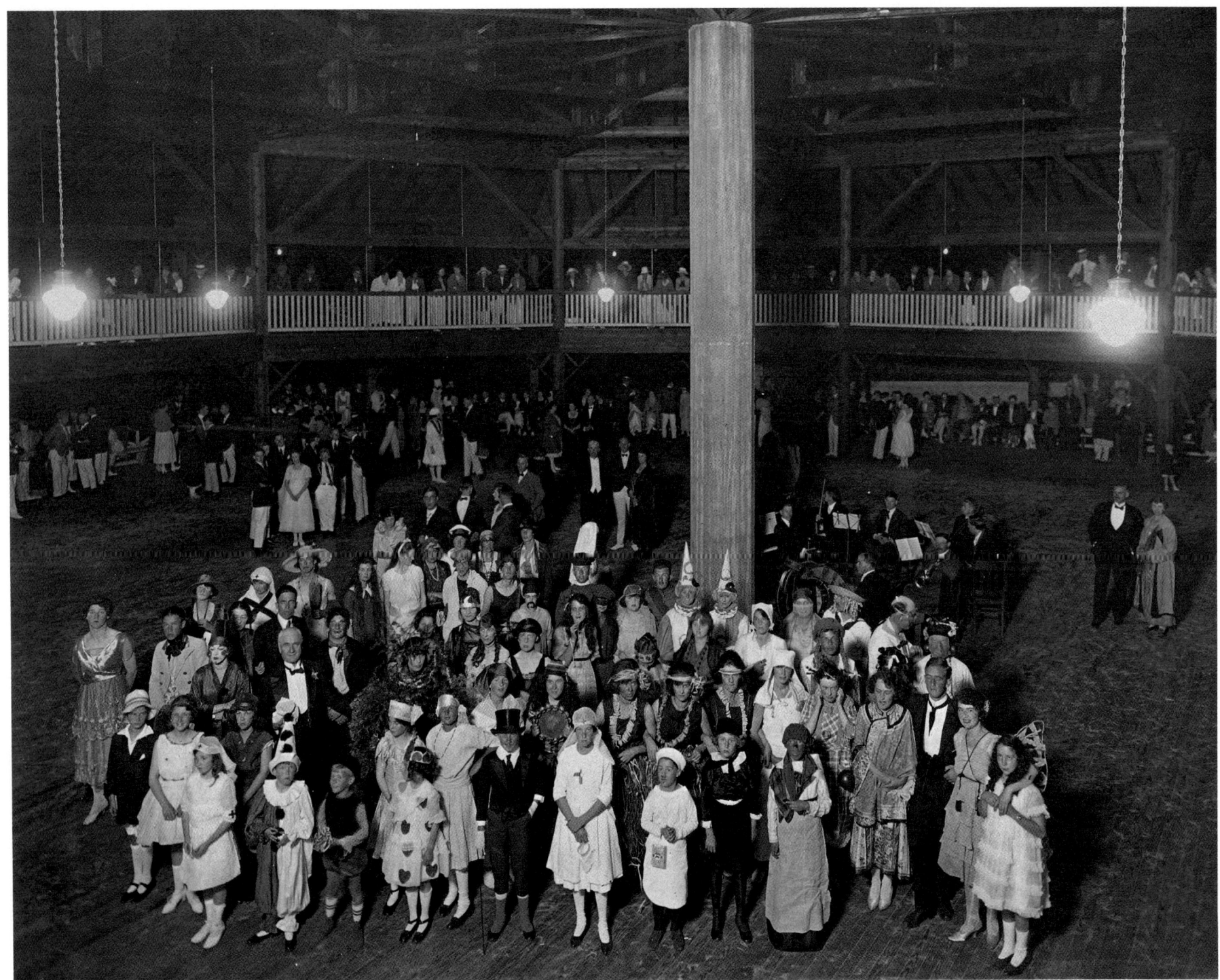

From the Gatsby-like era of the 1920s onward, glittering masquerade balls in the Pavilion were highlights of the operating season with formal attire *de rigueur*.   - *Helen E. O'Connor*

Acknowledgements

The history of Bigwin Inn is one which spans several decades. Through those years, thousands of people came to know the magnificent resort. Today, the Muskoka landmark is still the subject of great interest and speculation as many reminisce about her glory days or travel to the island harbour to marvel at the majestic buildings that grace the shoreline.

Surprisingly little has been written on this great symbol of Canadian heritage. Recapturing some of the rare moments in Bigwin's colourful history has required the assistance of many people. The author extends his sincere appreciation to them all for their kind assistance and co-operation:

Additional words of thanks go to the Royal Netherlands Embassy, Global Television News, CBC Radio's Ontario Morning, Canada Life Assurance Company, Manulife Financial, Muskoka Publications Group Limited, McMichael Canadian Art Collection, Muskoka Pioneer Village, Canadian National Exhibition Archives, Simcoe County Archives, Ontario Archives, National Archives of Canada, Artists' Legal Advice Services, Central Reference Library of Toronto and the public libraries at Baysville, Bracebridge and Huntsville.

Mr. Hal Avery
Mr. James Mackay Avery
Mr. Frank Bogart
Mr. Bill Butt
Mr. and Mrs. Bill Bramah
Mrs. Edith Cardy
Mr. Gregory J. Clark
Mr. Abbott Conway
Mr. Douglas Conway
Mr. J.B. Cookson
Mr. Walter Cracknel
Dr. Hugh B. Croxton
Mr. Hillel Diamond
Mr. Tony DiNardo
Mrs. J. Dixon
Mrs. Phyllis Dodds
Mr. Donald J. Donahue
Dr. James Duthie
Mr. William G. Elliott
Mr. S. Moir Forsythe
Dr. Paul W. Fox
Mr. Charles Gill
Mr. Luke Hawkins
Mrs. H.C. Hindmarsh
Mr. and Mrs. Dennis Hook
Mrs. Sandra (Lobraico) Horkins
Mrs. Roxie Joy Hosking
Mr. George LaFleche
Mr. Gordon Langille
Mr. Jack Leacock
Mr. Frank Mills Leslie
Ms. Gisele MacKenzie
Ms. Mary Mastin
Ms. Lois Maxwell
Mr. Robert McLennan
Mrs. Barbara Mills
Ms. Jennifer Mills
Mrs. Helen O'Connor
Mr. Mario Pesando
Ms. Ann (Reid) Platt
Mr. and Mrs. Walter Preston
Ms. Jill Ransom
Mr. Robert Ransom
Mrs. Shirley (Kirby) Ransom
Mrs. Marye Sefl
Mr. Allan Thaxter Shaw
Mr. Charles Wellington Shaw
Mr. Donald R. Shaw
Mr. Geoffrey B. Shaw
Mr. Walter Brackley Shaw
Ms. Darlene Solomon
Ms. Linda Stanford
Mr. and Mrs. Alan Tasker
Mr. Ed. Terziano
Miss Ruth Tinkiss
Mrs. Margaret (Kirby) Tolton
Ms. Marie Rose (Reid) Tosoni
Mrs. Chicho Valle
Mr. Mike Wain
Mr. Hart Wheeler
Mr. Glen Williams
Mr. and Mrs. John McAllister Wilson

Bigwin Island (or Bigwin's Island as it was noted on an 1864 map) was the meeting place of native hunters and white traders. After the signing of the Williams Treaty, native camps, trails and portages fell silent.
- *DGM*

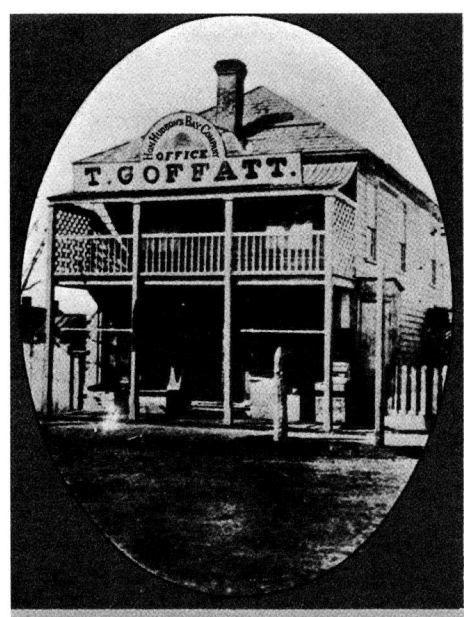

HUDSON'S BAY FACTORY, AT ORILLIA, 80 YEARS AGO

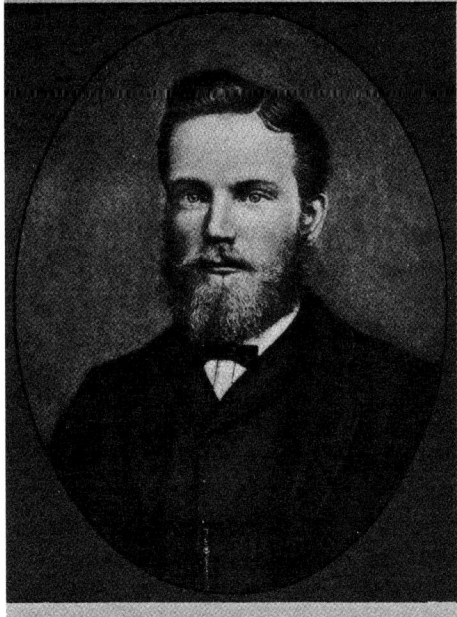

THOMAS GOFFATT, FACTOR, MUSKOKA POST, UPPER CANADA

ROMANTIC TRAILS OF THE FUR TRADER

Bigwin Island has an historic and storied past through which the shadows of Indian hunters, fur traders and hardy settlers come and go with the passing of the years. In the ancient days of unrecorded history, Iroquois warriors prowled Muskoka's frontiers in search of furs and scalps, only to withdraw in snarling defeat.

Bigwin Island was named after a noted Ojibway warrior and hunter, Chief Joseph Big Wind, whose village stood a short distance from Bigwin Inn, back in the first half of the last century. In the Sixties, the Hudson's Bay Co., established a trading post under the jurisdiction of Factor Thomas Goffatt, at Orillia. It was a small, roughcast building and the clerk-in-charge lived above the store where the trading was done.

When the air was brittle with frost and evergreens bent under their heaping weight of snow, the crunch of snowshoes would be heard on ice-locked waterways, as men of the Bigwin post, beards frosted white, would drag toboggans loaded with furs to the main factory at Orillia. In the time of the Spring Beaver Hunt, these "runners" would go forth into the district, camp at the regular points of trade, usually where the fresh-running rivers emptied into Lake of Bays, set up their duck tents and wait for the Indians to come.

In these days of the winter break-up the shore-line would take on a strange appearance. Camp fires would burn against the dark outline of the forest and Indian wigwams would stand black in the flame's red flare. It was here that the trading was done. Mink, otter, fisher and martin, beaver, bear, raccoon and muskrat were taken for money and credit at the Hudson's Bay factory, at Orillia. Then the furs were freighted by canoes to the Orillia storehouses.

So great was the catch of furs each season that Lake of Bays was once known as "Trading Lake"; but the Indians withdrew before the settlers and towns, such as Huntsville and Bracebridge, grew up where the forest once stood. The sweep of Lake of Bays is so long and wide that much of it escaped the settler's axe, and Bigwin Island, today, is magnificently wooded, providing an ideal setting for one of the finest summer resorts on the continent.

INTRODUCTION

Awakening

The story of the Bigwin Inn is like the saga of a small town, one that was born in the Ontario wilderness and flourished for over five decades. Its historical roots reach back to the early development of Muskoka, when Indians canoed the lake waters, explorers first attempted to chart the unknown land, and settlers and industries eventually moved to the new frontier.

The first known human inhabitants of Muskoka's wilderness were a nomadic group of Algonquin Indians. The Ojibway tribe (whose name, translated, means "people whose moccasins have puckered seams") traditionally came to the pristine lakeland to hunt, fish and collect wild berries. For generations, they continued to summer in the Muskoka area, particularly on the lake named "Nagatoagomon" (or Nun-ge-low-e-nee-goo-mark-lak-a-hagan), an extensive water system with short portages that offered a viable travel route to and from various hunting grounds and trading posts. In time, this great body of water also became known as "Baptiste Lake," named by Lieutenant Henry Briscoe of the Royal Engineers; "Forked Lake" or "Lake of Two Bays," named by the early surveyor David Thompson; and was finally renamed "The Lake of Bays" by Alexander Murray of the Geological Survey of Canada in 1853.

The various explorers who travelled the Lake of Bays were often captivated by its spectacular scenery. Its sublimely beautiful shoreline of thickly wooded forest winds around the many bays for over 350 miles, with gently sloping hills at one end and rising cliffs at the other. In many of the lake's bays, golden sand beaches stretch into sparkling blue-black waters which drop to a maximum depth of 231 feet. Rising from these dark depths are numerous sylvan islands, among them Bigwin, Burnt, Crown, Fairview, Langmaid's and Maria Bianca.

Bigwin Island, the largest of them, measures 2½ miles in length by ½ a mile in width and is located mid-channel on the Lake of Bays. Both the island and a small lake situated south of it are named for Chief Joseph Big Wind of Lake Simcoe, whose signature endorses several land surrenders of the 1830s and 1850s. Chief Big Wind and his tribe established three large, sacred burial grounds on the island, though the specific grave sites were respectfully undocumented. Also on the island, the tribe established a summer settlement facing the rising sun and Haystack Bay. The tribe traded beaver, marten, bear and raccoon pelts for money, credit or various supplies brought by the Hudson's Bay Company to a site near the Ojibway encampment. This trading site was established by Thomas Goffat, the company's factor at Orillia, in the late 1860s.

In the same period, the Muskoka area was opened up to pioneers under the Homestead Act. With an influx of settlers, significant native land holdings were acquired through various treaties. Many Indians were relocated to reserves, such as Rama on the east side of Lake Couchiching. Others faced the horror of residential schools, where they were stripped of their religion, mythology and language, and forced to assimilate into white culture. With the brutal rape of the Indian society, the native trails, portages, encampments and villages soon fell silent.

In exchange for $242.66, two-thirds of Bigwin Island was patented by the Crown to Clark Benton Bridgland of York on November 23, 1875, and registered in 1881. The remaining third of Bigwin Island (excluding the 66-foot-wide road allowance around the perimeter) was patented to Henry Hugh Bridgland for $121.33.

As white society established itself on this new frontier called Muskoka, great new industries developed. The timber industry boomed in the 1880s and vast tracts of land were logged, including Bigwin Island, where a local resident, Edward Boothby, felled stands of softwood trees. As land was cleared around the lakes, various homesteads sprang up and an attempt was made at farming. When the shallow soil of the Precambrian Shield proved unfit for farming, many settlers opened their homes to tourists as an alternative means of generating income. From the log home of Edmund James Gouldie, telegraph company operator Harvey Prentiss Dwight (later president of the Great Northern Telegraph Company) and renowned newspaper editor Erastus Wiman led hunting and fishing expeditions to Bigwin Island and elsewhere on the Lake of Bays.

As the Muskoka lakes grew in popularity, there was a greater demand for tourist facilities. The Northern Railroad was one of the first to capitalize on this burgeoning new industry by establishing reliable and, most importantly, quicker transportation from Toronto to the town of Gravenhurst. By 1899 the Grand Trunk Railroad had laid a rail line between Gravenhurst and Huntsville. From the town's wharf, the Huntsville Navigation Company's boats extended service, penetrating the interior wilderness through the vast network of lakes. Through the years, dozens of boats would ply the waters while serving as work, freight, mail, supply and passenger conveyances.

With increased accessibility to the northern Muskoka lakes, a growing number of settlers and tourists from both American and Canadian cities travelled north to Muskoka. Property values rose as droves of visitors stayed in all types of available accommodation, from the rustic camp to the fashionable grand frame hotel. By the late 1800s, the flourishing villages of Baysville, Dorset and Dwight began to support a broad selection of tourist facilities on the Lake of Bays. Hotels operating around the turn of the century or shortly thereafter included Gouldie House, Hotel Britannia, Ronville Lodge, Iroquois Hotel, Ganoseyo, Port Cunnington Lodge, New Moon Lodge, Burlmarie House, Langton House, White House and Point Pleasant. While many people simply visited for their summer holidays, others took advantage of the new employment and business opportunities available in the bustling hamlets and towns.

In 1859 a gentleman named Brackley Shaw II travelled from the United States to Canada to assess the economic viability of operating a leather-tanning business. Subsequently, F. Shaw and Brothers acquired the tannery of John Pratt at Roxton Falls, Quebec. In the following years, other tanneries were established in Quebec and Ontario, where an abundance of hemlock trees offered ample supplies of tan bark. In Muskoka, the year 1891 saw Shaw, Cassils and Company establish a tannery along Huntsville's riverside, on the former Centre Street property of Allan Shay. A member of the Shaw family would eventually play an unprecedented role in the development of this industry and, in turn, the region of Muskoka. His name was Charles Orlando Shaw.

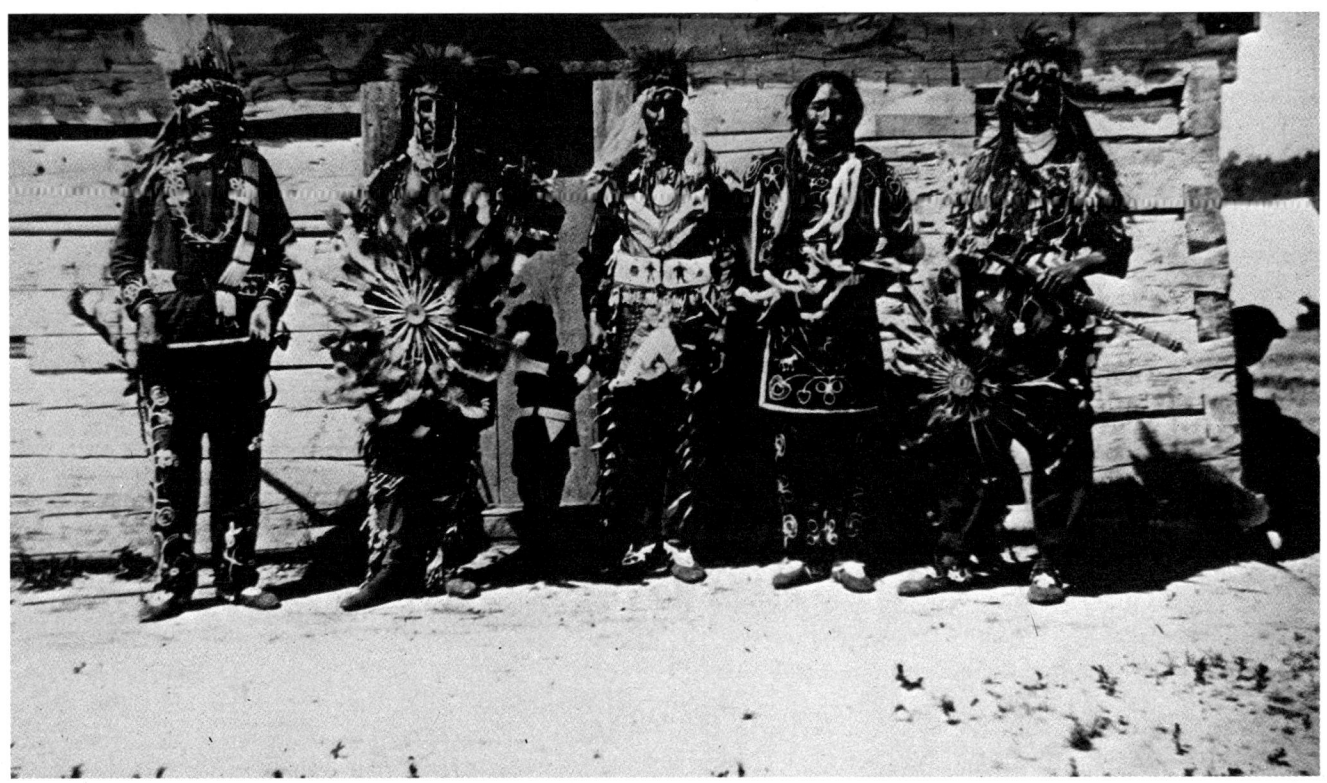

By the 19th century, Ojibway (Chippewa) ceremonial dress was significantly influenced by European trade. Glass beads, thread, woven cloth and silver brooches were often used in the composition and adornment of work executed for symbolic, magical or heraldic purposes.
- *Ontario Archives 6785 312251*

Chief Bigwin

During the summer months, particularly in the 1930s, Chief John Bigwin was a familiar sight in Huntsville and Bracebridge, riding in the sidecar of a motorcycle, playing his autoharp or singing hymns.

Descendant of Chief Joseph Big Wind, Chief Bigwin was a member of the Salvation Army, having joined in 1905. He gave up the use of tobacco and liquor, and would often warn of the horrors which its excesses brought to men. One of his many great stories recounted the day when he placed his last bottle of liquor on a log chute and let it drift downstream.

In 1936, with limited sight, Chief Bigwin led a colourful war dance on the steps of the Huntsville Town Hall and was the honoured guest at a subsequent banquet in celebration of the town's Golden Jubilee.

In 1938, at the age of 100, Chief Bigwin participated in a protest against the laying of criminal charges against four Indians for what was alleged to be illegal fishing. Attired in full Indian regalia, the small Chief travelled to an Orillia court of law and demanded that his children not be prosecuted. Supporting his case, he waved a declaration from Queen Victoria stating that "as long as the grass grows and the water runs, he and his people may hunt and fish." During his life, Bigwin was also presented to the King and Queen of England, welcomed Lord Tweedsmuir to Muskoka, and went to Ottawa to participate in a lengthy discussion of treaty rights.

Shortly after the discussion, he returned to Bigwin Island to select his burial spot. In spite of his age and handicaps, Chief Bigwin easily found one of the sites where over 30 graves were located. Kneeling over the graves of his parents, his brother Bob and his Aunt Maria, Chief Bigwin began to softly sing a beautiful Indian burial ritual. When it was finished, he designated the specific spot where he chose to have his body buried. However, because the Chief survived those who knew of the site, he was never laid to rest in the spot which he had chosen on Bigwin Island.

On July 13, 1940, after ten days of illness at the Rama Reserve on the shores of Lake Couchiching, Chief Bigwin (his name, translated, was Chevodin, which means "big tent") passed away at the age of 102 years or 1,223 moons. The hereditary leader of his tribe had survived his wives and children. His great-grandson Bill Bigwin, the last remaining male relative, returned to Bigwin Island aboard the *Wanda III* in the summer of 1990. It was the first time that he had visited the island since his early childhood. In the spring of 1991, he passed away at approximately 81 years of age.

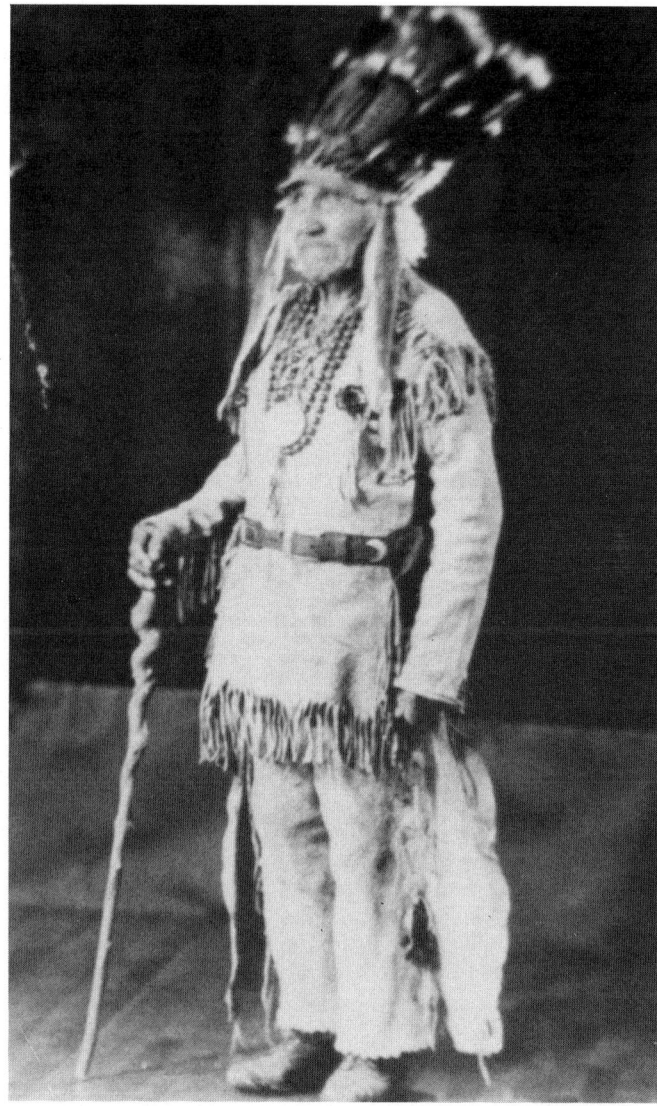

Bigwin Island is located in an area that was once the most northern sector of Ojibway hunting grounds. In the 1940s, Chief John Bigwin said: "My grandfather had over 2,000 acres of land before white men took some of it. Mackenzie King is one of the greatest of the chiefs of the white men. I went to see him one time to make him give back to the Indians the land the bad white men stole from us long ago. Mr. King shook my hand and said he was glad to meet a chief like myself, but he was sorry he couldn't make the bad white men give back my land because it happened so long ago."
- *Hal Avery and James Mackay Avery*

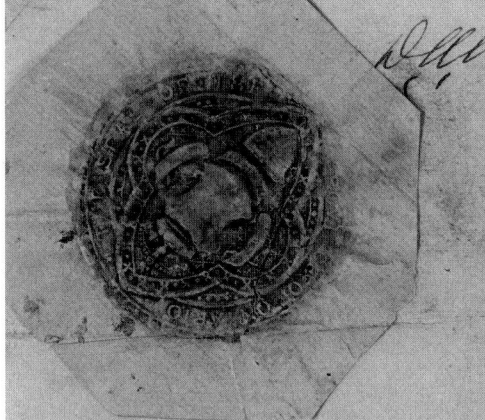

Province of Ontario.

Victoria, by the Grace of GOD, of the United Kingdom of Great Britain and Ireland, QUEEN, Defender of the Faith, &c., &c. &c.

To all to whom these Presents shall come—GREETING:

Whereas, *Henry Hugh Bridgland*, of the *Township of York* of the *County of York, Yeoman*,

hath contracted and agreed for the absolute purchase of the Lands and Tenements hereinafter mentioned and described, at and for the price or sum of *One hundred and Twenty one Dollars and thirty three cents* of lawful money of Canada, and of which Lands We are seized in right of Our Crown.

Now Know Ye, that in consideration of the said sum of *One hundred and Twenty one Dollars and thirty three cents* well and truly paid to Our use, at or before the sealing of these Our Letters Patent, We have granted, sold, aliened, conveyed, and assured, and by these presents do grant, sell, alien, convey and assure unto the said *Henry Hugh Bridgland* *his* Heirs and Assigns FOREVER: All those parcels or tracts of Land, situate, lying and being in the *Township of Franklin* in the County of *District of Muskoka* in the Province of Ontario, containing by admeasurement *Five hundred and Twenty acres* be the same more or less; which said Parcels or Tracts of Land may be otherwise known as follows, that is to say, being composed of *One undivided third part or share of Lots Numbers Nineteen, Twenty, Twenty-one, Twenty two, Twenty three, Twenty four and Twenty five being all the Lots composing Bigwin Island, the said Island being a part of the Township of Franklin and being situated in the Lake commonly called the Lake of Bays in the District of Muskoka in the Province of Ontario. Reserving nevertheless to Us Our Heirs and Successors all Pine Trees growing or being on the said lands save and except such Pine Trees as may be required for building and fencing thereon and as may be necessary to be cut and removed for purposes of clearing and cultivation and all such trees so cut as aforesaid and sold or disposed of to be subject to the payment of the dues ordinarily payable on Timber cut under License from the Crown. To have and to hold to him the said Henry Hugh Bridgland his heirs and assigns for ever.*

Documents from the 1861 census note that Chief Bigwin and his wife lived in a wigwam on Bigwin Island, Trading Lake (or as it was later renamed, Lake of Bays). In exchange for $242.66, two-thirds of Bigwin Island was patented by the Crown to Clark Benton Bridgland of York on November 23, 1875, and registered in 1881. 110 years later, in 1991, local publications noted that Bigwin Island was part of a land claim issue specified in the Williams Treaty of 1923.
— Robert McLennan

~~To have and to hold,~~ the said Parcel or Tract of Land, ~~hereby granted, conveyed and assured unto the said~~ ~~heirs and assigns for ever~~: saving, excepting and reserving, nevertheless unto Us, Our Heirs and Successors, the free uses, passage and enjoyment of, in, over, and upon all navigable waters that shall or may be hereafter found on or under, or be flowing through or upon any part of the said Parcel or Tract of Land hereby granted as aforesaid.

GIVEN under the Great Seal of Our Province of Ontario: Witness the Honorable DONALD ALEXANDER MACDONALD, Lieutenant-Governor of Our Province of Ontario.

At TORONTO, this *Twenty third* day of *November*, in the year of Our Lord one thousand eight hundred and *Seventy-five* and in the *Thirty-ninth* year of Our Reign.

Ref. No. 39761
Sale No. 36163 }C.L.S.

By command of the Lieutenant-Governor in Council.

Secretary. Thos. H. Johnson
  Assistant Commissioner of Crown Lands

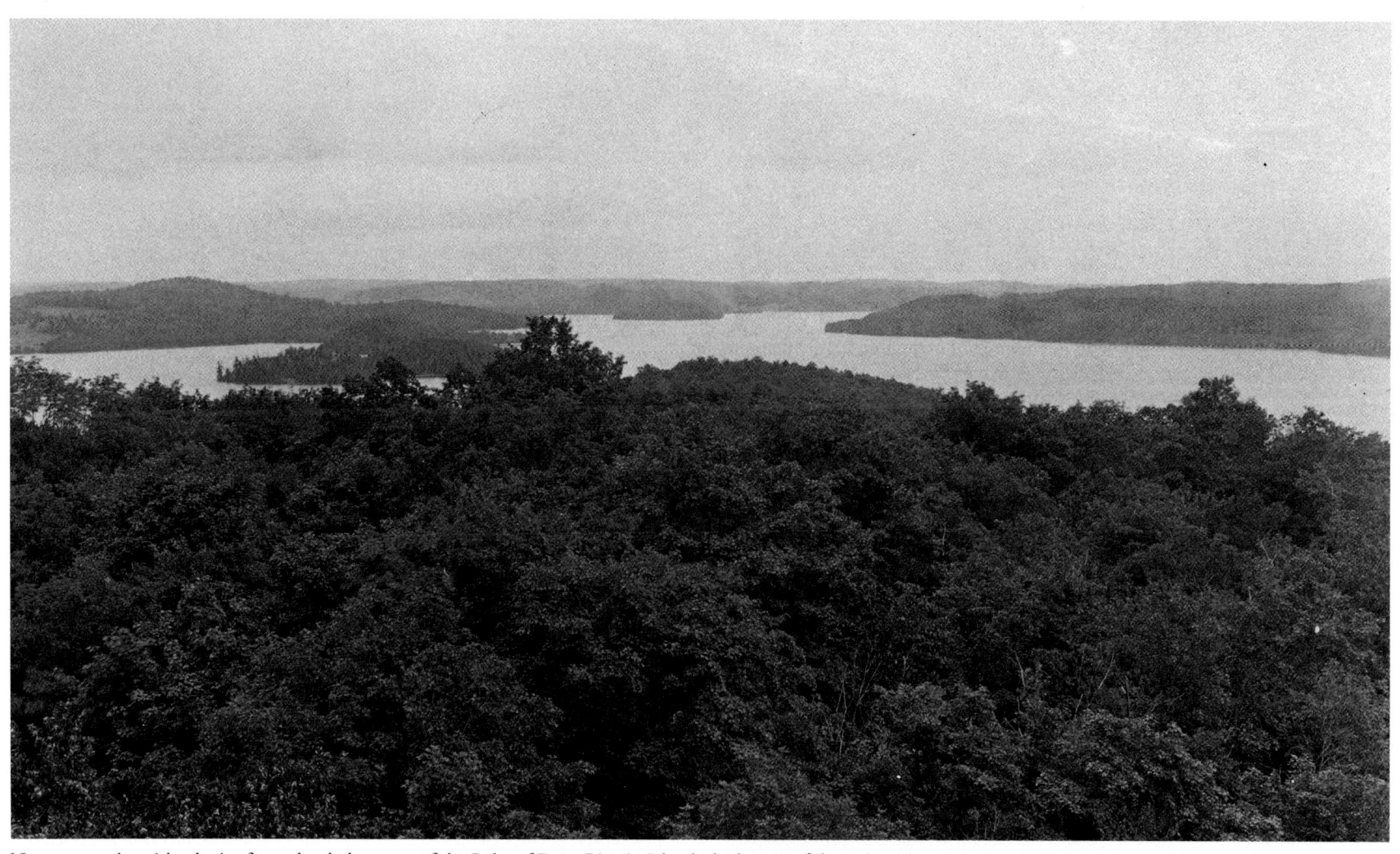
Numerous sylvan islands rise from the dark waters of the Lake of Bays. Bigwin Island, the largest of them, is an important part of Muskoka's environmental and archaeological heritage.
- *Helen E. O'Connor*

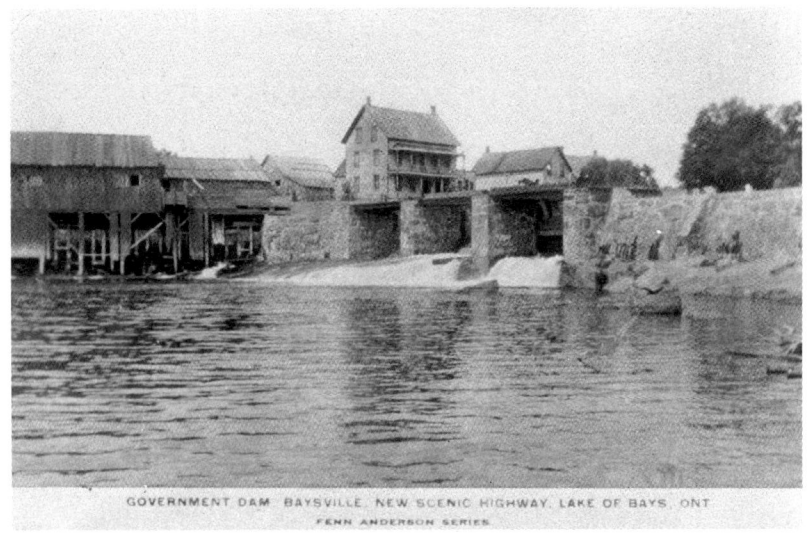
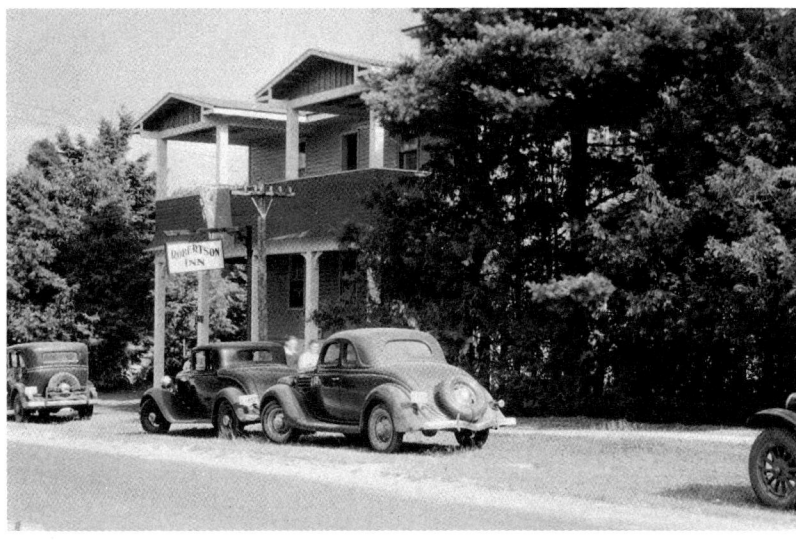
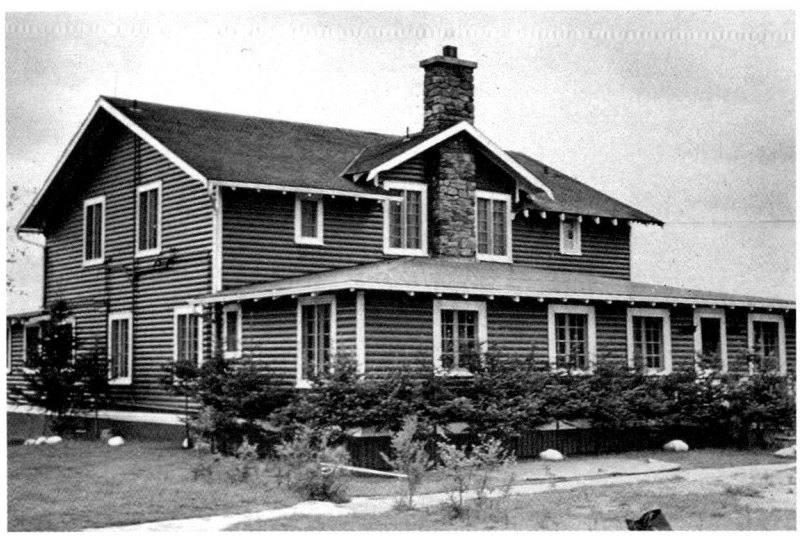
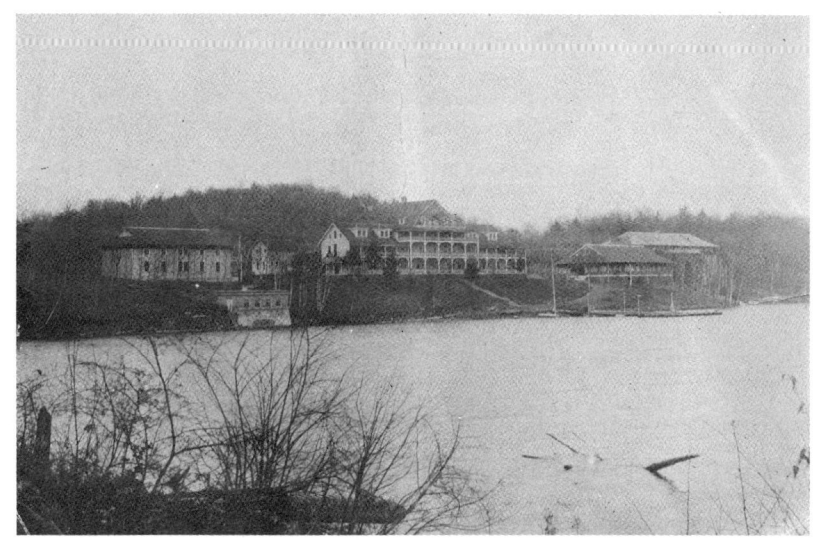

Lincoln Lodge, Robertson Inn, New Moon Lodge, Hotel Britannia, Port Cunnington Lodge and Ronville Lodge offered tourists a varied selection of accommodations.
- *Alan Tasker and DGM*

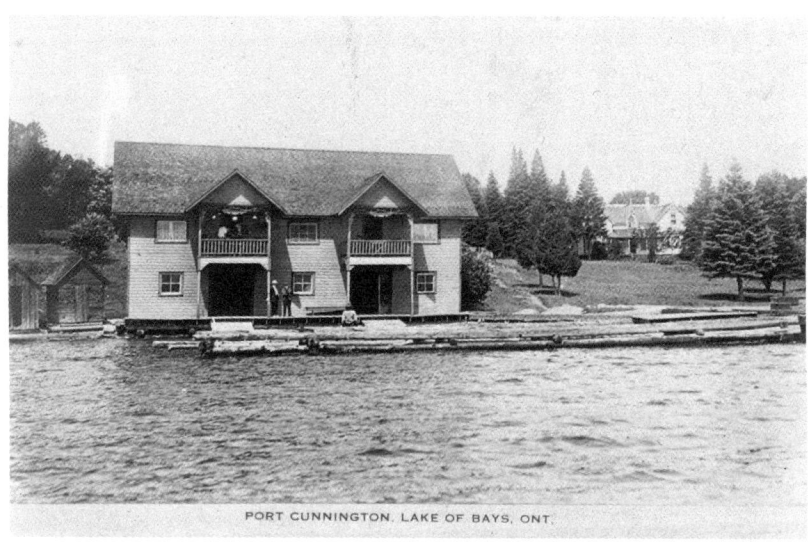

PORT CUNNINGTON, LAKE OF BAYS, ONT.

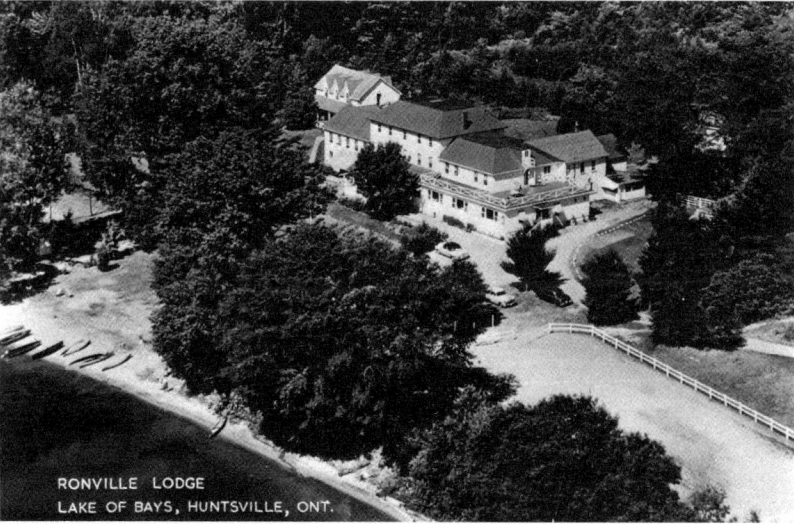

RONVILLE LODGE
LAKE OF BAYS, HUNTSVILLE, ONT.

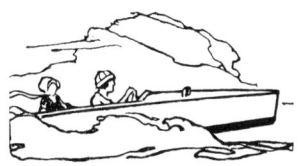

HOTELS AND BOARDING HOUSES

Name of Hotel	P.O. Address	Proprietor or Manager	Accommodation	Rates Per Day	Rates Per Week
LAKE OF BAYS					
Bigwin Inn	Bigwin Inn (via Huntsville)	Bigwin Inn Co.	500	$5.50 up	$30 up
Britannia Hotel	Kingsway	Britannia Hotel Co.	250	3.50 up	20 up
Ronville	Birkendale	D. G. Cole	100	4.00	21-24
Point Ideal	Huntsville	E. P. Boothby, Jr.	75	3.00 up	17-23
Port Cunnington	Port Cunnington	B. H. Cunnington	60	2.50	14-18
The Hemlocks	Birkendale	C. W. Irwin	30	3.00	15-18
Fairview Farm	Brown's Brae	John E. Brown	10	2.00	12
Grandview Resort	" "	Mrs. A. Robertson	50	3.50	18-22
Glenmount	Glenmount	Jas. C. McGarvey	40		
Island View	Fox Point	Thomas Salmon	60	2.50	13-17
Grove Ave. Lodge	" "	H. C. Schwenker	40	2.50-3	12-16
Garryowen Lodge	Dorset	Shirley B. Ball	40	4.00	20
The Maples	"	J. G. Burk	20	2.50	10-14
The Narrows	"	Thos. J. Woods	40		
Bunny Lodge	"	Mrs. L. A. Western	20		
Ganoseyo	"	W. M. Miller	50		
Whitewood Lodge	"	L. J. Fisher	10		14-16
Pine Grove Inn	Dwight	Harry A. Corbett	115	2.00-3	14-18
Nor Loch Lodge	"	Barker & McKay	40		
Gouldie House	"	A. G. Gouldie	80	2.00-3	12-15
Dwight House	"	Peter F. Newton	30	2.00	12-14
White House	Baysville	J. Alldred	40	2.00	12-14
HOLLOW LAKE					
Mountain Trout House	Dorset	Ben. W. Russell	40	3.00	18
Anglers Retreat	"	The Manager	20	On application	
FAIRY LAKE			40		
Haverland	Huntsville	Ethelred Rowe	50	2.00	10-12
Fairy Port Inn	"	E. J. Ecclestone	65	2.50	16
Grandview Inn	"	M. Cookson	25	2.50	15
Holinshead Resort	"	Thos. Holinshead		2.00	10-14
MARY LAKE					
Clyffe House	Port Sydney	Robert Jenner	85	3-3.50	16-20
River View	"	Chilton Rumball	25	3.00	15
The Balsams	"	E. Clarke	20	2.50	14-16
Vue du Lac	"	G. E. Cadieux	20	3.50	18-20
Muskoka Lodge	"	A. A. Gilmore	40	2-2.50	12-15
PENINSULAR LAKE					
Malvern House	Canal, P.O.	Mrs. A. M. Conroy	15	2.00	10-12
Wequash Resort	Hillside	J. V. Robinson	20	2.50	12-14
Deerhurst Resort	Huntsville	C. W. Waterhouse	100	3.00	On app.
Portage Lodge	Penlake	John Allison	40	3.50	18-20
Burnbrae	Canal	S. J. Ware	30	2.50	12-15
CLEAR LAKE					
Limberlost Lodge	Hillside	R. J. G. Hill	60	3.00	16-20
BELLA LAKE					
Camp Billie Bear	Antioch	Mrs. H. N. Hill	45	3.00	15-18
BAYSVILLE RIVER					
Point Pleasant	Baysville	P. B. Bastedo	50	2.50	10-12
Idlwyld	"	Peter A. Brown	40	2.50	12-16
Langton House	"	John L. King	35	2.50	12-15
Rosebank Farm	"	J. Lea Roberts	25	2.50	12-15
Pulford House	"	John J. Robertson	50		
MUSKOKA RIVER					
Hotel Kent	Huntsville	Chester Blake	50	3.50	21
Hotel Dominion	"	T. W. Simmons	40	2.50 up	
Vernon House	"	The Manager	30	3.00	10 up
LAKE VERNON					
Lakeview Villa	Ravenscliffe	Jno. Blackley	20	2.00	10
Wayagamack	Huntsville	Jas. S. Hubbard	15		

Note —This information is the latest available. Travellers should arrange for and confirm their reservations in advance. All rates American plan. Many resorts grant specially reduced rates during month of September, which is one of the loveliest of the year in the Highlands of Ontario.

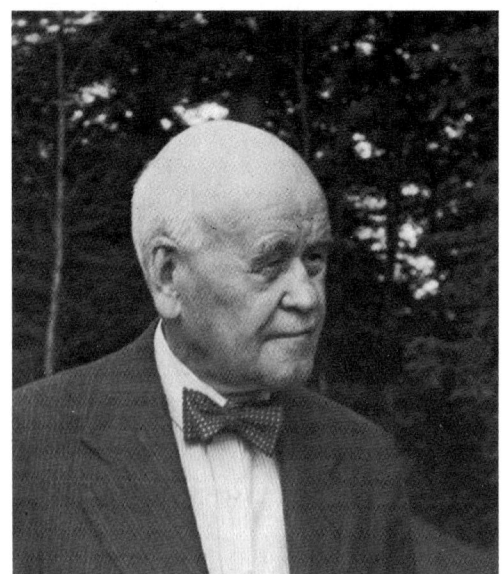

Charles Orlando Shaw.   - *S. Moir Forsythe*

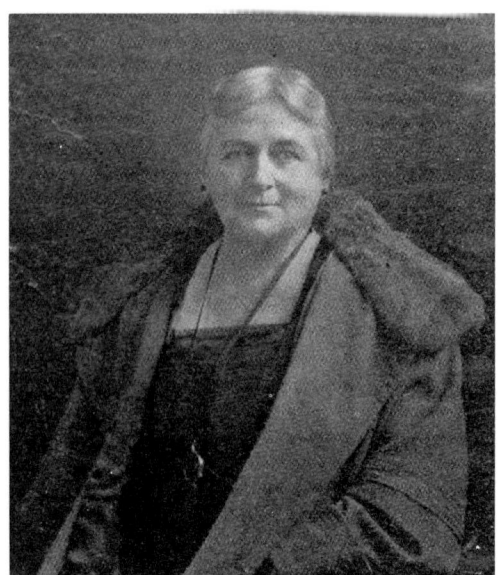

Jennie Lavinia Shaw.   - *Muskoka Pioneer Village*

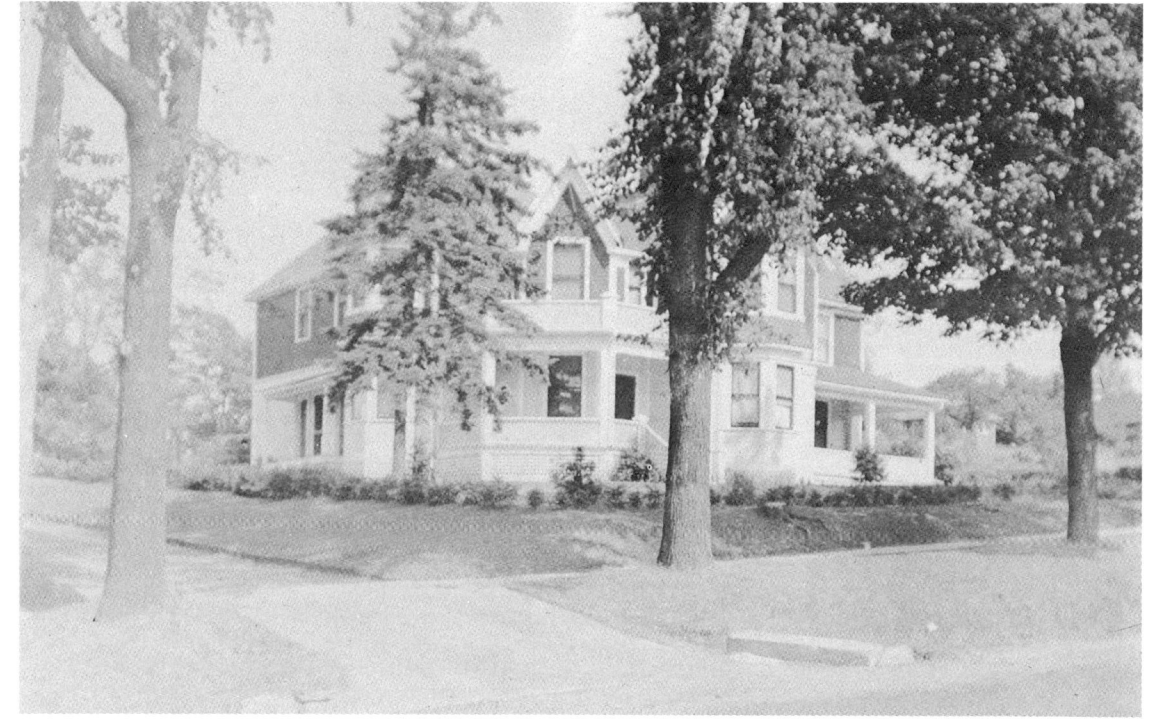

The Shaw's residence on Centre Street, Huntsville.   - *Allan Thaxter Shaw, Charles Wellington Shaw, Walter Brackley Shaw.*

CHAPTER 1

Foundations

The journey of Charles Orlando Shaw began with his birth in 1858 in Dexter, Maine. On October 26, 1886, he married Jennie Lavinia Abbott, and for a time they lived in Boston, Massachusetts, where their two daughters, Pauline and Jennifer, were born. The Shaws later moved to Cheboygan, Michigan, where their only son, Charles, was born. In the late 1890s C.O. Shaw moved his family to a large frame house on Centre Street in Huntsville, Ontario.

Mrs. Shaw, a woman of many talents, had trained as a contralto singer in Boston under the tutelage of the renowned teacher Charles Adams. In Huntsville, she continued to sing, leading the Saint Andrew's Presbyterian Church choir for many years. Her cultural interests inspired her to participate in other organizations, among them the Huntsville Literary Club.

Upon the family's arrival in Huntsville, Charles Orlando Shaw, a civil engineer and a man of great vision, assumed the position of vice-president at the tannery. Because he refused to compromise the integrity of work done under his name, C.O. Shaw appeared to be quite the autocratic individual. With perfection as his standard, Shaw cast himself as a martinet in the business world. His unrelenting commitment to excellence and his business acumen — together with an initial municipal tax exemption for ten years — helped cultivate the tannery into one of the province's earliest business empires. In 1905 the flourishing enterprise became known as the Anglo Canadian Leather Company Limited, one of the largest in the British Empire and a cornerstone of Muskoka's economic structure for over half a century.

Shortly after C.O. Shaw took over the reins of the Huntsville tannery, the company's building was renovated and enlarged as a fireproof facility. Housing a work force of over 150 men, the tannery generated an annual payroll exceeding $70,000, by far the largest in Muskoka. In addition to wages earned, many of the tannery's workers were provided with company housing in a nearby valley known by many as "The Hollow." Over 30 employees were covered by Canada Life Assurance Company's first group policy, issued on January 12, 1920, for approximately $300,000.

Through regular tours of inspection, Shaw became well acquainted with tannery employees and quite familiar with their capabilities. From them all, he demanded "an honest day's work." Guarding against tardiness and the disruption in production which it brought, C.O. Shaw occasionally waited with a watch as company workers arrived at the start of the business day. Those who dared to arrive late were often excused for the day without pay. However, other situations were more negotiable. An employee once recalled Shaw persuading him to stay with the Anglo Canadian Leather Company after he had resigned from its ranks. The employee stated that he would need a total of $2 per hour to stay. Recognizing the worker's ability, Shaw readily agreed but qualified his enthusiasm with the words, "Don't come back asking for three dollars per hour."

The talented musicians among the Anglo Canadian Leather Company's employees brought immense pleasure to the people of Muskoka and launched one of the great stories of the Canadian music world. When the group asked whether their small band might practise in his garage, C.O. Shaw, a virtuoso cornetist since childhood, empathized with their request and granted permission. Sunday-afternoon rehearsals were led by Vincent Grosso, who directed the players, many of whom had emigrated from northern Italy. Inspired by their talents, Shaw began attending the sessions, thus tempering his business life with his penchant for music. Shaw participated with the band in every aspect, from setting up concert equipment to financially supporting the venture. As his interest heightened, he retained revered instructor George R. Simmons of Bracebridge and procured the best of musical instruments, together with the finest uniforms available. Despite Shaw's enormous capital outlay, the band was available for any worthy cause, with admission rarely charged at any of its performances. While the organization would have been a daunting responsibility to the average man, it was simply a change of pace

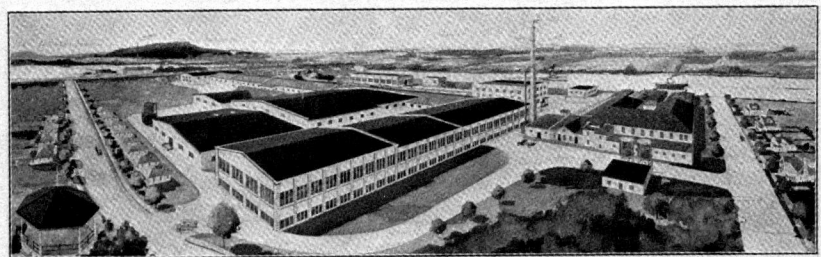

The above is a reproduction of the large and modern SOLE LEATHER TANNERY of the ANGLO CANADIAN LEATHER CO. LIMITED, at HUNTSVILLE, ONTARIO, where the MAPLE LEAF BRAND HUNTSVILLE OAK LEATHER is produced.

Buildings all solid concrete fireproof construction and all equipped with the most modern up-to-date machinery known. Capacity 1600 SIDES A DAY or 10,000,000 LBS. OF LEATHER A YEAR.

ANGLO CANADIAN LEATHER CO. LIMITED

Head Office
MONTREAL, QUEBEC

Branches
Toronto, Ontario & Quebec City, Quebec

Tanneries
Huntsville, Ontario & Bracebridge, Ontario

Tanners of Sole Leather exclusively (MAPLE LEAF BRAND)

Below is a reproduction of the ANGLO CANADIAN LEATHER CO. LIMITED Sole Leather Tannery at Bracebridge, Ontario, about twenty miles from the Huntsville plant. Here also the buildings are all solid concrete fireproof construction fully equipped with modern machinery, with a capacity equal to the Huntsville plant.

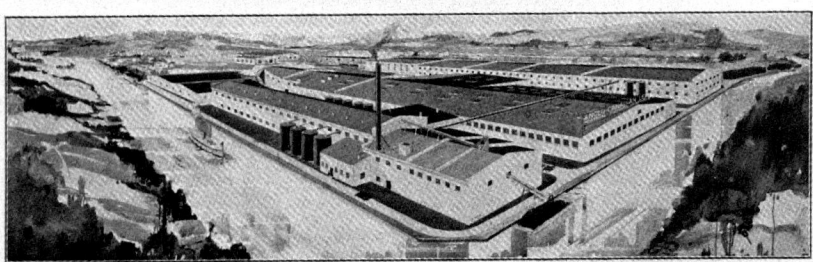

The Anglo Canadian Leather Company Limited was a cornerstone of Muskoka's economic structure for over half a century.
- *Robert McLennan*

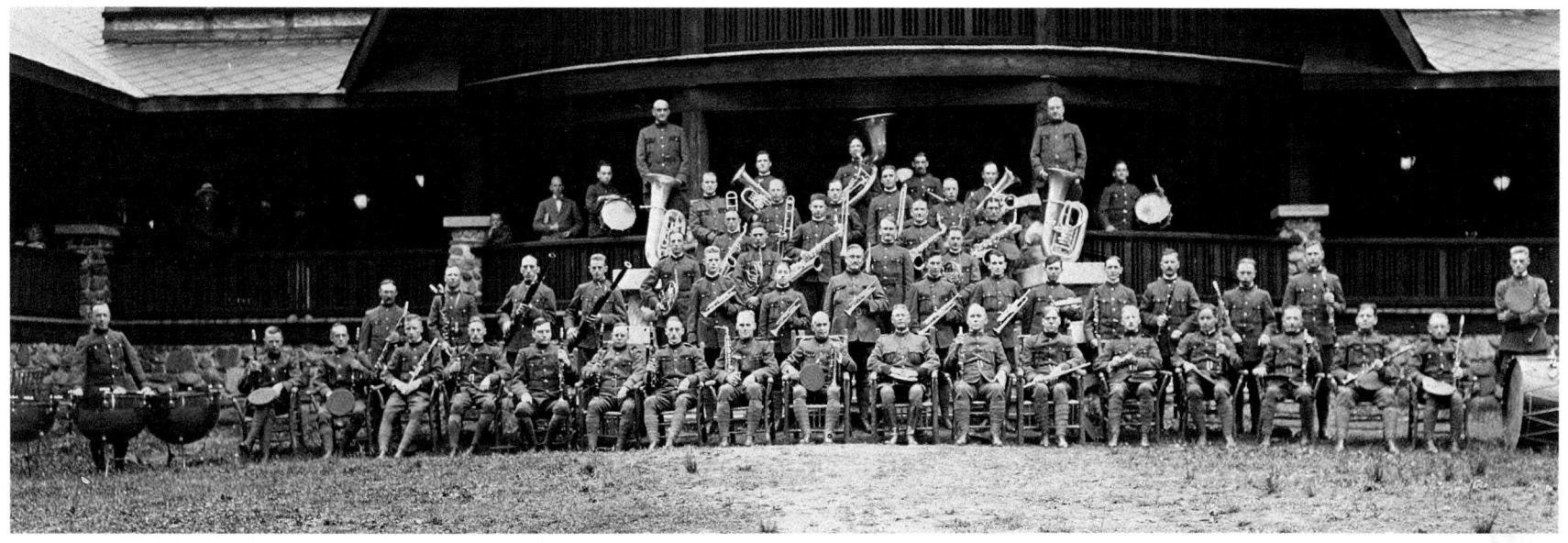

Members of the Anglo Canadian Concert Band strike a pose on the front steps of Bigwin Inn's Rotunda circa 1920. Standing on the far left is the hotel's manager, James G. Reid. C.O. Shaw is seated tenth from the left and the bandmaster, Herbert L. Clarke, is seated on C.O.'s left.
- *Robert McLennan*

Programme of Concerts
BY THE
Anglo Canadian Concert Band of Huntsville

Friday Afternoon, Sept. 8th, 3.30 to 5.30 p.m.

GOD SAVE THE KING

1. March — "Bigwin" — Clarke
2. Overture — "The Bartered Bride" — Smetana
3. Piccolo Solo — "L'Oiseau du Bois" — Le Thiere
   Mr. John T. Collins
4. Suite — "At the King's Court" — Sousa
   a. Her Ladyship, The Countess.
   b. Her Grace, The Duchess.
   c. Her Majesty, The Queen.
5. "Fackeltanz" — Meyerbeer

INTERMISSION

6. Selection from "Parsifal" — Wagner
7. Concert Waltz — "Sweet Memories" — Clarke
8. Clarinet Solo — Fantasie on "Puritani" — Bassi
   Mr. Edmund C. Wall
9. Overture — "Beautiful Galatea" — Suppe

O CANADA

While living in Huntsville, Herbert L. Clarke composed various pieces of music, including "Bigwin," "Lake of Bays," "Twilight Dreams," "Helen," and "Lavinia."
- *DGM*

for Shaw, who once said that his participation was almost a release for him and that "the principal delight of the band was that it took me out of myself. After two or three hard hours of practice or rehearsing I would be refreshed and confident." The band was much more than just a release for many of its talented members. Highly successful musical careers were launched after association with the organization. Shaw once confided, "That sort of thing brings a man happiness."

C.O. Shaw quickly attracted the finest teachers and performers to the Huntsville musical group, including clarinetist E.A. Wall Sr. from Chicago. Later, practising in a remodelled schoolhouse on Caroline Street, the band swelled from 60 pieces to 72 pieces. Then, Shaw financed the greatest of musical engagements. With a five-year contract amounting to over $75,000, 51-year-old Herbert Lincoln Clarke was brought to Huntsville from the United States on April 16, 1918, to direct the band. The genius of this conductor, arranger and pioneering musician brought the Anglo Canadian Concert Band to new heights of accomplishment.

Clarke, a premier cornet soloist, had been the principal soloist and assistant conductor with John Philip Sousa's band for many years. During the first summer under his direction, the Anglo Canadian Concert Band performed by invitation at the Canadian National Exhibition (CNE). Before long, the band was billed as one of the foremost musical organizations on the North American continent, with its success likened to that of the bands of Goldman, Sousa and Pryor. On September 4, 1919, the Huntsville musicians gave an outstanding performance at the CNE which included the playing of Clarke's new arrangement, "Bigwin." Other pieces composed by Clarke while living in Huntsville include "Lake of Bays," "Twilight Dreams" and "Lavinia," as well as "Helen," which was written especially for C.O. Shaw's granddaughter.

Performances beyond bandshells and concert halls included engagements at Timothy Eaton Memorial Church and Saint Paul's Anglican Church, where great pleasure was brought to Toronto congregations. Performances by the band were sometimes transmitted over telephone lines from Muskoka and broadcast from CFRB Radio in Toronto to audiences across the country and to U.S. listeners as far away as Miami Beach, Florida.

A man of great diversity, C.O. Shaw had many other professional interests. In 1905 he became the major shareholder in the Huntsville, Lake of Bays and Lake Simcoe Navigation Company. His acquisition of the steamer fleet and the Portage Railway facilitated the transport of harvested bark for the tannery as well as mail, freight and tourists. With an almost inexhaustible energy, he also served on the Huntsville town council and was involved in the development of the famous WaWa Hotel at Norway Point on the Lake of Bays. To commemorate this association with the WaWa, in 1908 Shaw was presented with a baton from Henry Birks and Sons Limited and promised special accommodation in the hotel at any time. The following summer, two incidences would compel C.O. Shaw to build the Bigwin Inn.

John W. McKee, a colleague of Shaw and secretary-treasurer of the Lake of Bays Navigation Company, noticed that the steamer fleet's profits were not as encouraging as they had been in previous years. In a similar situation William Cornelius Van Horne, vice-president of Canadian Pacific Railway, had built the Banff Springs Hotel to lure tourists to use the rail lines. Adapting the CPR's success formula, McKee suggested to Shaw that a hotel be built on an island where the only means of getting to and from it would be aboard one of the Navigation Company's steamers. While C.O. Shaw was somewhat intrigued by the idea, it would take a greater influence to completely convince the wealthy Huntsville tycoon to build a hotel.

One afternoon in that summer of 1909, Shaw arrived at the beautiful WaWa Hotel, built in 1907 for the colossal sum of $195,000 on a former farm site. The WaWa (which, translated, means Canada goose) was a frame structure with a three-storey central building and a two-storey wing to either side, accommodating a total of 300 guests. Rising from the centre of the building was a five-storey tower crowned with a powerful searchlight that could be seen for miles. The lavishly finished interior was panelled with Georgia pine and appointed with the most luxurious of furnishings. At the height of the season and to the pleasure of the management, Canadian Railway News Company, the hotel attracted so many visitors that it had to offer sleeping tents to accommodate the overflow. When C.O. Shaw went to register at the front desk, he found that his personal suite had inadvertently been given to one of the many guests. Realizing the immense profitability of the WaWa since its opening in 1908, Shaw vowed to establish a much larger, safer and more tasteful resort of his own, one that would rival any hotel and enable his companies to capitalize on the tourist trade.

In 1911 C.O. Shaw and John McKee bought 562 acres of Bigwin Island, as tenants in common, from George Rutherford for $3,000. In 1912, the Crown gave a patent for $210 for the island's outstanding 42 acres of shore road allowance to C.O. Shaw, who retained two-thirds interest in the lands, and to John McKee, who retained one-third interest in the lands. At the time of the sales, the purchasers consented to protect and preserve the island's archaeologically significant burial sites from desecration and to allow Chief John Bigwin (Anglo corruption of "Big Wind") to be laid to rest with his ancestors. In 1912 C.O. Shaw and John McKee sold Bigwin Island (concession lots 19-25 inclusive) to their company, Bigwin Island Land Company Limited, for $1.

At the same time, the company registered a plan for subdivision of 76 lots around the perimeter of Bigwin Island. However, this was later reduced to 69 lots, with the outstanding pieces of property being

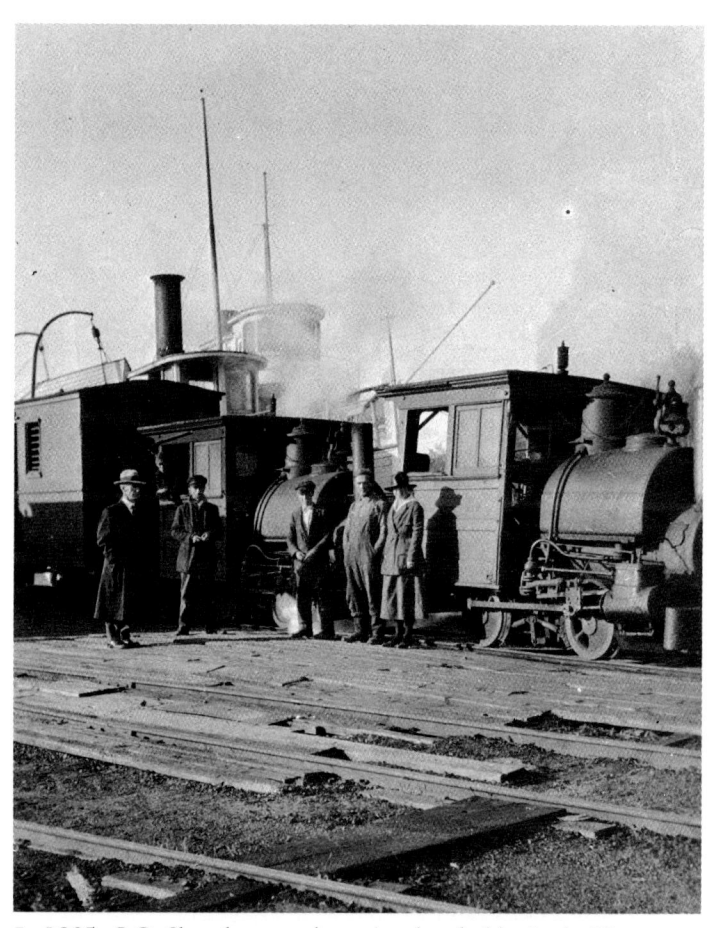

In 1905, C.O. Shaw became the major shareholder in the Huntsville, Lake of Bays & Lake Simcoe Navigation Company. His acquisition of the steamer fleet and the Portage Railway facilitated the transport of tan bark, mail, freight and tourists.
- *Ruth Tinkiss*

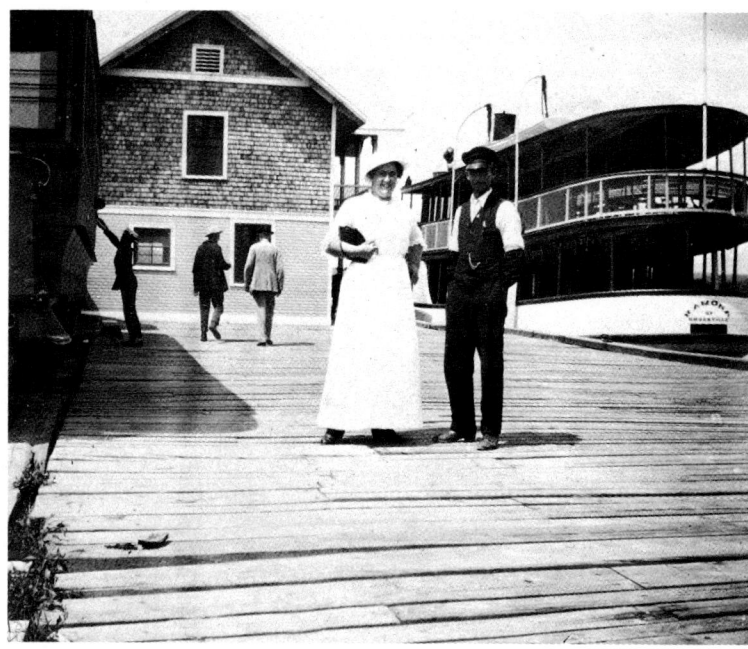

August 1, 1914, Captain and Mrs. William P. Tinkiss at the Huntsville wharf.
- *Ruth Tinkiss*

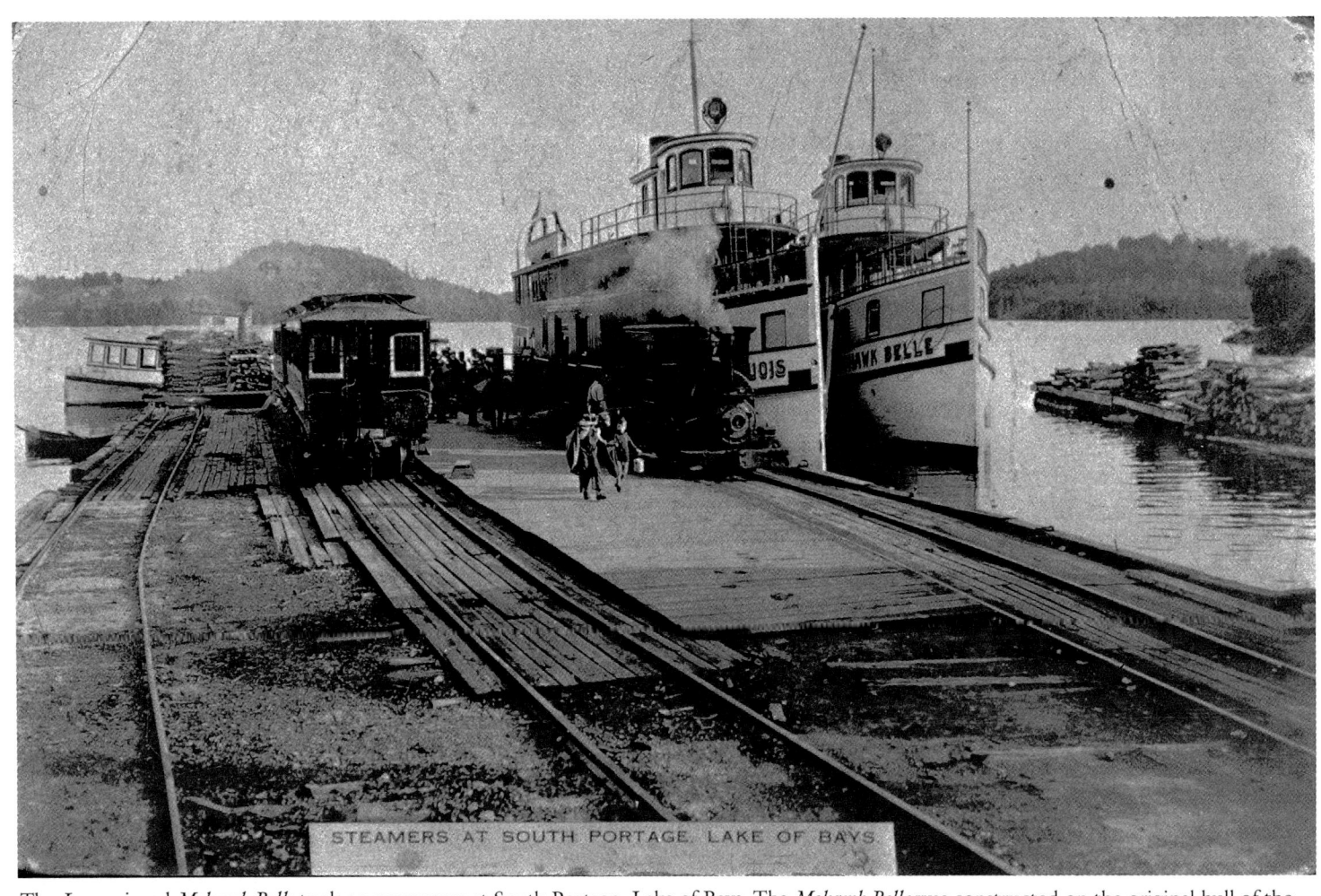

The *Iroquois* and *Mohawk Belle* took on passengers at South Portage, Lake of Bays. The *Mohawk Belle* was constructed on the original hull of the *Florence Main*. Its steam engine was built in 1901 by John Inglis and Sons, Toronto.
- *Alan Tasker*

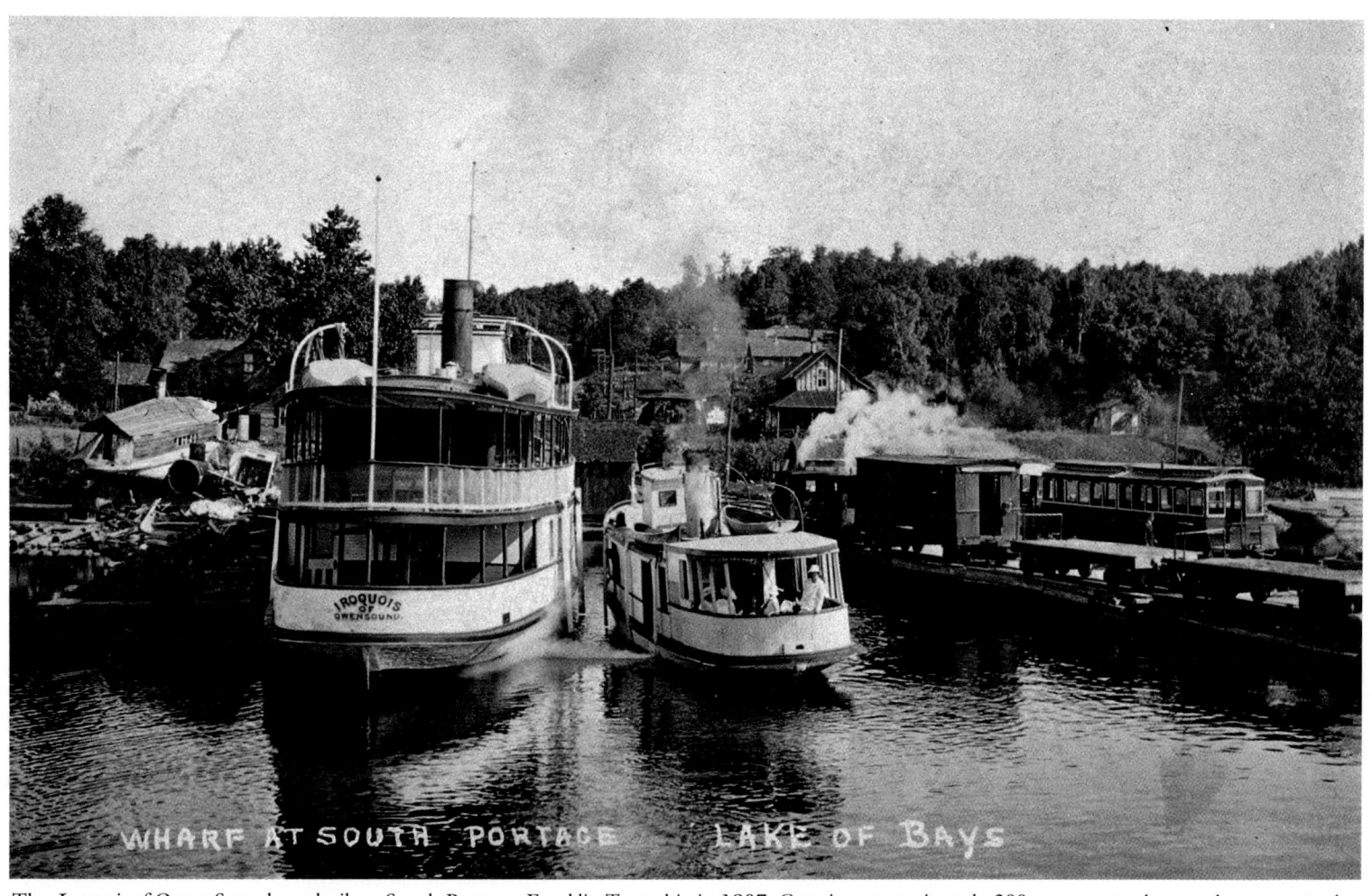

The *Iroquois* of Owen Sound was built at South Portage, Franklin Township in 1907. Carrying approximately 300 passengers, the vessel was powered by a 28.16 horsepower steam engine.
- *DGM*

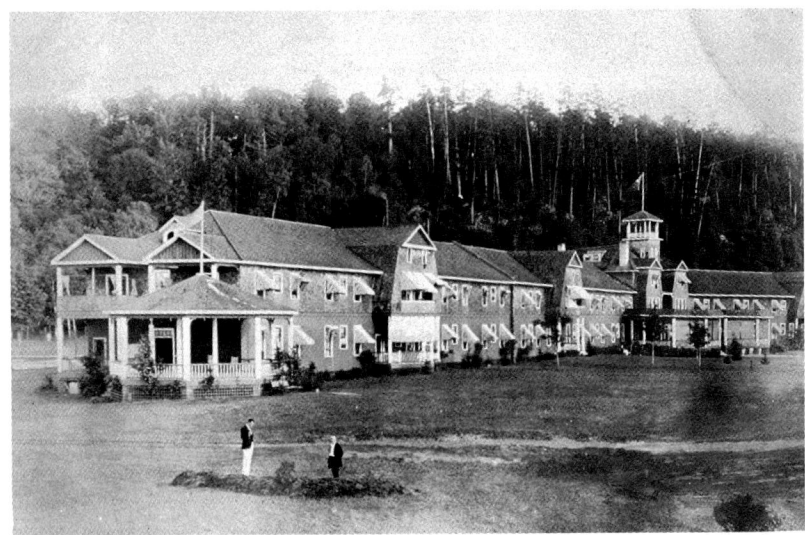
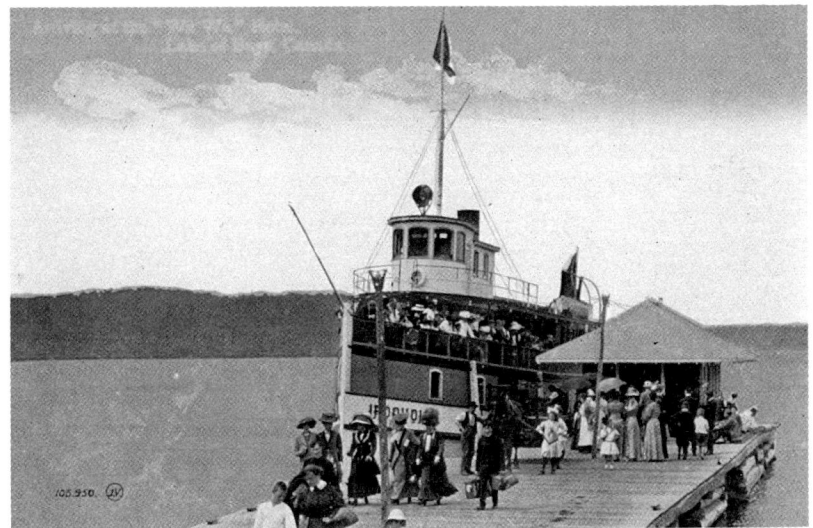
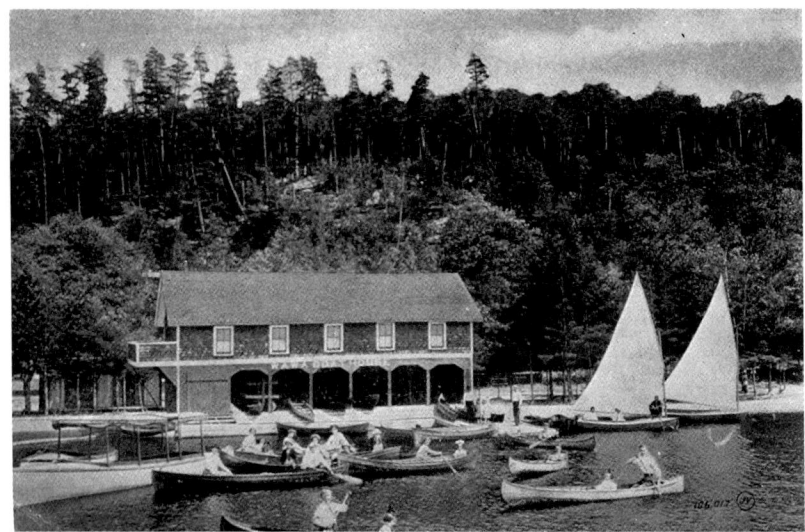
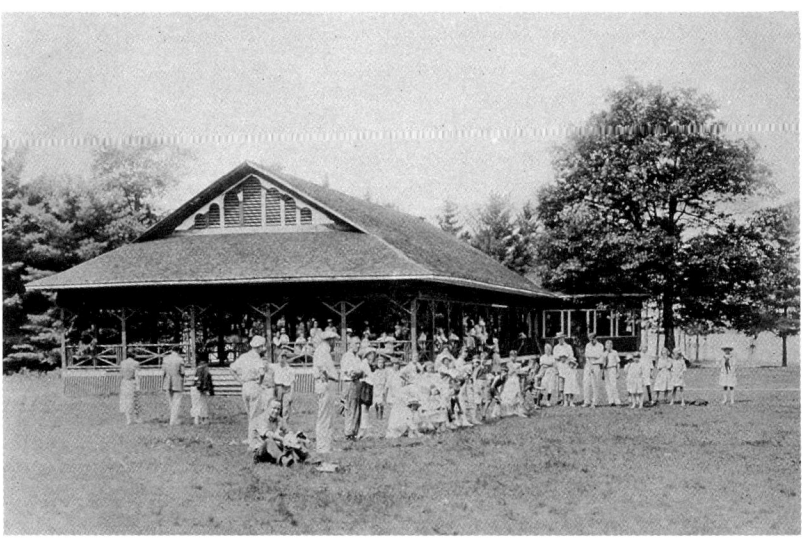

The WaWa Hotel was constructed on a farm previously owned by the Robertson family who later established the Robertson Inn at Baysville. In addition to the main hotel building, the WaWa's structures included a boat house, steamer dock, waiting room and pavilion. All luxuries aside, the hotel would *rendez-vous* with disaster some years later.

- *DGM*

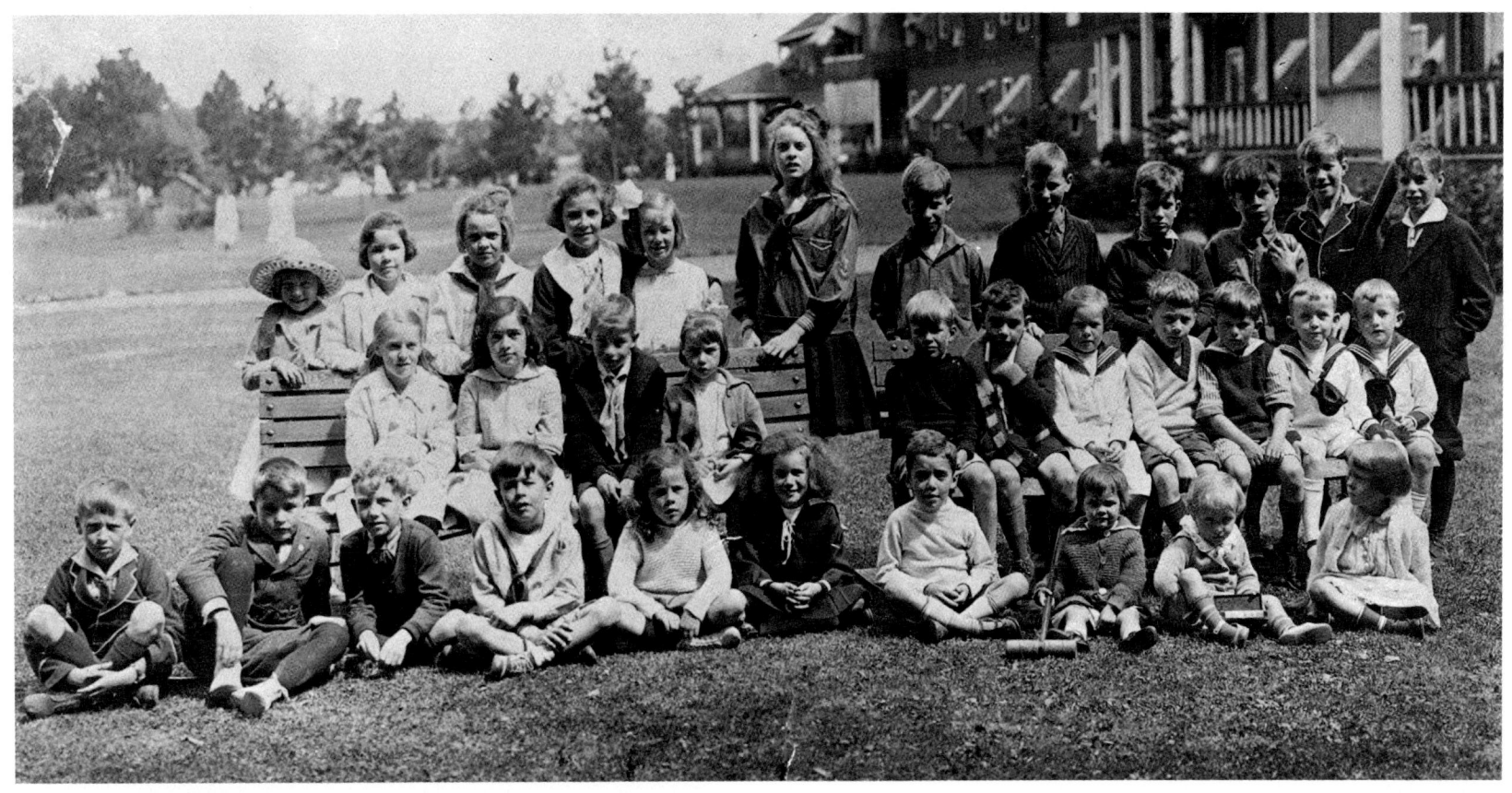
Young guests at the WaWa Hotel, Norway Point. - *Mrs. Jamieson*

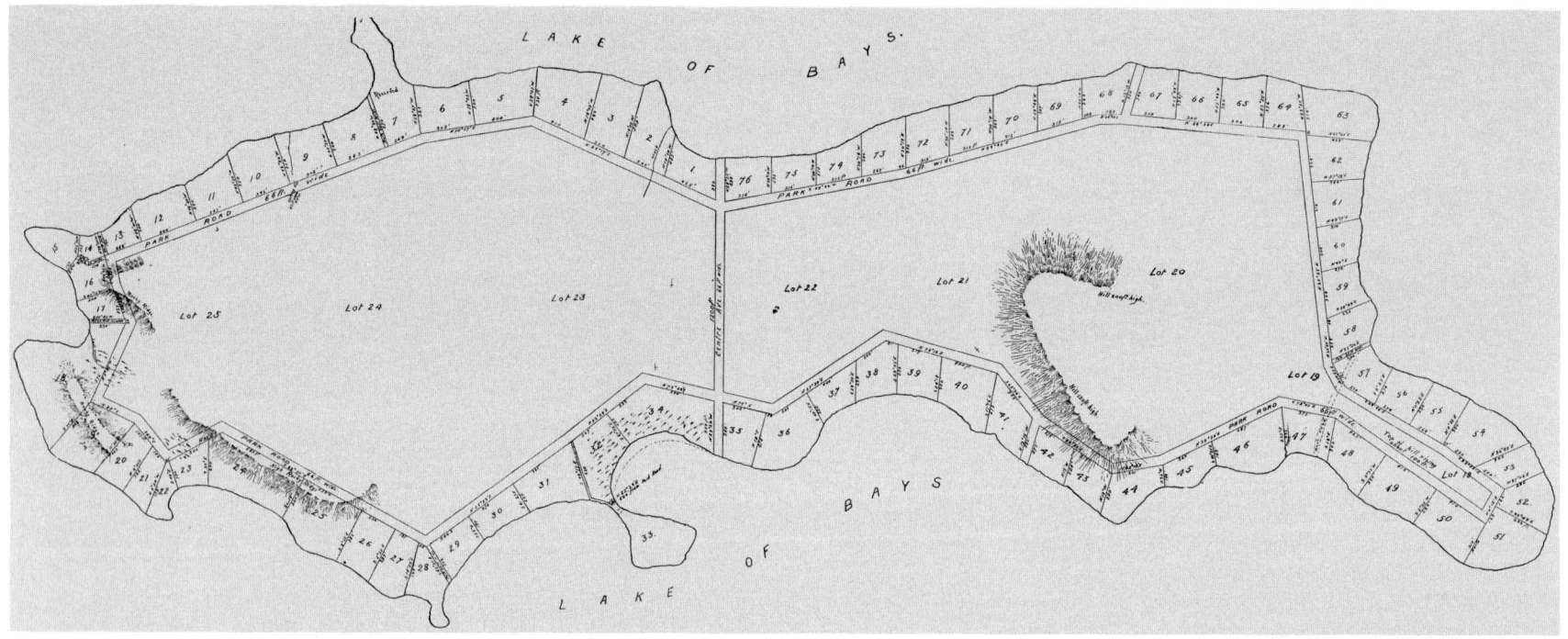

In 1912, C.O. Shaw and John McKee sold Bigwin Island to their company, Bigwin Island Land Company Limited, for $1.

- *Robert McLennan*

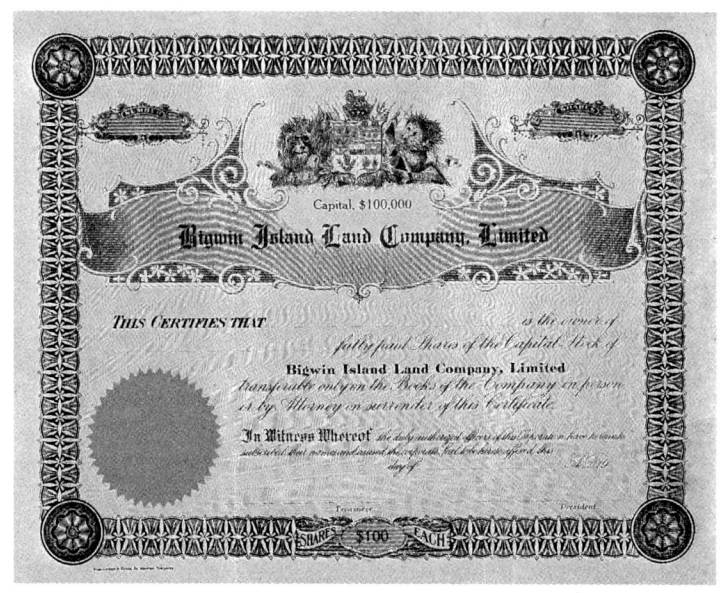

reserved for the proposed resort. A Lake of Bays travel brochure produced by the Grand Trunk Railway System in 1913 advertised, "There are innumerable choice sites available in the Lake of Bays region for those who desire to erect summer homes, camps or cottages. Besides those already enumerated might be mentioned the following: Bigwin Island, comprising about 550 acres, beautifully wooded with timber, both hard and soft woods and located in the most picturesque part of the Lake of Bays, in close proximity to Norway Point, Port Cunnington, Grove Avenue and other resorts. Building sites are for sale on this island in lots of any size."

In 1915 Bigwin Island Land Company Limited sold 65 acres of property to the newly formed entity, the Bigwin Inn Company Limited, for $1. With the exception of the lots around the perimeter of the island, the remaining land was transferred to the Bigwin Inn Company Limited between 1915 and 1932. Shortly after the acquisition of Bigwin Island, Shaw retained renowned Simcoe County architect John Wilson of Collingwood to design the new resort.

John Wilson had recently designed Hotel Britannia on the site of the old Patmore House and had met C.O. Shaw through its owner, Thomas J. White of White's Limited, Collingwood. Britannia's main building was situated above the beautiful sand beach of a protected bay. The frame hotel's large verandah and three balconies afforded some 350 guests a wonderful view of the Lake of Bays from any level. Other features enjoyed by visitors over the years included a dance pavilion, stage, golf course and tennis courts. Shaw was impressed with the outstanding quality of Wilson's work and began to describe to him the general layout of the Bigwin Island resort as he envisioned it.

Wilson and Shaw worked closely on the design of Bigwin Inn, ensuring that it would be the finest resort on the continent. From the start, nothing was spared in its planning or construction. While many of the era's grand hotels were architecturally significant, none compared with the Bigwin Inn. Bigwin was the perfect embodiment of the era, a time when man's ability to master nature with massive and indestructible projects was very much in vogue. In an equally impressive project across the Atlantic Ocean, designers had recently outfitted the luxurious ocean liner *Titanic*. While the White Star Line had built the *Titanic* to be enormous, luxurious and unsinkable, Shaw and Wilson designed Bigwin Inn to be enormous, luxurious and fireproof.

By arranging the buildings along the natural curve of the shoreline, Shaw and Wilson created a series of relationships between these imposing concrete structures that was aesthetic and integrated with the natural surroundings of the island. Roughly sketching the preliminary plans with pencil on paper and drawing the final plans with India ink on linen scrolls, Wilson tastefully combined various schools of architecture, including Classical, Mediterranean, Dodecagon, Craftsman, Tudor and Victorian, collectively creating an architectural masterpiece.

Equally important to the design of the buildings, and a great part of their substance, was the space that the buildings defined. Most of the rooms, both public and private, were built on such a grand scale that to this day they are virtually unparalleled in size. To complement the interiors, Wilson manipulated the use of natural light with the placement of doors, windows and fireplaces. Together, Shaw and Wilson produced a collection of buildings uniquely invaluable to Canada's architectural heritage.

Soon after the designs were completed, construction of the colossal project began. With delays resulting from World War I, it would be some time before Wilson's elaborate drawings materialized as structures of plumb and level lines. Nonetheless, many curious people ventured over to see the gradual evolution of the almost inconceivable project.

During the years of construction, dozens of workmen travelled to Bigwin Island, where camps were set up on the small, adjacent island nicknamed "Little Bigwin" or, more officially, "Shaw's Island." The craftsmen, many of them European born, laboured strenuously for $30 a month and were sustained by camp meals which cost the modest amount of 11 cents a plate at the start of the project.

Expansive areas of land were cleared and the building sites were staked. Vast amounts of timber, steel, concrete, stone and gravel were brought to the island by steamers such as the *Joe*, as well as by various tugs and barges. Many boats broke down under the strain of their huge loads. Some sank; others were simply retired to the depths of the lake. The steamer dock, one of the first features to be built, received most of the heavy supplies. From there, they were moved about by the sheer strength of the workmen, as few pieces of equipment, such as stone-crushers and tractors, were steam powered.

Much of the work was done during the colder months of the year. In the winter, when the lake iced over, supplies were delivered on sleighs drawn by teams of horses. Taking advantage of the ice-locked waterways, the craftsmen began construction on the southwest side of the island, facing Norway Point. There, they began the herculean task of building on the ice an extensive crib structure that would drop down to the lake's bottom during the spring thaw. The workmen pushed tons of boulders and crushed stone around massive, reinforced cement pillars and cribbing. With a huge area reclaimed from the lake, they began the construction of the dining-room complex.

The season's harsh temperatures never kept the fiery Charles Orlando Shaw from supervising the island project. Although McKee was overseer of the endeavour as builder-in-charge, C.O. Shaw himself worried over matters such as the mixing and setting of cement in such frigid weather. To ensure that the work was not substandard, Shaw tested the integrity of the buildings' 6-inch concrete walls by slamming them with a sledgehammer — with no effect, much to the relief of the craftsmen responsible for their construction.

It would take several years of meticulous designing, arduous construction and tedious delays before the monumental Bigwin Inn would open its doors to island visitors.

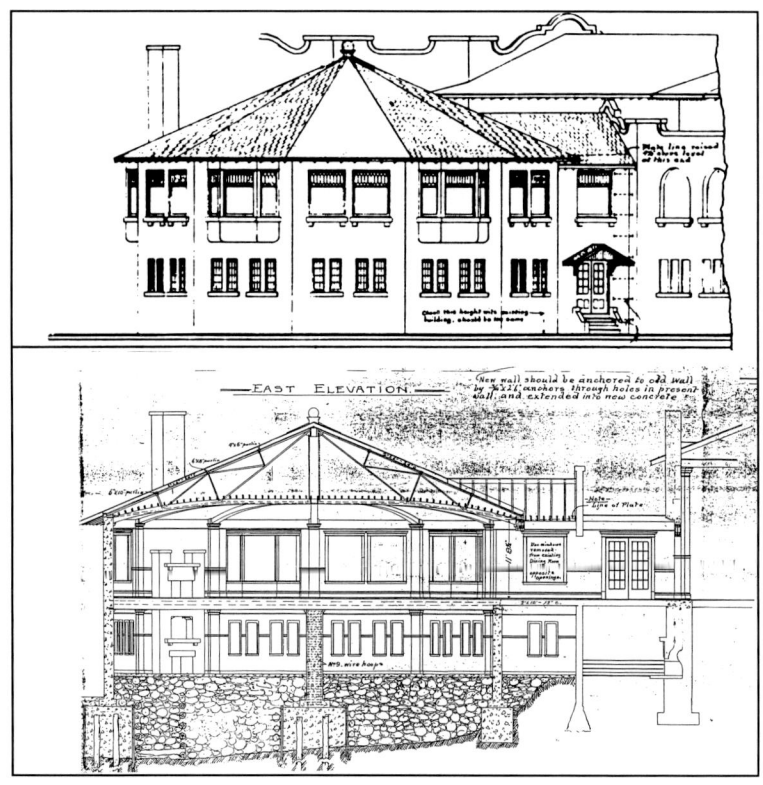

Eclectic in his design, Wilson synthesized the relationships of the magnificent concrete structures that collectively defined his consummate piece of artistry, Bigwin Inn. — *Simcoe County Archives and DGM*

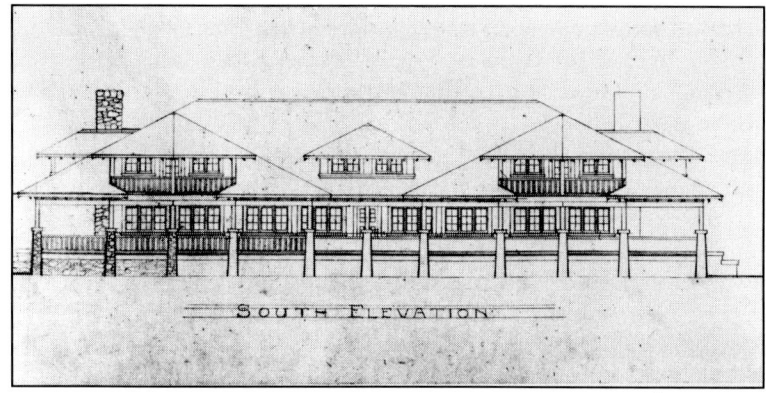

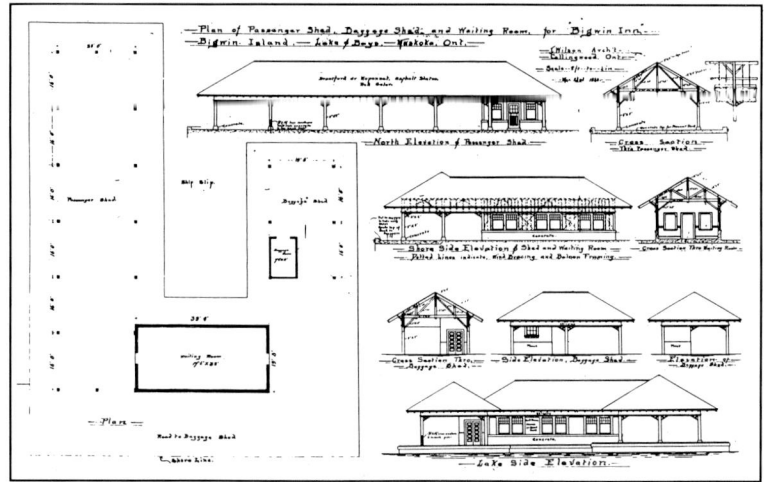

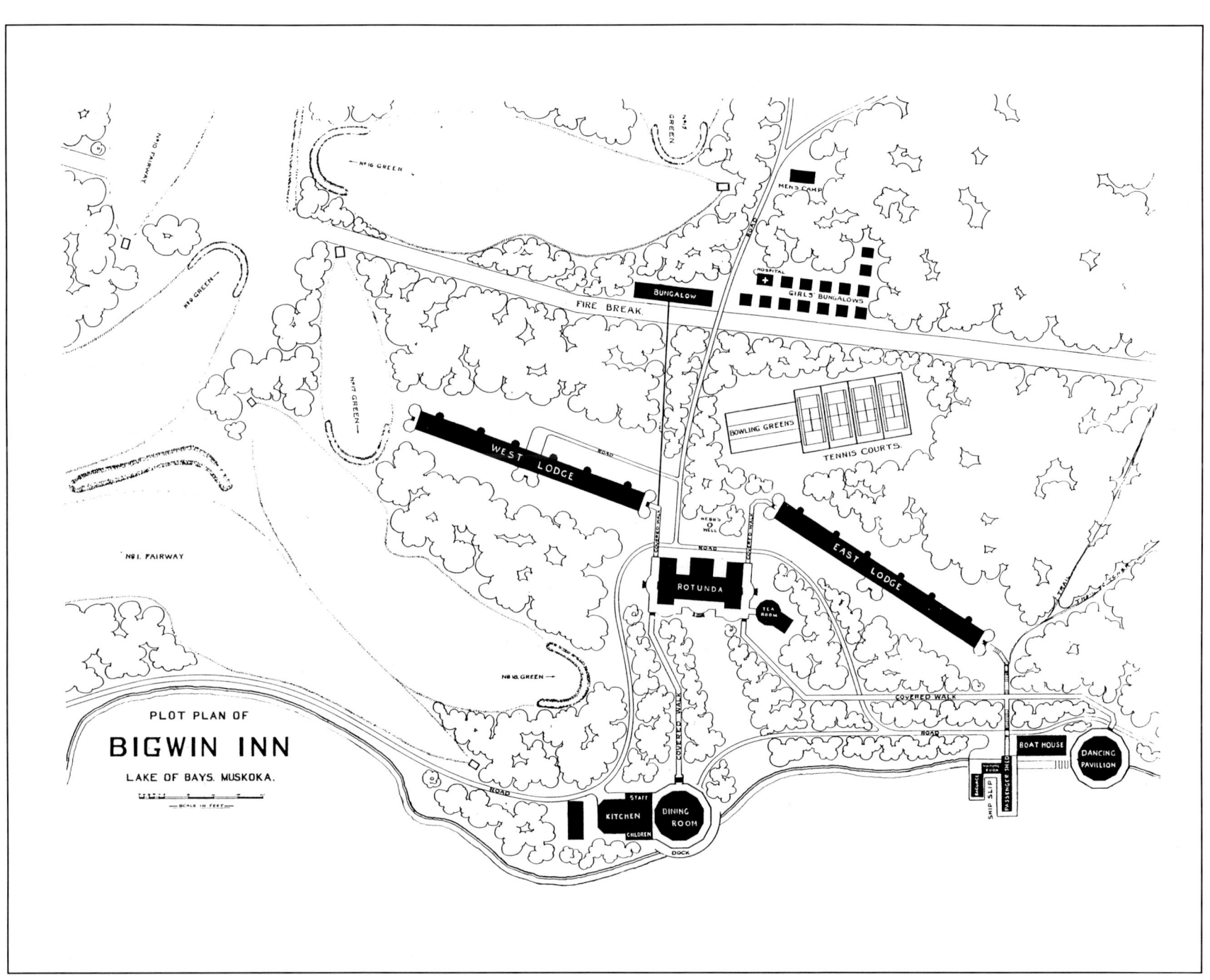

John Wilson

Walter C. Wilson immigrated to Canada from Islay, Scotland, in 1853 aboard the barque *Ann Harley*. The Atlantic crossing took nine weeks. Living first in Quebec, Walter Wilson later moved to Nottawasaga, where he married Ann McAllister of Jura, Scotland, on August 22, 1856. Their son John was born in Collingwood, Ontario on August 17, 1863.

As a boy, John Wilson became interested in the construction of buildings. At the young age of 14 he began working in the building trade and quickly learned its fundamentals. Within three years, he completed his elementary training. Three years later, at the age of 20, he undertook one of his first jobs, the building of Victoria School in 1884. At the time his mentor was Fred T. Hodgson, a great Collingwood architect and author of many volumes on building construction. In 1888 John Wilson and his brother Daniel established Wilson Brothers at the rear of 175-179 Hurontario Street. There they manufactured and distributed various building materials. One of their specialties was manufacturing wooden washing machines and refrigerators called "iceboxes." From an early age, John Wilson held true to his ideal: "Never work for another; you are worth twice as much to yourself." As their business grew, the brothers moved to a new facility at 1st and Walnut streets. (This factory was later consumed by fire.)

Though he never attended university, John Wilson studied the science of architecture through the American School of Correspondence. In 1899 he was listed in Dunn and Bradstreet, and by 1901 he had become a full-time architect. Before long, he was recognized as the leading architect of Simcoe County and among one of the most talented architects in Canada. In 1924 he was formally recognized by the Ontario Association of Architects under certificate no. 0365. During this period, he lived on the southwest corner of Saint Marie and Ontario streets.

At the Glen Huron School, he devised a system whereby spring water was collected in a reservoir and piped to the building for running water and flush toilets. Fascinated by the novelty of this luxury, the young students of the school depleted the entire water reserve in a matter of hours.

As for his personal character, John Wilson never charged for services rendered to hospitals or veteran's allowance homes. When asked to build the factory for the Collingwood Meat Packing Company, he travelled to Chicago to study a fully operational plant. After seeing the facilities, he subsequently refrained from eating processed meat. Wilson was well recognized for his participation in the community and was respected by many townspeople as an honest, upstanding man of unusual integrity. During his 63 years as a member of the Masonic Lodge Manito, Number 90, Wilson was presented with a jewel as a past master in 1896, a fifty-year jewel in 1939, and in 1949 a 60-year jewel. He was a member of All Saints Anglican Church in Collingwood, a town councillor in the 1920s, chairman on a vocational committee of the Board of Education, and a member of the first Public Utilities Commission, established in 1906.

Wilson continued to practise architecture with a young man named Bill Carswell, who "assisted him with much of the leg work." Wilson's last professional undertaking was the renovation of the Gayety Theatre. On Monday, November 17, 1952, he inspected the project. Shortly thereafter, he suffered a weak spell and was taken home. Less than an hour later, he suffered a fatal heart attack and passed away at 90 years of age. He was interred at the Presbyterian Cemetery on Poplar Sideroad. In his later years, his relationship with his family had been particulary close, especially after his wife, Ethel's, death on May 29, 1937.

John Wilson was survived by four children: Walter A. (Bill) of Farnham, Surrey, England; John McAllister of New Hamburg; J. Donald of London; and Margot Hanley of Collingwood. A second daughter, Mary J., had died in December 1936. John Wilson was also survived by his sister, Mrs. Walter Beer of Owen Sound, his brother Robert Wilson of Oakville, eight grandchildren and one great-grandchild.

In many respects, Wilson's various works stand as testimony to his unusual and seemingly innate talent. Having worked as an architect for decades, the plans and designs of his buildings numbered in the hundreds. While some of them went for safekeeping to John Wilson's friends, the Russ family, others inadvertently fell out of family hands.

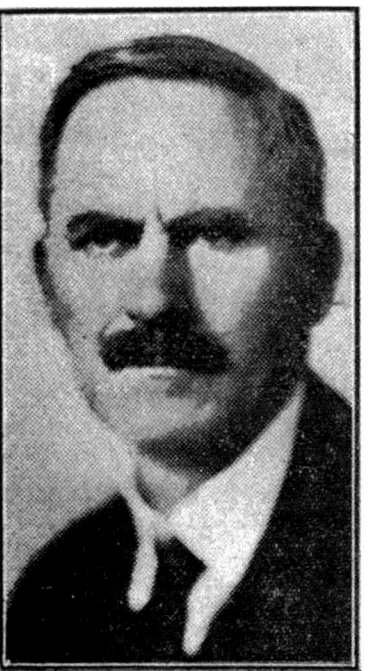

While Addison Mizner's architectural vision defined elegance in the island villas of Palm Beach, John Wilson's architecture defined grandeur in the summer retreat of Muskoka. Wilson's work on Bigwin Island is an experience in line, form and colour. Pictured is architect John Wilson of Collingwood, Ontario.
- *Mr. and Mrs. John McAllister Wilson*

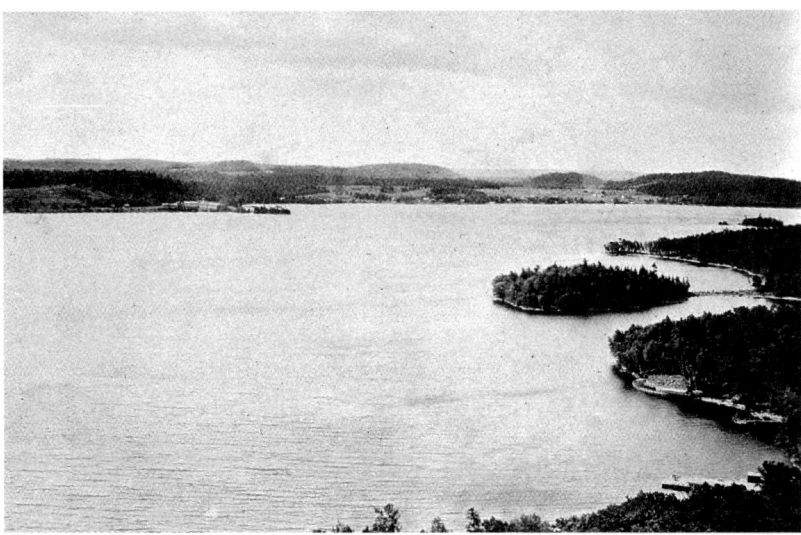

With a huge area reclaimed from the lake, workmen began the herculean task of building the massive dining-room complex. - *DGM*

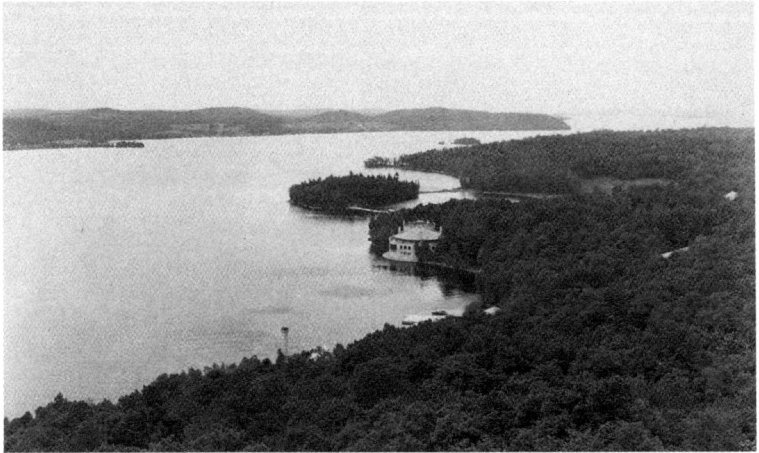

Amid the majestic pines, maples and birches of Bigwin Island, wood, stone, steel and mortar were transformed into the powerful architecture of the dining-room complex, something more grand and extravagant than anything previously erected in Muskoka. - *Helen E. O'Connor*

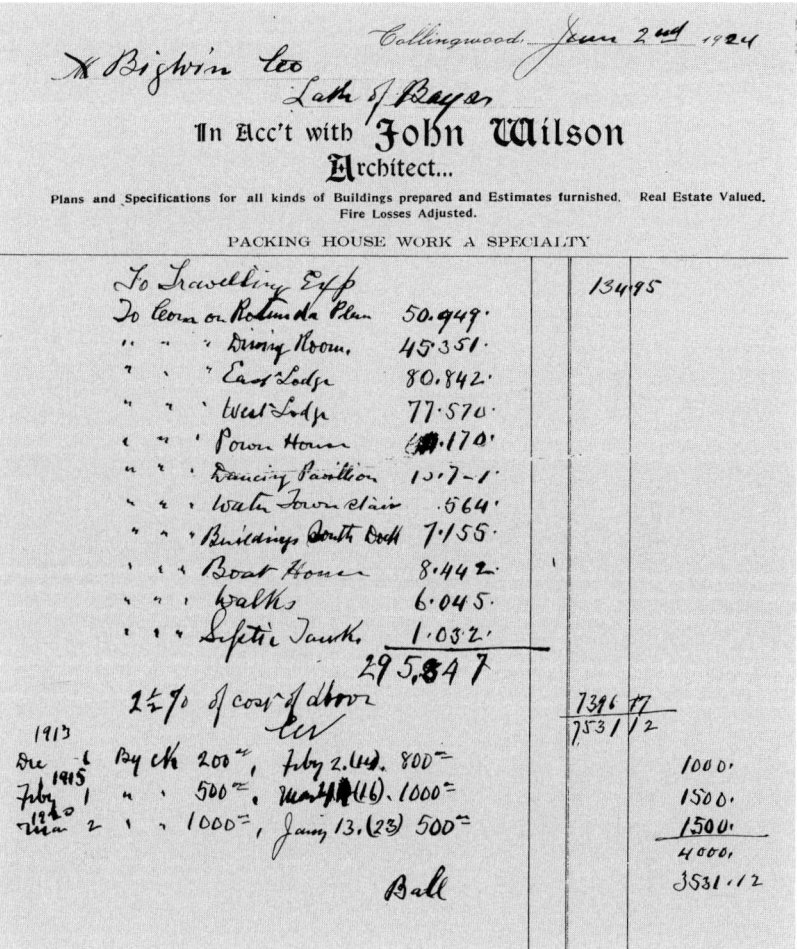

The cost of this ferroconcrete building — a pioneer Canadian structure using this material — was $45,351. - *Mr. and Mrs. John McAllister Wilson*

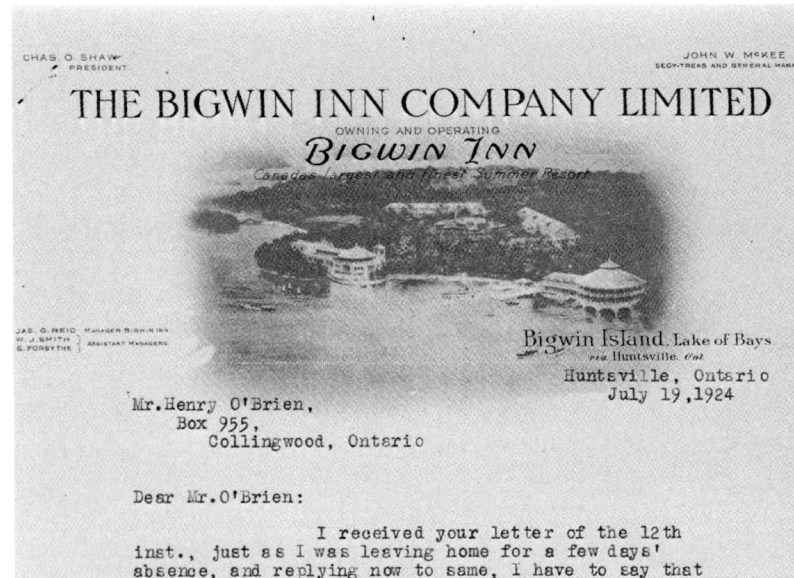

THE BIGWIN INN COMPANY LIMITED

Bigwin Island, Lake of Bays
Huntsville, Ontario
July 19, 1924

Mr. Henry O'Brien,
    Box 955,
    Collingwood, Ontario

Dear Mr. O'Brien:

I received your letter of the 12th inst., just as I was leaving home for a few days' absence, and replying now to same, I have to say that Mr. John Wilson, Architect, of your town, was the sole architect for the buildings at Bigwin Inn. After discussing with Mr. Wilson, as I did at the start and at various times later, and giving him as nearly as I could, my idea of the general lay out of Bigwin as I wished it to be, it was left entirely to Mr. Wilson to provide plans and details of the various buildings which have been erected there. The style of architecture of the various buildings was left entirely to Mr. Wilson, and he is responsible for same. Mr. Wilson was always willing to discuss with me, and to consider my wishes in connection with the general ideas as carried out by him in the planning of all the buildings, but further than to convey to Mr. Wilson my ideas as to locations of the buildings, general dimensions, etc., etc. which I wished to have carried out, I am entitled to no credit, nor is anyone but Mr. Wilson entitled to credit for the architecture and character of the work as it stands today at Bigwin. I would like to go further to say that never in my experience have I found a more practical, in fact as practical and common sense and architect as Mr. Wilson,- always ready and desirous of constructing with the utmost economy, consistent with good work, and showing always more than an ordinary architect's knowledge as regards practical working out of the various details of construction work and operating of same. Were I to have more work of this class to do, Mr. Wilson would unquestionably be my choice as architect and advisor. I can say that in all

---

Mr. Henry O'Brien -2- July 19, 1924

the construction work at Bigwin, and general planning and architecture, I have no regrets nor criticisms as to the general result, and this I think, is about all that could possibly be said, as a result of such an undertaking of construction work.

I might say further, that when the town of Huntsville recently decided to erect, and did erect, a large and substantial addition for their high school, on the recommendation of myself and other directors of our Company, Mr. John Wilson was selected as the architect for such addition, and it was carried out most satisfactorily under his supervision, and according to his plans.

I am pleased to be able to express the satisfaction which I have had in connection with all the work which Mr. Wilson has ever done for the Companies with which I have been associated.

With sincere regards to yourself and Mrs. O'Brien, I remain

Yours very respectfully,

COS/ES

John Wilson's work on Bigwin Island brought him many future commissions. As testimony to Wilson's talent, C.O. Shaw composed a letter of recommendation.
- *Mr. and Mrs. John McAllister Wilson.*

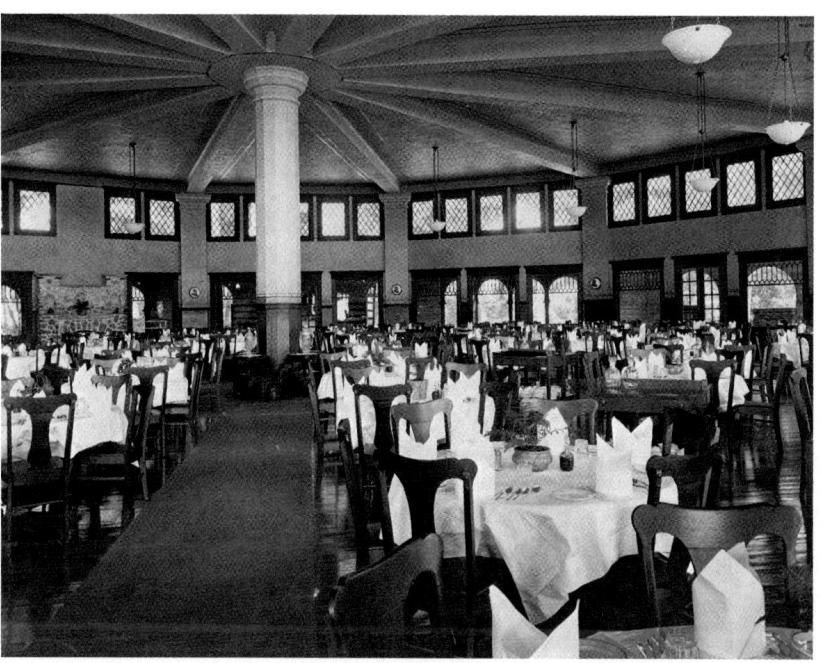

Equally important to the design of the buildings, and a great part of their substance, was the space that the buildings defined. To complement the interiors, Wilson manipulated the use of natural light with the placement of fireplaces, doors and windows. The fenestration of lattice windows in the clerestory captured daylight and cast decorative patterns over the tables below.
- Helen E. O'Connor

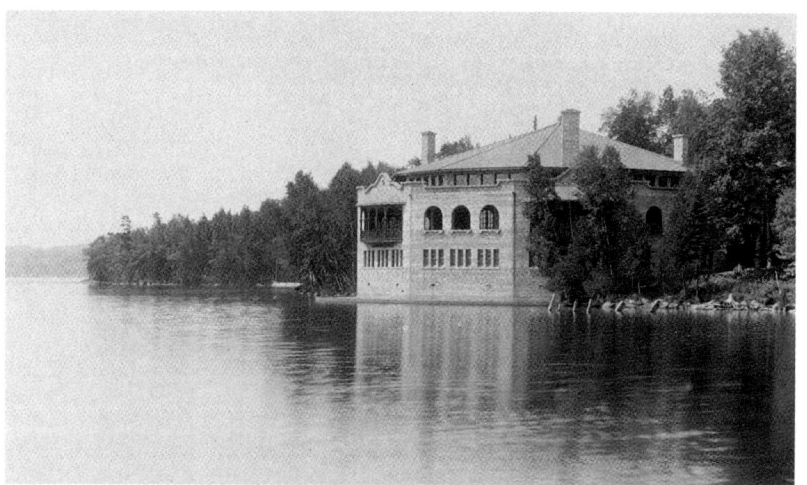

Breathtakingly romantic, the dining-room complex resembled an Italian villa and embodied Wilson's perfect sense of proportion, balance and simplicity.
- DGM

To reach the awe-inspiring Indian Head Room, guests were ushered up a few stairs beneath a campanile-like tower with arched apertures and Romeo-and-Juliet balconies, then through the formal entrance doors.
- DGM

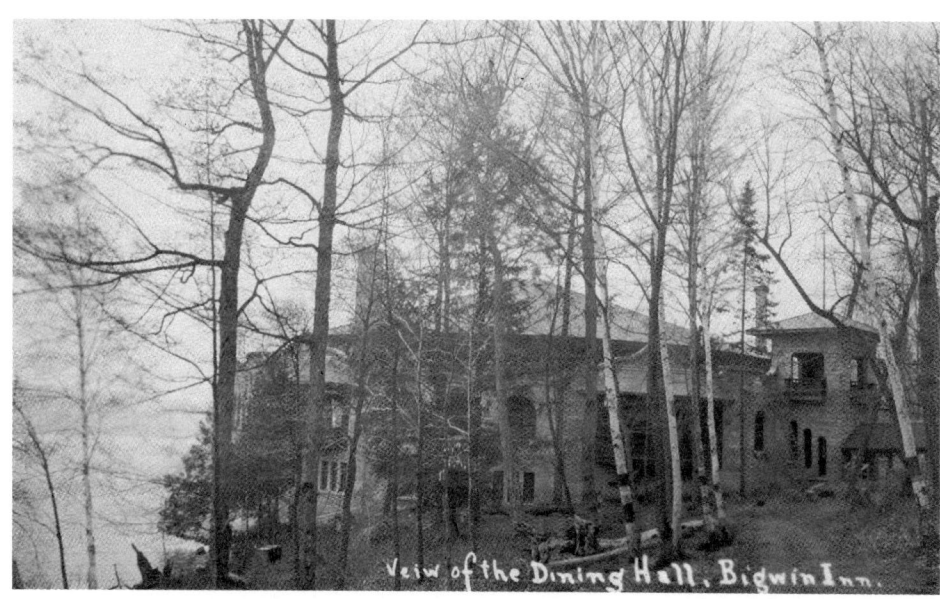

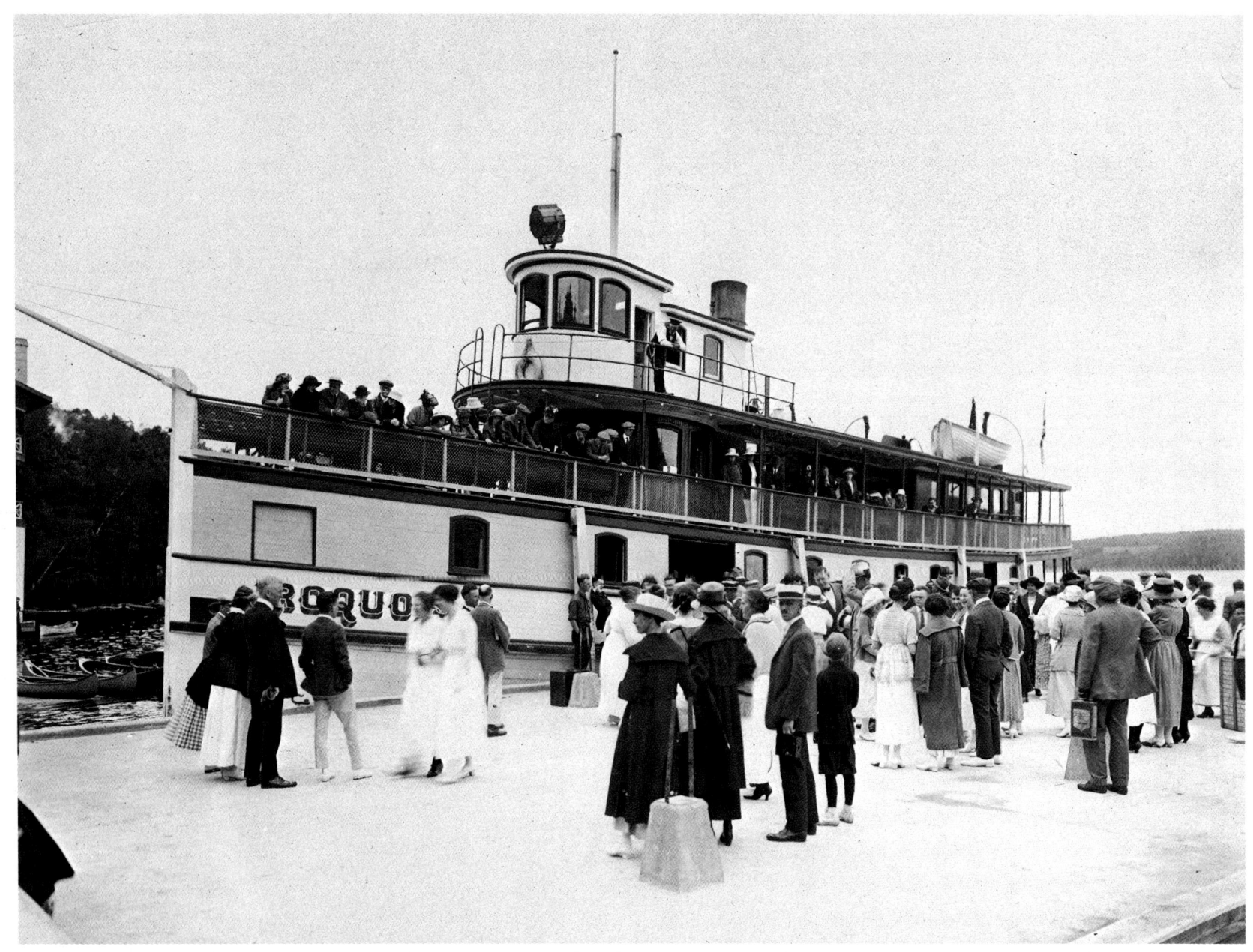
Arriving at Bigwin's wharf in the Roaring Twenties, the steamer *Iroquois* delivered passengers to the exclusive island retreat. Fashionable during that decade were Al Jolson, Mary Pickford, Mickey Mouse, Florenz Ziegfeld's Follies, flapper dress and the Charleston.
- *DGM*

CHAPTER 2

Island Holiday

With the dawn of a glorious golden sun, Canada's finest and most luxurious summer resort, the Bigwin Inn, opened its doors to receive guests on June 26, 1920. Advertisements and brochures for the grand opening boasted that "no hotel could surpass Bigwin Inn in beauty of design, luxuriousness of appointments, excellence of service or charm of natural surroundings." In an age of conspicuous affluence, this was no more than proper self respect on the part of the hotel. With excellent reviews from the Grand Trunk Railway and the Editorial Association of Canadian Papers and American Papers, the news of Bigwin's opulence spread rapidly.

The opening of the Inn added a new oasis to the list of magnificent bastions already enjoyed by some of the world's wealthiest travellers. Fashionable sites such as Florida's Palm Beach Inn, West Virginia's Greenbrier Hotel, the Grand Hotel on Mackinac Island, Michigan, and the Algonquin Hotel of Saint Andrews by the Sea, New Brunswick, would no longer dominate the North American tourist trade. With its striking grandeur, its unique appeal and inherent prestige, the Bigwin Inn immediately established an international clientele of discriminating taste. Socialites soon came to know that this exclusive island retreat was *the* place to see and to be seen at.

The Inn's first season was booked well in advance, and it would become increasingly difficult to get accommodation at the resort for some years to follow. Quite often, those wishing to summer at the Inn were obliged to stay at other hotels on the Lake of Bays and travel to Bigwin by launch to enjoy its amenities. The management reflected this magnetism in most of its promotional brochures, advising, "In order to avoid disappointment or possible failure to obtain accommodation on arrival, the management requests that those who intend visiting Bigwin will give reasonable notice in order that they may be advised as to the acceptance and confirmation of their reservations. All applications not necessarily accepted." The hotel's outstanding social success also meant financial prosperity. Reportedly, "the largest summer resort in the British Commonwealth" paid for itself in its first seven seasons of operation.

To summer at Bigwin Inn was like going to see a great theatrical production. From the high decks of an approaching lake steamer, passengers could view the Inn from afar. Nearing the harbour, the curtain began to rise as many of the buildings came into full view. As the production began, guests were enveloped in the enchanting scene. Against the magical island backdrop, John Wilson had designed elegant sets. C.O. Shaw was the enterprising producer-director, the hotel personnel were the talented performers, and the resort's guests played the role of a spellbound audience.

The Dining-Room Complex
Over 30 feet from the shoreline, Bigwin's dodecagonal dining hall rose dramatically from the watery depths of the Lake of Bays with a Venetian élan. Designed in Mediterranean Revival style, the imposing structure captured the interest of many passengers aboard incoming steamers.

Guests were ushered up a few stairs beneath a small tower with arched apertures and Romeo-and-Juliet balconies, then through the formal entrance doors at the rear of the dining room. Those visiting Bigwin for the first time were often awestruck by the size and atmosphere of the main room. With over 55,000 square feet, the dining complex was enormous and seated up to 750 guests at a time.

The grand hall, known as the "Indian Head Room," was designed by John Wilson to be very simple, open and bright during the day. He accomplished this in various ways. The steel beamed, vaulted ceiling, rising over 35 feet above a floor measuring over 130 feet in diameter, was supported in the middle by a large structural column. From the top of the column, 12 beams fanned out to a series of finely moulded cornices, thus giving the huge room a sense of symmetry and lightness. During the day, windows around the perimeter of the ceiling let sunbeams trickle in and gently reflect off the gleaming wood floors; at night, the focus of the room shifted to the three grand fireplaces. French doors and gallery

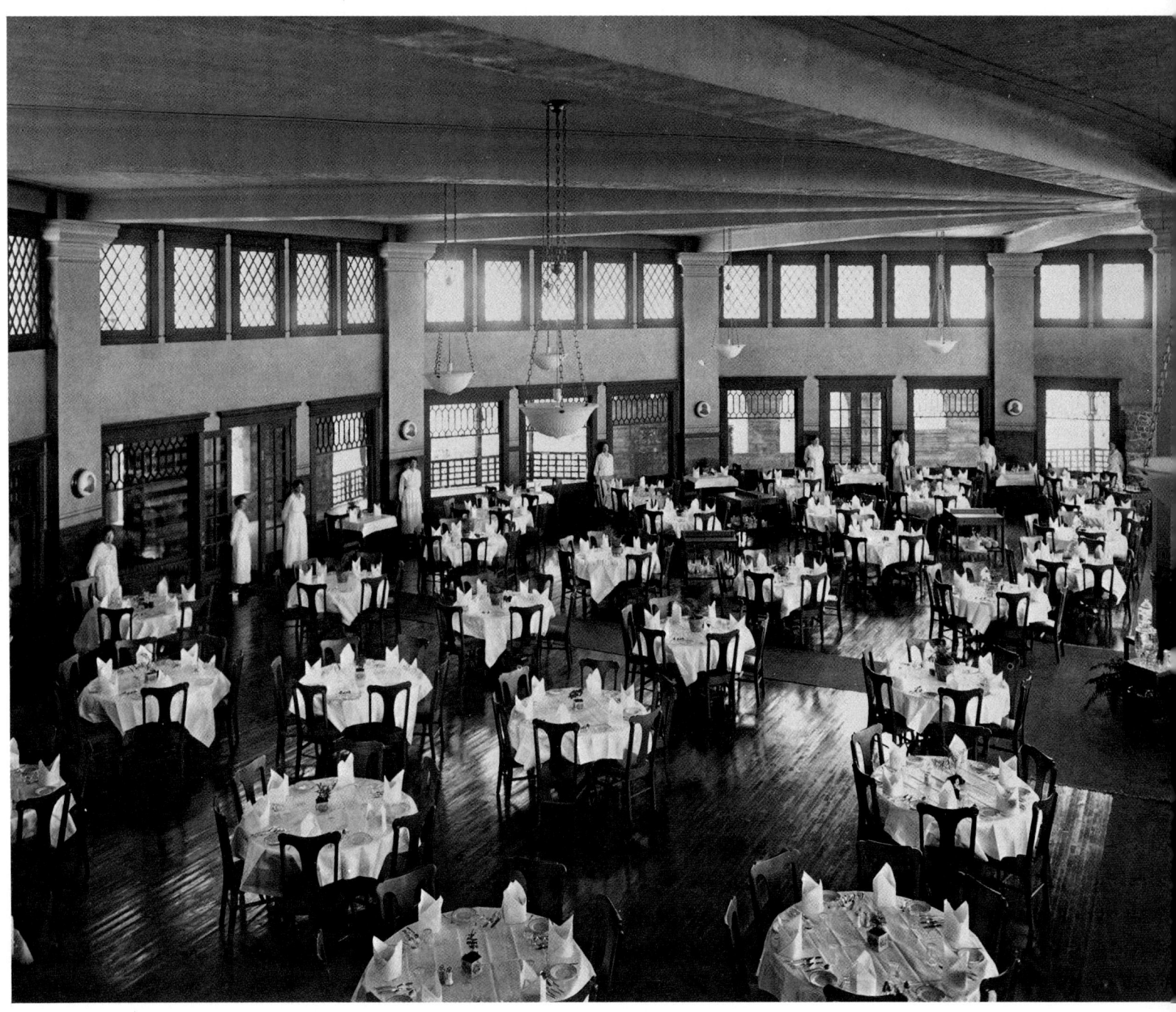

Aesthetically compelling, the Indian Head Room was designed by John Wilson to be very simple, open and bright. By 7:30 each morning, waitresses would station themselves and await the arrival of the first breakfast guests.

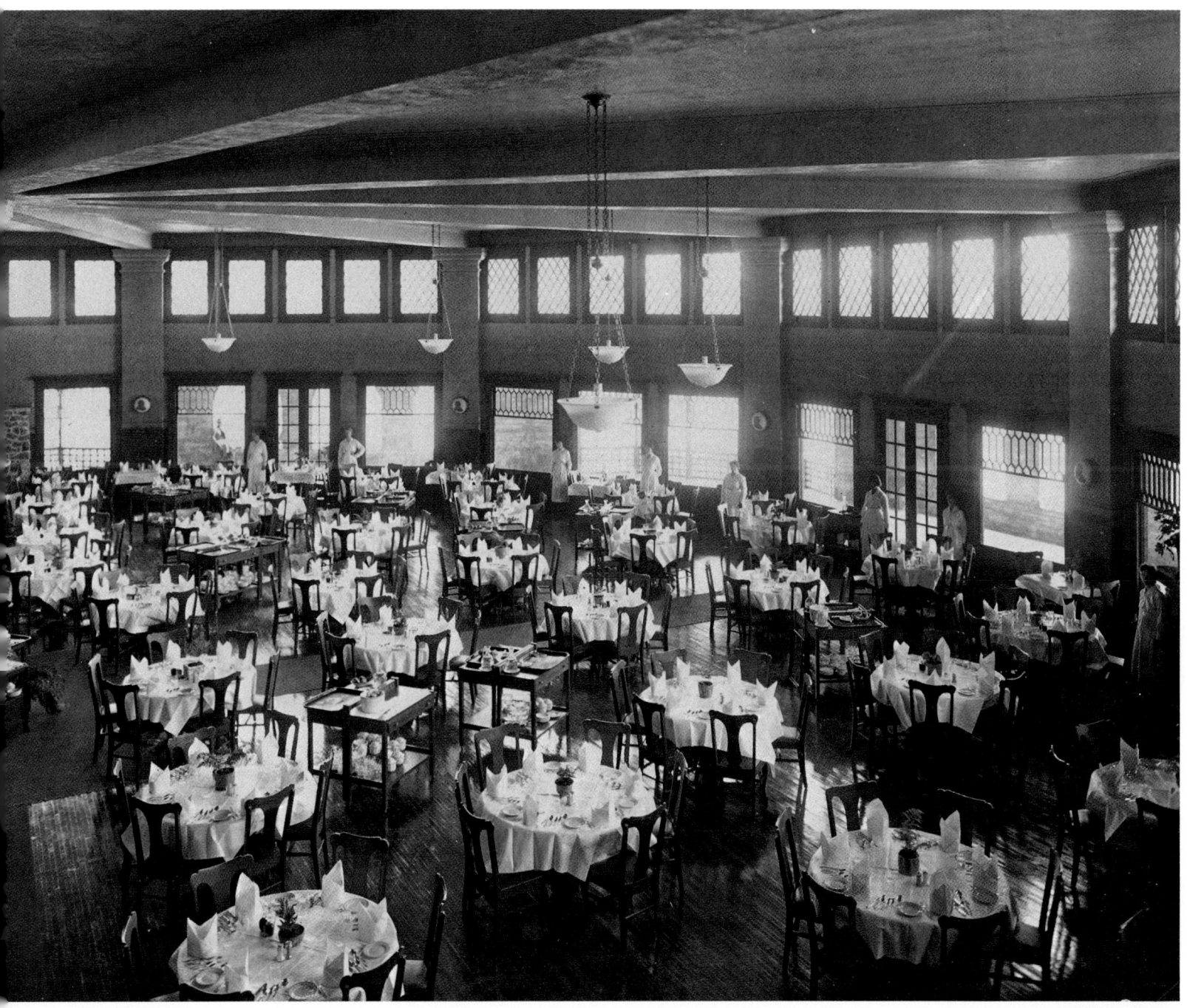

- Robert McLennan

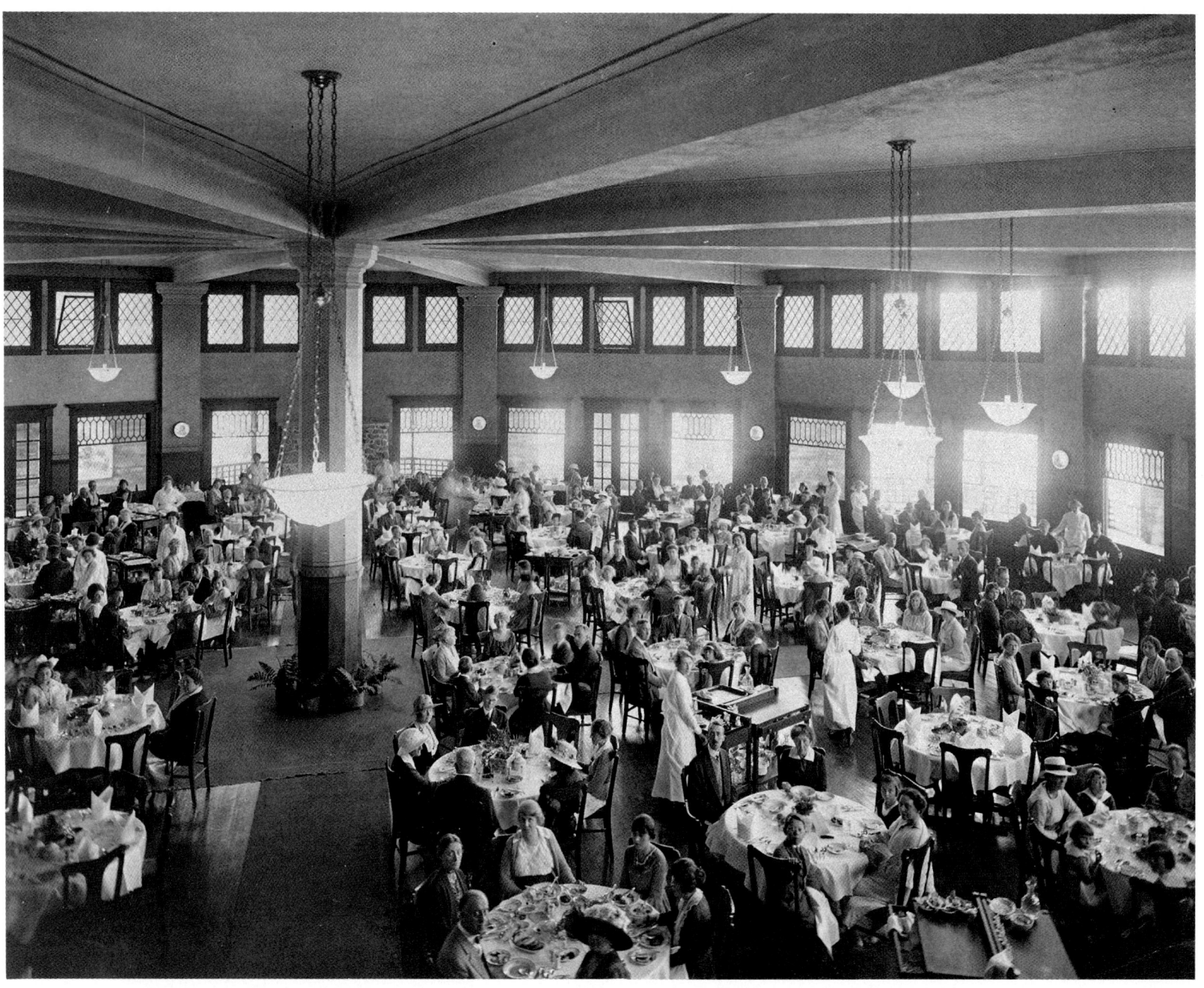
By 8:15 a.m., most tables were full. Chelsea buns, brioche, fresh farm eggs, bacon, California oranges, buttermilk, Shirriff's Good Morning marmalade, hot cocoa and pure spring water were favourites of guests.
- *DGM*

windows were located around the perimeter, informal entrances were available, and wonderful views of the lake or forest could be had from anywhere in the room.

Seating up to six people, the maple pedestal tables were dressed with crisp, white damask cloths and appointed with the hotel's extensive dinner service of blue-and-white crested china, glassware and silverware, as well as freshly cut flowers or potted ferns. In preparation for the hotel's debut, the linens were voluntarily prepared by members of the Ladies Aid of Saint Andrew's Church in Huntsville. As a token of his appreciation, C.O. Shaw invited the Ladies Aid to a rehearsal luncheon served two days before the resort's grand opening.

The dining facility demanded an extremely large staff. To C.O. Shaw's standard, most of the 95 girls who waitressed in the dining room were university students. They abided by a strict set of rules established by Shaw and enforced by the dining-room hostess, who choreographed the performance from start to finish.

After checking the list of arriving guests and cross checking it with her guest-history files, the hostess welcomed the visitors and guided them to their tables. Once the guests were seated and given an opportunity to review the menu, waitresses in black-and-white uniforms approached the tables (spare aprons, collars and cuffs were kept ready to ensure each waitress a spotless appearance at all times). With orders memorized, they retreated to the kitchen to place them with the executive chef. Shortly thereafter, the waitresses re-entered the room carrying serving trays high above their shoulders. The tables were re-approached and the trays lowered in unison. This procedure was repeated for various courses, with hot and cold dishes always carried separately. The delivery of hundreds of finger bowls signalled the meal's end. After the performance had concluded, both Mr. and Mrs. Shaw reviewed the operation, and by correcting any imperfections immediately, ensured a perfect dining experience for all future visitors.

Ensconced in a large loggia overlooking the dining room, the hotel orchestra enhanced the opulence of the entire production by performing delightful classical music each day during luncheon and dinner.

The only indulgences denied guests in the dining room were smoking and the consumption of alcohol. One of the many stories of Bigwin recounts the instance when a major automobile tycoon from the United States was asked to leave the island after insisting on smoking in the Indian Head Room.

Protecting the serenity and elegance of the Indian Head Room, the resort offered an auxiliary dining room to the right of the building's main entrance. There, infants, nurses and nannies could be comfortably accommodated and, in the words of the hotel's brochure, be "free from petty restraint." To encourage the room's use, the management afforded a discount to guests whose servants, nurses and children utilized this alternative facility.

Surrounding the Indian Head Room was the broad "Venetian Terrace," furnished with hickory and wicker furniture, most of which came from Eaton's College Street store and Barrymore's of Toronto. The terrace's many wide arches and latticed balconies proved popular for viewing boats and waterfront activities during afternoon teas or games of bridge. At one end of this arcade was a "glass enclosed apartment where breakfast for late risers" was "served until 10 o'clock in the morning without extra charge."

Directly below the Venetian Terrace was the staff dining room. While this cafeteria was decidedly more simple than the Indian Head Room, a beamed ceiling, narrow-paned windows and a modest fireplace gave the room a sense of refinement. All newly employed waitresses began their extensive training in the canteen, working there until their skills were perfected for the formalities of the Indian Head Room.

Designed in early February 1929, a second dodecagon structure was built for the 1930 season as an annex to the main dining room. The new addition, the "Marine Dining Room," was connected by a short passageway where the third fireplace of the Indian Head Room had once stood. The room had a vaulted ceiling and handsome fireplace of its own. Over 150 guests could enjoy a more intimate dining atmosphere and spectacular views of the ever-changing lake waters. In addition to the victuals served in the dining room, the management offered "room service with a small charge for the busboy's delivery of trays to private rooms." Picnic hampers could also "be prepared with notice by the evening prior to any intended excursion."

Below the Marine Dining Room was a large hall complete with a tiered stone fireplace. In this room, originally known as the "Casino," the hotel's office staff took their meals. From time to time, the area was also used by guests as a cinema or by conventions as a function room.

A labyrinth of hallways and service staircases allowed employees to hurriedly thread themselves through to all rooms, unseen by guests. The busiest of these rooms were the serving rooms, pantries and kitchens. Servicing them was an ensemble of the most modern equipment available, including a dumbwaiter which could hoist supplies from the meat lockers, root cellar, bakery and storage rooms below.

The Inn's culinary masterpieces were the responsibility of a dietician and various chefs well versed in all aspects of European cuisine. Their day began shortly after 5 o'clock in the morning, when the hotel engineer would complete his inspection of the complex and let in the first of the dining room staff. Later, as guests began to filter in for breakfast, the fragrant aroma of freshly baked breads and chelsea buns drifted through the rooms and outside, where it mingled with the scent of the forest's pine trees. In spite of their many talents, the kitchen artisans were not completely immune to the occasional predicament. When a guest requested that rice pudding be added to the luncheon menu, the kitchen

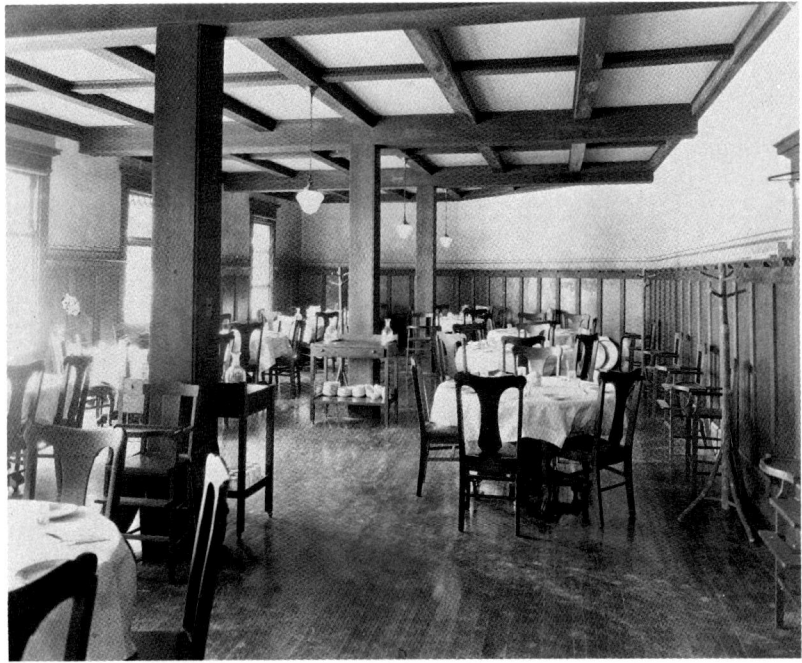

The management encouraged young children, nurses and nannies to dine in the auxiliary dining room, "thus protecting the serene elegance" of the Indian Head Room.
- *Helen E. O'Connor*

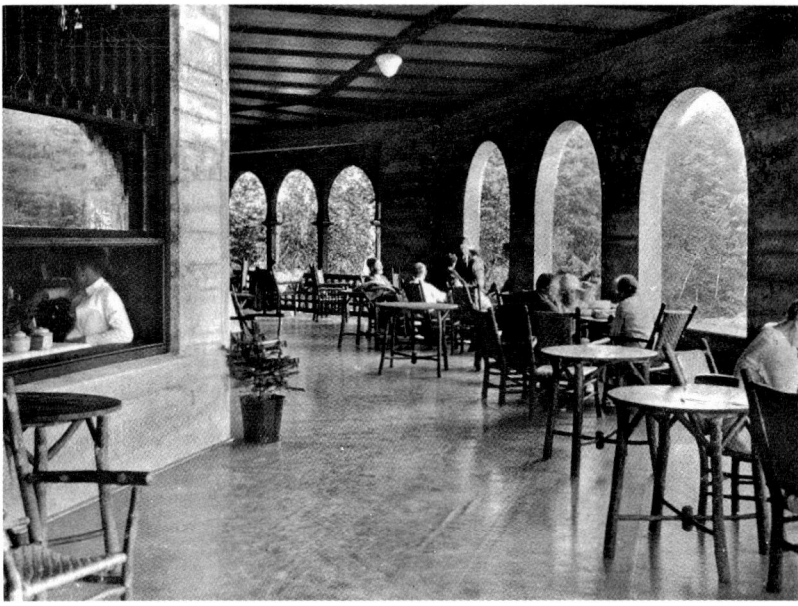

The Venetian Terrace was furnished with hickory and wicker furniture. Framed by Roman archways, guests could enjoy magnificent views of waterfront activities and passing mahogany launches while listening to the strains of Mozart or Gershwin.
- *DGM*

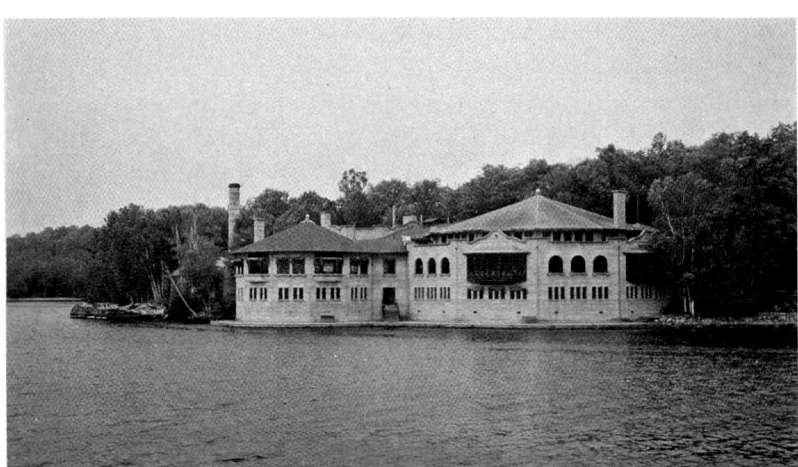

Like a DeMille movie set, the dining rooms were designed on a grand scale and conveyed an overwhelming sense of elegance, conjuring up exotic images of Spanish castles.
- *DGM*

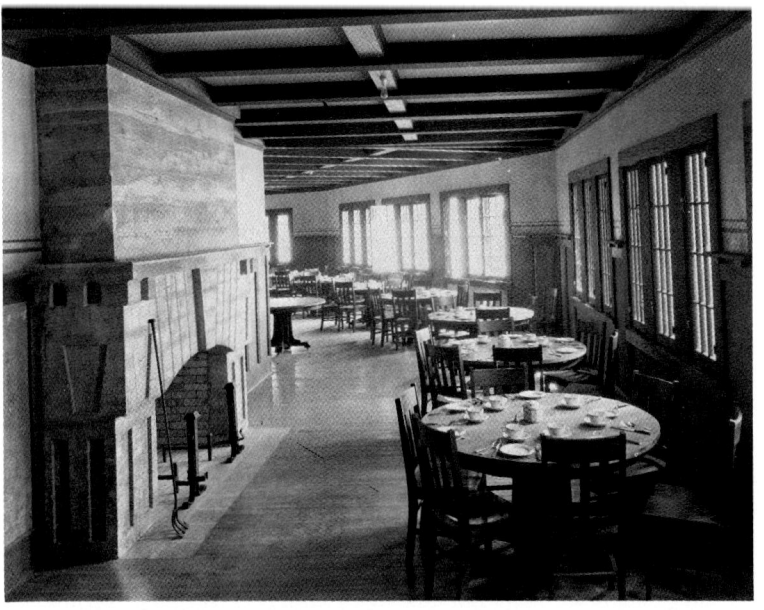

The staff dining room was located directly below the Venetian Terrace.
- *Helen E. O'Connor*

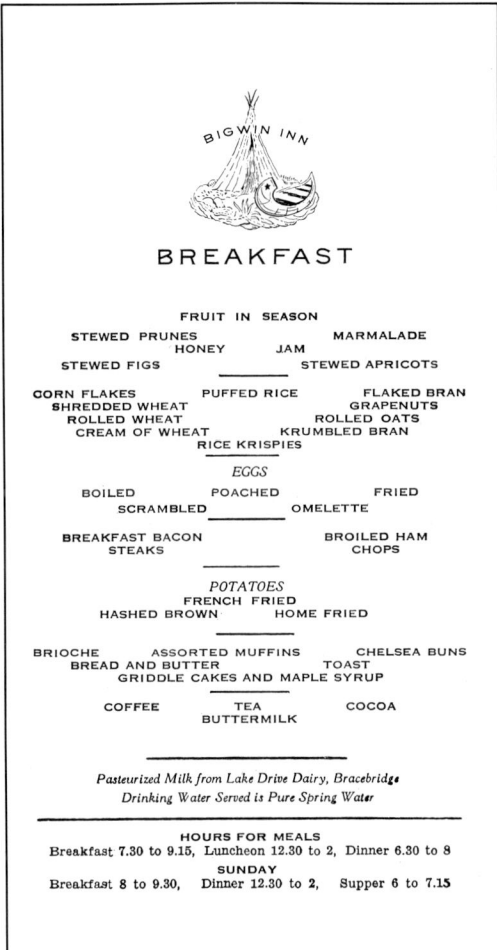
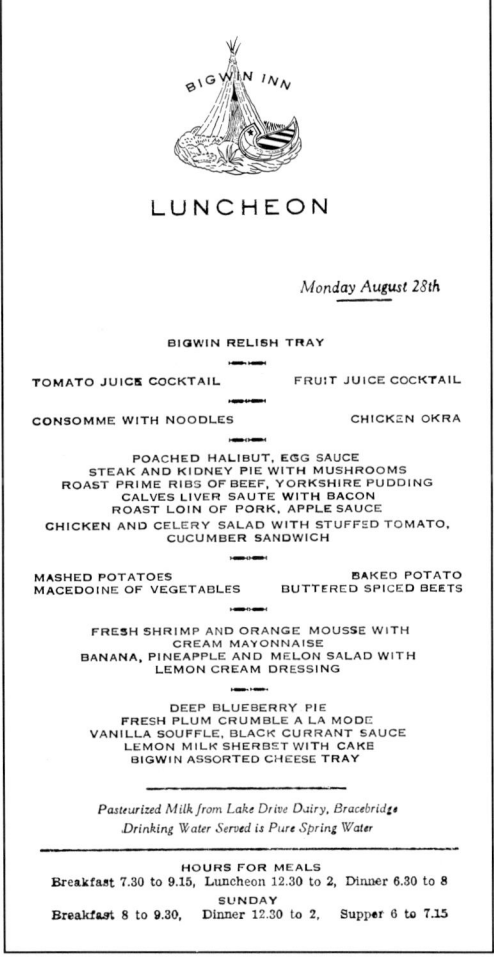
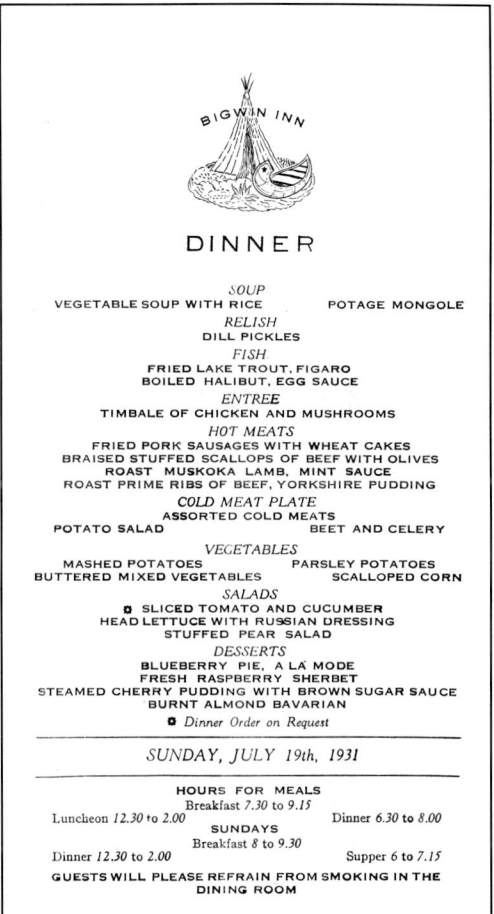

Bigwin's menu continued to be quite impressive during the stringent times of the Great Depression and rationing measures of W.W. II. Fearing shortages, some guests attempted to negotiate the purchase of personal supplies from the Inn prior to their trip home.

— *DGM and Mr. and Mrs. John McAllister Wilson.*

staff found themselves without a recipe. Samuel Forsythe, the resort's first assistant manager, anxiously telephoned his wife. She recounted a recipe over the telephone, and the dining-room staff was saved from considerable embarrassment.

The highest-quality ingredients for gastronomic delights were often obtained from the resort's own vegetable and dairy farm, which was located in Huntsville, overlooking the Muskoka River, across from the tannery and behind the Bigwin Laundry. There, the farm's herd of 50 Holstein cows supplied the purest milk for cream and butter. Just below the farm and along the river bank, the steamer *Algonquin* docked. Though she was already laden with passengers and freight on their way to North Portage, her deck hands picked up all dairy products, produce and clean linens for subsequent delivery to the hotel.

On the southwest side of Bigwin Inn's dining-room complex was a series of small, wooden freight docks where crates and casks of such cargo were unloaded by crews of the steamers *Mohawk Belle* and *Iroquois*. Just beyond these docks, perishables were stored in a vast icehouse kept cool by massive blocks of crystalline ice that had been packed in sawdust after being laboriously cut and hauled from the lake during winter months.

The Sun Terraces, Offices, Steamer Docks and Bigwin Boat Livery
Southeast of the dining complex, flagstone terraces afforded guests lakeside views of "Bigwin Bay" while lounging in the warmth of the summer sun. Colourful umbrellas offered shade for delicate complexions and an attendant served chilled glasses of iced tea or lemonade from a beverage trolley. With a Monegasque vivacity, stone steps led down from the terraces and met a golden sand bathing beach where a special hostess offered morning and afternoon lessons to inexperienced swimmers. By the mid-1930s, a large swimming dock, diving board and three diving towers had been added to the harbourfront facilities for greater comfort and more challenging recreation. Numerous swings, slides and pathways delighted children and encouraged them to enjoy the perfumed zephyrs of the island, consequently leaving the buildings quiet for the adults or, as one early brochure stated, "the Victorians who read their books in the lounge."

As they tapered into the curving shoreline, the terraces merged with the baggage and steamer docks. In the berth between the wharves, vessels such as the *Iroquois* pulled in twice daily. Tourists disembarked from her starboard side, and baggage and mail were unloaded from her port side. Guest swimming was permitted from either of these wharves, but staff aquatics were restricted to the baggage dock. By 1922 a crimson-tiled roof sheltered the wharves. In the same period, a management and printing office were added, where various items were printed, including menus for the dining rooms, regatta posters for the Livery, and a weekly newsletter entitled *The Bigwin Banter*, which included notice of forthcoming musical concerts at the hotel.

An early mishap in hotel operations occurred one morning when bellboys, suited in handsome grey uniforms embroidered with red stitching, focused so intently on standing at attention to greet the resort's first guests that they neglected to collect the baggage from the *Iroquois*, which continued on her journey to Dorset. Understandably, the event was much to the consternation of the management and to the dismay of the guests, a Mr. and Mrs. Reid and their two children, from Napanee, Ontario. Later, in somewhat similar instances, and at the discretion of the boat's owner, Charles George Shaw, the speedboat *Marco* came to the rescue. Capable of travelling at high speed, the launch was able to catch up to the *Iroquois* or *Mohawk Belle*, subsequently delivering urgent mail or guests who had missed the returning boat destined for South Portage.

Next to the steamer wharf was a two-storey, gabled boathouse. This 5,100-square-foot building housed staff quarters above and storage facilities below for the Bigwin Boat Livery Company Limited. The Livery, which operated in conjunction with the hotel, stocked over 100 canoes, dinghies, gigs, sailboats and skiffs, each available for short-term or seasonal rental.

The Lake of Bays Regatta was traditionally held at Bigwin Inn in August. On this festive annual occasion, people hired many of the marina's vessels and competed in such spirited events as aqua-planing, canoe-tipping, log-rolling, walking a greasy pole, sailing and swimming races.

For sightseeing, guests could charter any one of the Inn's five motor launches. Boats like *Annetta*, *Clarion*, *Kingfisher*, *Rambler III* and the *Wanda III* carried tourists around the Lake of Bays for day or evening cruises. In the event of inclement weather conditions, the Livery offered passengers the comforts of slickers and hats. Of course, some people smuggled on board a flask of their own type of comfort, as Bigwin Inn was a temperance hotel and therefore completely "dry."

The Pavilion
Across the bay from the dining-room complex and adjacent to the Livery, an imposing panelled dodecagonal building rose over the water with a Victorian gracefulness. Architect John Wilson designed the structure to be both grand in appearance and versatile in function.

One of the most unique features of the "Pavilion" was that it was cantilevered over the water. With four boat slips beneath it, all classes of watercraft could be moored and their varnished or painted finishes protected from the elements.

The exterior fir walls of the edifice featured detailed woodwork, including ornamental railings which incorporated the design of the Union Jack. Topping the 12,000-square-foot hall was a gently sloping, crimson-tiled roof with a large windowed lantern. Inside, the roof was reinforced with steel beams which were supported by a large structural

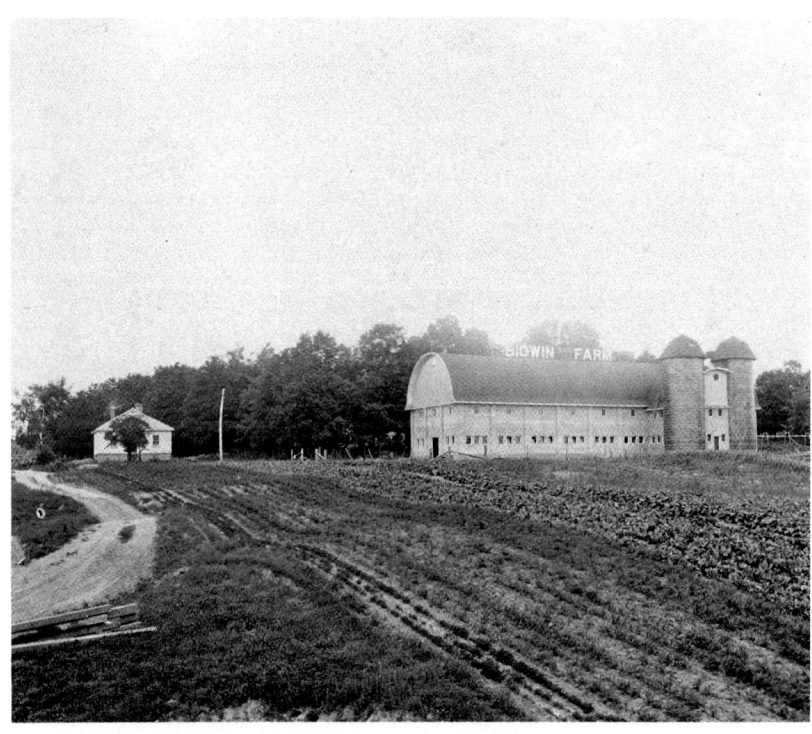 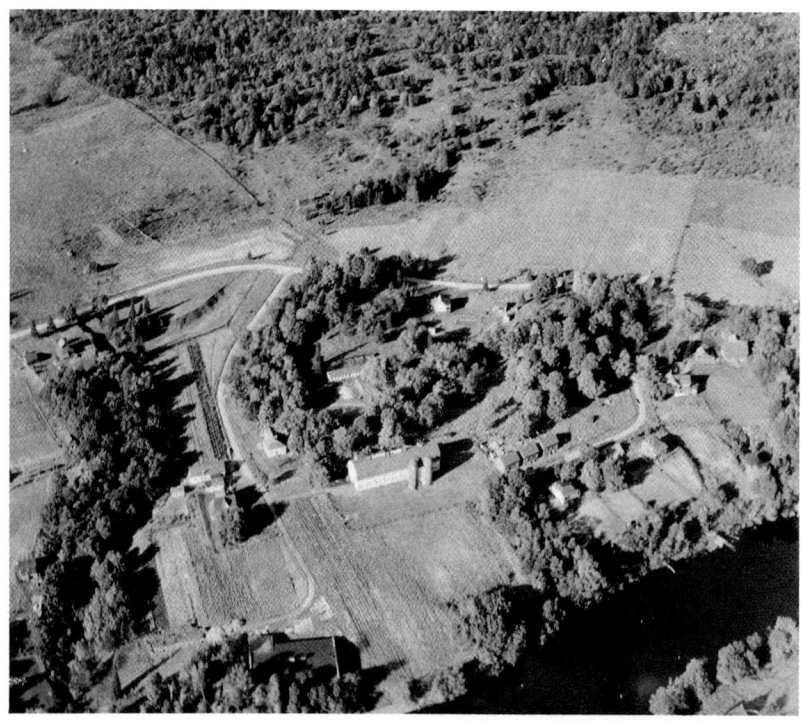

A great deal of the hotel's produce and dairy products were shipped by the Navigation Company from the Bigwin Farm at Huntsville. Other supplies were procured from National Grocers Company Limited and delivered to the resort by Kelly Transport or Hutchins Transport. A *Bigwin Banter* of 1937 read: "One of the busiest sections of back stage at Bigwin is the Salad Pantry. No need to comment on the goodness and beauty, yes beauty, of these delectable creations! Have you ever seen such gorgeous looking affairs served on any dining room table? Bigwin's salads are famed the continent over, and it really is an interesting operation to watch skilful fingers put them together. Two of Toronto's ablest dieticians are responsible for this most important course on the menus — Miss Helen Irvine and Miss Irene Miller. Orchids to you both — clever ladies."

- *Helen O'Connor and DGM*

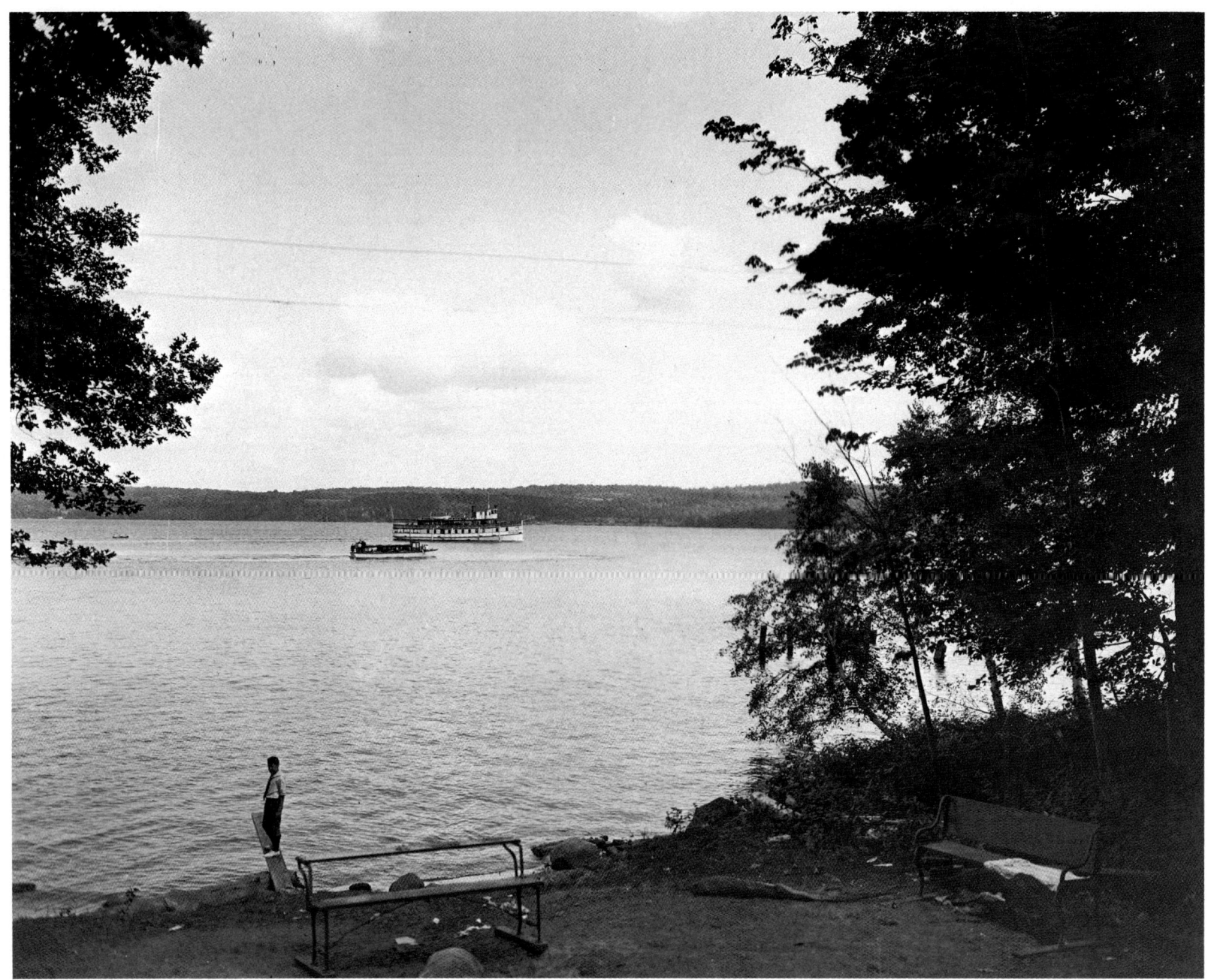
Flagstone terraces built along the waterfront by the late 1930s transformed the original bathing beach. *- Helen O'Connor and DGM*

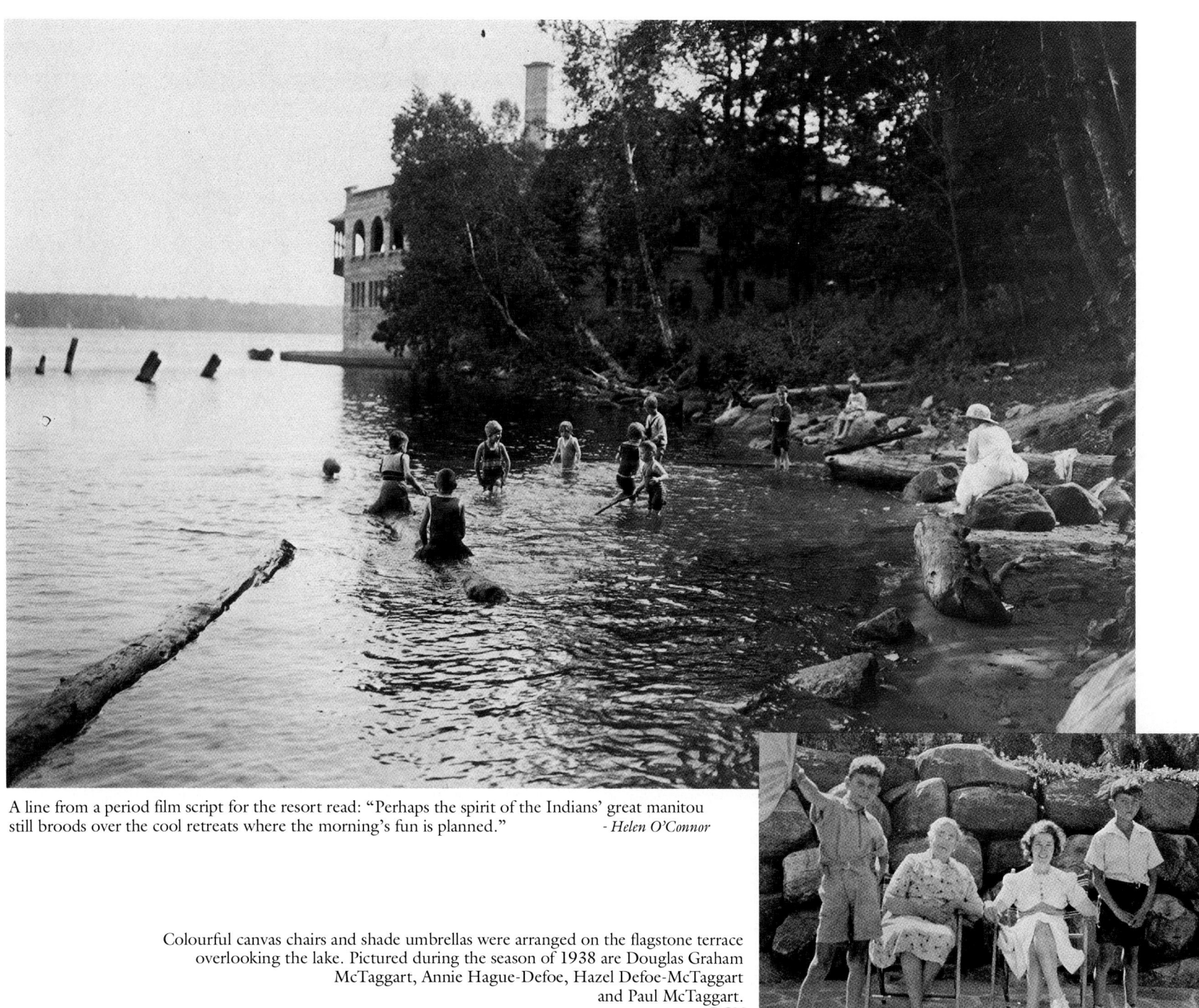

A line from a period film script for the resort read: "Perhaps the spirit of the Indians' great manitou still broods over the cool retreats where the morning's fun is planned."
- *Helen O'Connor*

Colourful canvas chairs and shade umbrellas were arranged on the flagstone terrace overlooking the lake. Pictured during the season of 1938 are Douglas Graham McTaggart, Annie Hague-Defoe, Hazel Defoe-McTaggart and Paul McTaggart.
- *DGM*

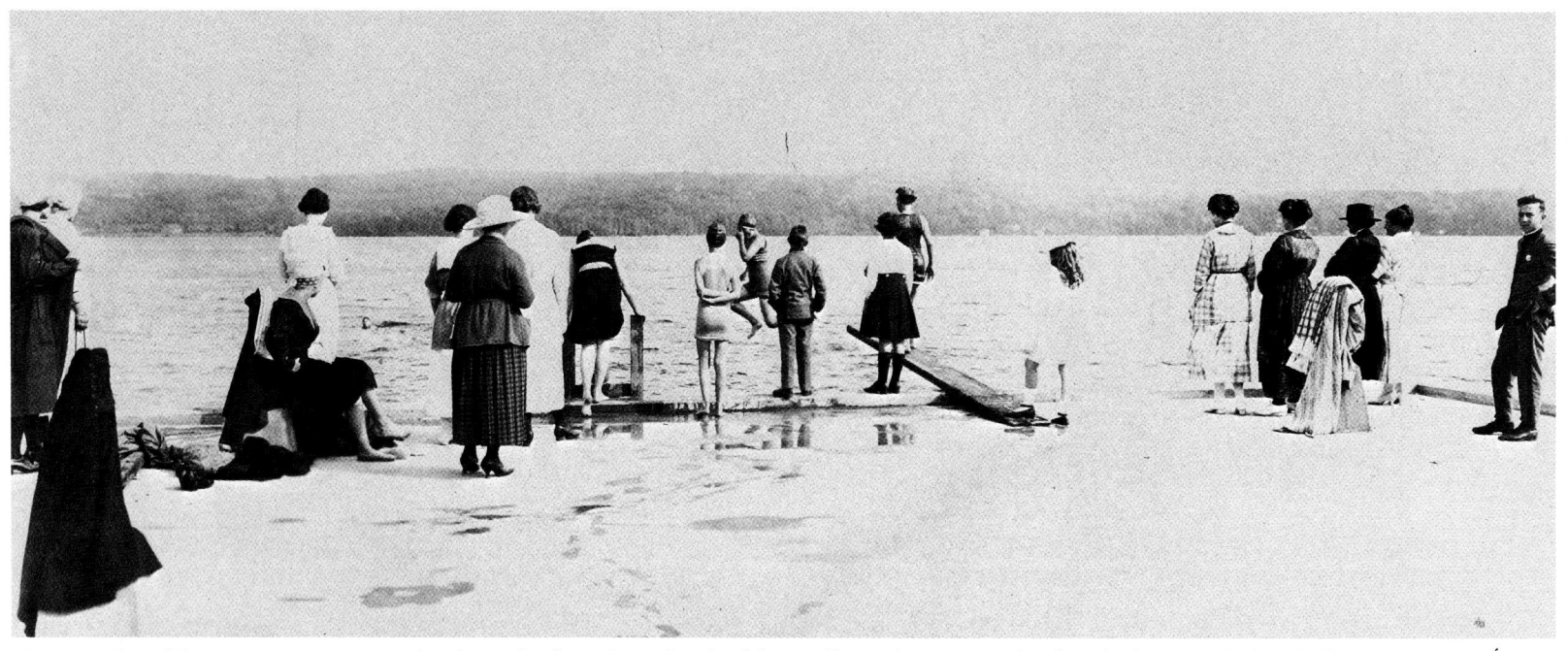

Guests at the wilderness retreat were permitted to swim from the main wharf, but staff aquatics were restricted to the baggage dock. A bellboy, far right, awaits the arrival of guests by private launch.
- *Helen O'Connor*

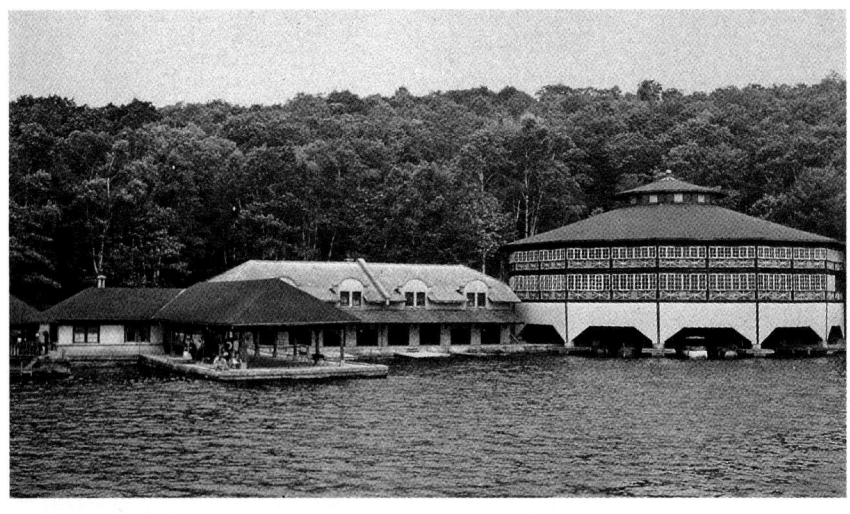

Pictured are the manager's office, steamer dock, Bigwin Boat Livery and Pavilion. A newsletter from the 1930s featured this enticement: "The John Holden Players scored a singular triumph with 'Accent On Youth' last year, when they gave its first stock showing in Winnipeg, and we know their interpretations of the clever lines will move you with tenderness — yet leave you happy with enjoyment. Tickets for 'Accent On Youth' are on sale Monday morning at the desk. Curtain goes up at the Pavilion, 8:45 Monday evening."
- *DGM*

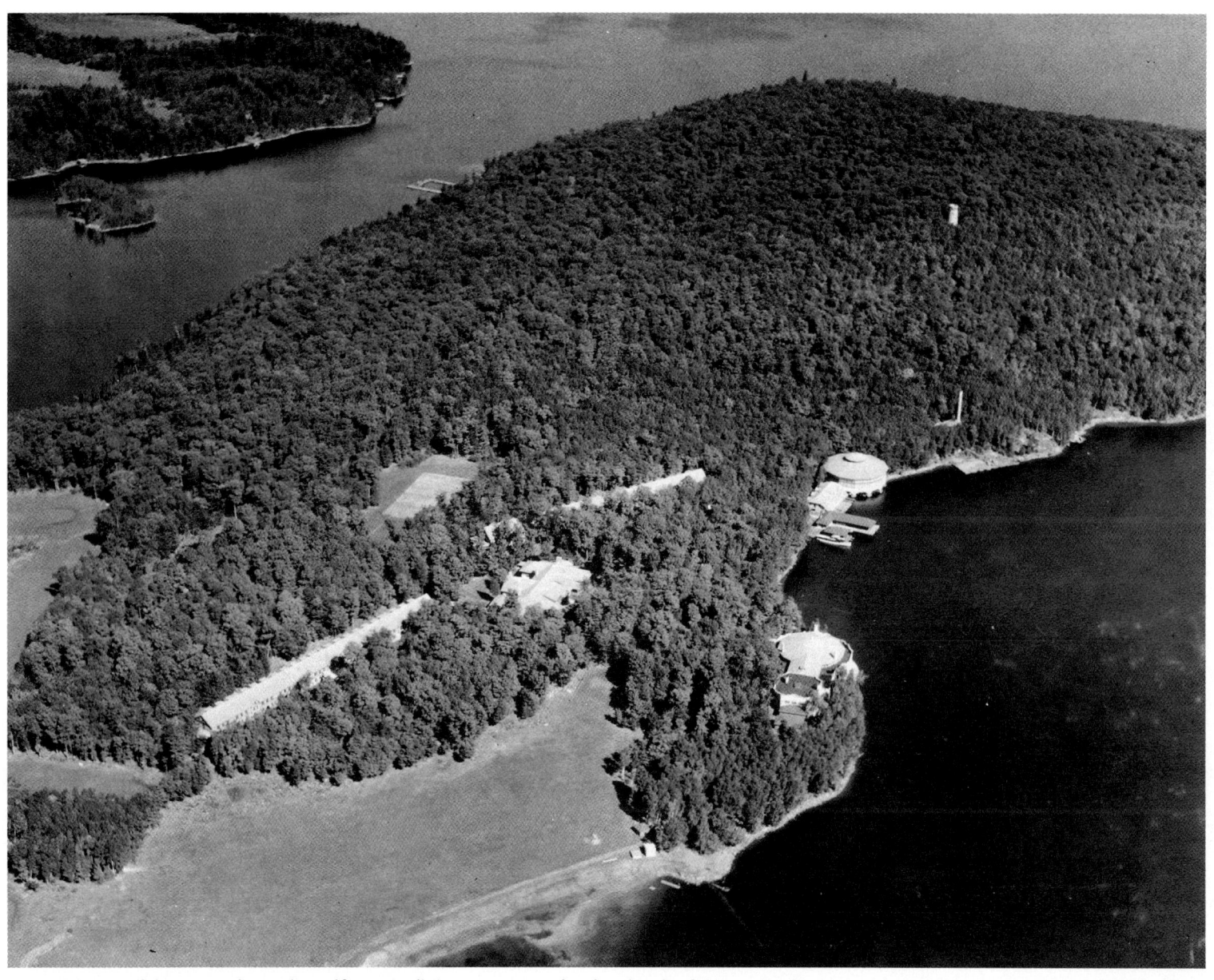

An aerial view of the resort shows the golf course, dining-room complex, beach, wharf, Livery, Pavilion, powerhouse, Observation Tower, East Lodge, Rotunda, West Lodge, tennis courts, bowling greens, and on the north shore of the island, the dry docks.
- *Robert McLennan*

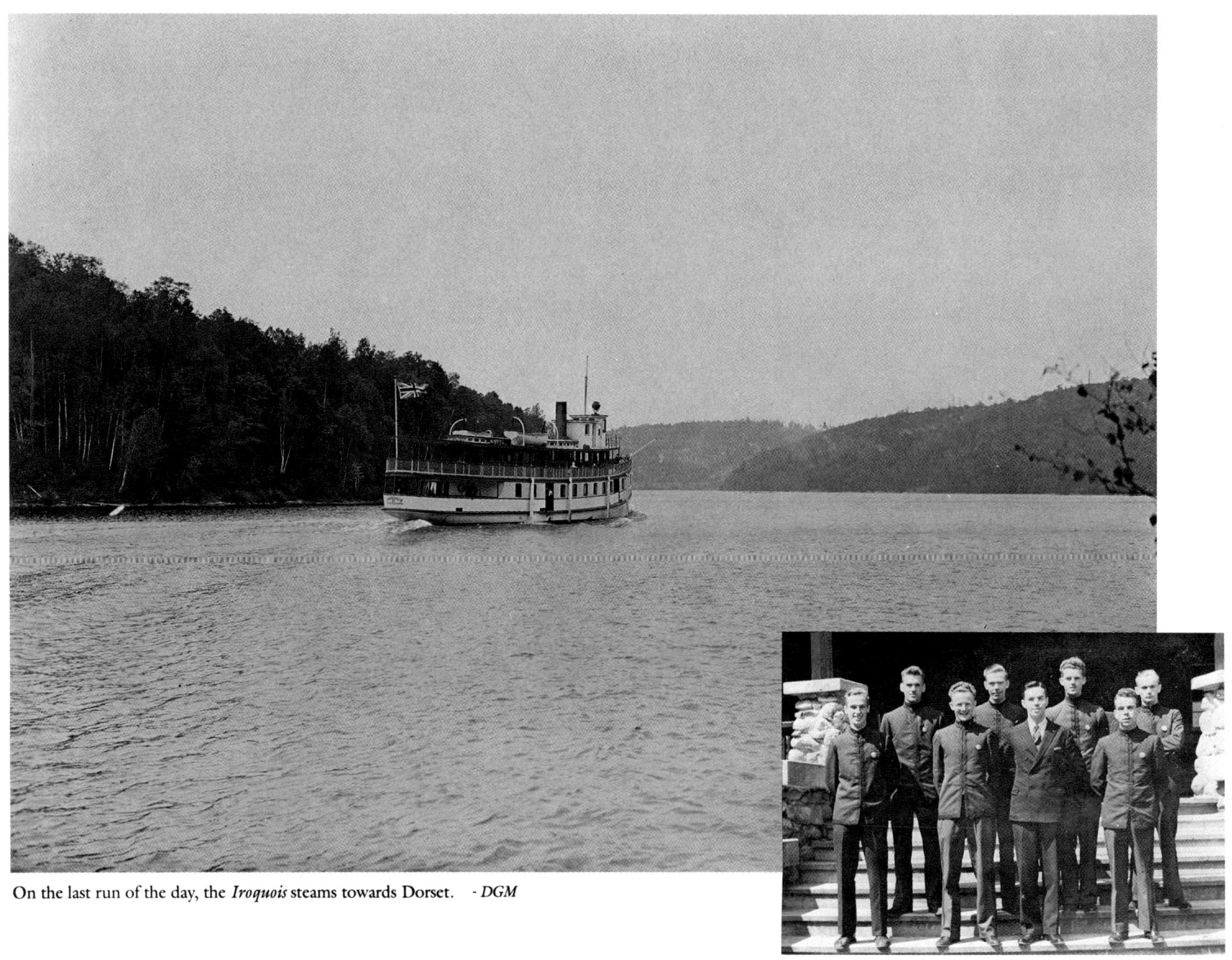

On the last run of the day, the *Iroquois* steams towards Dorset. - *DGM*

Upon their arrival, guests of the Inn were welcomed by bellboys who escorted them to the front desk of the Rotunda. In later years, C.O. Shaw's V16 Cadillac chauffeured guests to the Rotunda. - *Robert McLennan*

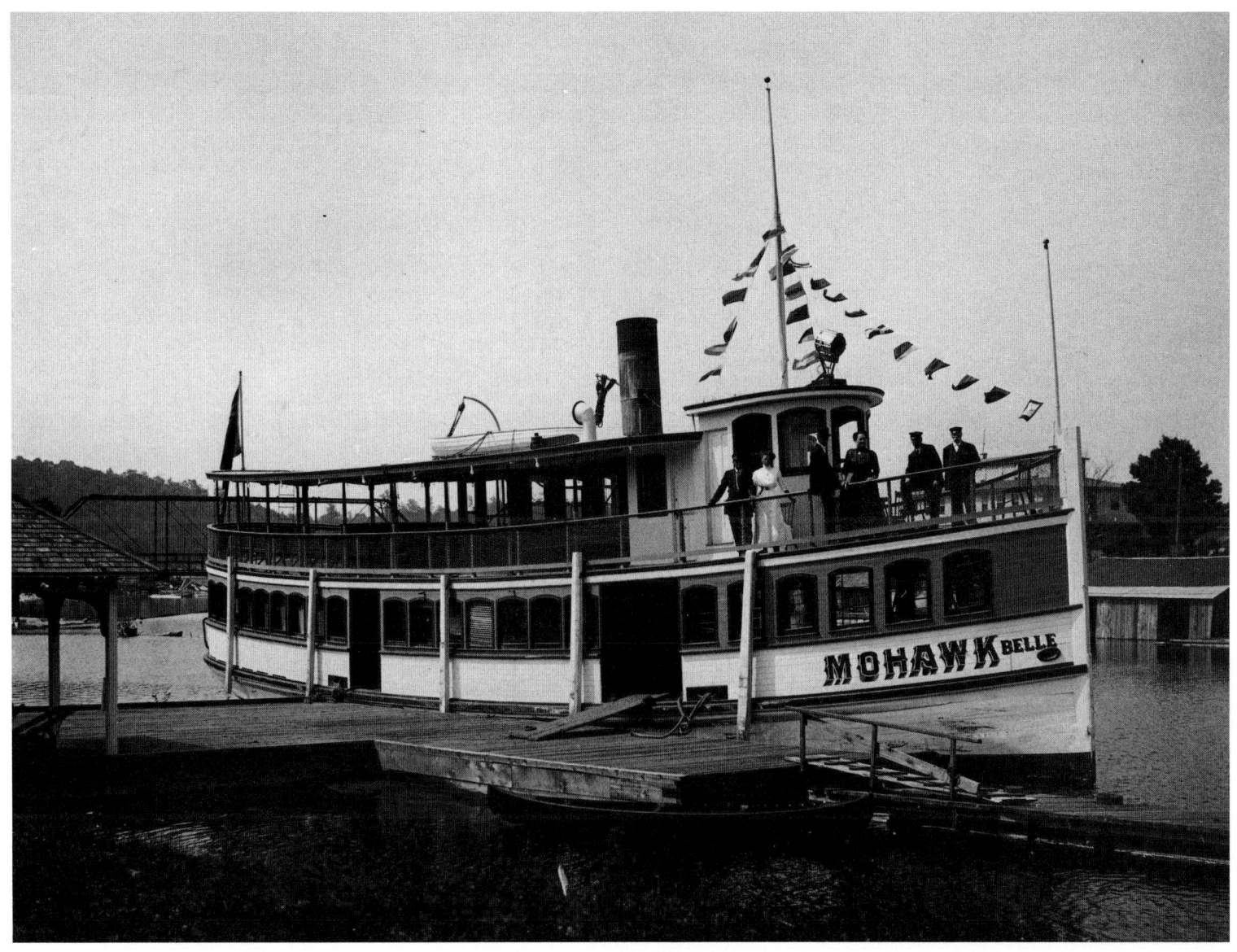

Pictured is the *Mohawk Belle* moored at the government dock in Baysville. The steamer plied the lake waters between South Portage, Dwight and Baysville.
- *Ruth Tinkiss*

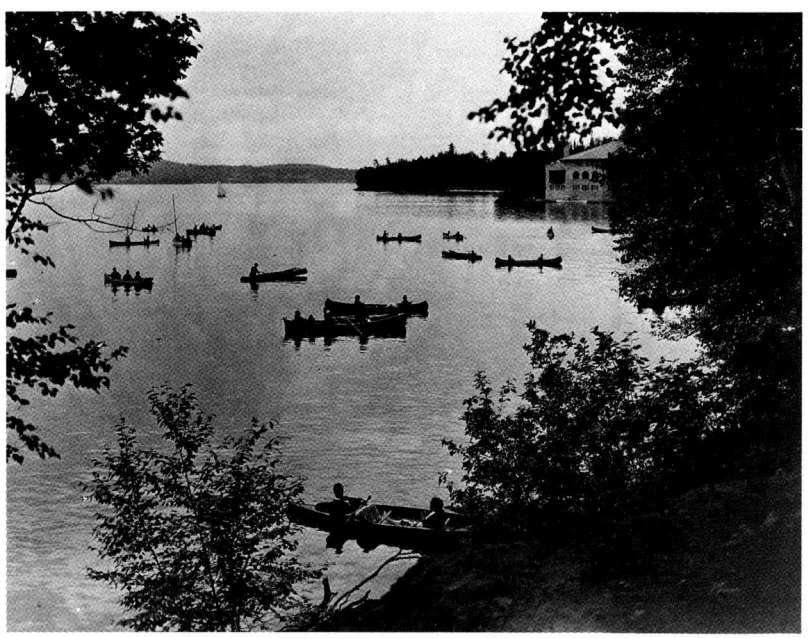
The Bigwin Boat Livery Company Limited stocked over 100 canoes, dinghies, gigs, sailboats and skiffs.
- Helen O'Connor

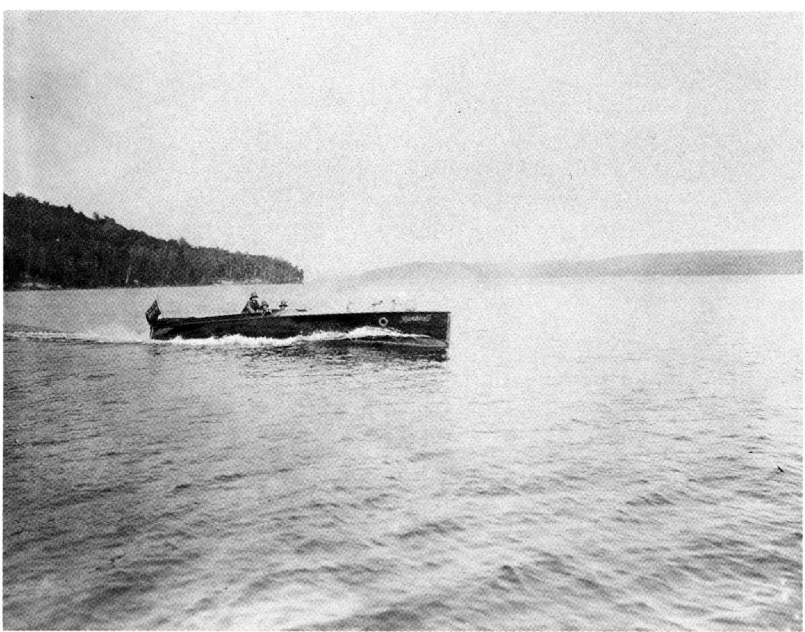
The mahogany launch *Rambler III* plies the lake waters of Bigwin Bay.
- Robert McLennan

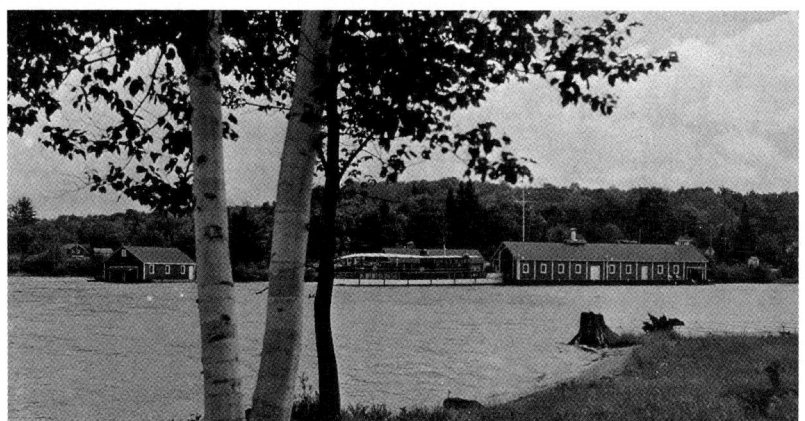
Once Lady Eaton's steam yacht on the lower Muskokas, the *Wanda III* was eventually added to the Bigwin Boat Livery's flotilla. The original brass bell of the ship is engraved with the inscription "*Wanda III* 1915." During a refitting of the vessel, the bell was chrome plated.
- DGM

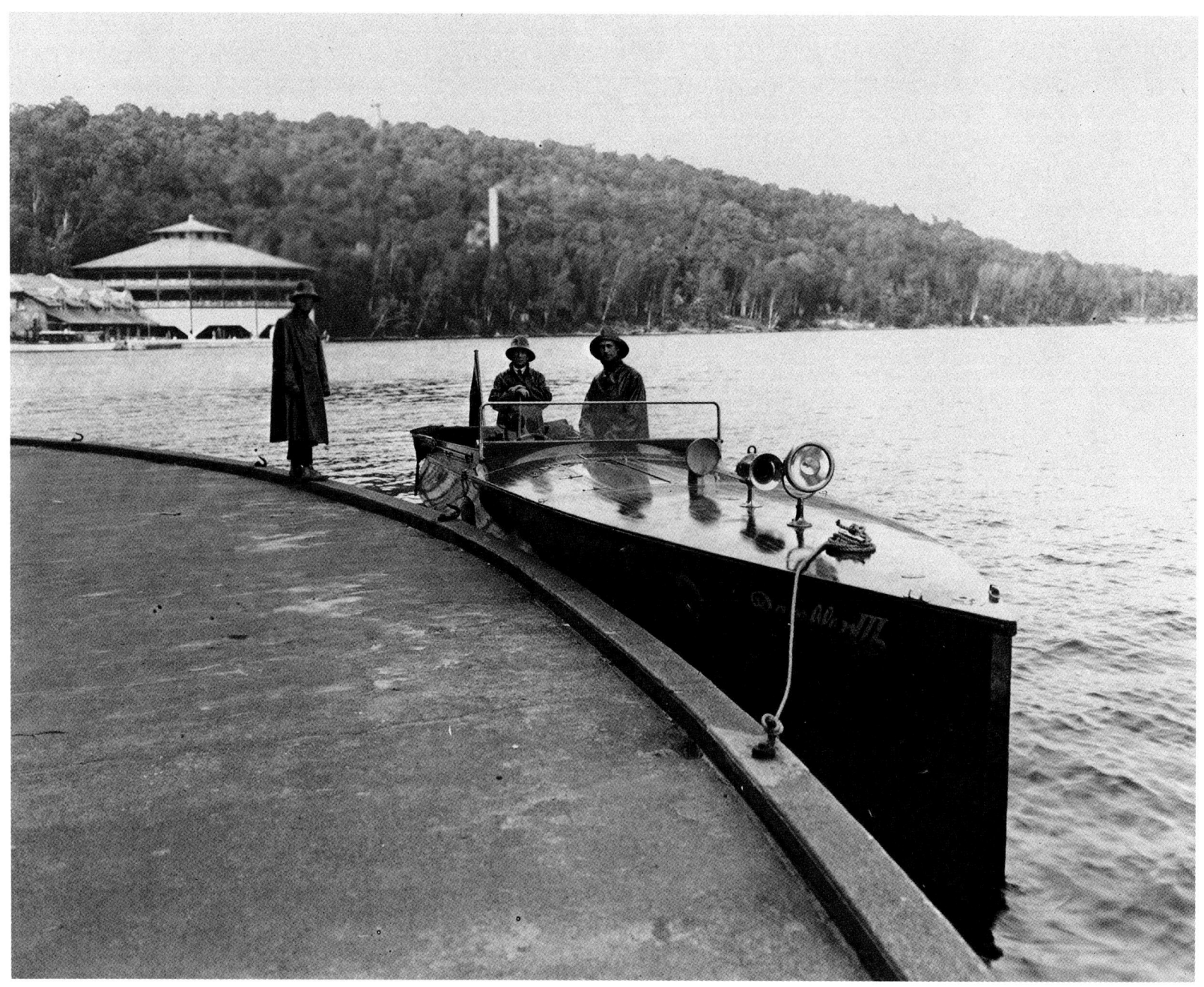

Despite a rain shower, the *Rambler III* prepares to cast off for an afternoon cruise. In the event of such inclement weather, the Livery offered passengers the comforts of slickers and hats.
- *Helen O'Connor*

column rising from the centre of the room's maple dance floor. Later, an acoustic ceiling was suspended from these beams and painted cerulean. The Pavilion was originally open-air, but it was eventually enclosed with two levels of windows, one level encircling the main dance floor and another encircling the observation gallery running around the perimeter of the second floor. Thus, the management boasted, "On warm evenings the cool lake breezes would blow through the hall and when the nights were chill and late in the season, the numerous windows were closed and the Pavilion steam heated."

Comfortably seating over 1,000 people, the vast room was frequently used as a convention hall during the day. In 1949 the Fourth Commonwealth Conference was held in the Pavilion. Wrote one official, "The Canadian Institute of International Affairs is happy that it was able to act as host to this important conference. It is greatly indebted to five generous Canadians — Mr. J.S. McLean, Mr. J.W. McConnell, Mr. H.R. MacMillan, Mr. Garfield Weston and Mr. John David Eaton, whose substantial contributions to the conference fund make it possible to hold the meeting in the pleasant and retired atmosphere of Bigwin Inn." Equally impressed, the president of the 1925 and 1927 Beta Theta Pi Fraternity Convention, Frank G. Ensign, wrote, "We therefore desire to convey to the Bigwin Inn Company the thanks of the Convention, and to commend to all organizations similar to our own the facilities of the Inn. We depart with regret, and hope that at some future time the Fraternity may again enjoy the hospitality of this pleasant place."

On rainy days and when conventions had not reserved the hall, the Pavilion afforded athletic guests the use of indoor badminton courts which had been laid out on the dance floor. For players' refreshment, a round cobblestone fountain just outside the main doors of the Pavilion offered an endless supply of cool water piped directly from one of the island's three known natural springs.

With the softness of summer evenings, the Pavilion became a centre for musical concerts and dances, as these were an integral part of the entertainment agenda at the Inn. The pageantry of Friday and Saturday festivities began at 9:30 p.m. when the hall flooded with coloured reflections from a conical, glass and mirrored light built at the Huntsville tannery. The music of the nine-piece Bigwin Orchestra was entrancing as women in long gowns and gentlemen in "tails" danced countless circuits around the ballroom floor. Employees occasionally joined in these celebrations but were only permitted to dance in the Pavilion's gallery if invited by one of the hotel guests or when the main orchestra was at rehearsal. From various boats in the harbour, many spectators simply enjoyed watching the dancers' blue silhouettes floating across a gilt background and listening to the music as it drifted over the water.

Plays and vignettes were performed on the Pavilion's stage on Monday evenings. John Holden and the Actors' Theatre Colony Players, the Straw Hat Players, and Bala's Summer Theatre Group made many appearances and became quite popular through their engagements. From time to time, guests themselves donned costumes for masquerade balls and carnivals. The annual guests' and employees' masquerades were highlights of the season, with C.O. Shaw making a rare appearance at the black-tie occasions in one of his many tuxedos. Throughout the evening galas, the orchestra performed an extensive selection of music, and at the stroke of midnight, the playing of "God Save the King" signalled the conclusion of festivities.

Over the years, the Pavilion was host to many great international entertaining talents and the site of some of the most outstanding cultural performances in Canada's history. Early entertainers who contributed to this great heritage included Herbert L. Clarke, Ernest Pechin and the Anglo Canadian Concert Band. Later entertainment at the Inn included the celebrated talents of Bob Armstrong, Count Basie, Mario Bernardi (later conductor of Ottawa's National Arts Centre (NAC Orchestra), Frank Bogart, Howard Cable, Larry Elgart, Duke Ellington, Graeme Forber, Art Hallman, Mart Kenny, Benny Lewis, Guy Lombardo, Gisele LaFleche MacKenzie (who went on to perform on "Meet Gisele," "The Woolworth Hour," "Your Hit Parade" and "Bob Crosby and the Modernaires"), The Happy Gang, Jim McHarg, Ellis McLintock, Al Nicholas, Bert Niosi, Bob Shuttleworth, Frank Sullivan, Chicho Valle, Moxie Whitney (who was popular at the Royal York's Imperial Room), cellist Donald Whitton (later cellist with the NAC Orchestra), and Mohawk Indian bass-baritone Os-Ke-Non-Ton.

Os-Ke-Non-Ton (Running Deer), also known as Louie Deer, was born on the Caughnawaga reservation near the shores of the St. Lawrence. His mother passed away while he was still young, and by the time Os-Ke-Non-Ton was ten, his father had died. The sole inheritance given to him were the words uttered by his father just prior to his death. "I am going on a long journey," he said. "Some day you will follow me. Life is a thing of changes — many trails. Whatever happens, remember never to lose courage." After his father's death, the orphan received some schooling in Caughnawaga, in Munsey, Ontario, in Montreal, and for three years at Parkdale Collegiate in Toronto. In Toronto, he lived in an unheated, unlighted and unfurnished attic room. "My trail was from my school to my attic room and I never left it," he once said. During the summer months, he managed to travel to the Lake of Bays, where he earned a living from the tourist industry as a hunter and guide.

One summer, Os-Ke-Non-Ton pitched his tent beneath the fragrant pines of Norway Point and at night made quivers, moccasins and birchbark boxes to sell to tourists. Cloaked in his Hudson's Bay blanket, he would sing by a flickering campfire and the rich sound of his bass-baritone voice would carry across the still, dark waters of the Lake of Bays.

Leonora James-Kennedy, of Toronto, was a coloratura soprano soloist who often performed at Norway Point Church and in Toronto at the

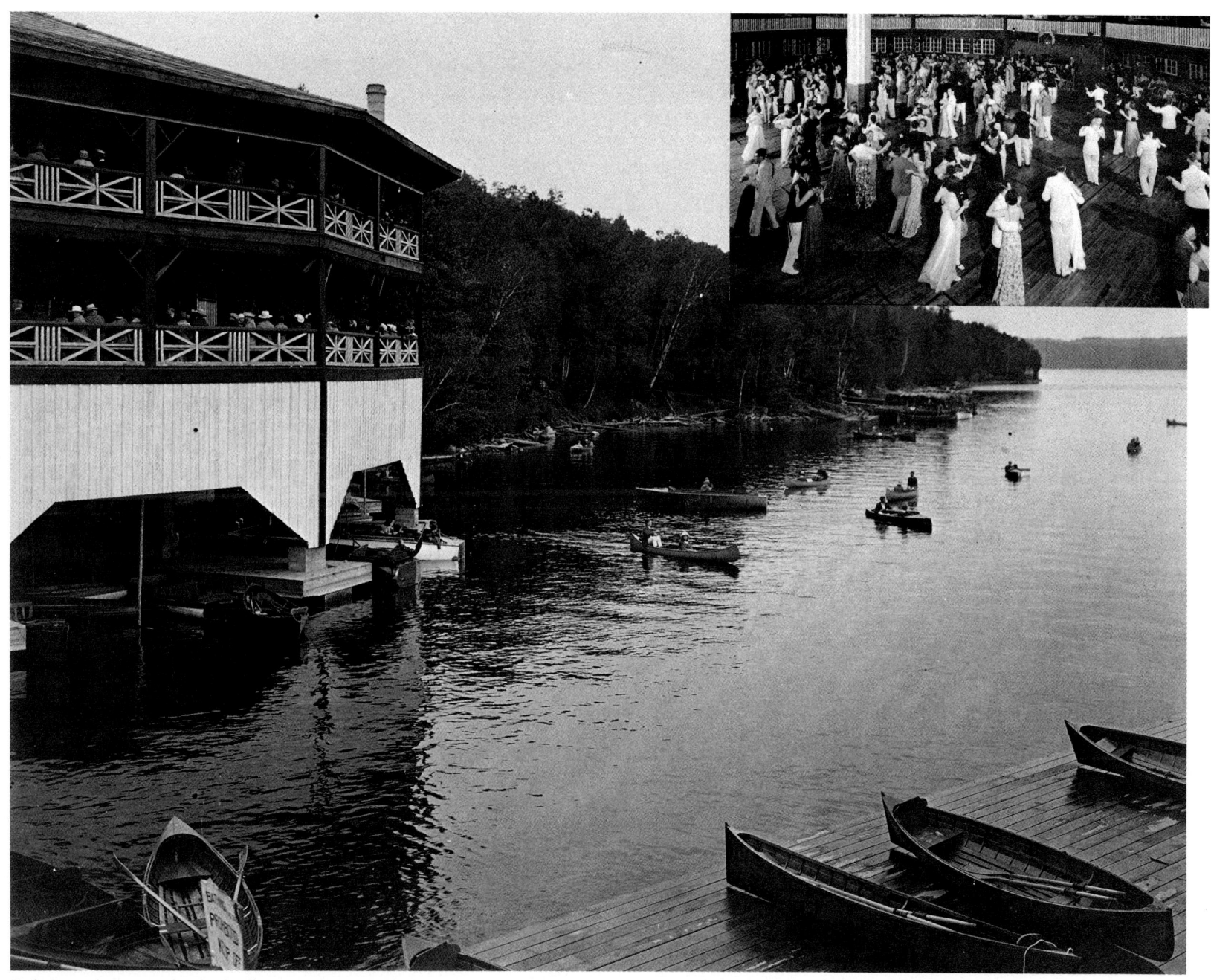

Relative to human scale, the Pavilion was massive in size. Built over the water, the edifice provided a sense of architectural drama in balance with the dining complex. Beneath the gently sloping roof and overhanging eaves, the exterior fir walls featured detailed woodwork, including ornamental railings which incorporated the design of the Union Jack. Inside, the Pavilion's concerts, revues and recitals attracted hundreds of guests.

- *Helen O'Connor*

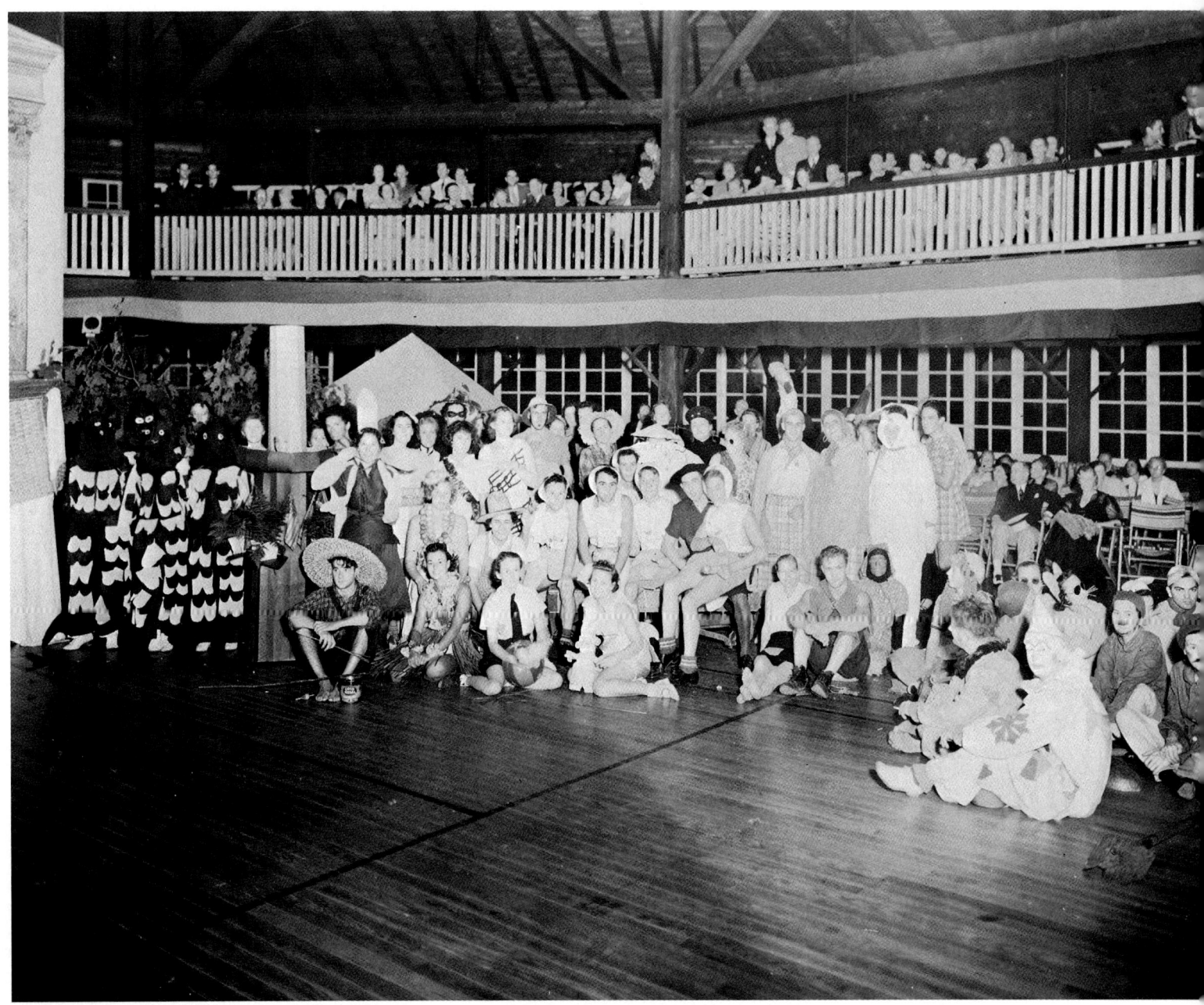
Spectators enjoy the Bigwin Masquerade of August 1939. C.O. Shaw is seated in the gallery's front row, above the Bigwin Inn teepee.

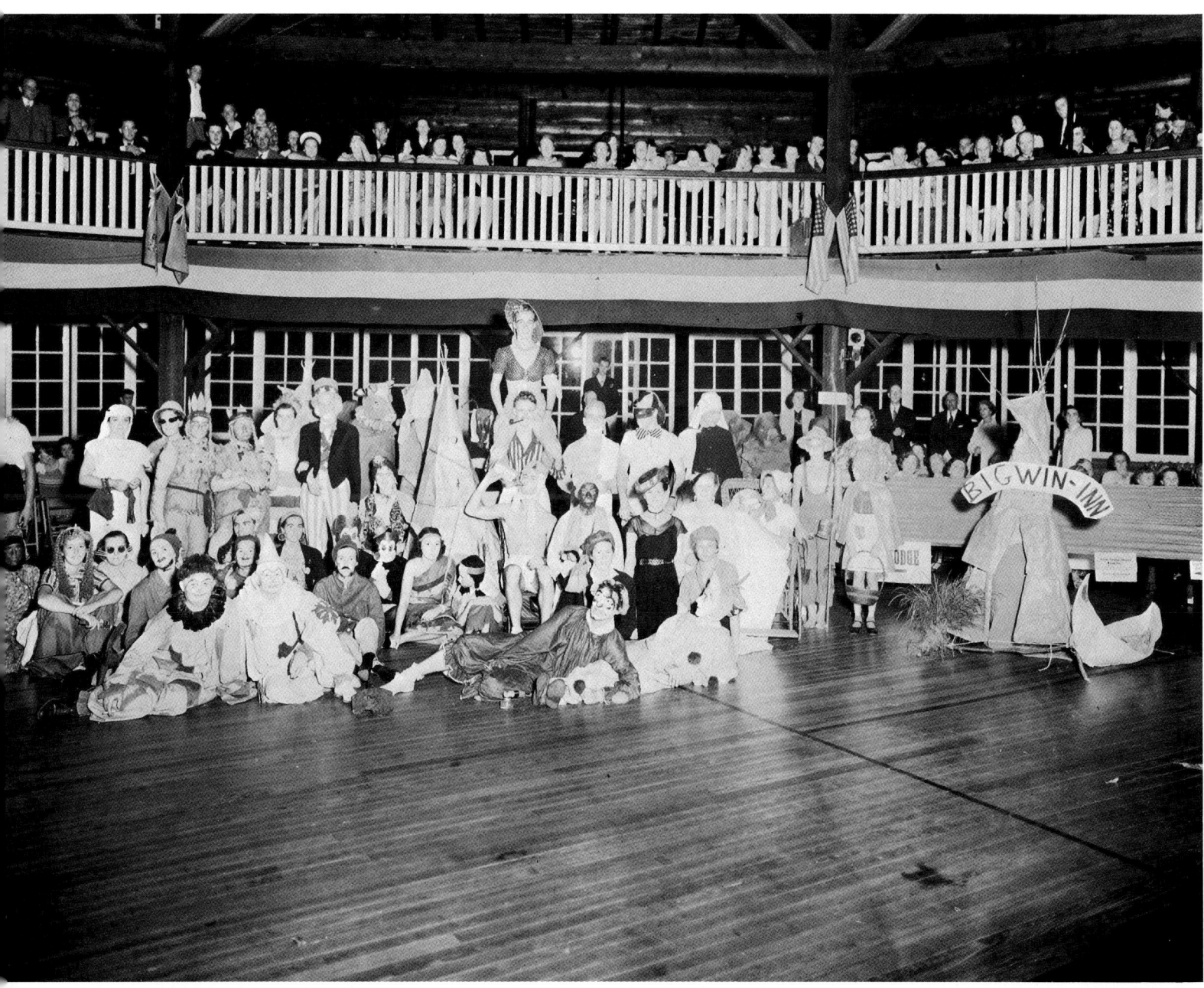

- Robert McLennan

VOL. 1   NO. 8

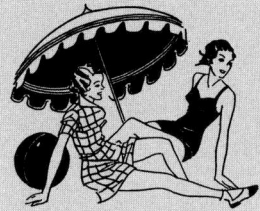

The Weather	The Water
Clear and Warm	Nice and Warm

BIGWIN BANTER
LAKE OF BAYS • ONTARIO CANADA

SATURDAY, AUGUST 1st, 1936

WELCOME

A hearty welcome is extended to the following guests who are returning again to Bigwin:

Mr. and Mrs. H. E. Walker and Miss Marion Walker, Mrs. E. McIsaac and Miss Shirley McIsaac, Mr. and Mrs. E. A. Thomas and Mary Susanne, Mr. and Mrs. T. A. Russell, Mr. and Mrs. L. A. Morine, Dr. Lockwood, Mr. and Mrs. C. M. Canfield and Bob, Mrs and Mrs. R. A. Batten and Reg Jr., Dr. Colin Campbell, Mr. and Mrs. Samuel Lowther, all of Toronto; Mr. and Mrs. H. M. Marsh, Mr. and Mrs. J. J. Byrne and Mary Ellen, Mr. and Mrs. R. R. Evans, Rannie and Helen, Miss Annie Ainslie and George W. Robinson, all of Hamilton; Mrs. Harold Sharp and Mr. W. G. W. Dewar, of Ottawa; Mr. and Mrs. R. S. Archer, of Chicago; Mr. and Mrs. Ernest Mayo, of Evanston, Illinois; Mr. and Mrs. J. B. Stewart Jr. and daughter, of Cincinnati; Mr. and Mrs. C. C. Shively, of Columbus, Ohio; Mr. and Mrs. F. B. Dangler, of Willoughby, Ohio; Mrs. S. L. Henderson, of Cleveland; Judge Fraud and Mrs. Geiger, of Springfield, Ohio; Mr. and Mrs. Joseph Stelwagon, of Merion, Pa.; Mr. and Mrs. Arthur Sherin, of New York City; Dr. and Mrs. Earl Osborne, Mr. and Mrs. E. C. McCormick, Mr. and Mrs. E. C. Schlenker, Mr. and Mrs. G. M. Fiero, Mr. E. K. Paul and party of eight, all from Buffalo; Mr. and Mrs. F. P. Wilcox, of Chevey Chase, D.C.; Mr. and Mrs. Edward Burlage, of Brosse Pointe, Mich.; Mrs. Abott and Mr. Jere Abbott, of Dexter, Maine, Mr. and Mrs. F. T. Huffman, F. T. Huffman III, and Ira, and Mrs. Huffman Sr., of Dayton, Ohio.

NEWS OF THE JUNIOR GUESTS

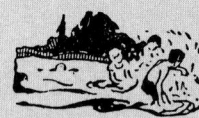

If you should wander down to the swimming dock any morning you will find Bigwin's Junior Guests hard at work learning all sorts of acquatic feats under the direction of Molly Maw, who seems to be able to work wonders with even her tiniest pupils, the youngest of whom, Eve Cassels, age three and a half years, is stroking and kicking valiantly and will soon be swimming off "on her own." Michael Cox, another young pupil, took eight strokes by himself yesterday. Virginia Steele mustered up courage enough to jump off the dock and the next step forward will be a dive; Gordon McKay has reached the diving stage and Bill Collins is probably the star of this little crawl stroke, sign up for the ten thirty a.m. class

THE PLAYERS EXCEL

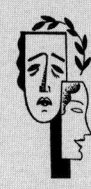

PLAYING to a capacity audience last Monday night, John Holden and his Actors' Colony Players scored the biggest hit of the season in the first Canadian Production of the Broadway hit "Blind Alley," by James Warwick. Jack Holden was outstanding. His role as Hal Wilson, the gangster, whose mind gradually broke down under the verbal battering of the Professor of Psychology, in whose house he and his gang took refuge, was the finest piece of acting we have seen in many a moon, summer or otherwise. His skilled handling of the dramatic tension through the whole three acts kept the audience simply breathless.

The part of the Professor of Psychology (by Robert Christie) was keenly interpreted. Warwicks clever use of popular psychology in the build up of the role of the professor fighting with the only weapon he knew was given its full contrast by Robert Christie against the gangster mentality of Wilson.

Grace Matthews as the gun-moll and Betty Boylen as the Professor's wife both turned in splendid acting—Miss Matthews was so thoroughly tough we wonder if she will ever smoke a cigarette gracefully again.

The supporting cast, Isabel Price, Robert McRae, Kay Gibbons, Dick Fonger, Alex McKee, Jack Richardson and Harry Beattei all fitted each in their own character, to make a smooth running and harmonious background for the principals. The highest praise should be given the Actors' Colony Players for their make-up, properties and stage settings—this professional attention to details was well rewarded in the extremely fine comments we heard on it from all sides among the audience.

NEXT WEEKS' PERFORMANCE

"Dangerous Corner," by J. B. Priestly, will be the Actors' Colony presentation on Monday evening, when Jane Mallett will make her bow to the members of Bigwin Inn audience, who have been looking forward to this date with a great deal of pleasure as Miss Mallett is so well and favorably known for her work with Freddie Manning in "Town Tonics." "Dangerous Corner" is a mystery play filled with thrills and baffling situations, skillfully written and cleverly interpreted by John Holden and the players, who received unstinted praise for their acting when they gave

Bigwin's Sunday Evening Musicale to be in Aid of the Star Fresh Air Fund

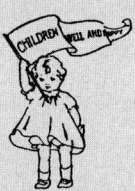

FORTUNATE are we to be spending the glorious summer days at beautiful Lake of Bays and Bigwin. For this reason our thoughts turn to those less fortunate, especially the little children, who have to live through Toronto's recent torrid heat spell, penned up in dingy city living quarters, with nothing larger or greener than a backyard to play in out of doors. What would some of these little kiddies think and how would they feel if they were turned loose on Bigwin Island or some other country spot equally as lovely? It is not difficult to picture in our minds the joy such a vacation would prove to the hundreds of youngsters who are hoping and longing that by a wave of some magic wand, they will be transported from their pent-in quarters in the city to a fresh green country for a week or ten days at least.

Most of Toronto's needy children and their parents know of the Star Fresh Air Fund and hundreds of applications are still unfilled for undernourished children to be sent to the camp this summer. These will remain unfilled unless more money is forth coming in order to meet the cost of sending these kiddies to the country. The Star Fresh Air Fund Editor told us that the prolonged hot wave had taxed their resources to the limit as they found it imperative to send so many more kiddies than they had expected, away at that time. They had thought that the cash they had in hand on July first would tide them over the balance of the summer, but this whole amount has been spent and more money is urgently needed in order to carry on through August.

So, that we all may have an opportunity of helping, it has been decided to make Sunday's musicale a benefit for the Fresh Air Fund and a collection will be taken up that evening. Only seven dollars is required to give some unfortunate little kiddy a whole week in the country, a small amount indeed in comparison to what this child receives in return through the well organized operation of the Star Fresh Air Fund. That the opportunity will be taken full advantage of is a certainty. How very splendid it will be if we of Bigwin, can make it possible for many little ones to enjoy a week in the country during the month of August. Five of Toronto's finest musicians are giving their talent for this

generous response will be made by all when one of these charming young ladies comes to you on Sunday evening.

The Programme

Not often has Bigwin had the honour of welcoming so many distinguished artists at the same time. The renowned two piano team, Malcolm and Godden will be our most interesting performers. Torontonians know these fine pianists so well they need no further introduction to them, but to our guests from across the line may we say that a rare treat indeed is in store for them on Sunday evening. Add to this three such prominent soloists as Alice Strong, soparno; Jean McLauchlan, contralto, and Harvey Doney, baritone and we have an aggregation of artists which outstrips some of Toronto's best musical presentations. The great lounge will be filled to overflowing Sunday night without a doubt, and many little kiddies will have a week or two in the country as the result of the concert.

BIGWIN'S ANNUAL GOLF TOURNAMENT

Open to all amateurs opens on Tuesday, August 4th, and will be 36 holes medal play, 18 of which will be played Tuesday, and 18 on Wednesday. A splendid entry list is expected, most of last summer's winners having signified their intention of taking part again this year. Prominent golfers who are now registered include Mr. Stanley Biggs of Toronto and Mr. W. N.

The *Bigwin Banter* updated guests on the latest news at the hideaway of the rich and famous: "Each week night a fine orchestra plays for dancing and on Monday evenings, an excellent summer stock company presents current Broadway successes. Sunday evening musicales feature Amy Fleming, contralto, and Harvey Marshall, tenor. The Bigwin orchestra, under the direction of James Wiggins will add their usual fine contribution to the programme. Sunday at 8:30, in the Rotunda."

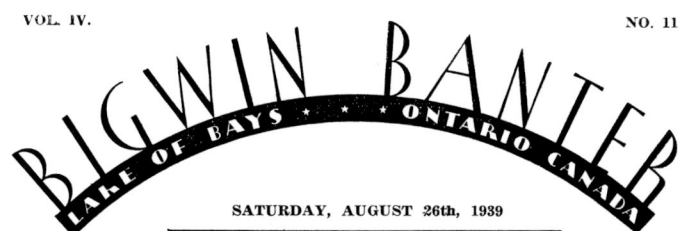

VOL. IV. NO. 11

BIGWIN BANTER
LAKE OF BAYS ★ ★ ONTARIO, CANADA

SATURDAY, AUGUST 26th, 1939

Two Days in the Life of a Bigwin Guest

Proving You Can be as Active or as Lazy as You Please

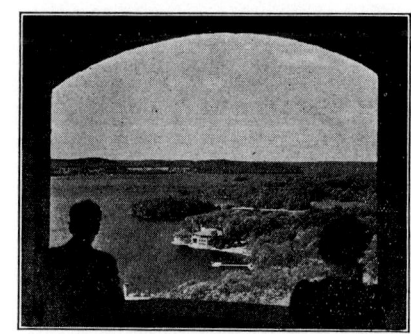

Bigwin Inn from the Tower

GAY DECEIVERS

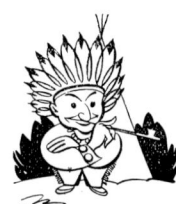

thronged the pavilion for the Bigwin Masquerade in costumes that set a new high for color and originality! Bigwin guests, cottagers from across the lake and visitors from other Muskoka resorts heartily applauded the choice of the judges, Mr. A. H. Sherin, Mrs. David Gourlay, Mrs. Moffat Woodside, Mrs. L. B. Robinson, Judge W. T. Henderson and Colonel Goodwin Gibson. The programme presented after the grand march included dance numbers by Dorothy Goulding and Miss Louise Burns, songs by Olive Barlowe Blakely and Dr. Harvey Doney, and a specialty act by clowns Moffat and Turpin. C. B. C.'s special microphone made it possible for the hundreds present to enjoy the music. The final awards were as follows: Special Prize to the archeologist and his Egyptian mummy. (Dode Sullivan deserved a medal for endurance in her yards and yards of crepe paper bandage and the mud pack on her face, and Wes. Clare another for wheeling her around all evening). Single prizes were won by the Dining-room Centre Post, complete with ferns and flags; Aunt Jemima, the Fishing Boy, Bigwin Inn, Day and Night, Laundry Basket, Salad Tray, Hawaiian Girl, Huck Finn, and the Birch Tree. Pair winners were the Bigwin Family, Mickey and Minnie Mouse and the Pirates, whose treasure chest turned out to be flash bulb equipment with which they "shot" everyone in the grand march. The realist replica of Cabin 6, complete with clothes-line and policeman, carried off the group prize; the well-made Covered Walk with bench, waste paper can and trading Indian, came second, and the farmer's wife and her three blind mice third. Cecil Farrar was Popularity Prize-winner. As for skits see if you can ask the girls in the dining-room how they got the idiosyncrasies of the guests . . . and staff . . . down so pat without both of you blushing!

* * * *

TEA ON THE WANDA III.

was a delightful part of the cruise over Lake of Bays to which Mrs. C. O. Shaw invited thirty ladies, guests at Bigwin Inn. During the cruise Miss Amy Fleming, Toronto, and Mrs. Olive Barlow Blakely, Hamilton, sang for them from the deck of the Wanda. On the return trip a presentation was made to Mrs. Shaw on behalf of the Bigwin Ladies' Friendship Club by the president, Mrs. Graham Lackner.

* * * *

"HELLO AGAIN"

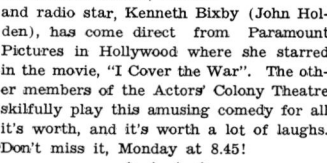

is a poor title for the Holden Players' farewell performance of the season at Bigwin Inn, but it's a good play for you to remember them by when they are far away in Winnipeg. Gwen Gaze, who plays the part of Anne Rogers, secretary to the famous author, lecturer and radio star, Kenneth Bixby (John Holden), has come direct from Paramount Pictures in Hollywood where she starred in the movie, "I Cover the War". The other members of the Actors' Colony Theatre skilfully play this amusing comedy for all it's worth, and it's worth a lot of laughs. Don't miss it, Monday at 8.45!

* * * *

JOHN HOLDEN'S PLAYMATES

in the Actors' Colony Theatre gave him a birthday party last week. Everyone dressed as a favorite play! John sported a broken wrist watch and a handfull of tragedies for "No Time for Comedy". A bouquet of goldenrod carried by Gwen Gaze meant "Hay Fever" to most. Bill Needles stuck a pin cushion in his lapel and left it to the others to guess "Pins and Needles". Mary Ericson was pretty clever with a halo-effect about two feet above her head for "Ceiling Zero". Susan Goulding wore mourning-black and a bustle like a funeral wreath. How's that for "Dead End"!

* * * *

SUNDAY EVENING MUSICALE

is featuring Amy Fleming, contralto, and Harvey Marshall, tenor. The Bigwin orchestra, under the direction of James Wiggins will add their usual fine contribution to the programme. Sunday at 8.30, in the Rotunda.

* * * *

OLIVE BARLOW BLAKELY

is the pretty little brunette who sings in the Rotunda after dinner. Her father, mother, two brothers and sister all used to sing so Olive comes naturally by her rich contralto voice. She has studied with Campbell McInnis and Francis Coombs. Olive tied for first place in open competition in the North American National Music Festival at Utica, in 1935, and last year, with her partner, won the opera duet contest in London, Ontario. She has had charge of her own radio variety programme, has played violin with two orchestras, and has sung as guest soloist with the Hamilton and Centenary Symphonies and Bach and Elgar choir. At present Olive is soloist in the Central Presbyterian Church, Hamilton, and radio artist for C. B. C. Quite a career for the girl who

THE LIVELY LIFE

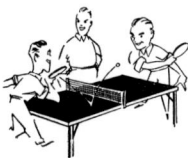

Up for a swim before breakfast, working up an appetite for Bigwin's famous griddle cakes with hot butter and maple syrup, m-m-m-m! Then for eighteen holes of golf on the sporting course, so beautiful it's hard to keep your eye on the ball. Cooled off with a swim before lunch. Then sailing on Lake of Bays . . . some breeze . . . and back on land, climbed to the Tower for a marvelous view of the island and lake. Went horseback riding for an hour, had a hot bath, and joined the gang in a get-together before dinner. Played a set of ping pong. Then to the pavilion for a dance, and finally to bed and right to sleep.

THE LAZY LIFE

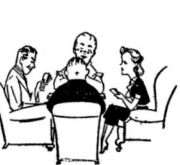

Slept in, just making the deadline for late breakfast in the dining-room. Chose a novel from the Bigwin library and sat on the sun terrace, reading and chatting with other guests. Then moved into the shade of the trees by the tennis courts and watched others play tennis or bowl on the greens near by. After a leisurely lunch joined the cruise up the Ox Tongue river in one of the Bigwin launches. The falls near Dwight are beautiful! Back in time for a game of bridge and a rest before dinner. Chatted in the Rotunda till it was time for the weekly play by the John Holden Players to begin in the pavilion. A bed-time snack in the tea house

- Robert McLennan

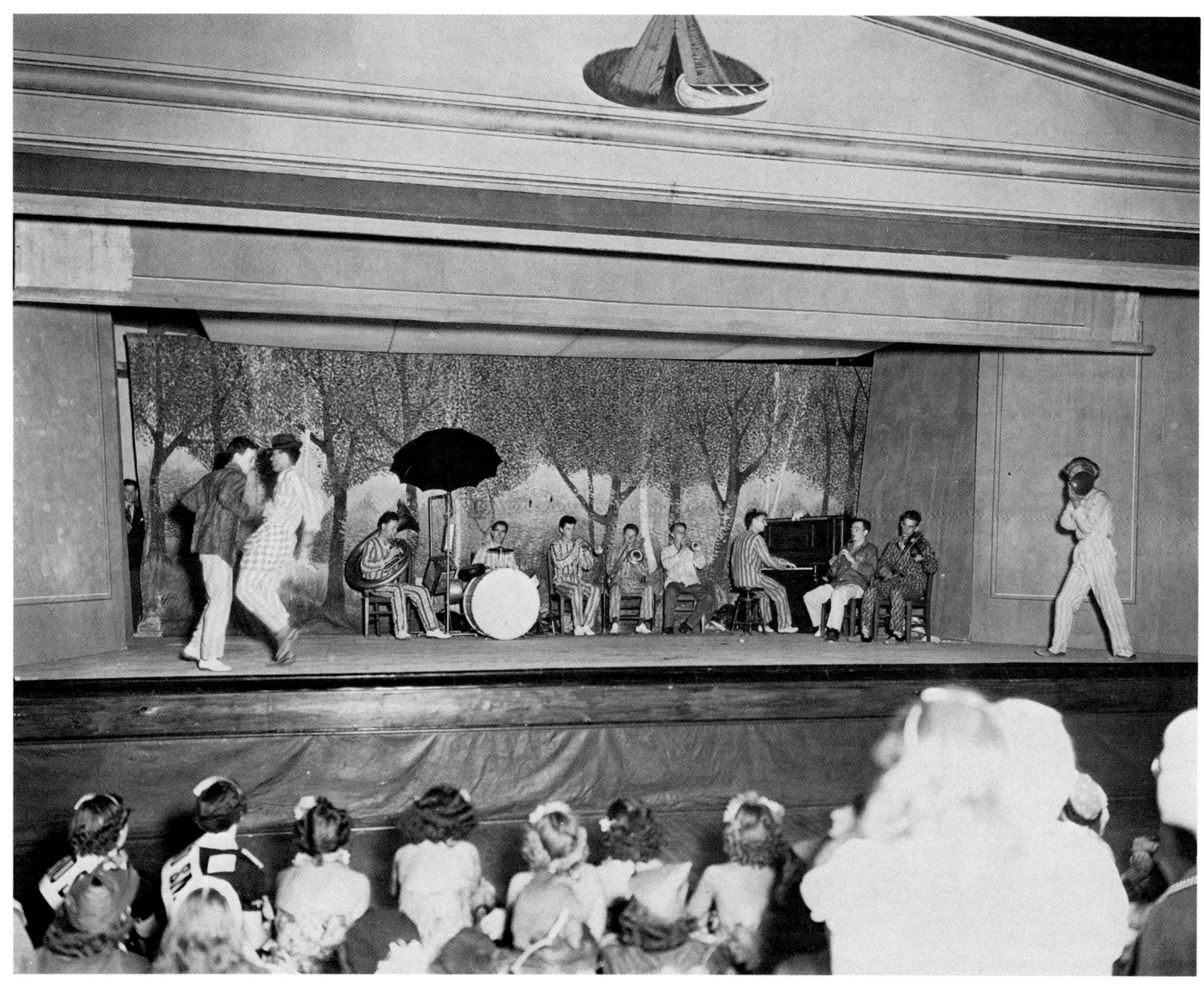

With spotlights shining down from the gallery above, golf caddies perform a skit on the Pavilion's stage (dancing is Bob Hughes; announcing is Sid Grewar; on violin is Jack Young; on trombone is Lorne Rayfield, on trumpet are Jack Martin and Ed Terziano).
- *Ed Terziano*

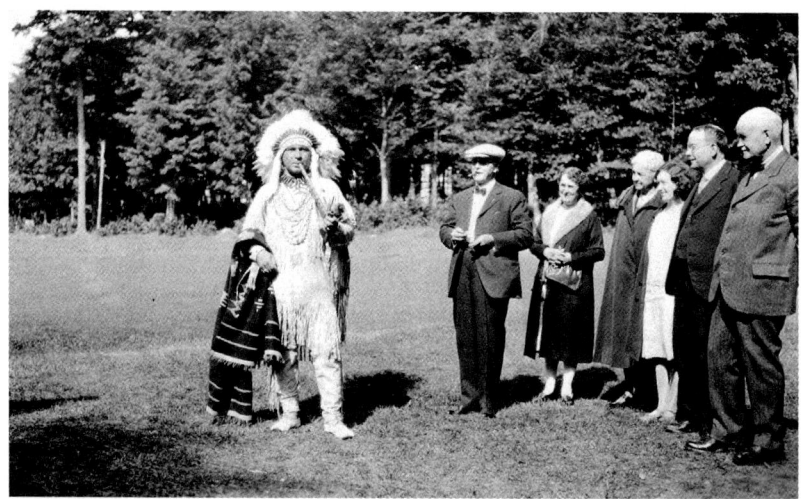

Bass-baritone singer Os-Ke-Non-Ton smokes a peace pipe on the first fairway of the resort's golf course. Standing on the far right is C.O. Shaw. - *Jennifer Mills*

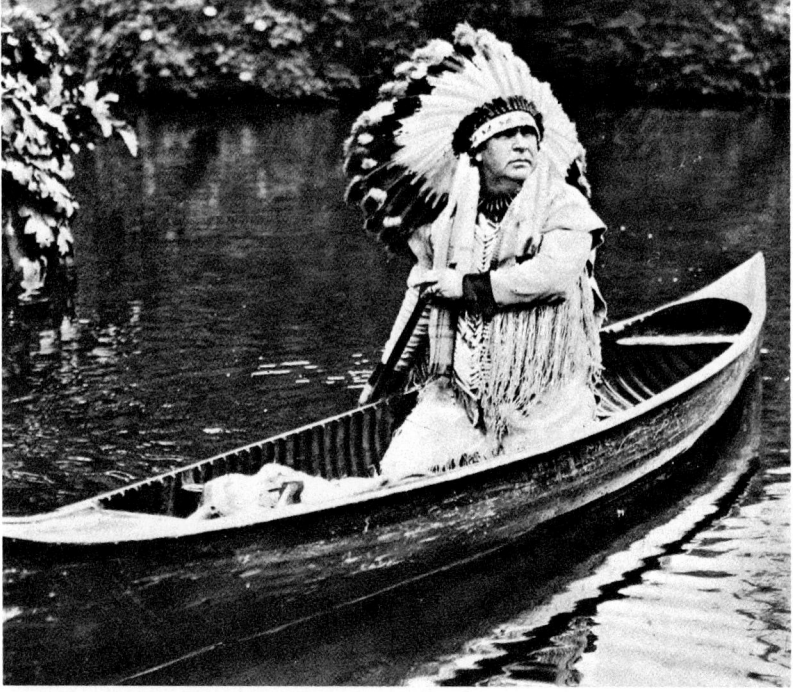

Attired in full regalia, Os-Ke-Non-Ton paddled his canoe in the lake at Regent's Park, England. During the evenings he performed in Coleridge Taylor's opera *Hiawatha*. - *Marie Rose Tosoni*

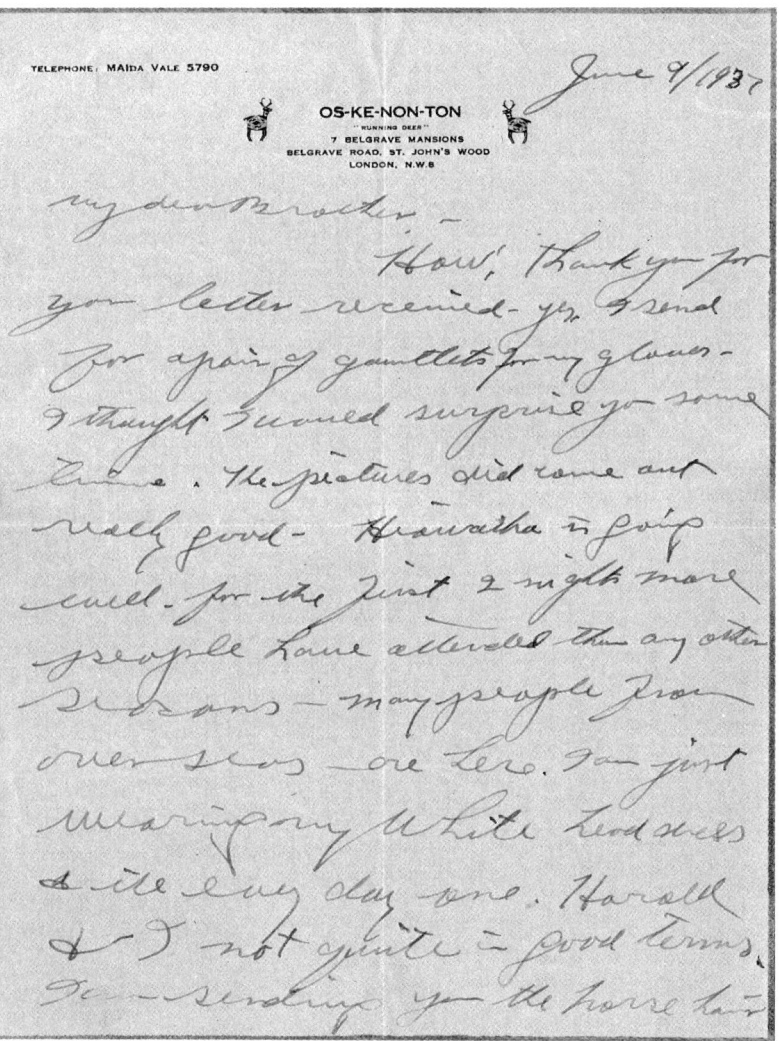

In June 1937, Os-Ke-Non-Ton wrote a close friend and advised him that "*Hiawatha* is going well, for the first 2 nights more people have attended than any other seasons — many people from overseas are here." - *Jennifer Mills*

Bloor Street Presbyterian Church. One summer evening she travelled from her cottage at Black Point to visit with her friend Mrs. C.O. Shaw, who was staying at the WaWa Hotel during the construction of Bigwin Inn. Mrs. James-Kennedy discovered Os-Ke-Non-Ton during a stroll and later persuaded him to pursue a singing career. As his instructor and sponsor, she encouraged him to travel to New York City, where his talents could be properly rewarded. He began work in the metropolis as an usher at Carnegie Hall. On one occasion, Os-Ke-Non-Ton ushered Andrew Carnegie to his box for an evening performance. Having met the young Mohawk previously, during a private engagement, Carnegie inquired, "How are you getting along?" "Splendidly," responded Os-Ke-Non-Ton, although he hadn't eaten in days. Oblivious to the Indian's plight, Carnegie replied, "I hope, my boy, I'll live to hear you sing on this very stage." Reflecting on their meeting, Os-Ke-Non-Ton felt it ironic to be starving in the presence of one of the world's wealthiest men.

However, great change would soon come to his life. Using his Mohawk name, Os-Ke-Non-Ton, he sang in public often, attired in a modest suit and paper shirt. Making his formal debut on the evening after Leonora James-Kennedy's unexpected death, he gave a strong performance, revealing his otherwise hidden emotion by the silent tears that flowed down his face. In August 1927, he travelled to Ontario and gave a benefit concert in her memory at the Bigwin Inn Pavilion. After singing songs to a full house, Os-Ke-Non-Ton walked in solitude through the island woodlands, singing softly to himself as he had done in childhood.

With the funds raised from the performance, Mrs. C.O. Shaw made arrangements to purchase an oak pulpit and three chairs for the Norway Point Church. Later, they were hand-carved with Indian symbols by Os-Ke-Non-Ton and the pulpit appointed with a bronze tablet that read:

> *In memory of Leonora James-Kennedy, Os-Ke-Non-Ton,*
> *A Mohawk, her friend sings these words.*
> *Her voice was like a thrush at ease*
> *Otsi-Tsia, bower in the forest*
> *My dark heart called her*
> *The wild swan to her nest in Spring*
> *Is not more faithful than Otsi-Tsia*
> *To her friends and to her songs*
> *Onen: Farewell Otsi-Tsia*
> *When the thrush sings in the high tree tops*
> *I will say your name. Onen.*

Os-Ke-Non-Ton went on to give many other performances, including annual appearances on Music Day at the CNE and at numerous events in the United States and "across the big pond" in Europe. Notably, he sang Charles Cadman's Indian opera *Chanewis* in the Hollywood Bowl. His European career was launched in London, England, where he invested his life savings to rent the Aeolian Hall under the auspices of the Over-Seas League. The performances sold out almost immediately. He later sang before Queen Mary of England at Royal Albert Hall, playing the roles of both the medicine man and the wedding minstrel in a production of Coleridge Taylor's opera *Hiawatha*. In spite of his extensive tours, Os-Ke-Non-Ton returned to Ontario many times, and from time to time sang over the radio on station CFCA. On recordings, his voice was accompanied by The Columbia Miniature Orchestra. Songs in his repertoire included "Tribal Prayer" (Omaha), "Lullaby" (Mohawk), "Happy Song" (Mohawk), "Shuffling Feet" (Sioux), "Every Day Song," "Moccasin Song," "Hunting Song," "War Song," "By the Weeping Waters," "Flute Melody," "By the Waters of Minnetonka," "Invocation to the Sun God" and "Peyote Drinking Song." Attired in full regalia, he also played a cameo role in some of Bigwin Inn's promotional movies.

The Ferry-house, Dry Docks, Powerhouse and Manager's Cottage
In the late 1920s, the hotel built an enormous 8,000 square-foot ferry-house on the east side of the Pavilion to provide storage space and to house the livery's boats. The vessels were raised from the water for winter storage by an extensive system of industrial hoists and pulleys.

The Livery's larger boats were serviced and stored in the dry docks on the north shore of the island. However, from its inception, the facility proved to be unreliable. The *Mohawk Belle*, once a proud passenger steamer on the Lake of Bays, was eventually stripped and used by the hotel as a scow. During the winter of 1949, pernicious ice in the dry docks pulled out the scow's oakum caulking, and after taking on water, she sank. The engine and boiler were salvaged by the owner of Port Cunnington Marina and attempts to tow the remains to deep water for scuttling were made, to no avail. The skeletal structure of the worthless red hull was simply left in the dry docks to deteriorate.

East of the Pavilion and ferry-house was a 2,000-square-foot powerhouse where twin power facilities assured the resort uninterrupted utility service. Farther along the shoreline stood a private, seven-room stone cottage where the secretary treasurer/general manager of Bigwin Inn, John McKee and his wife, Mary, together with their children, John and Mary, spent their summers.

The Observation Tower
Wooded trails led the Inn's visitors to the highest point on the island, Landmark Hill, where a concrete observation tower rose supremely from the forest floor. One of the first features of the resort to be built, the lofty Tower concealed a cavernous well which stored over 100,000 gallons of water for the hotel's consumption. By ascending the concrete steps around the outer wall, guests could reach a wooden staircase that wound

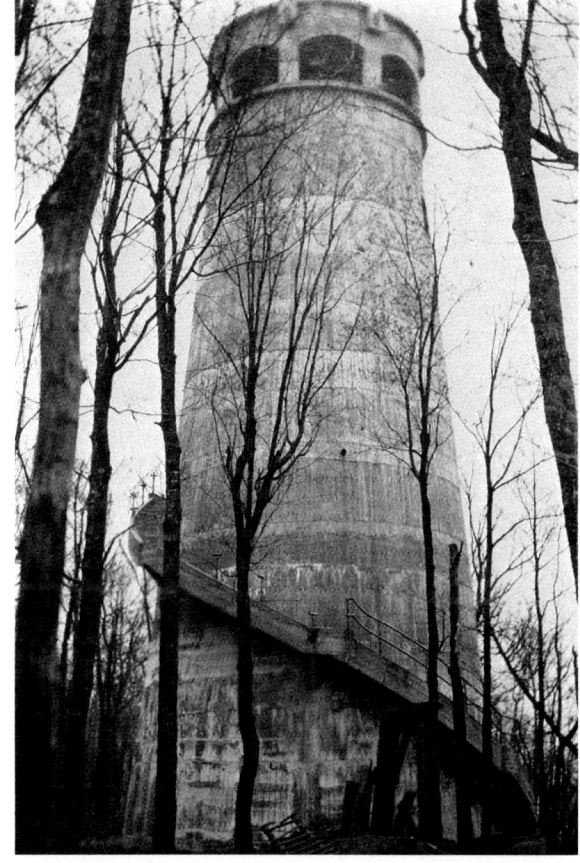

"A dominating landmark of Bigwin Island is the thickly-wooded hill, rising 200 feet above lake level and, on its crest, crystal clear water gushes out from a natural spring. This water, absolutely pure, is piped to the Inn for drinking purposes. The source of the spring is a mystery, for no body of water within an area of thirteen miles can be located high enough to force the spring to such an elevation." Sitting atop the hill, the Observation Tower concealed a cavernous well which stored over 100,000 gallons of water for the hotel's consumption.
- *DGM*

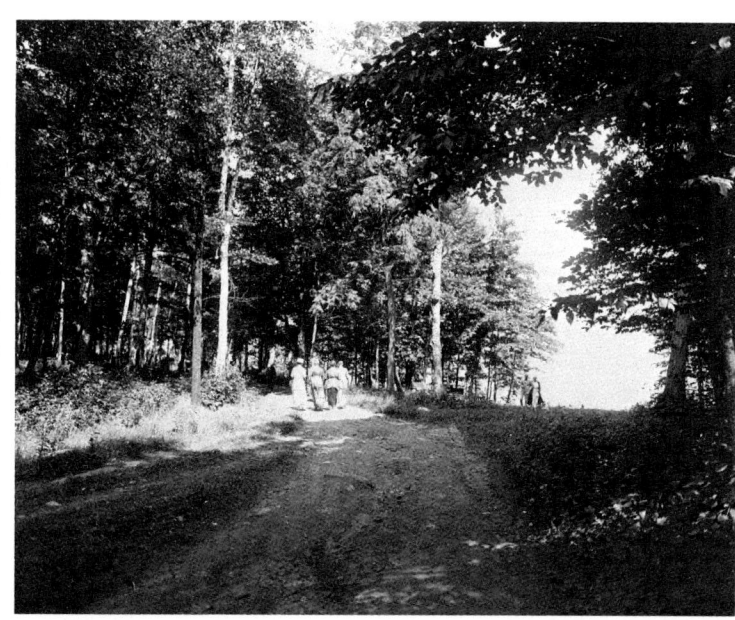

An early brochure stated: "You will treasure all winter the memory of hours spent roaming the lovely paths by the water's edge, leading you through bits of dusky virgin forest, cutting through peninsulas of stately pine groves and lovely silver birch with the sun playing among them."
- *Helen O'Connor*

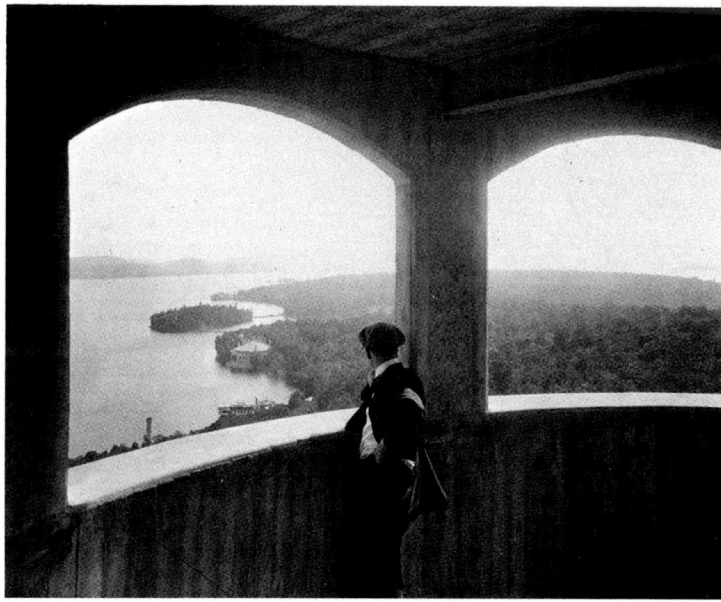

A brochure printed at the resort's zenith noted: "Nature was in her most lavish mood when she fashioned Lake of Bays and Bigwin Island, and in planning Bigwin Inn, we believe we created something worthy of its gorgeous setting."
- *Helen O'Connor*

around the interior. At the top of the stairs was an observation deck surrounded with arched apertures. For those adventurous enough to climb an iron ladder from the first deck, an open-air platform with steel railings crowned the Tower. At 350 feet above the Lake of Bays, guests could enjoy breathtaking views of the Inn and its setting, a vast wilderness of primeval forests and wind-swept waters.

The Cloisters
Outdoors, over half a mile of pillared and electrically lighted cloisters connected the formal entrances of the resort's main buildings. Exemplifying the unique layout of the hotel, the walkways gave a sense of unity to the arrangement of the Inn's structures. The earliest cloisters were built by German P.O.W.s of the Great War, who also assisted in building the Tower.

Parading down the avenues of these covered promenades, ladies bedecked in jewels and gentlemen sporting boutonnieres were completely protected from the heat of the summer sun or the inconvenience of a rain shower. As one hotel brochure advised, "Guests of the Inn are in no need of parasol or umbrella as all public buildings are conveniently connected by covered walkways."

From time to time, guests were offered another convenience beneath the cedar-lined roofs of the cloisters. With complimentary steamer passes provided by C.O. Shaw, natives would venture to the island aboard the *Iroquois* or *Mohawk Belle*, carrying with them colourful beaded necklaces, deerskin purses, model birchbark canoes and woven basswood baskets to sell to Bigwin Inn's guests and staff.

The Lodges
Very early in the hotel's development, management decided that the layout of buildings should be spacious in every respect and that "the wide variety of activities of a large cosmopolitan summer hotel should not be all under one roof." Embodying this idea, the two guest sleeping lodges were situated in shady stretches of maple, pine and birch trees, one to the east and one to the west of the main reception lounge. As these stately lodges were set well apart from the other buildings, the management could proudly claim to visitors that "no matter how early you retire, you are in no danger of being wakened by the sound of haunting waltzes or giddy foxtrots played by the orchestra for youthful dancers."

Designed in Tudor Revival style, each lodge had twin octagonal verandahs on the first two storeys at either end and in the centre of the building. From here, guests could enjoy panoramic views of the forests, lake, tennis courts or golf course in the bracing air, 316 feet above sea level.

To access each lodge, guests could choose one of three formal entrances. Three sets of staircases led from the main floors to two higher floors, where corridors stretched out over an eighth of a mile in length. Each lodge, measuring over 55,000 square feet, contained 142 rooms of more than 225 square feet and bathrooms of over 56 square feet, all having 12-foot ceilings. The spacious rooms had large clothes closets where full summer wardrobes and steamer trunks were easily stored. Accommodations provided hot and cold water, were steam heated during cooler days, and were appointed with the most modern comforts available. Designed by architect John Wilson for later construction, but never built, were baggage elevators, additional public lavatories and a third lodge facility.

Peace of mind was given to any guests wary of the devastating fires which had consumed so many of Muskoka's frame resorts, as each lodge was uniquely constructed of concrete and divided into three sections by concrete fire walls and sliding metal doors. As a further precaution, the roofs were tiled with thick fireproof shingles, and for any unlikely emergency, a barrage of firefighting equipment and dozens of fire hydrants were readily available.

For other guests, the greatest feature of the lodges was the substantial degree of privacy that their rooms provided. Cocktails could be enjoyed behind closed doors, exempt from C.O. Shaw's scrutiny. Shaw had been known to ask imbibing visitors to leave the island. However, such instances were rare, as most people were quite discreet in this regard and used room service to surmount any awkwardness. Two rings brought a bellboy, five rings brought cracked ice, and one ring brought icy spring water obtained from a round cobblestone structure named "Nubb's Well," conveniently located between the East and West lodges.

One humorous incident which took place in one of the lodges involved the hotel's manager and a disgruntled female visitor. Early one morning, loud noises outside the guest's bedroom window caused her to waken. Perturbed by what she thought were the sounds of maintenance men, she delivered a complaint to the hotel manager, James Garfield Reid. Apologizing profusely, he advised her that, unfortunately, the hotel had no control over the actions of woodpeckers in the forest.

The Juliana Cottages
To offer guests with large families a different type of accommodation, the hotel constructed two granite cottages for the 1927 season and two larger ones for the 1928 season. "The Bigwin Cottage Colony" was located along the winding shoreline of the island, west of the dining room, where guests enjoyed both proximity to the hotel and the privacy of a sandy cove. The stone bungalows were designed by John Wilson in Prairie/Craftsman style, with each having a deep flagstone verandah, hardwood floors, three bedrooms, living room, bathroom and fireplace. Inside, they were appointed with telephone service to the Inn, electric lights, steam heating and "a hundred and one little conveniences which

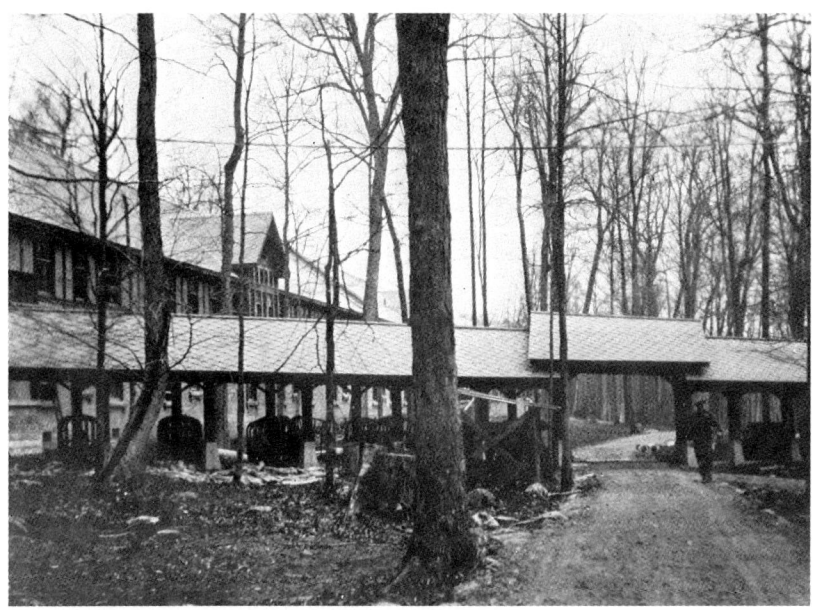

Giving a feeling of continuity and flow, covered walkways connected all formal entrances of the resort's main buildings. The earliest cloisters were built by German P.O.W.s of the Great War.
- *Alan Tasker*

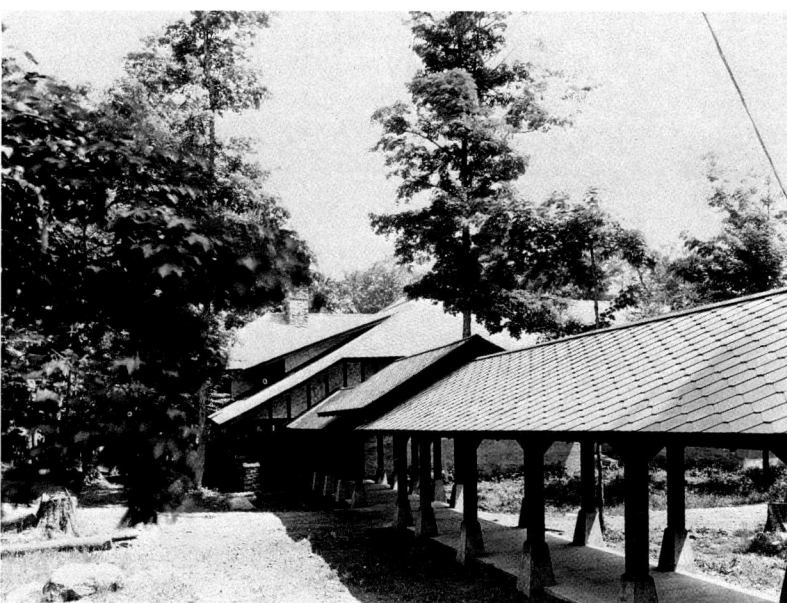

A newsletter from the resort noted that "every morning at five o'clock one of Malcolm Morden's men is up and busy, sweeping the walks clean and smoothing the tan bark paths that contrast so colourfully with the green of the grass."
- *Helen O'Connor*

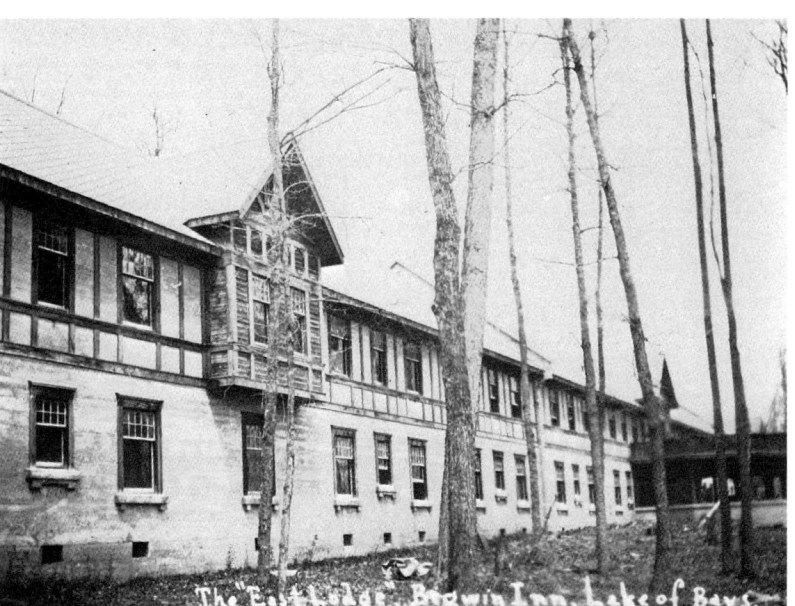

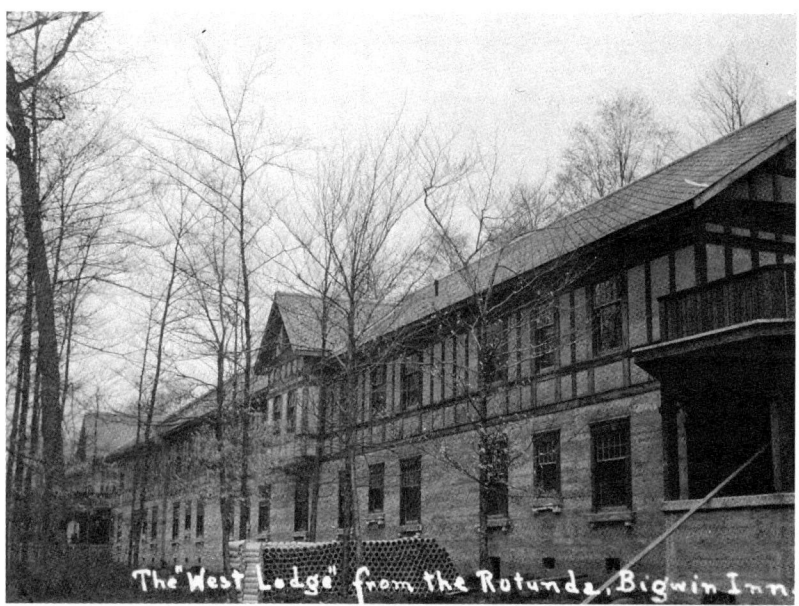

Designed in Tudor Revival style, the East and West Lodges offered guests panoramic views of the forests, lake, golf course or tennis courts. Together, the buildings are an important element of the architectural layout and stylistic composition of the entire complex as one single, unified whole.
- *DGM*

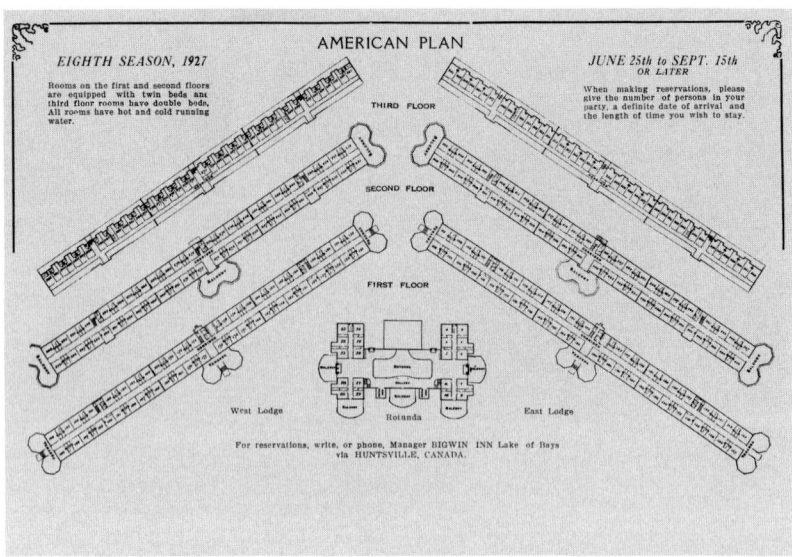

Bigwin offered patrons 284 rooms from which to choose when making their reservations. A resort newsletter noted: "On a flying visit was the young deer that wandered down to have a look at Bigwin Inn about three weeks ago. As soon as he was spied, he scampered up the hill, not even waiting to take the tower trail. Mr. McKee, who was telling us about it, says the unregistered guest probably swam over from the mainland."
- *Robert McLennan*

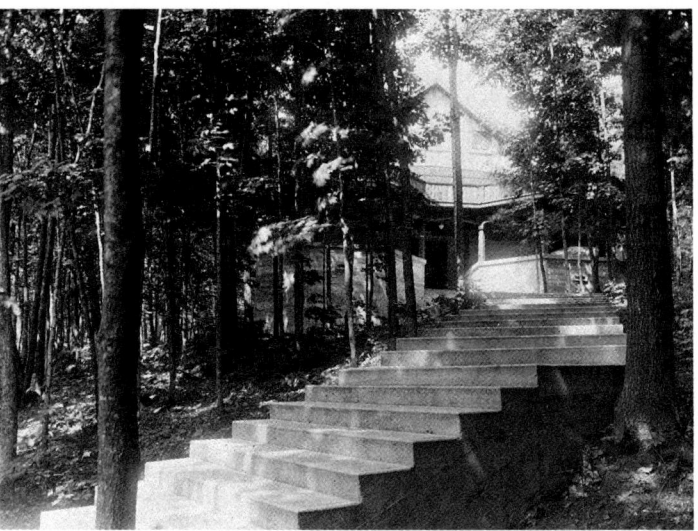

Midnight strolls often began beneath the treetops where winding concrete stairs led from the side door of the East Lodge to the covered walkways.
- *Helen O'Connor*

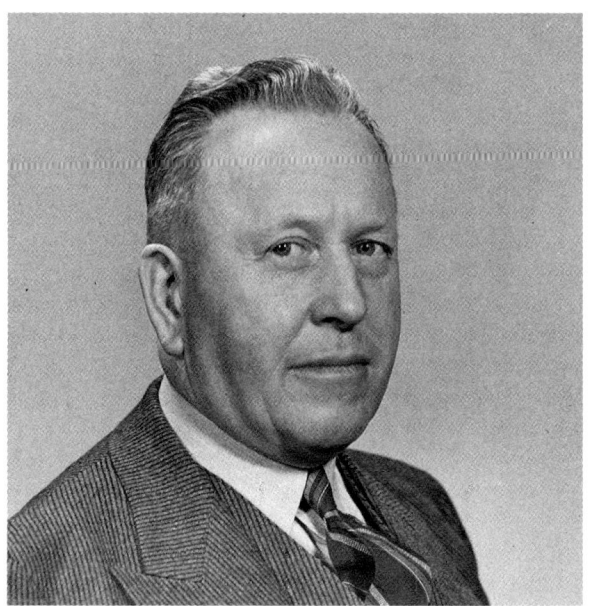

James Garfield Reid, manager of the resort for many years, spent summers on Bigwin Island with his family. The Reid's frame cottage stood on "Jimmy Reid Point," facing the mainland and Norway Point.
- *Marie Rose Tosoni and Ann Platt*

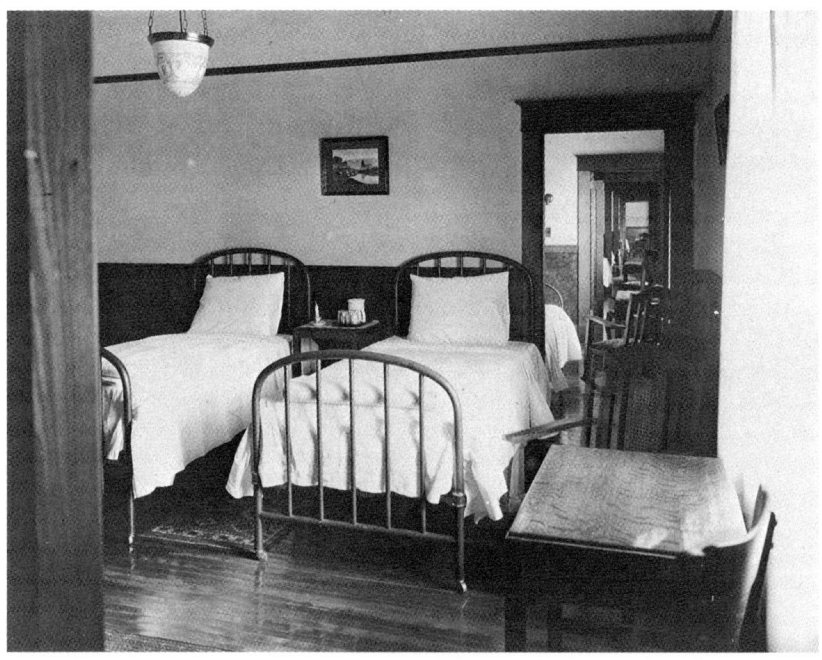

Guests wishing to imbibe often did so in the privacy of their own rooms, as C.O. Shaw operated Bigwin Inn as a temperance hotel.
- *Helen O'Connor*

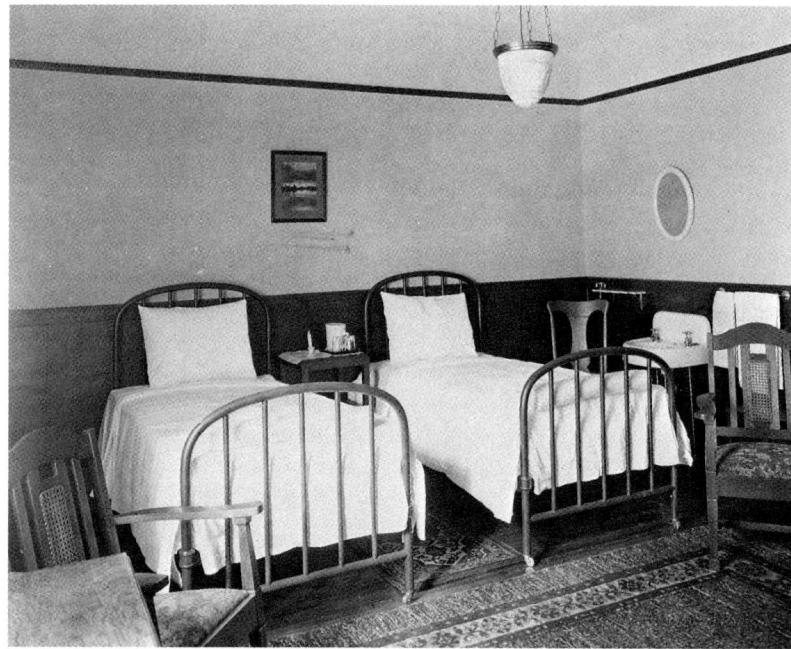

Not to be outdone by other hotels, Bigwin's rooms were redecorated in 1937, with cupboards built in third floor rooms and double doors added between rooms where needed. By the 1940s, most rooms had private baths, with the exception of the lakeside rooms of the East Lodge, which were reserved for family bookings.
- *Helen O'Connor*

Billed as "fireproof," both lodges were constructed of solid concrete. "Each contains large airy bedrooms and private bathrooms. These wing out east and west from the main lodge to which they are connected by covered walks. Good beds and a plentiful supply of hot water are two of the essentials included in the equipment."
- *Helen O'Connor*

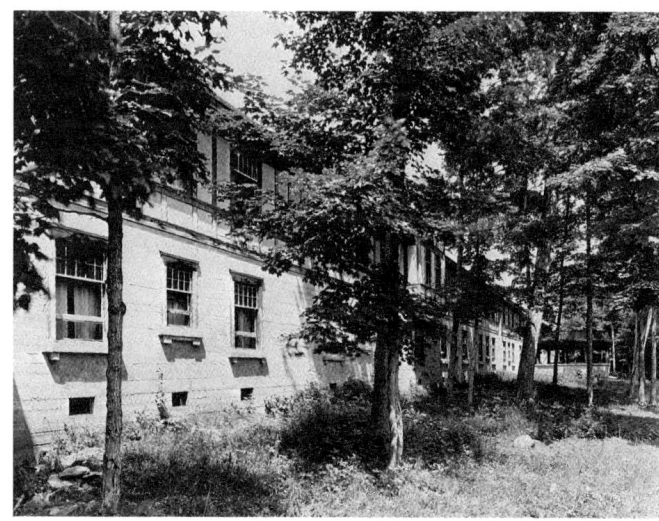

Concrete and Stone Construction—
—Fire-proof

Three Bed Rooms—
—Twin Beds

Living Room—
—Open Fire-place

Spacious Verandah—Screened—
—Appropriately Furnished

Bath Room—
—Running Hot and Cold Water

Private Boat Landing for
Cottage Community

Telephone Connection with Hotel

Electric Lighted

Maid and Bell Boy Service

Ice and Fireplace Wood

Location—Water's Edge

Launch Service to Dining Room—700 yards
—if raining during dining hours.

ALL FACILITIES OF HOTEL AVAILABLE
For Reservations, Write, Wire or Phone:
MANAGER, BIGWIN INN, BIGWIN ISLAND, LAKE OF BAYS
via Huntsville, Canada

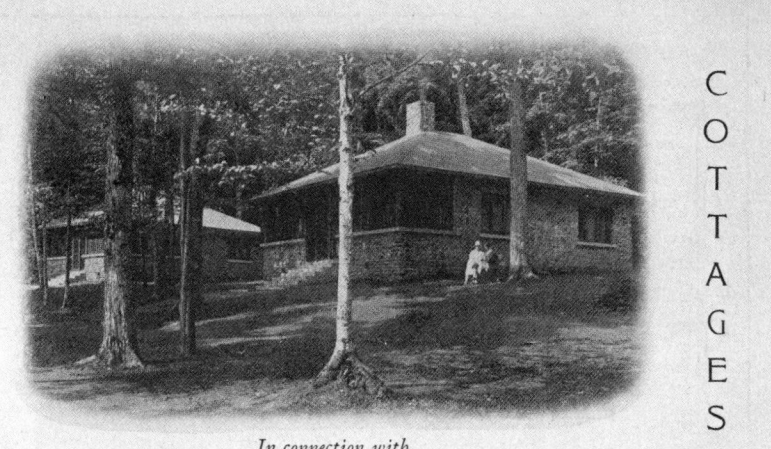

COTTAGES

In connection with
BIGWIN INN
CANADA'S FINEST AND LARGEST SUMMER HOTEL

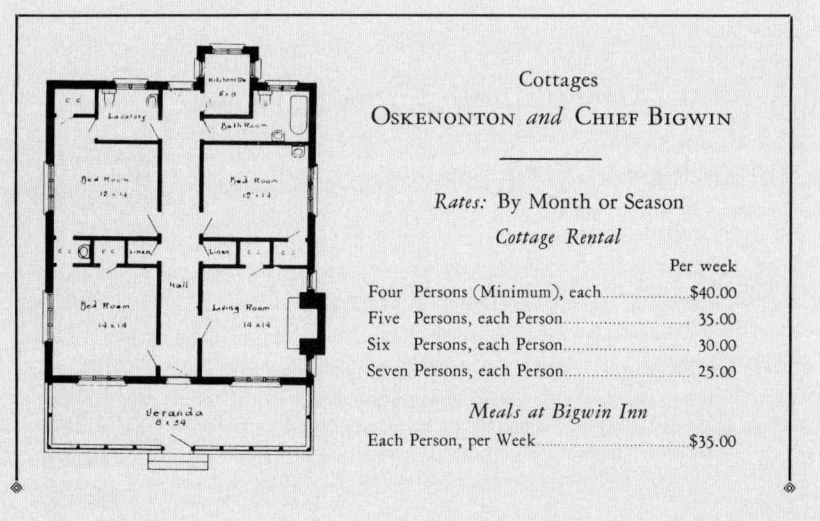

Cottages
HIAWATHA *and* MINNETONKA

Rates: By Month or Season

Cottage Rental

Per week
For not less than four and up to six persons $150.00
If more than six persons, each person $25.00

Meals at Bigwin Inn
Each Person, per Week..................................$35.00

Cottages
OSKENONTON *and* CHIEF BIGWIN

Rates: By Month or Season

Cottage Rental

Per week
Four Persons (Minimum), each.............$40.00
Five Persons, each Person.................... 35.00
Six Persons, each Person.................... 30.00
Seven Persons, each Person.................. 25.00

Meals at Bigwin Inn
Each Person, per Week..................................$35.00

For families, four cottages of the "Bigwin Cottage Colony" were designed by Canadian architect John Wilson in a Craftsman/ Prairie style. Popular from the early 1900s to the 1930s, the style was typified by long horizontal lines, low proportions and quiet skylines. South of the border, in the U.S.A., architect Frank Lloyd Wright used the style in many of his houses. Both architects advocated a close relationship between buildings, their landscape, and the materials used in construction. This was later termed "organic architecture."
- *Robert McLennan*

characterize the finest service of the big city hotels." Through the years, many visitors summered in these charming cottages known as "Os-Ke-Non-Ton," "Minnetonka," "Hiawatha," and "Chief Bigwin," but one guest who stayed in the westernmost dwelling, "Cottage Number One, Chief Bigwin," was particularly well remembered by those who staffed the resort at the time.

During the 1943 season, 34-year-old Crown Princess Juliana Louise Emma Marie Wilhelmina of Orange-Nassau, Duchess of Mecklenburg, and her children spent a month in the stone cottage as war guests of the Canadian government. The only child of Queen Wilhelmina I of the Netherlands and Prince Consort Henry had fled her homeland one day prior to the 1940 Nazi invasion. Her Royal Highness Princess Juliana, wife of Prince Bernhard of Lippe-Biesterfield, and her daughters, five-year-old Beatrix Wilhelmina Armgard and four-year-old Irene Emma Elisabeth, escaped to England and later were evacuated to Canada, where third daughter Margriet Francisca was born in 1943. (To assure the newborn Royal the conveyance of Dutch citizenship, that portion of the hospital where the baby was delivered was specially declared Dutch territory by the Canadian government.) During Her Royal Highness Princess Juliana's stay in Canada, she maintained a very low profile and only occasionally stepped into the spotlight with public broadcasts to her people. In keeping with this policy, the arrival of the Royal Family at Bigwin Inn late one evening was known only to a very select group of individuals.

Among that select group was Roxie Joy Hosking, who had worked for many years with C.O. Shaw. During the stay of Her Royal Highness Princess Juliana, important documents of the Netherlands were placed in the interior deposit box of Bigwin's cast-iron safe, the combination to which was held only in the minds of top officials of the company. While this proved advantageous for the security of valuables, it also provided humorous inconveniences. In one instance, general manager John McKee was unable to unlock the safe. To confirm its combination he telephoned Mrs. Hosking, who at the time was in northern Quebec. Through the poor telephone connection of a party line, Mrs. Hosking relayed the combination to Mr. McKee, who again tried to unlock the safe. After many attempts, the safe finally relinquished its stronghold, much to the relief of all individuals involved.

As the news of Her Majesty's arrival at Bigwin Inn spread through the surrounding towns, countless curiosity seekers arrived at the resort hoping to catch a glimpse of her. However, Her Royal Highness Princess Juliana was seldom distinguished from other guests unless accompanied by her bodyguards, and she took only her evening meal in the dining room. On occasion, Her Royal Majesty attended the weekend galas in the Pavilion. Generally refraining from dancing in the absence of her husband, she was said to have made one exception during her stay. After observing festivities from the gallery, she danced with a young boy by the name of Charles Shaw, the grandson of C.O. Shaw.

After a one-month stay, the Royal Family moved elsewhere for security reasons. On the day of her return to the mainland with her lady-in-waiting, Madame Roell, Her Royal Highness Princess Juliana and her children boarded the ferry with the youngest Royal cradled in the arms of the steamer's captain, William P. Tinkiss.

Following Her Majesty's visit at Bigwin, the stone bungalows collectively became known as the "Juliana Cottages." As part of the planned development of the hotel, other beautiful stone cottages were designed, complete with private dancing pavilions. They failed to materialize, however, leaving the collection of Juliana Cottages as a unique element of the island's architectural and social heritage.

The Rotunda
The main reception building, the "Rotunda," was designed by John Wilson to be darker and more stately than the resort's other buildings. Its foundation was constructed of large native boulders which supported broad verandahs trimmed with balustrades. Flanked by lush greenswards, the expansive decks surrounded the main building on three sides and were appointed with dozens of hickory rockers, chairs, tables, and swings.

Beneath the crimson-tiled gambrel and gabled roof, the interior of the edifice featured a great centre hall which stretched the entire length of the main building. Upon entering the Rotunda, the guests' attention was immediately drawn up from the reception desk to a high, heavily beamed and raftered ceiling. A second-level gallery surrounded the lounge on three sides and was reached by wide staircases. From it, guests could access various writing alcoves as well as five covered balconies. The balconies were later enclosed with windows, the south-central balcony becoming the children's playroom and the others used for table tennis, billiards, games of bridge or as the hotel's library. Like an English manor house, the lounge and all the adjoining rooms were appointed with gleaming wood floors, plush Persian rugs, potted palm trees and ferns, ceramic vases of freshly cut flowers and leaves, mounted moose- and deer-head trophies, chintz-covered chesterfields and rockers, oversized wicker chairs, burnished writing tables and benches.

Adorning the walls of the Rotunda's main lounge were eight huge fireplaces, some with stone armchairs built into them on the interior of the building and with benches, pedestals or urns built on the exterior. Each of the smaller ones used over 200 tons of stone in its construction and was built with a deep hearth designed to accommodate 5-foot logs. Fireplace designs were sketched on shingles and crafted by James McFarlane, a stonemason and farmer from Huntsville who received $5 a day and board for his work. His masonry was so exceptionally beautiful that it received many favourable comments from visitors to the Inn. One summer, an architect from the United States so greatly admired the

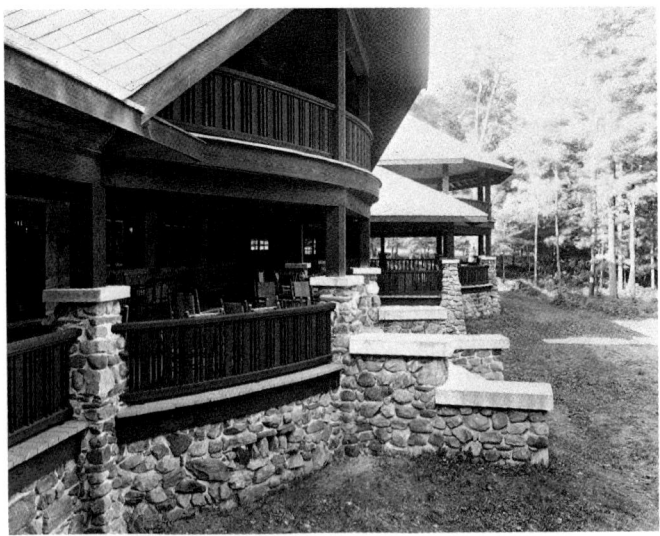

Wilson's use of native stone and timber symbolically linked the art of architecture with the natural surroundings of Bigwin Island. A building of baronial proportion, the Rotunda's foundation was constructed so that large native boulders supported broad verandahs. The architect designed the verandahs to eliminate visual and psychological barriers between indoors and out, thus uniting the two in harmony.
- *DGM*

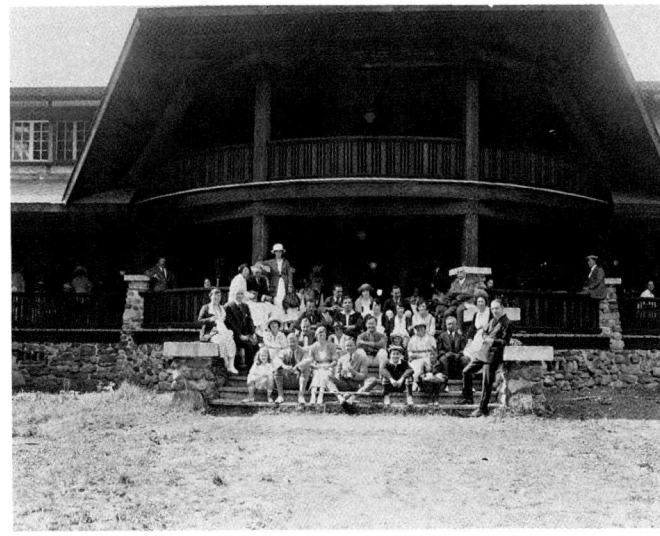

With gloves and hats the vogue, a trip to Bigwin Inn during the 1920s began with a visit to the nearest haberdashery and millinery shop.
- *Helen O'Connor*

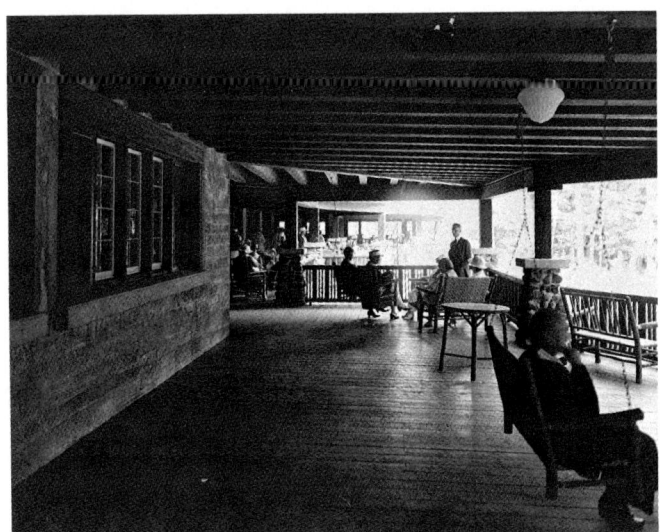

Overlooking the lake and a short distance from the dining room, the southwest corner of the Rotunda's verandah was a popular spot to meet dinner guests. Those who felt a chill in the evening air could purchase a Glenayr-Knit cardigan or pullover from the gift shop inside.
- *Helen O'Connor*

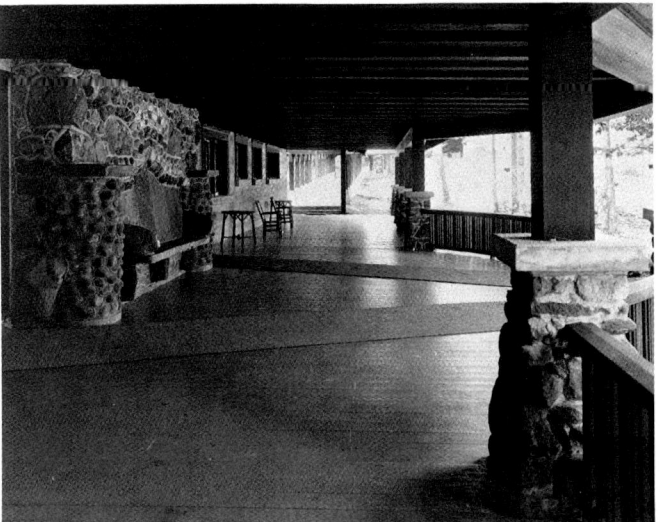

The elaborate masonry work on the walls of the Rotunda offered a visual symphony of natural forms. On cooler evenings, the stone benches on the outer wall were warmed by the fireplaces on the inner wall.
- *Robert McLennan*

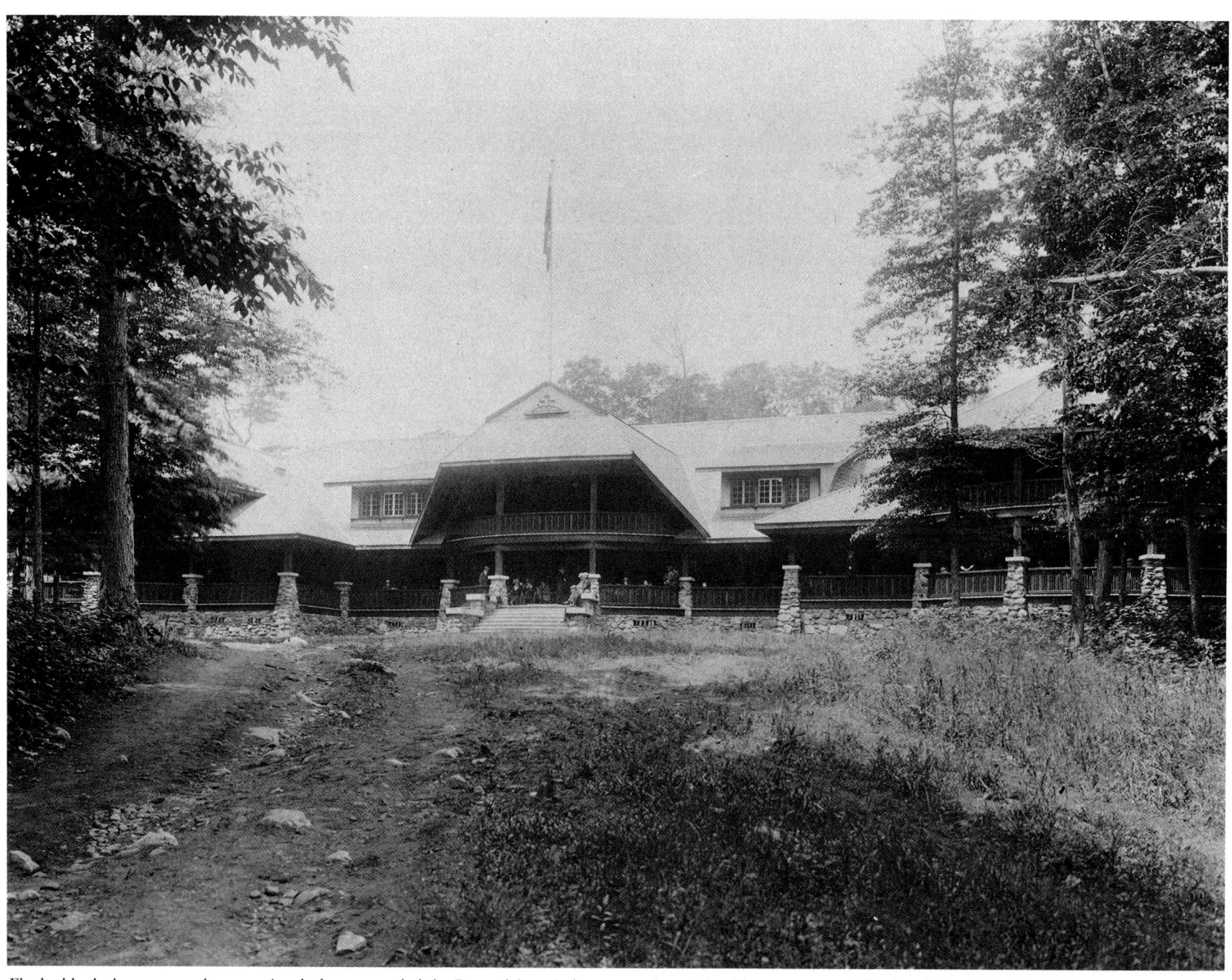

Flanked by lush greenswards, expansive decks surrounded the Rotunda's main lounge on three sides. There, guests could enjoy the perfumed air of the nearby gardens. A folding postcard from 1929 stated: "The clear invigorating air of Lake of Bays, the cool nights, and the freedom from the blight of 'heat waves' offers an immunity to hay-fever, which makes Bigwin Inn an ideal spot for rest and relaxation."
- *Robert McLennan*

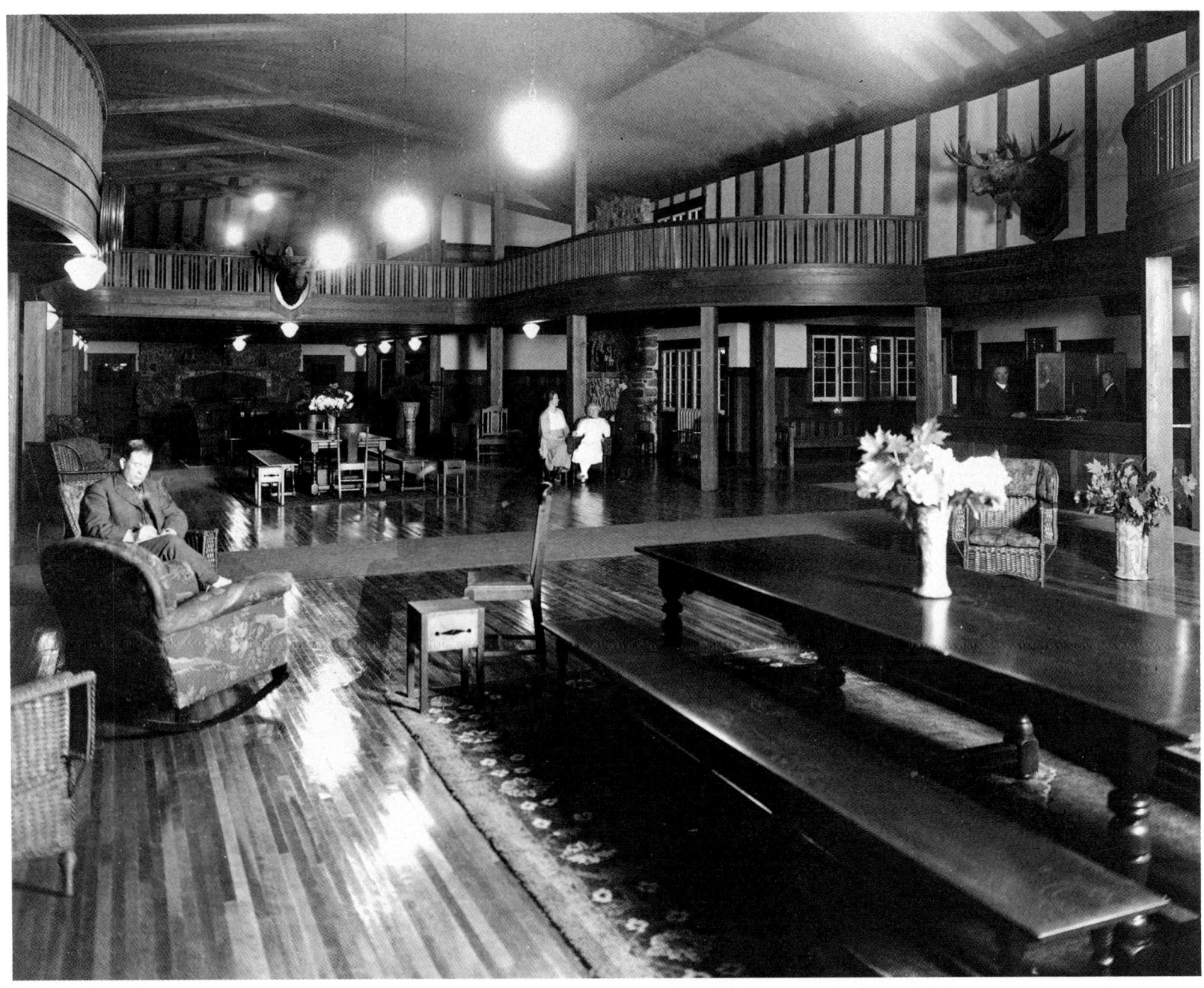

Dusted by housekeeping staff twice daily, three royal-tined moosehead trophies "stood guard" over the main lounge and front desk. (They were the first accessories brought to the island during construction of the resort.) The Rotunda's gallery was a popular spot to catch a glimpse of the aristocratic elite, including the Rockefellers, Princess Juliana of the Netherlands and Canadian Prime Ministers Arthur Meighen and John Diefenbaker. - *DGM*

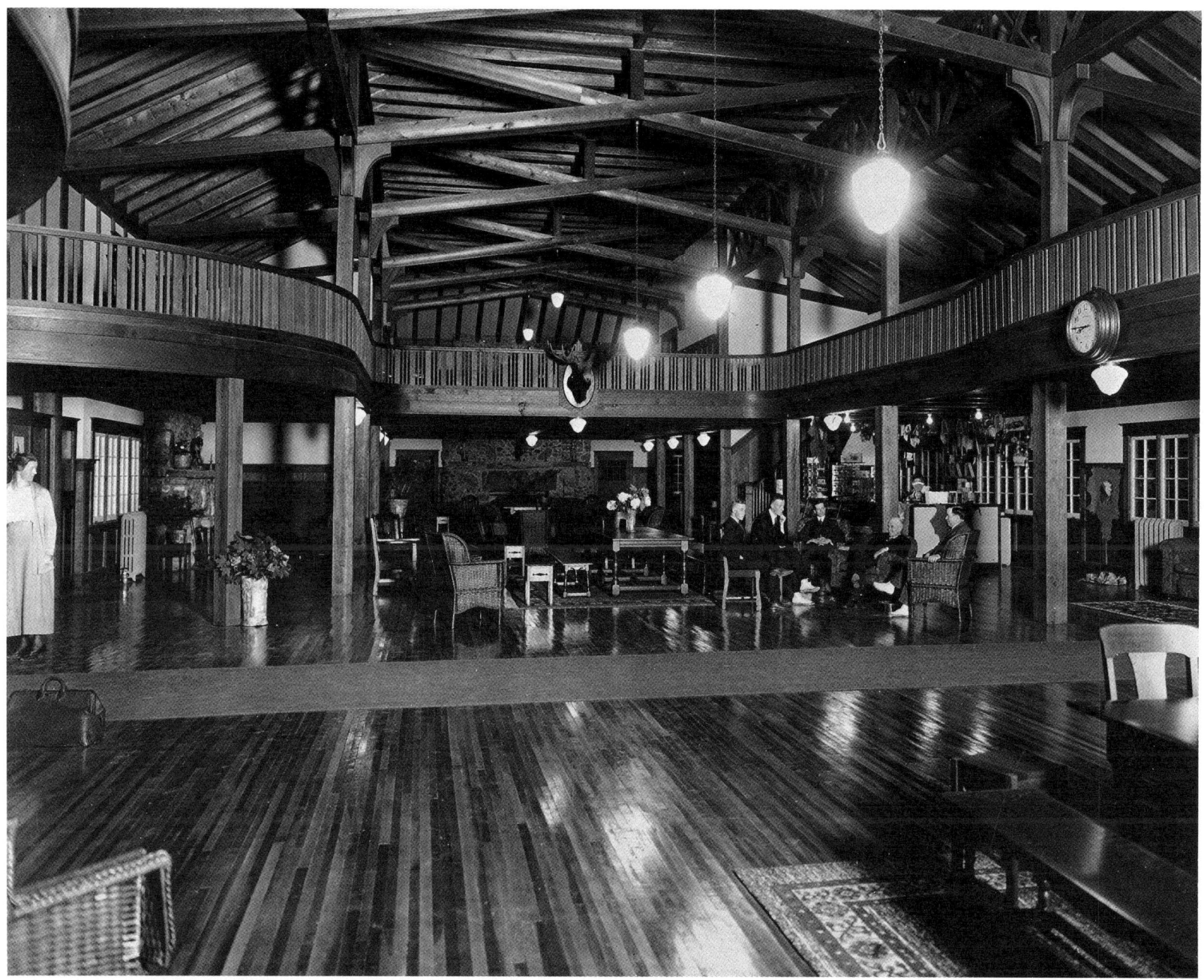

Upon entering the Rotunda, visitors' attention was immediately drawn upward to a high, heavily beamed and raftered ceiling. "The giant redwoods of California have relations at Bigwin. Look up at the beams in the ceiling of the Great Lounge, and you'll see the grandfathers and great-grandfathers of our northern forests. You can't cut trees like those today, there just aren't any such giants left. We planed the last of them for the Bigwin Lounge, and built a monument to the forests of Canada. Next time you're in the Great Lounge, glance up and measure the length of one single beam; it will surprise you," read the *Bigwin Banter* on August 14, 1937. Lounging in regal splendour in a wicker chair, fourth from the left, C.O. Shaw chats with a group of men in the east end of the Rotunda's Great Lounge.

- *DGM*

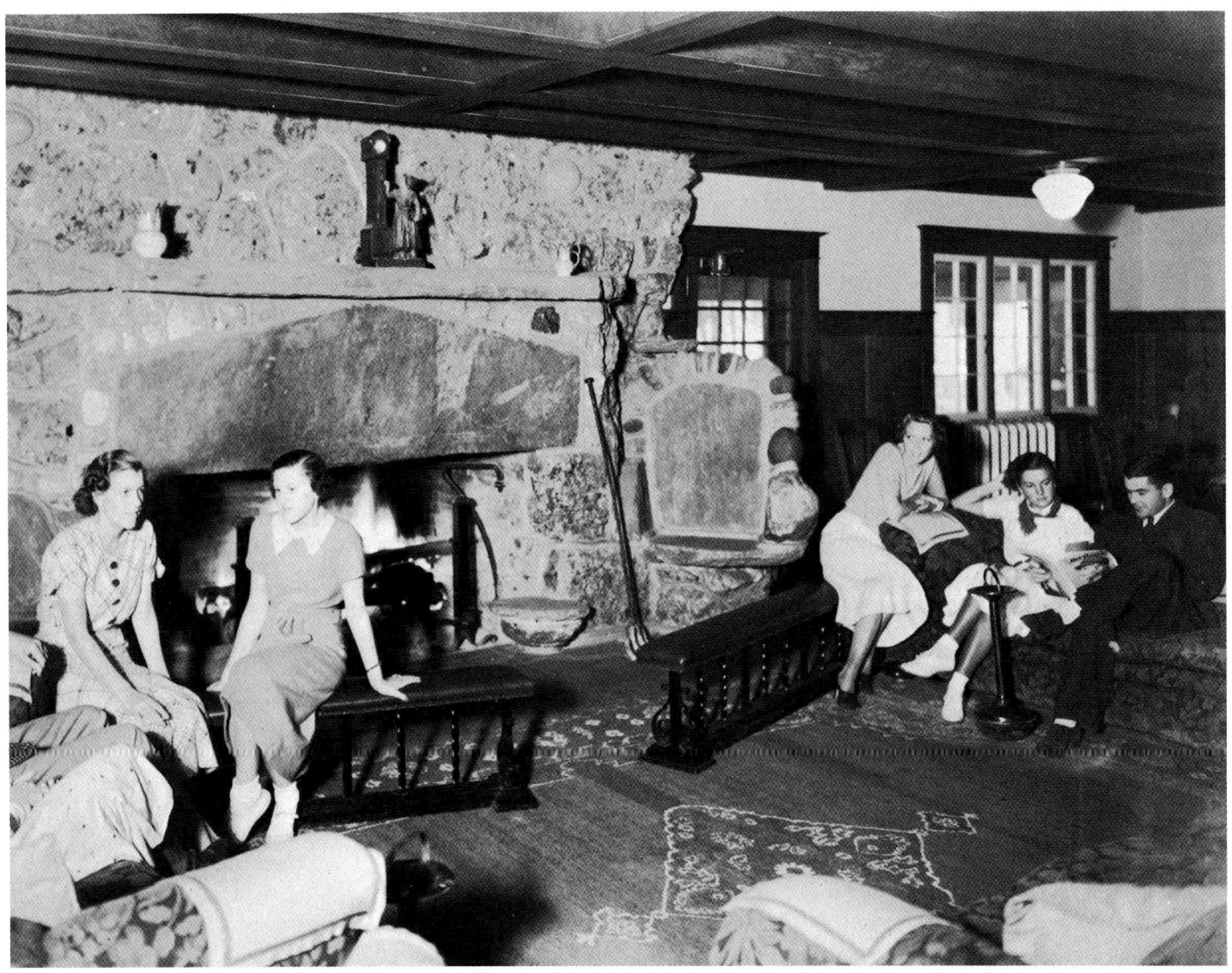

A quiet corner of the Rotunda offered debutantes and their suitors a convivial place to chat and to read the latest editions of *Town and Country, Mayfair* or *American* magazines. The newsstand and gift shop nearby offered guests a myriad of products, including postcards, stamps, McIntosh toffee and Neilson Burnt Almond chocolate bars. In later years, visitors could also purchase Black Cat, Buckingham and Phillip Morris English Blend cigarettes. A *Bigwin Banter* of 1937 noted: "Goody, goody, these are the things that will solve our gift problem. Purses of English leather, hand tooled with conventional designs, hand-painted work bags that will harmonize with almost any costume, English tapestry bags that can be used with fall and winter frocks as well as darker summer rigs, gorgeous homespun scarves, triangles, belts and bags to match from the Shuttle in Oakville, and last but by no means least, swanky runners and cushion tops to match, all with hand patterns in blending colours: at the gift shop in the Rotunda. And they are going like hot cakes too, so hurry, hurry and make your selections before the choice pieces are all gone."

- *Frank Mills Leslie*

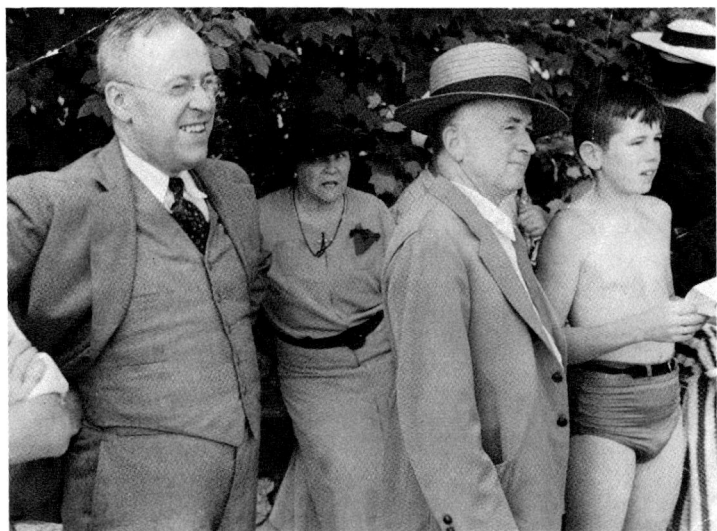

Samuel Forsythe, Greg Clark and his son observe the festivities of the annual regatta. Many of the resort's regattas were won by contestants from nearby Camp Otter, where E.B. White, author of the children's book *Charlotte's Web*, spent his summers. - *S. Moir Forsythe*

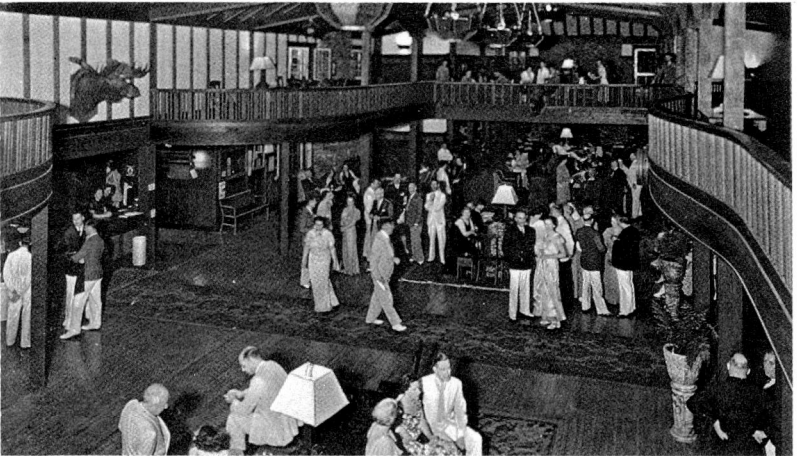

"Meet Jocko! That's what we all call him, behind the scenes — but off duty he's Signor Pesando — and he's been on the Bigwin staff since the first concrete foundation was poured on the island. Jocko is our Master Electrician. He's responsible for the artistic lights in the Rotunda —including the wrought iron and stained wood fixtures — and he also constructed the clever kaleidoscope of colour suspended from the cupola in the pavilion. Born in Piedmonte, at the edge of the French border, Jocko came to Canada when he was sixteen years of age, and has, since then, given his time and ability to Bigwin. Congratulations on your lights, Jocko — they're clever, and artistic and to your assistant, Ross Cameron, who helped no little bit in turning them out," read a *Bigwin Banter* in August of 1937.

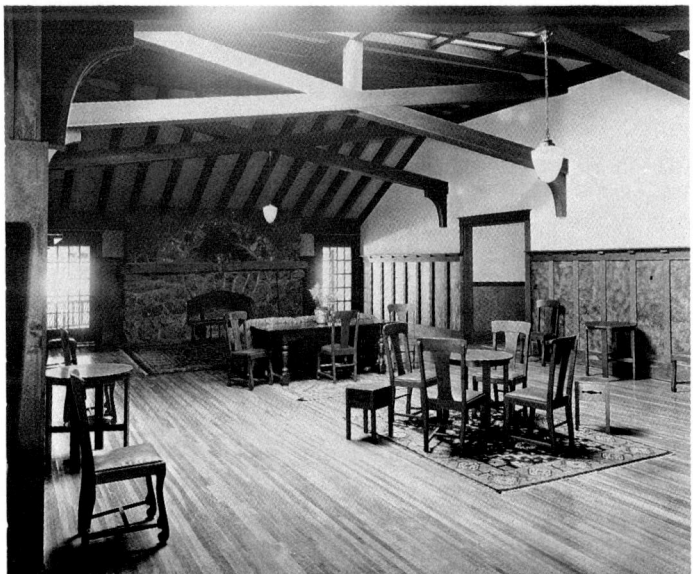

The gallery of the Rotunda contained various writing alcoves where guests could write postcards and letters or "play a rubber of bridge." Two of the alcoves were equipped with sky lights - a modern convenience for guests. "At night, guests may look at the twinkling sky that sparkles like diamonds." - *Helen O'Connor*

fireplaces' originality of design and composition of colours that he enquired where he might obtain copies of their blueprints. "I am sorry," replied C.O. Shaw, "but the man who built them made his plans on shingles and the shingles were thrown away."

With over 26,000 square feet of space, the Rotunda contained many other rooms in its adjoining wings. Behind the reception desk, the north-central wing contained the 24-hour switchboard and telegraph office, a pop stand, the hotel safe, staff parlour and C.O. Shaw's office, complete with fireplaces of its own. A service staircase led to the second floor, where the mailroom, post office and publicity office were located. The northwest wing contained the doctor's office, nurse's office, key room, beauty parlour and ladies' cloakroom, with executive offices and accommodations for staff on the second level. The northeast wing contained the barbershop, valet and gentlemen's cloakroom, and above, additional executive offices and employee accommodations. Opposite this wing, on the first floor, were the newsstand and gift shop.

Sunday-afternoon musicals were performed in the Rotunda, often in aid of the *Star* Fresh Air Fund. Twice monthly, the Anglo Canadian Concert Band would perform at Bigwin Inn, and these concerts were periodically broadcast, much to the acclaim of radio audiences across Canada and the United States.

The Rotunda was a popular social area during the evening hours. One Bigwin brochure stated, "Each evening after dinner, the Rotunda is the scene of a gay, colourful pageant when hundreds of interesting looking men and beautiful women, some in evening clothes, some in afternoon costume and others in smart sport togs, gather to chat, play cards, read, write in one of the alcoves or just sit by the blazing fires. However, there are no rules at Bigwin Inn calling for the wearing of formal evening dress, it being the desire of the management to have the guests feel that their own comfort and convenience is the first and only consideration." Of course, many people dressed as elegantly as they could and changed their clothes frequently, in keeping with the period and the sophisticated surroundings.

Countless visitors returned over the years, and checking in at the Rotunda's reception desk was a reunion for many, as Bigwin Inn had all the tradition and familiarity of a private club. Among those registering in the resort's guest books were Judge Barton, Stuart Darling, Mr. and Mrs. R.A. Batten, Mr. and Mrs. F.H. Schmidt, and Mr. and Mrs. H.C. Hindmarsh. Other social luminaries visiting the resort included the Bassetts, Joseph E. Atkinson (president of the Toronto *Star*), Sir Beverley Baxter (Canadian-born journalist famous for his *Maclean's* column, "London Letter"), William "Billy" Avery Bishop (Canadian flying ace decorated with the Victoria Cross in WWI), Franklin Carmichael (of the Group of Seven), Glenn Gould, Ernest Hemingway, E. Pauline Johnson (poet), Gregory Clark (Canadian journalist and author), Donna Douglas (Ellie-Mae on the CBS series *The Beverly Hillbillies*), Clark Gable (screen star), Mr. and Mrs. Donald Fleming Hunter (of Maclean Hunter Limited), Carole Lombard (screen star), Cameron Peck (Chicago's milk magnate), the Rockefellers, Gordon Sinclair (Canadian broadcast journalist), the Southam family (of Southam Communications), Franchot Tone (actor), William Wrigley (of Wrigley's Gum), Her Royal Highness Princess Juliana of the Netherlands and her children, and Canadian Prime Minister Arthur Meighen and his family.

An enduring Bigwin tale involved John McAllister Wilson, the son of Bigwin's architect, who first started to work at the resort as a bellhop in 1924. That year, the 15-year-old had travelled from Collingwood to the Inn for the summer. Shortly thereafter, his father sent him a loan of $25 dollars to tide him over until he earned sufficient remuneration to cover his expenses. One day, young John Wilson was sitting on the bellhop bench alongside the reception desk when he was summoned to deliver a message to a wealthy railway tycoon staying at the resort. The young boy dutifully began scouring the island to make his delivery. Eventually, he found the gentleman, but surprisingly was given no tip for his services. The incident was cause for the pages, porters and bellhops to worry, as it was thought that this behaviour might set a precedent among guests. Within a few days, however, tips amounted to such an enormous sum that young John Wilson promptly returned the uncashed money order to his father. Proudly displaying it, the architect of the resort recounted the great success of his fine young son at Bigwin Inn.

The Tea House
To keep Bigwin Inn abreast of other fine hotels, C.O. Shaw established a 25-year plan to expand and constantly improve the resort's facilities. A small part of the plan was executed in 1929, when the management erected a beautiful stone building known as the snack room or "Tea House." Leading from the southeast verandah of the Rotunda, the 4,000-square-foot dodecagonal building boasted yet another vaulted ceiling, two handsome stone fireplaces and a glazed, terra cotta-tiled floor. Adjoining the main room was a service wing where the kitchen, pantry, serving room, scullery, meat locker and cloakrooms were located. Planned in October 1940 by architect John Wilson, but never built, was a larger two-storey tea house annex designed in the fashion of the Marine Dining Room, with a similar domed ceiling and elaborate stone fireplaces.

One hotel pamphlet described the Tea House as "a boon to the late sleeper who has missed breakfast and to guests who arrive tired and hungry between meals, as snacks or lighter repasts are always available." Tea was served each afternoon at 4 o'clock, and visitors were entertained by a chamber trio that played piano, cello and violin. After taking tea, guests often retired to their rooms and changed into formal apparel in preparation for the exciting evening events ahead.

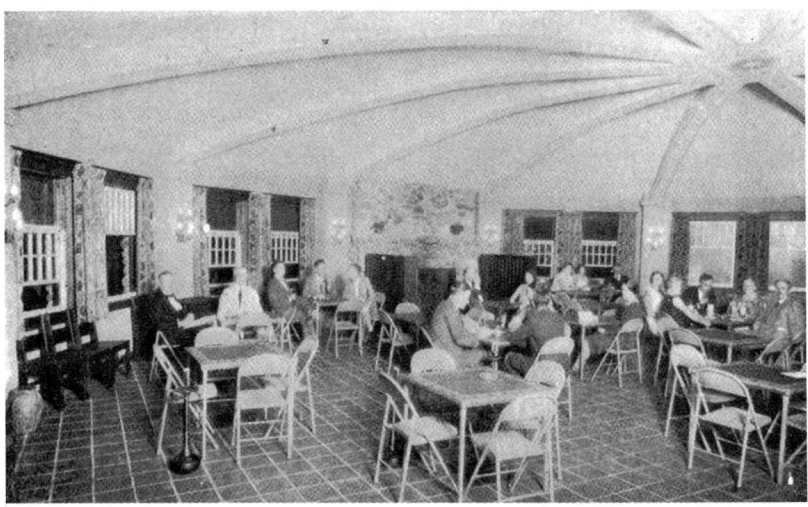

To keep Bigwin abreast of other fine hotels, C.O. Shaw established a 25-year plan to expand and improve the resort. A small part of the plan was executed in 1929, a year remembered for the stock market crash, with the construction of the stone Tea House. A line from a 1930s movie script read: "In the evening, logs blaze cheerily in the great fireplaces, there's music and laughter, friendships, romance and over the coffee cups are recounted the highlights of a world of pleasure on Bigwin Island."
- DGM

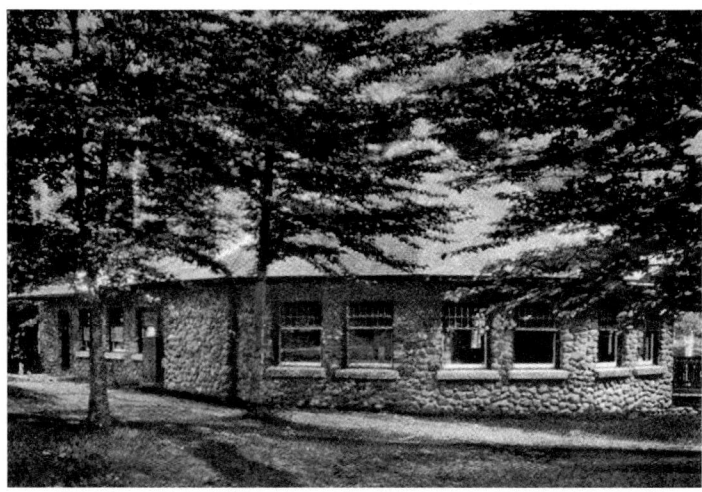

"Connecting with the Rotunda verandah is the Tea House, a most hospitable apartment of soft greens vying with the colouring of the little natural park in which it nestles. From ten in the morning until midnight, the Tea House serves you, a real boon to the late sleeper who has missed breakfast or guests arriving tired and hungry between meals — refreshing hot drinks, tempting iced drinks, dainty lunches. Here prevails a camaraderie that is delightful, happy groups gather about the two great fireplaces with their chummy settles. We all love wood fires and can sympathize with our pagan ancestors in their worship of fire." declared one hotel brochure.
- DGM

In 1936, C.O. Shaw produced *Pleasure Island* under the direction of Gordon Sparling of Associated Screen News. The 11-minute, 35mm film was shown at various cinemas in North America prior to a theatre's main feature. The *Bigwin Banter* of Saturday, August 14, 1937, read: "Were you here last year when Bigwin Island became the 'location' for the talkie, now showing in hundreds of American theatres? That talkie — *Pleasure Island* — will be shown in the Casino on Thursday night — along with the regular feature, comedy and short. If you want to see yourself out-doing 'Garbo' on the screen — don't miss Thursday night's program and even if you weren't on Bigwin Island last year when the picture was taken, you'll enjoy seeing Bigwin in the movies. The show starts at nine o'clock Thursday night. Tickets on sale at the Casino door."
- DGM

> Huntsville, Ont.
>
> "Pleasure Island", the very lovely Moving Picture taken at Bigwin Inn last summer, will be shown at
>
> **BELLE CINEMA THEATRE**
> Brooklyn N. Y.
> July 15th - 17th
>
> We know you will be interested and hope you may find it convenient to see this very attractive sound film. It is delightful entertainment. For those who were not at Bigwin Inn last season it will give an excellent idea of the added beauty and charm recent improvements have given. Do see it.
>
> The Bigwin Inn Co., Limited
> per Chas. O. Shaw,
> President.

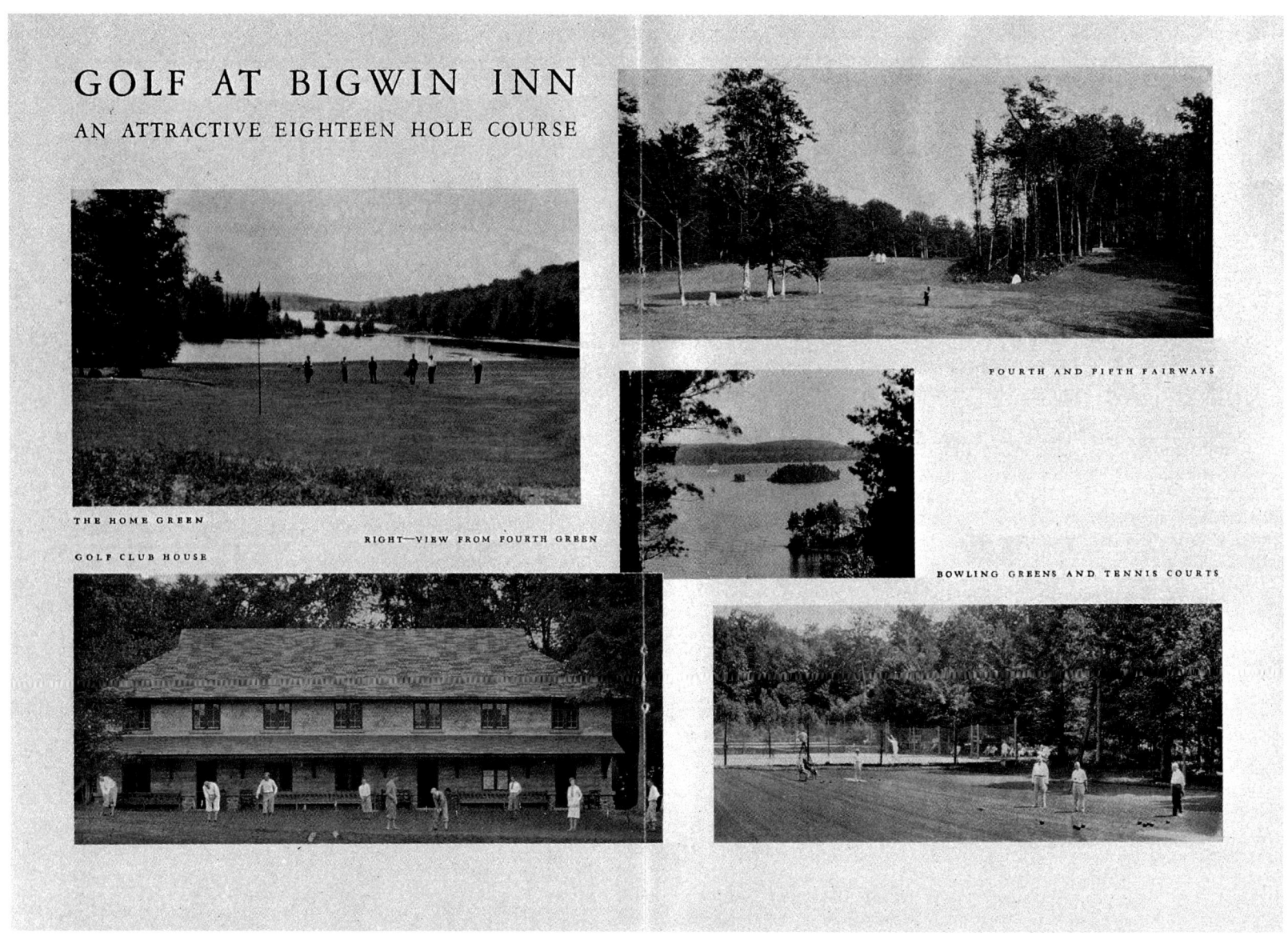

The hotel's golf course opened on July 1, 1922. By 1930, 18 holes were in play and a clubhouse had been erected by the home green. Period brochures read: "Amid such heavenly scenery, even the business of hunting for a lost ball becomes less conducive to profanity." Tennis was also a popular pastime. The Northern Ontario Tennis Championship was traditionally held at Bigwin in August.
- *Robert McLennan*

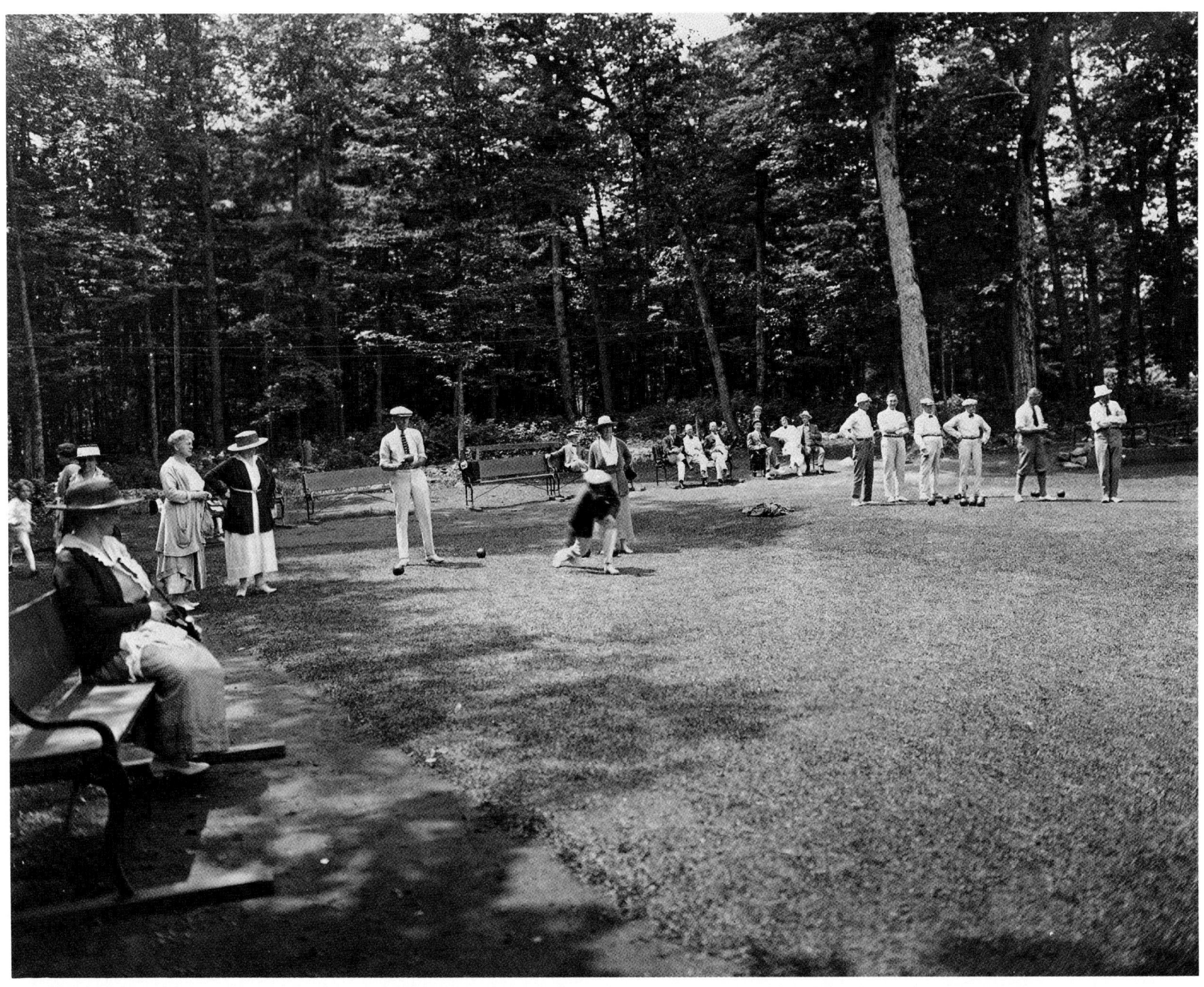
Outdoor activities were extensive and included shuffleboard, croquet and lawn bowling. "Three smooth bowling lawns and four fast clay tennis courts are in close proximity to the lodges. Their wooded setting provides cool shady spots for the spectators who invariably gather to watch the games."   - *Helen O'Connor*

The Great Outdoors

For outdoor recreation, Bigwin's extensive facilities appealed to the most discriminating of guests. In addition to the waterfront activities, there were four tennis courts, badminton courts, horseshoe pits and three bowling greens, all behind the East Lodge, and a baseball diamond behind the West Lodge. In front of the Rotunda, there were croquet lawns and shuffleboard courts. The fragrant air of the island's gardens, lawns and forest glades could also be enjoyed by relaxing beneath great groves of maple, pine, oak, birch and beech trees, where various cobblestone benches were situated.

The hotel's nine-hole golf course opened on July 1, 1922, and shortly thereafter was thought to be the finest in Muskoka. It was built under the supervision of Stanley Thompson, the noted landscape architect. Characteristic of the times, the course was ingeniously designed around the natural landscape of the island, with the dual purpose of preserving its irreplaceable environmental heritage and affording intermittent firebreaks throughout the forest. The first tee was located by the dining room and the ninth green near the verandahs of the Rotunda. As part of the progressive development of the entire hotel, the management added another three holes to the golf course for the 1926 season, two more holes in 1928, and another four holes in 1930, despite the fact that C.O. Shaw never partook of the sport. For players' comfort, eight rain shelters and numerous benches were scattered across the course. A handsome two-storey clubhouse was erected in 1930, replacing the "Caddy Tent." Complimentary lockers were available, as well as a repair shop, an accessory shop and a resident professional who was in attendance at all times.

Caddies, often Boy Scouts, were obtained from a camp located along Bigwin Island's north shore. As a tribute to their founder, Lord Baden-Powell, the Scouts erected cobblestone cairns with historic plaques at their campsite. Each day at sunrise, the bugle would sound and flags would be raised on poles atop the cairns. After a morning meal, the young men would march down to the clubhouse and begin the painstaking task of weeding the course by hand. As the day wore on, they would take turns caddying for the Inn's golfers. With over 350 players a day, each caddy would often carry three bags of long, hickory-sticked clubs just to keep up with the traffic. In addition to their normal duties, caddies would occasionally deter deer from bolting across the fairways or foxes from snatching golf balls as they rolled along the greens of the 6,000-yard course.

Hotel staff were allowed to play the golf course but were not permitted to tee off at the clubhouse. One summer, a waitress at the Inn played the challenging course and hit her first hole in one. As another player congratulated her, she commented that her friends would be sceptical of such an unusual accomplishment. The gentleman kindly offered to sign a golfing hat as witness to her achievement. He did so, signing "Gordon Sinclair."

Norway Point

The summer of 1923 brought disaster to the Lake of Bays. On Sunday, August 19, one of Muskoka's greatest tragedies occurred at the WaWa Hotel. Early that morning, shortly after a dance and after most of the 240 guests and 95 employees had retired to their rooms, two gentlemen noticed the ominous glow of light beneath a door. On closer examination, they discovered that one of the baggage rooms in the frame structure was ablaze. Amidst great confusion, one man aimed a fire hose at the baggage room while the hotel's bellboys quickly sounded the alarm. But the fire already raged beyond control. As guests and staff clambered to escape, flames raced through the tinder-dry hotel at all levels and up the elevator shaft, erupting into the tower. Within a fleeting 35 minutes, flames engulfed the hotel, it weakened, and then collapsed into a sparking pile of scorched timbers, glowing cinders and white ash. Among the 11 killed were Margaret Bowker (daughter of the CNR's general manager) and Mrs. James McNally of Rand, McNally Publishing Company. Those who survived the blazing inferno were quickly evacuated to various locations, including Bigwin Inn, where a temporary hospital was established. Many Bigwin guests gave up their rooms and donated clothing from their wardrobes to the survivors of the gruesome disaster at the WaWa Hotel.

Days later, the blackened ruins continued to smoulder amid a field of incinerated debris littered with shattered plumbing fixtures, broken bricks, melted panes of glass, and deformed kitchen pots. After the smouldering coals were finally extinguished, "treasure hunters" raked through the tangled wreckage, searching for any caches of jewellery that might have escaped the calamity. All that survived of the once beautiful WaWa Hotel's buildings were a small gazebo on the point, pavilion, boathouse and a baggage and waiting room on the steamer dock. As reporters flocked in from surrounding areas, many colourful rumours arose concerning the rebuilding of the WaWa Hotel. It failed to happen. Little could compare with the elegance and safety of Bigwin Inn, just a short distance across the shimmering lake waters.

Realizing that an increasing number of tourists chose to motor to the Inn, Shaw negotiated the purchase of land at Norway Point, where the WaWa had been. Until this time, many guests had come to the Inn via CNR train number 55, Muskoka Express, from Union station to Huntsville, where bonded baggage was inspected by a customs official. From there, tourists walked to a nearby dock to board a steamer such as the *Algonquin*, which travelled into Hunter's Bay, then down the river, where the swing bridge was opened to Fairy Lake, through a narrow canal to Peninsula Lake, and eventually to North Portage. Mail, supplies, laundry and guests were transported by the Portage Railway along 1⅛ mile of 42" guage track to South Portage, and finally by a steamer such as the *Mohawk Belle* or *Iroquois* to Bigwin Inn. Trains that left on Friday assured guests of a Saturday-morning registry at Bigwin. The returning boat left the Inn at 7:30 p.m. on Sundays, guests being delivered to sleeping cars waiting in Huntsville, which ultimately arrived in Toronto the next morning. By purchasing the land at Norway Point, C.O. Shaw hoped to please his guests with a much simpler and faster means of getting to and from the island Inn.

Shortly after C.O. Shaw acquired ownership of the land, he erected a series of facilities along its sandy shoreline, including staff quarters, a stone utility cottage, dog kennels, gas pumps and six garages with capacity for over 100 cars. An 8,000-square-foot steamer dock offered visitors a small sitting room to use while waiting for a boat to take them across to the island. During the wharf's construction, rubble from the WaWa was cleared from the nearby site and buried in the dock's cribbing.

As the new facilities at Norway Point neared completion, C.O. Shaw began to search for a vessel to ferry guests over to the island Inn. In December 1924, he located the 15-year-old 24.64 ton Toronto-built steam screw yacht *Ella Mary*. With a length of 66 feet and a maximum breadth of 11.75 feet, the boat carried up to 44 passengers and steamed at a maximum speed of ten knots. C.O. Shaw assessed that the yacht might be suitable for his needs and had his son, Charles George, inspect the vessel's keel for dry rot. With his son's enthusiastic approval, C.O. Shaw purchased 64 shares of the craft on December 16, 1924, for $3,500 from Charles J. Gibson, an architect from Toronto. The boat was renamed *Bigwin* on July 4, 1925. After being rechristened and repainted with the Huntsville, Lake of Bays and Lake Simcoe Navigation Company's signature colours — a red water line, white hull, varnished cabin, red and black smokestack and details painted black, red or green — the "Lilliputian liner" was launched into the Lake of Bays. On March 23, 1928, C.O. Shaw transferred ownership of the steamer from the financially beleaguered navigation company to the Bigwin Boat Livery Company Limited of Bigwin Island for $6,093.81.

The ferry's captain collected the fare of 25 cents for individual passage to Bigwin Island. On Sundays, the steamer captain would ferry the Inn's guests to church services at Glenmount and Norway Point, in addition to the regular service runs. Some of the seasoned men who served the resort in this capacity were captains Tinkiss, Elder, May, "Nipper" Hill, Reg Leeder and Bill Scollard.

While the proud little steamer was an attractive vessel, many visitors were dazzled by the volume of luxurious automobiles parked on the Bigwin parking lot. During the 1920s and '30s the Inn's lot frequently overflowed with extravagant automobiles such as Packards, Lasalles, Pierce Arrows, Buicks and Cadillacs (including C.O. Shaw's 16-cylinder Cadillac).

Riding Stables And Staff Camps
Continuing its development of Norway Point, the Bigwin Inn Company Limited erected a 2,600-square-foot stable and paddock, making horseback riding available for the 1927 season. Horses were provided by the G.F. Smith Riding School and the Ward Riding Academy of Toronto, with guides and lessons available on request. Once trails had been groomed around the perimeter of Bigwin Island, horses were also boarded in beautiful stone stables located along the north shoreline.

Not far from the island's stables were the golf course drive sheds, the men's staff camp and women's staff bungalows. Both employee camps had housekeeping staff of their own, which left many workers with free time during the later evening hours. Escaping the curfew of the night patrol, hotel personnel would often secretly *rendez-vous* aboard launches en route to destinations such as the Hotel Britannia, Ronville Lodge or Lumina Lodge.

For various reasons, the decade of the Great Depression proved to be a severe strain on Bigwin's profitability, although it never reported a loss, according to founder C.O. Shaw.

Due to its exclusive island location, Bigwin had a very short season in which to operate. Running from mid-June to mid-September, with a staff of 250-300 people and an enormous maintenance budget, large and luxurious Bigwin had to operate near capacity during the months of its operation to sustain profitability.

During the economic storms of the Depression, fewer people had dollars to spend on such luxuries as staying for long periods at summer resorts. Even the very wealthy reduced their annual summer stay to a few weeks or days. Hundreds of steamer trunks gradually gave way to dozens of compact weekend suitcases.

Under the pressure of these times, tastes began to change. With the development of new roads through government projects during the Depression and the subsequent popularity of the private automobile in the post-Depression period, the ability of most people to holiday away from their cities increased greatly. Private cottages became increasingly popular as such a lifestyle became affordable. Tourists who had once flocked to the summer resorts no longer had need of steamer transportation nor hotel accommodation, and thus vacancies grew alarmingly, both on board the lake steamers and at many Muskoka resorts.

Aggravating the situation was the growth in popularity of air travel and the appeal of exotic destinations, which often captured both the individual tourist and the convention trade. Although travel patterns and rationing measures of World War II brought temporary relief to the Muskoka steamers and hotels, armistice soon made foreign destinations safe, affordable and fashionable once again.

Bigwin's failure to react to its shifting market niche resulted in an increasingly elusive clientele. Advertisements for the resort fell on deaf ears in that films and brochures, often produced under the direction of Canada's Gordon Sparling of Associated Screen News, seldom circulated beyond the province of Ontario and the northeastern United States. What was circulated often targeted an older generation of plutocrats already familiar with the beautiful island Inn, thereby leaving many potential markets unsolicited.

In the late summer of 1942, after the last guests had checked out, the staff at Bigwin Inn began to prepare for the winter months ahead. The dining-room employees carefully wrapped the hotel silverware in flannel sleeves and placed it in a crate to be shipped to the Huntsville tannery for safekeeping. The winter superintendents laid in food supplies for the duration of the lake's freeze-up, the Livery staff prepared the mahogany launches for winter storage, the plumber drained water from the pipes, and the housekeeping staff stripped all beds and placed dust covers over most of the furniture. As the Rotunda's rugs were rolled up, blazing hearth fires weakened to a few hot cinders amid deep piles of ash.

During these quieter days, C.O. Shaw would often sit in a chair on the steamer dock to enjoy the peacefulness which came at the end of the tourist season, or he would play a card game or two with one of the hotel personnel. Through the years, he had always made an effort to know his employees, and he credited much of the resort's success to "their hard work and faithfulness." Shaw had once said, "It seems a pity to me that the modern manager spends so much time in a chair behind a desk and so little time out among his men, where he can get to know them by name and by ability."

With the breath of autumn's wind, the leaves turned rich colours of chrome yellow, burnt umber and crimson. As the end of the season drew near, the skeleton staff left at Bigwin prepared for a long list of fond farewells until the following spring. No one realized the glory days of the resort would soon begin to set like a fiery evening sun consumed by the cool, purple vapours of night in Muskoka.

Colour Plates
In 1939, two classic MGM films made their debut, *Gone With The Wind* and *The Wizard of Oz*. While theatregoers were well acquainted with "talkies," many were dazzled by the introduction of colour motion pictures. Colour film also had an impact on still photography. In the summer of 1940, C.O. Shaw's son, Charles George, captured images of Bigwin Inn's heyday on colour film.
- *Allan Thaxter Shaw, Charles Wellington Shaw and Walter Brackley Shaw.*

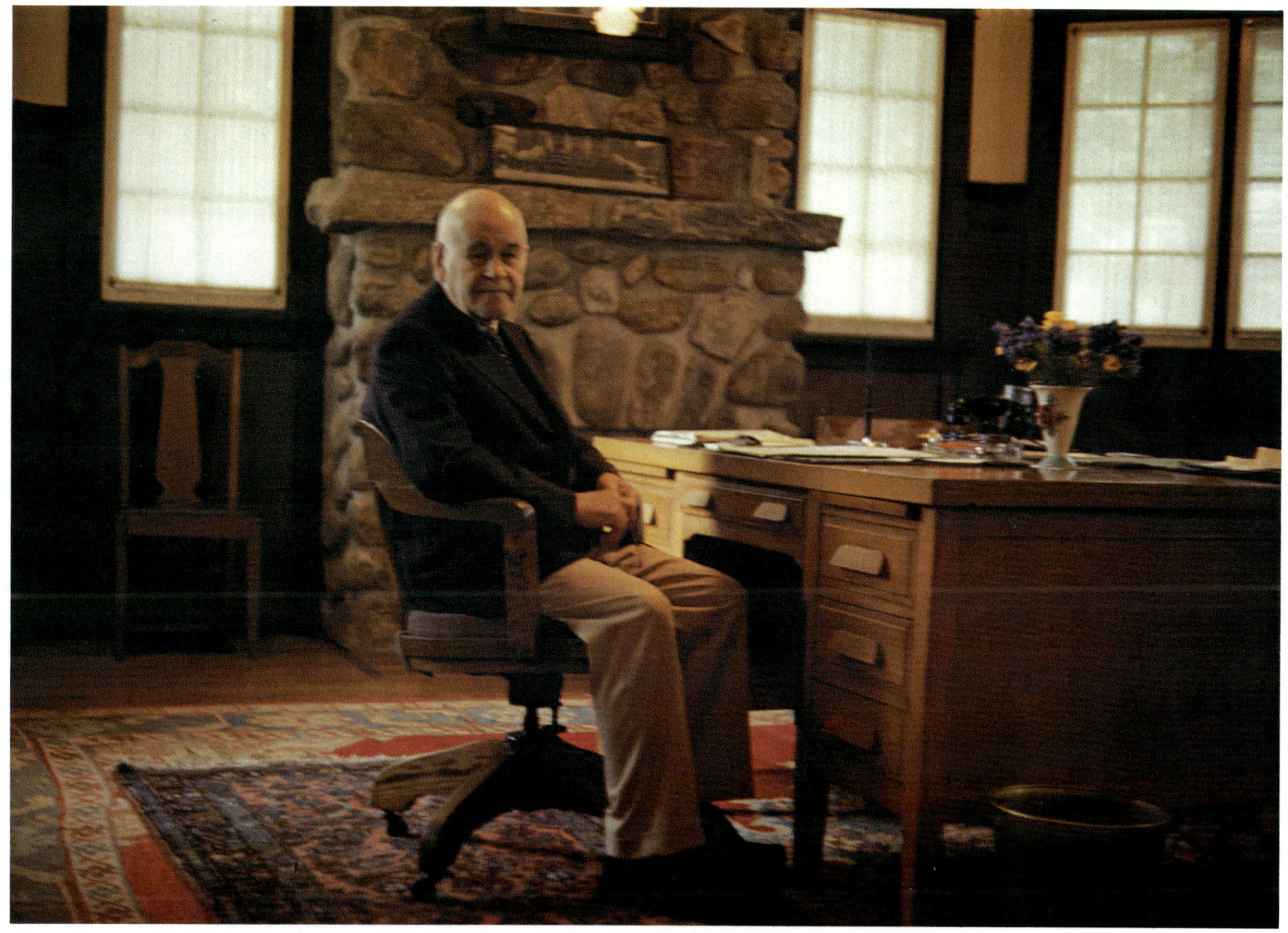

On the rare occasion, when not making a tour of inspection, C.O. Shaw could be found at his desk in the Rotunda. Over the office's fireplace hangs a photograph of the Anglo Canadian Concert Band taken in September 1925 at the CNE. The ink wells on the desk held C.O.'s signature colour of specially mixed ink, often a green or mauve colour.

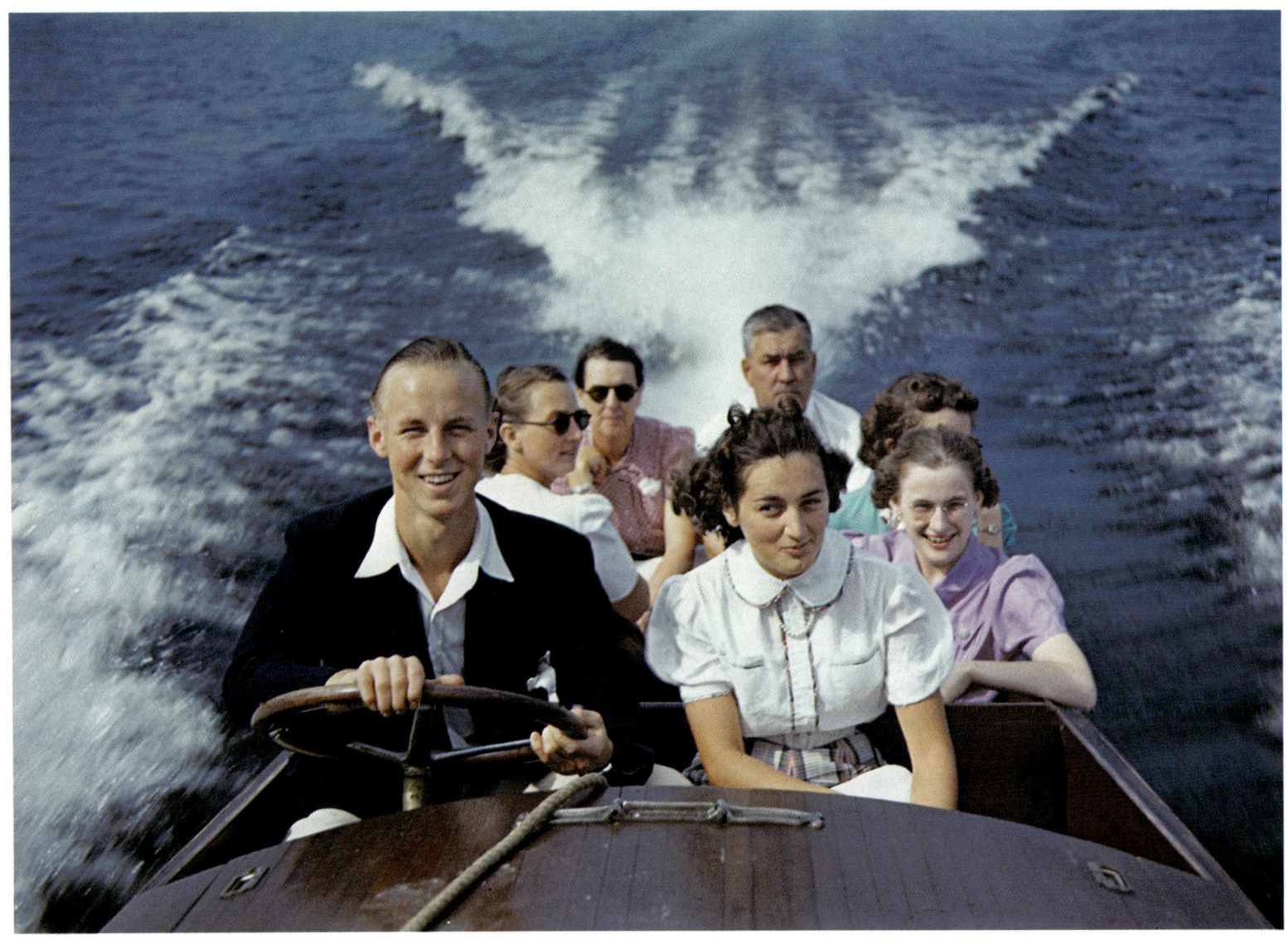
For some, gracious resort living entailed cruising on the Lake of Bays aboard the *Marco*. Aboard are Charles Shaw, Imogene Abbott, Betty Deyell, Mrs. C.G. Shaw, Christine O'Connell, Rena Shaw and Ralph Shaw.

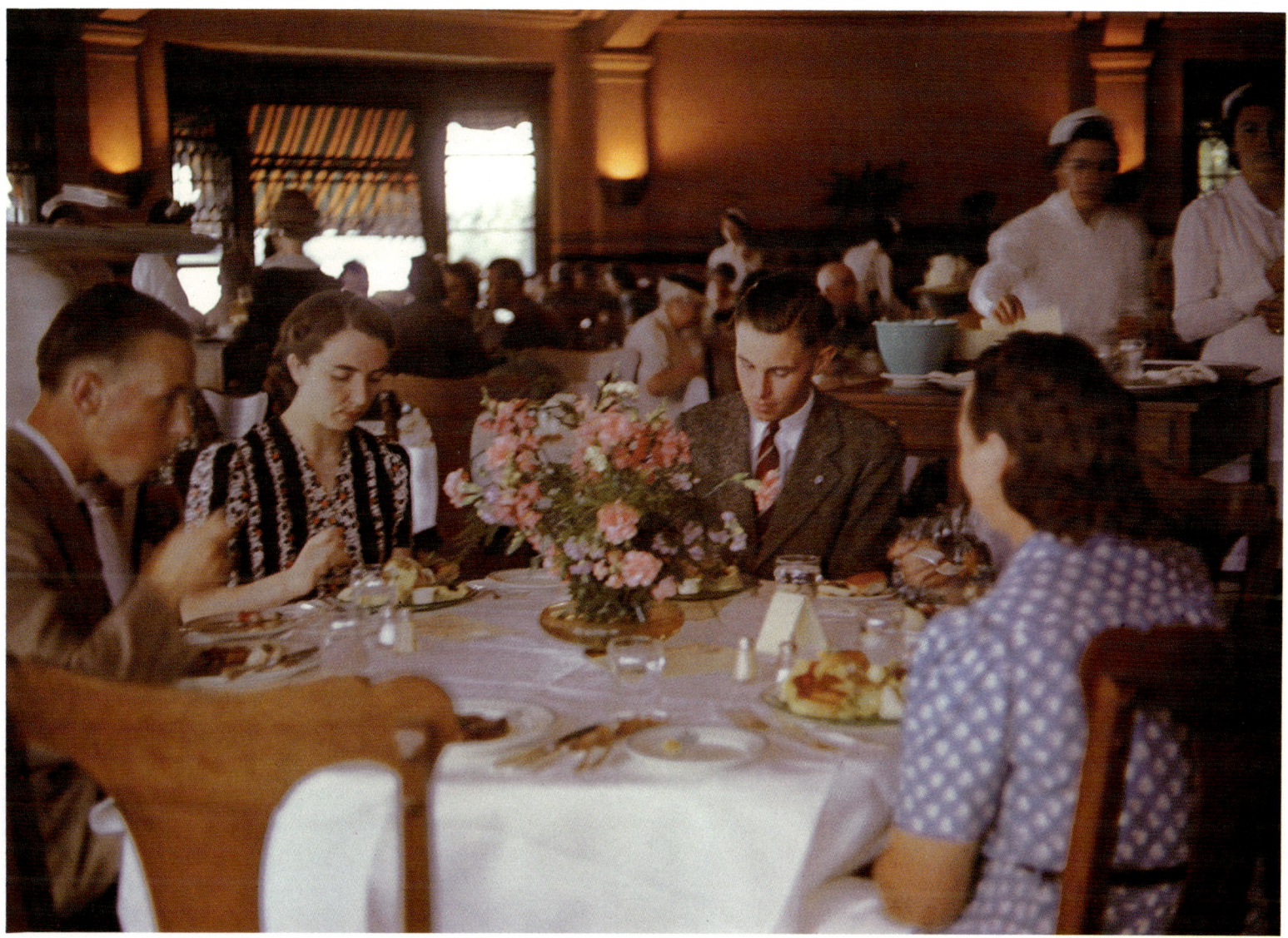

The 1940s saw W.L. Mackenzie King at 24 Sussex Drive, Franklin D. Roosevelt at 1600 Pennsylvania Avenue, and Winston Churchill at 10 Downing Street. A resort brochure printed at Bigwin during that decade noted: "With European travel now impossible, the management anticipates this summer will be a very busy and gay one at Bigwin Inn and we are planning for our guests such excellent service, meals and entertainment, good housekeeping and general comforts, as will deepen old loyalties and make us many new friends. To assure our American friends we should like to say, you have the assurance of our Canadian government that you will find in Canada none of the restrictions usually associated with a country at war." Seated in the Marine Dining Room are Charles Shaw, Christine O'Connell, Brackley Shaw and Mrs. Charles G. Shaw.

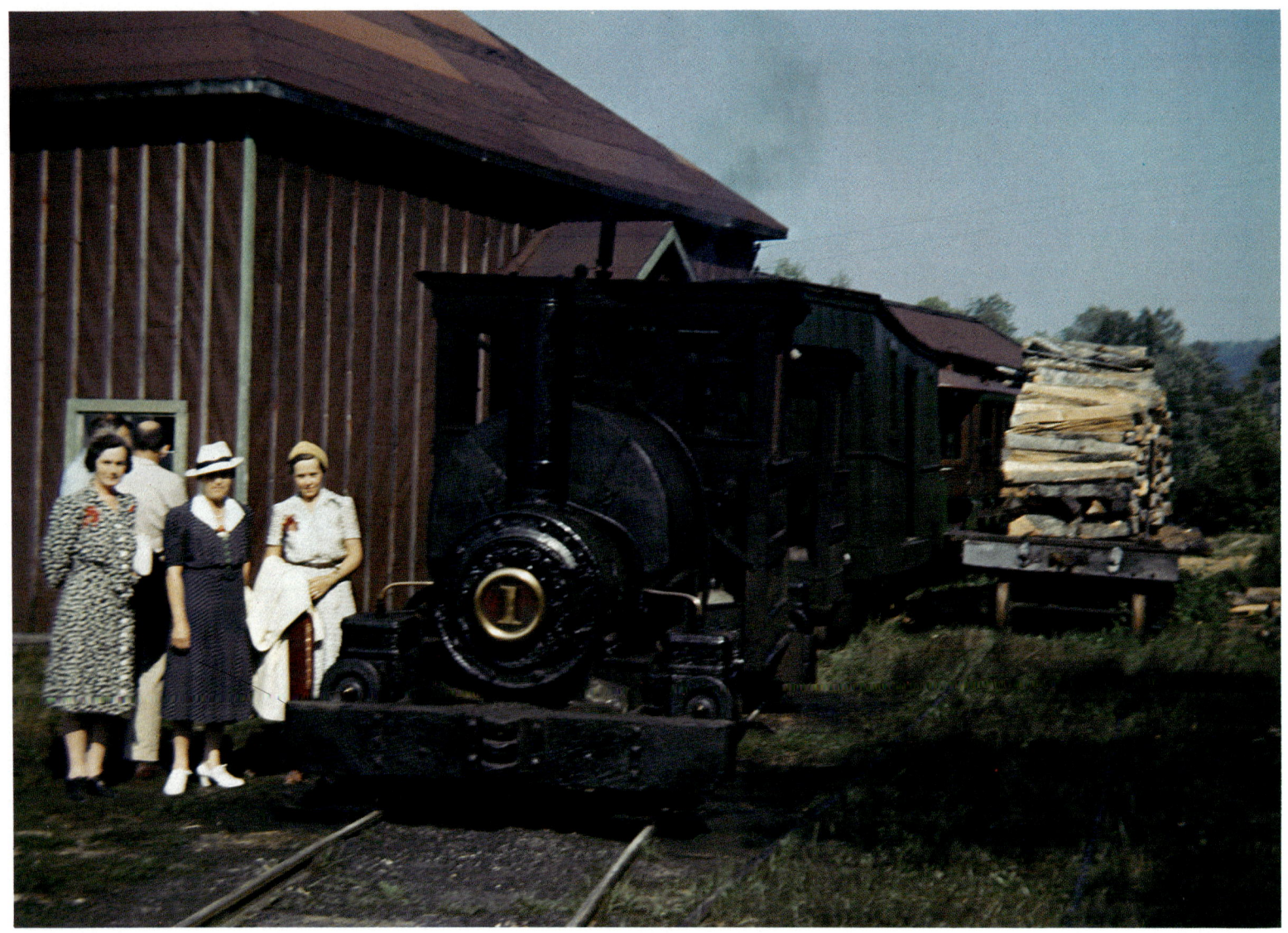
Built in 1903 for Captain George Francis Marsh's company, the Portage Railway linked North Portage, Peninsula Lake, to South Portage, Lake of Bays. Its rolling stock consisted of two locomotives, two passenger cars, two boxcars and two flatcars. The train, shown here at North Portage, was affectionately known as "The Hot Tamale."

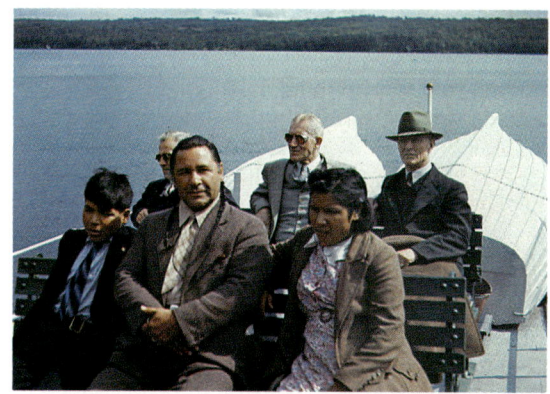

Seated centre in the front row atop the steamer *Bigwin*, Os-Ke-Non-Ton travels to Bigwin Inn, where he performed on many occasions. The *Bigwin Banter* of August 14, 1937, noted: "Os-Ke-Non-Ton is the grandson of Chief Bigwin — once the Lord of the Isle. Os-Ke-Non-Ton is not only a prince of the blood royal, he is also an artist of international repute. During the concert season, you'll hear him singing at Albert Hall in London, England, and this summer he is to be featured in the Hiawatha Pageant at the CNE, Toronto. Tomorrow evening you are to be honoured by a visit from Os-Ke-Non-Ton, who has consented to come to the home of his fathers, and entertain the guests of Bigwin Inn. Os-Ke-Non-Ton will dress in his tribal clothes, and sing the songs of his people. We are happy to present him as one of our guest artists at the Sunday Evening Musicale. The other guest artist of the evening will be Miss Edythe Shuttleworth, whose rich soprano has delighted you during the past week."

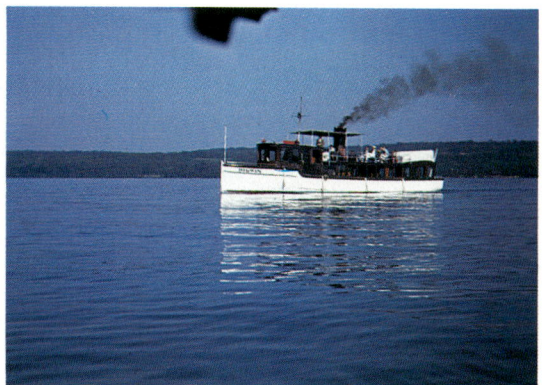

The steamer *Bigwin* was built by the Polson Iron Works Limited of Toronto and had an oaken hull, square stern and carvel build. Communication between the pilot house and the engine room was made with a system of bells and occasionally a voice tube. With the boat at rest, one ring signalled "engine forward," two rings signalled "engine reverse" and three rings signalled "reduce speed." With the boat in motion, a single ring ordered a full stop.

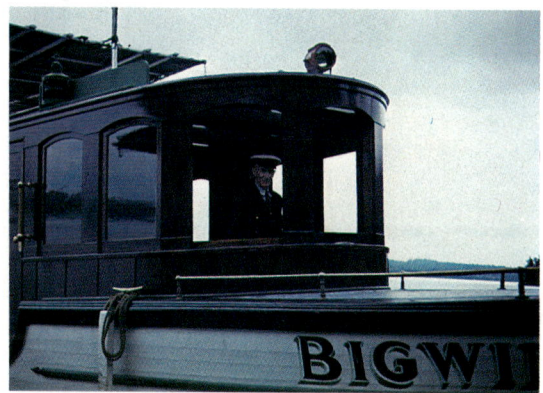

By 1925, the *Clarion* (a closed motor launch capable of carrying 18 people) and the steamer *Bigwin* serviced the resort. Pictured in the *Bigwin* pilot house is Captain William Henry Elder.

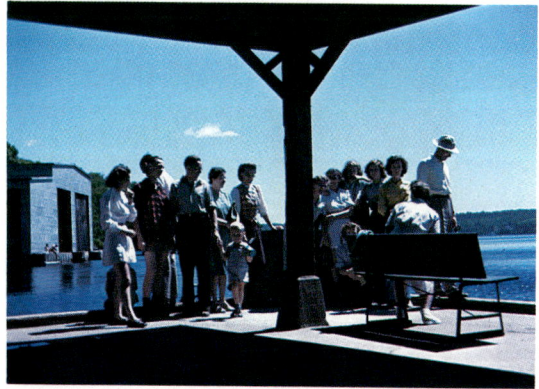

Telephone lines were quickly jammed when an issue of the Huntsville *Forester*, hot off the press, noted the arrival of Clark Gable and Carole Lombard in Muskoka in July 1940. En route to Bigwin Inn, the Hollywood couple stopped in Huntsville for a meal at the Dairy Lunch and later inspected silver fox pelts at Tink's Bait Shop. Reporters, on their trail for the latest scoop, followed the movie stars to Bigwin Inn. One reporter offered a young dock attendant on the wharf a crisp $10 bill with the understanding that he would point out the celebrities. As the deal was struck, Gable and Lombard evaded them, scurrying past disguised in casual sportswear and dark sunglasses.

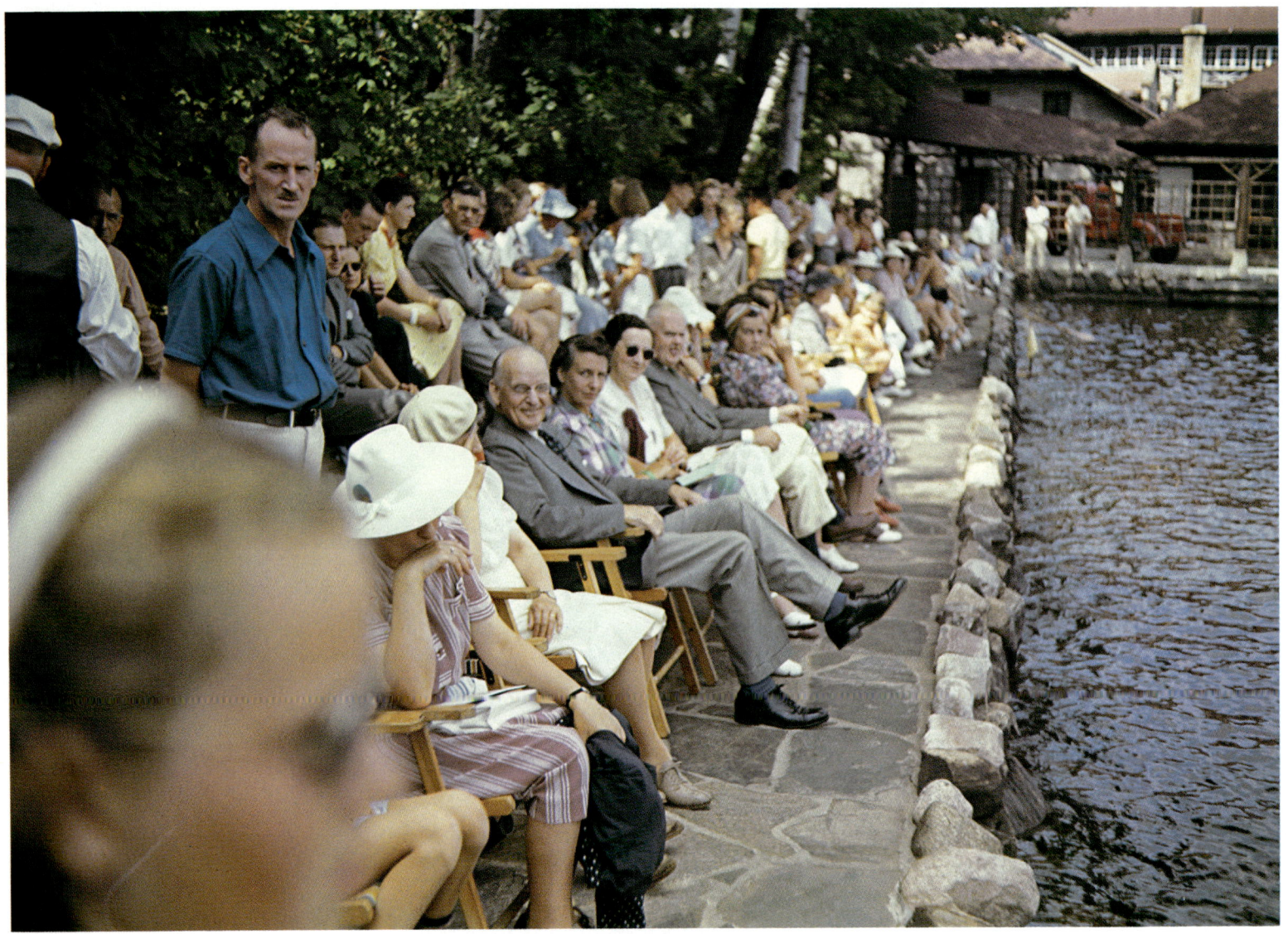
Fanned by lake breezes, members of the upper echelons of society crowded the shoreline's flagstone terraces to observe the activities of the annual Lake of Bays Regatta.

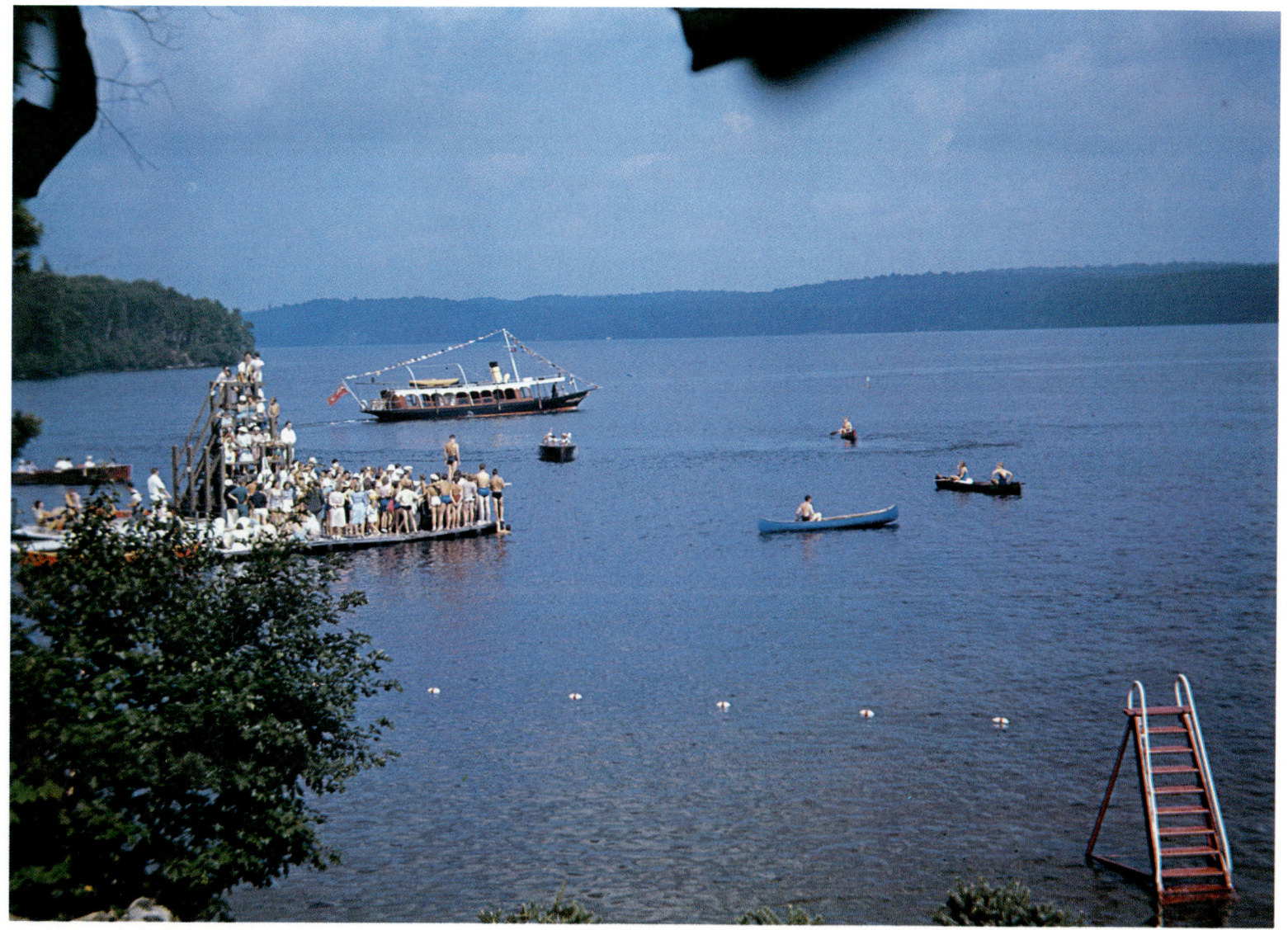
The steamer *Naiad*, owned by Chicago's milk magnate Cameron Peck, was occasionally loaned to Bigwin Inn for charter cruises.

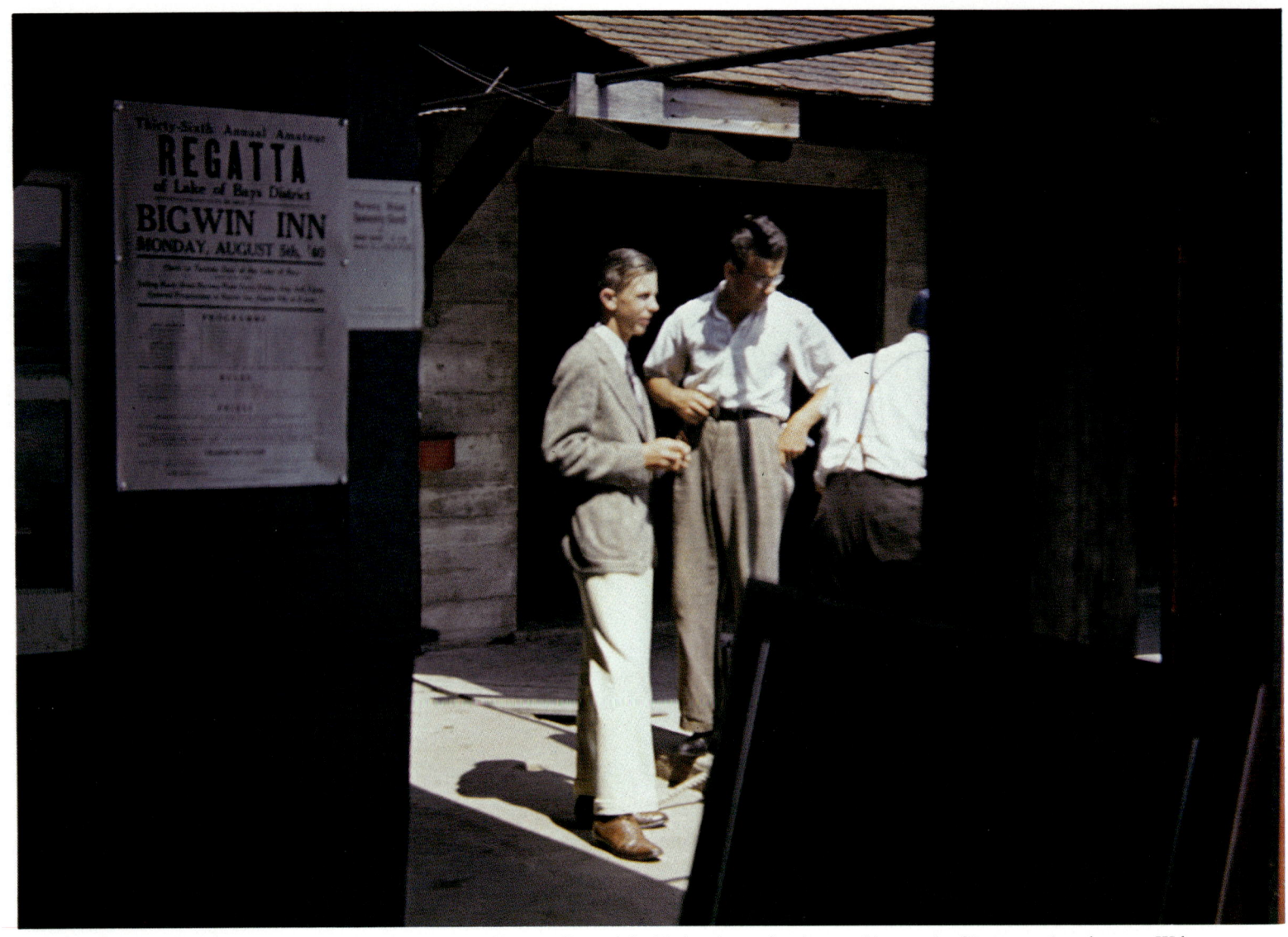
The Frantic Forties brought in victory bonds, jitterbugging, Glenn Miller and the big band sound, nylon stockings and refrigerators. Seen here are Walter Brackley Shaw and Mario Pesando.

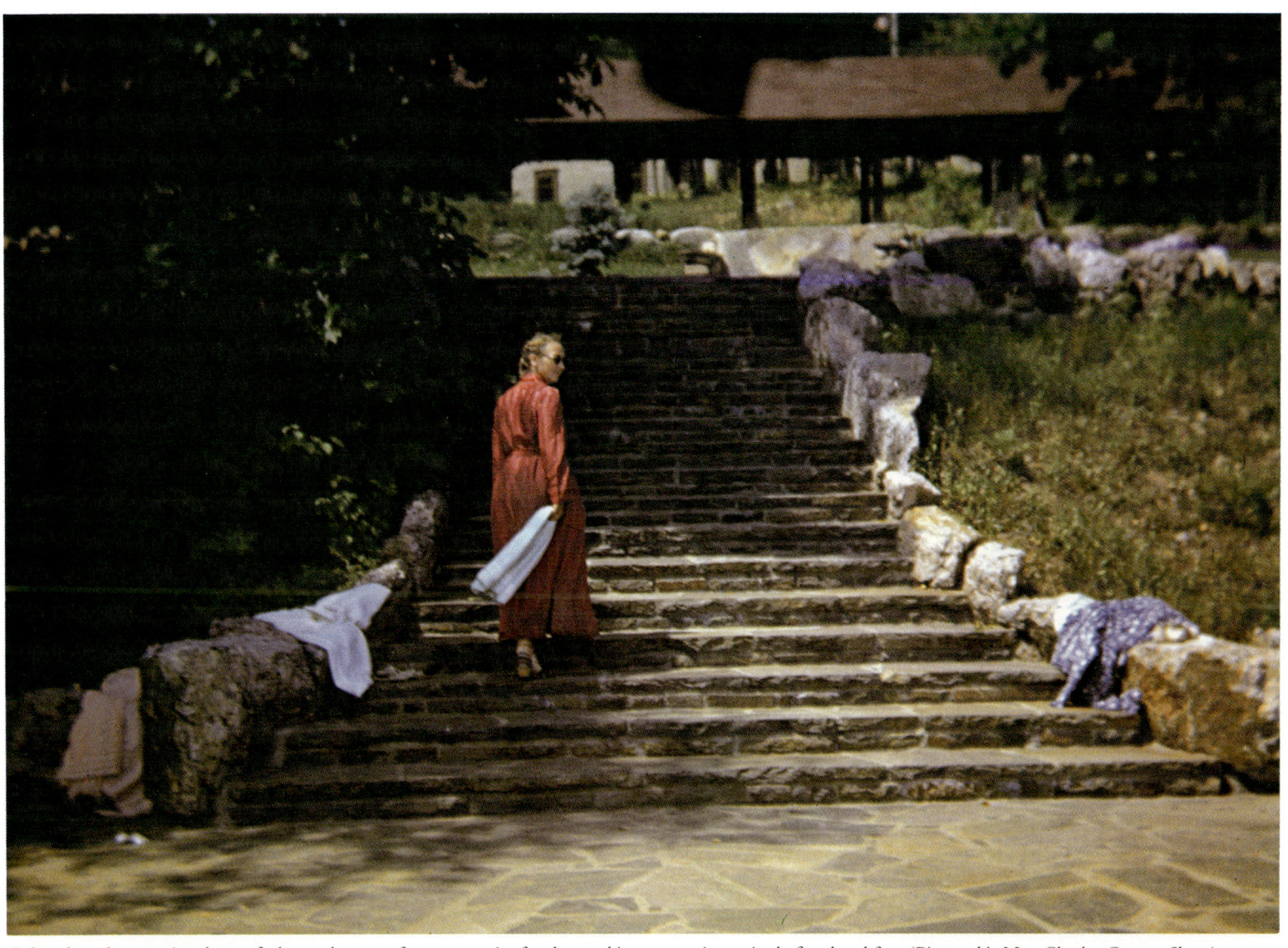
Other than the occasional cry of a loon, the waterfront was quiet for those taking a morning swim before breakfast. (Pictured is Mrs. Charles George Shaw).

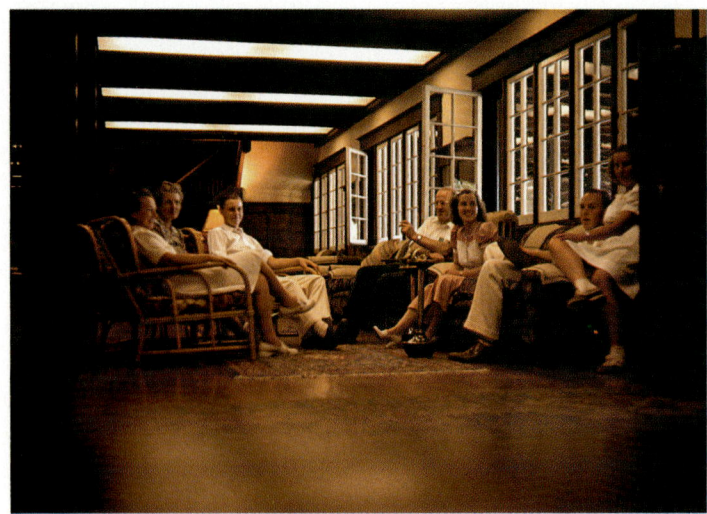 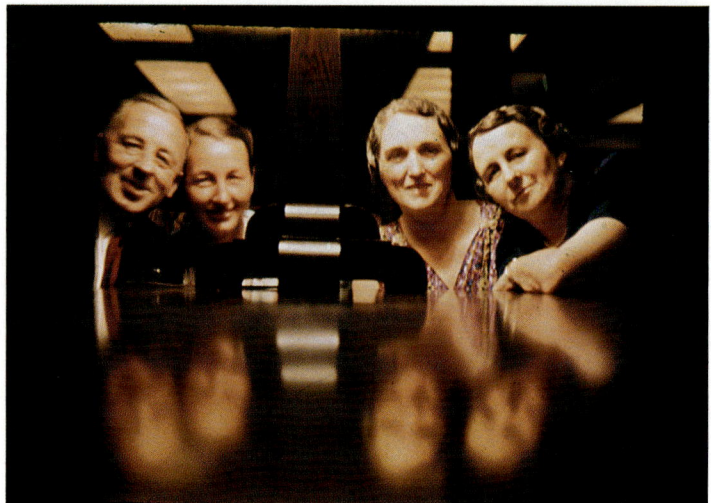

Waiting for the daily mail to arrive offered guests a moment to relax in the main lounge of the Rotunda. "Snap, snap went the camera — and little Johnnie had his picture taken. If you want yours taken by an expert, or if you want to try your own hand at photography, the Associated Screen News can set you up with films, camera or photographer — as you wish. Ask at their desk — east end of the Rotunda," read a 1937 *Bigwin Banter*. Seated are Mrs. C.G. Shaw, Mrs. Reid, Brackley Shaw, Mr. Reid, Elizabeth Shaw, Charles Shaw and Anne Shaw.

The Rotunda's interior was as lavishly decorated as an English manor house, with plush Persian rugs, chintz-covered chesterfields, and burnished wooden tables and benches. Casting decorative pools of light, indirect lighting fixtures were added in the Indian Head Room, Pavilion and Rotunda in 1937. Seated at a table in the Rotunda are Mr. Fred Abbott, Mrs. C.G. Shaw, Mrs. Fred Abbott and Pauline Gill.

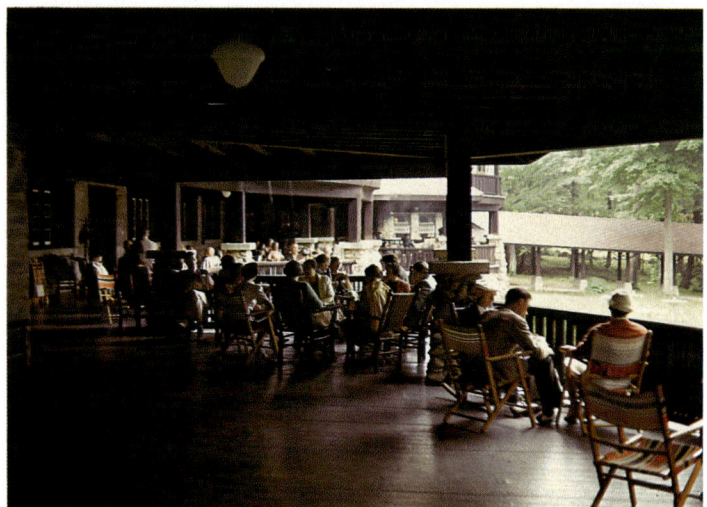 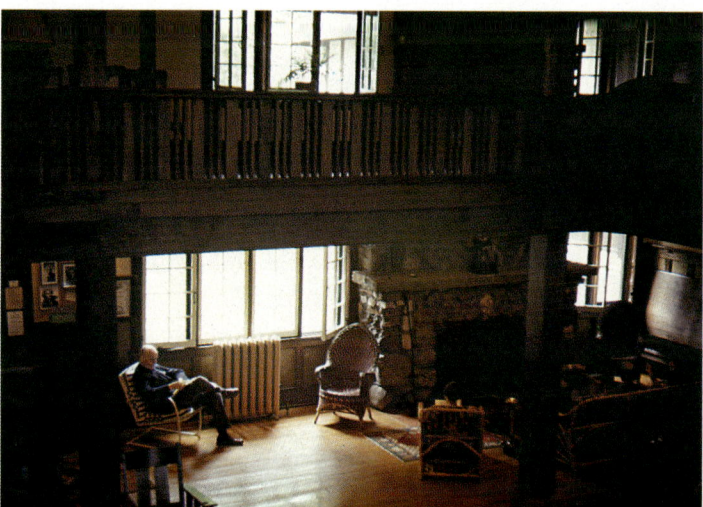

The Rotunda's verandahs offered magnificent views of the front lawns, shuffleboard courts and Lake of Bays.

Toronto Star publisher Joseph E. Atkinson reads the morning paper in a quiet corner of the Rotunda.

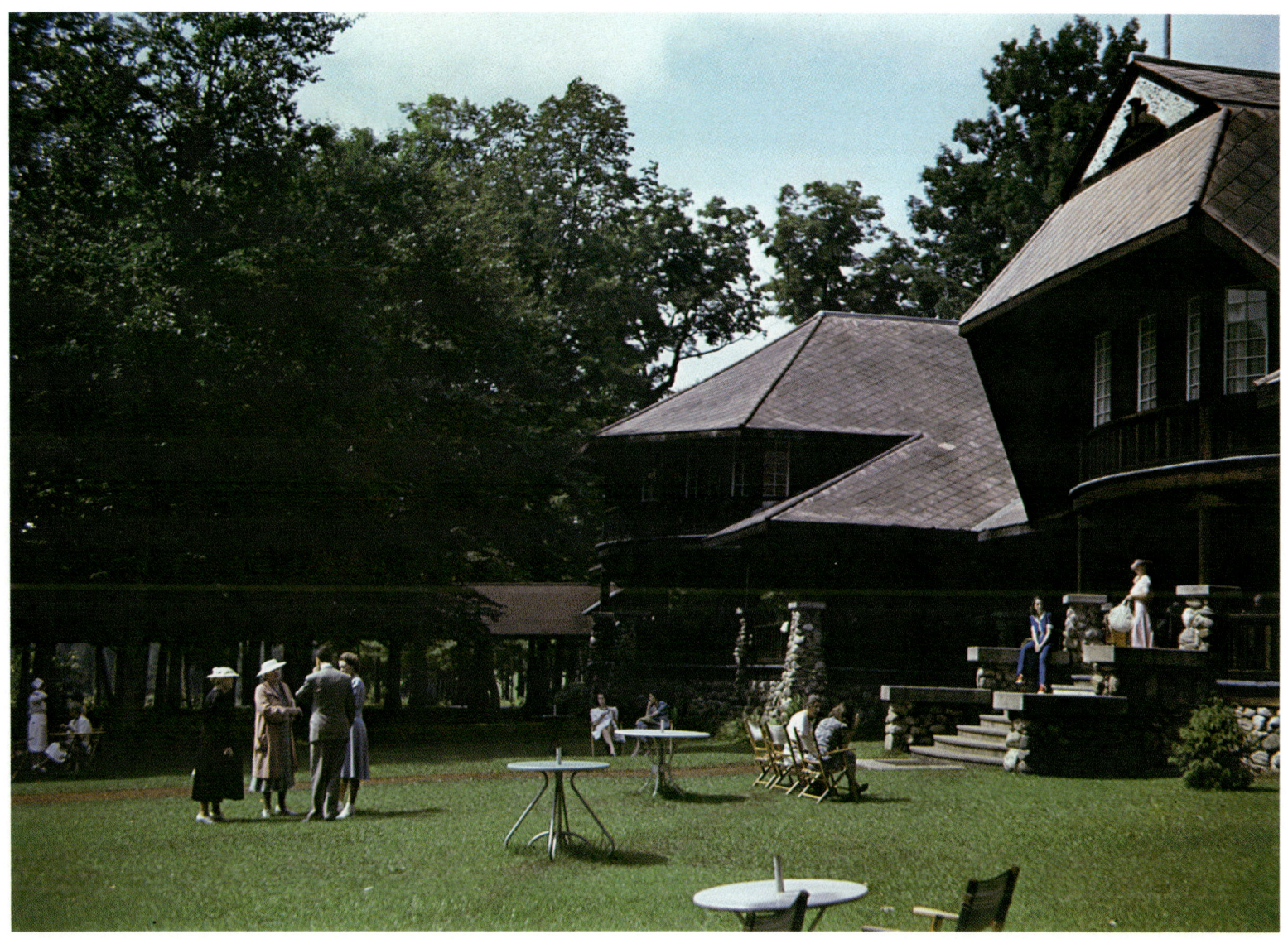
Lawn parties were popular among members of the Establishment. Visitors to the resort included Atkinsons, Bassetts, Blacks, Cookes, Creeds, Dodges, Eatons, Eastmans, Fords, Gardiners, Gooderhams, Hitchcocks, Jarvises, Kellogs, Labatts, Masseys, McLaughlins, Mellons, Neilsons, Oslers, Rogers, Seagrams, Shearsons, Siftons, Sinclairs, Southams, Taylors, Thomsons and Westons.

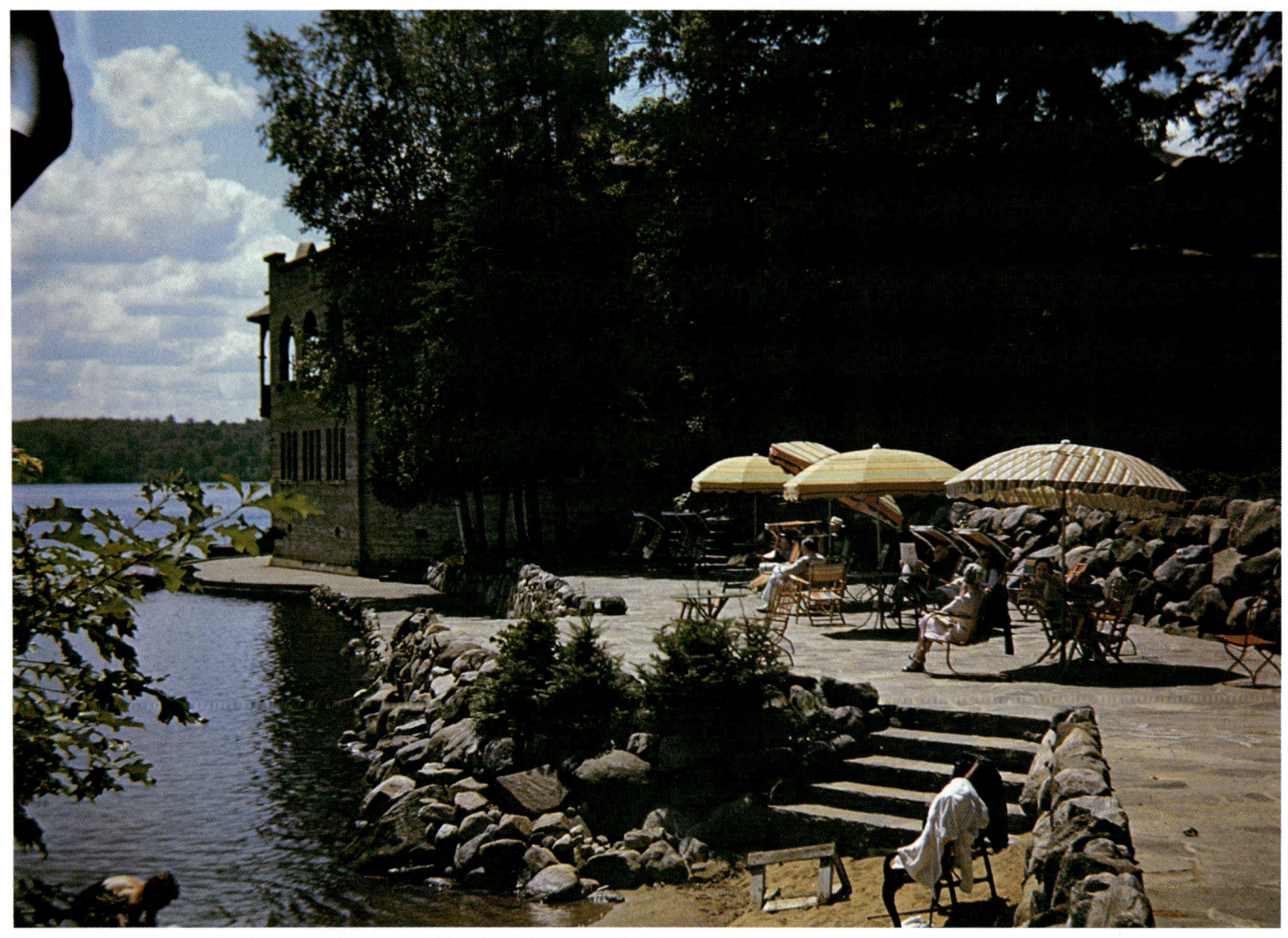
The flagstone terraces offered guests uninterrupted lake vistas. Stone steps led from the flagstone terraces to a golden sand beach. Rock gardens around the island were planned under the direction of Mr. Roy of the Grand Trunk Railway.

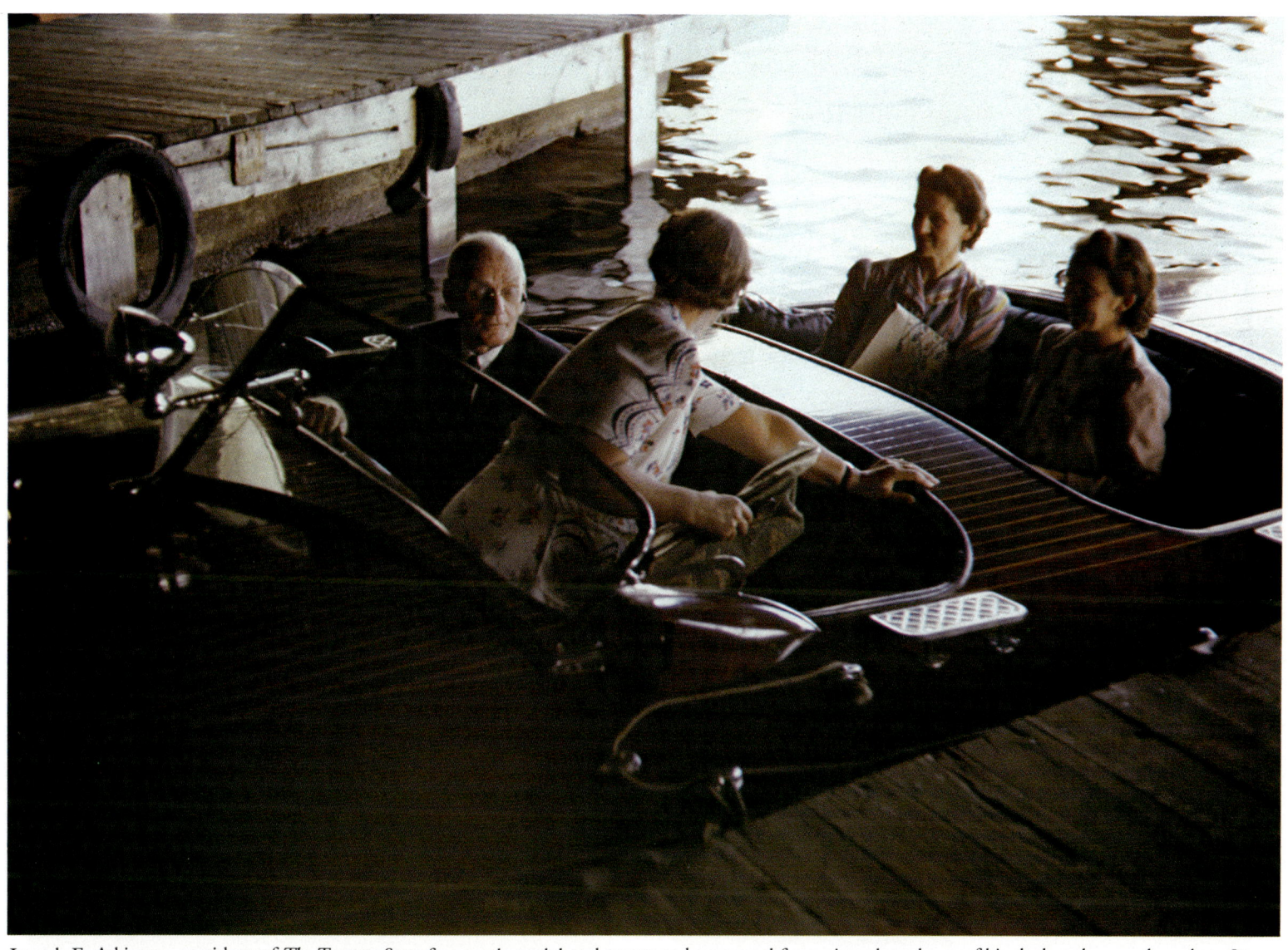
Joseph E. Atkinson, president of *The Toronto Star*, frequently took hotel guests and personnel for cruises aboard one of his sleek mahogany launches. *Star* writers said to have visited the resort during its heyday include Greg Clark, Ernest Hemingway and H.G. Wells.

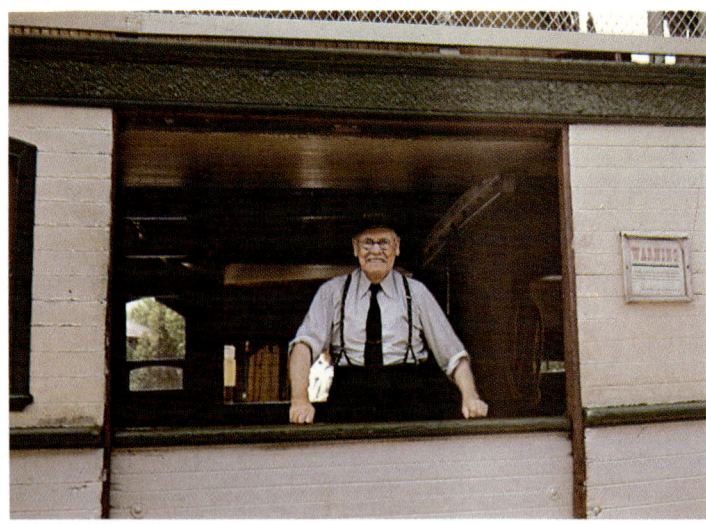

Purser George Rutherford looks starboard from the steamer *Iroquois*. The vessel's route ran between South Portage and Dorset.

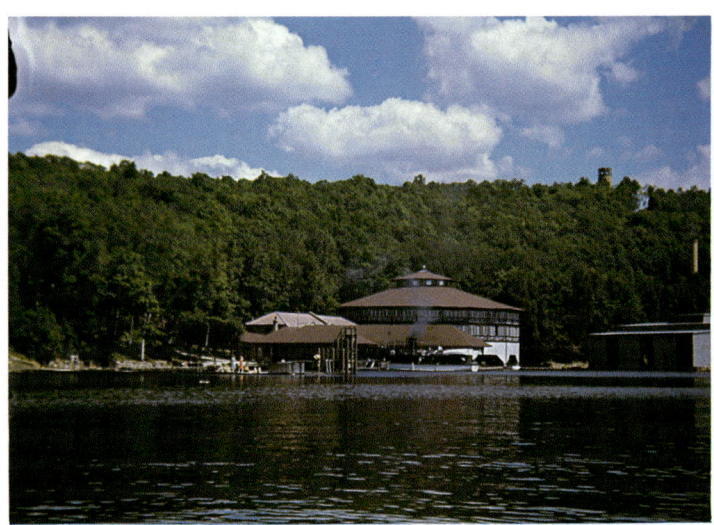

With howsers fastened to dock cleats, the "Lilliputian liner" *Bigwin* was moored at the resort's steamer dock.

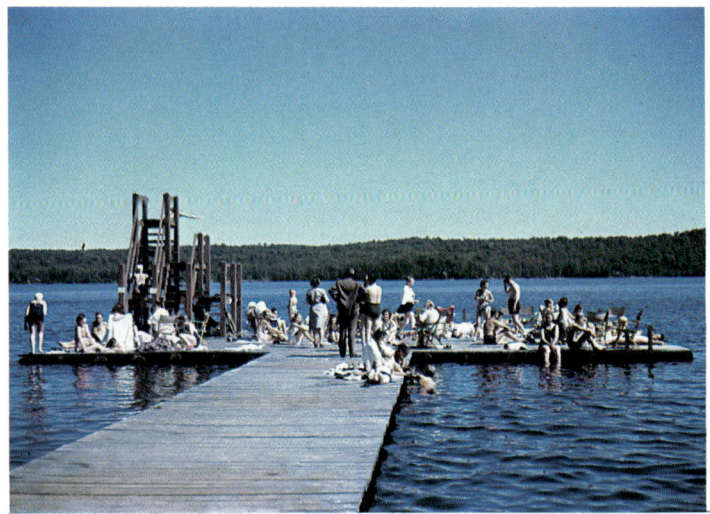

Trying to find a spot to sunbathe on the swim dock was a difficult venture on a hot summer's day. "Where do the Bigwin guests come from? Well — forty percent of the registrations are Canadian — but sixty percent come from our border neighbour — the U.S.A. We've even had guests from as far west as California, Oklahoma, Texas, Florida and Louisiana — and then of course the odd English guest arrives — and once in a while a guest from 'down-under' " read a *Bigwin Banter* in the summer of 1937.

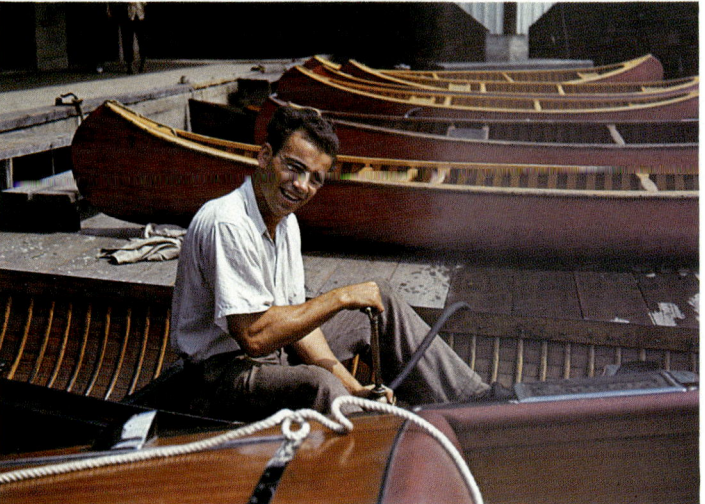

The Bigwin Boat Livery Company Limited stocked dozens of red cedar-strip canoes. Advertisements from the 1940s read: "Modern docks line the shore where the Indians once launched their great canoes. Skies clear, barometers steady. What more could the heart of a sailor desire as he sets his sail for the blue waters of Lake of Bays?" Pictured is Mario Pesando, purser on the *Bigwin*, who began working at the Inn during the 1935 season.

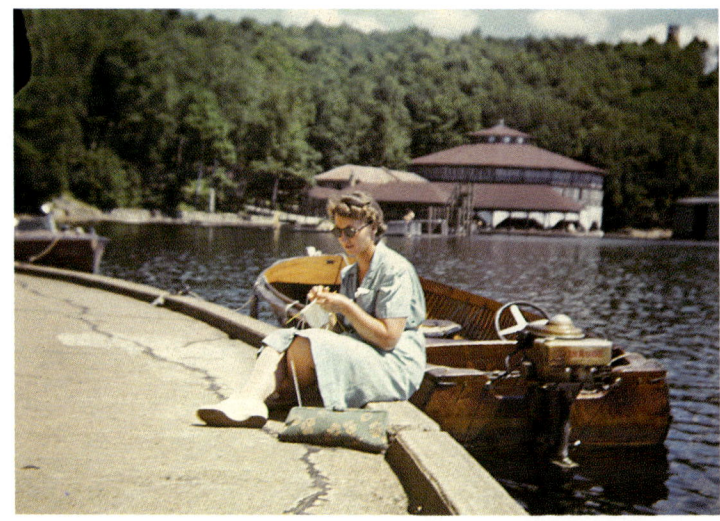
Mrs. Charles George Shaw spends a few moments relaxing in the warmth of the summer sun.

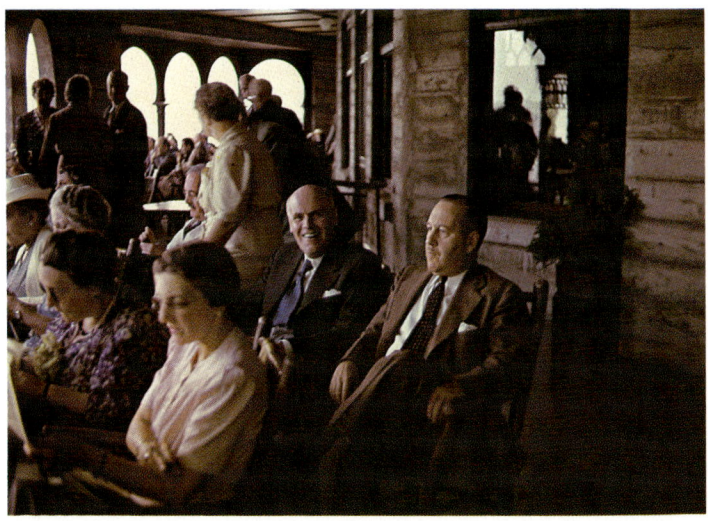
One hotel brochure noted: "Hundreds of the smartest, most fashionable and discriminating people from all parts of the continent spend summer after summer beneath the smiling roof tree of Bigwin Inn."

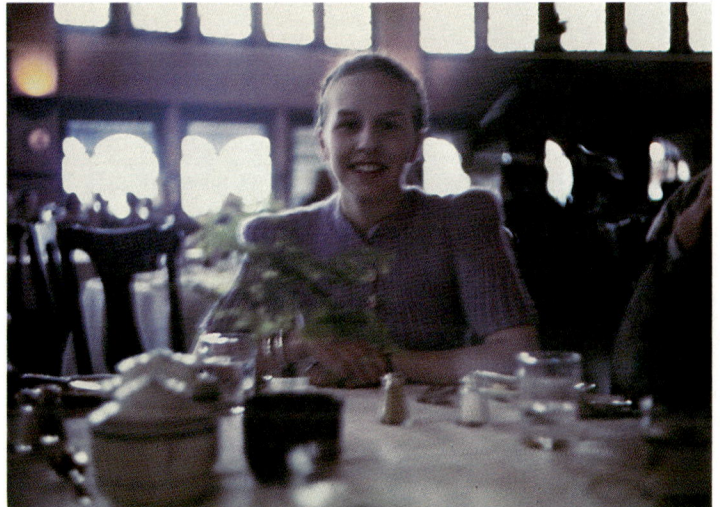
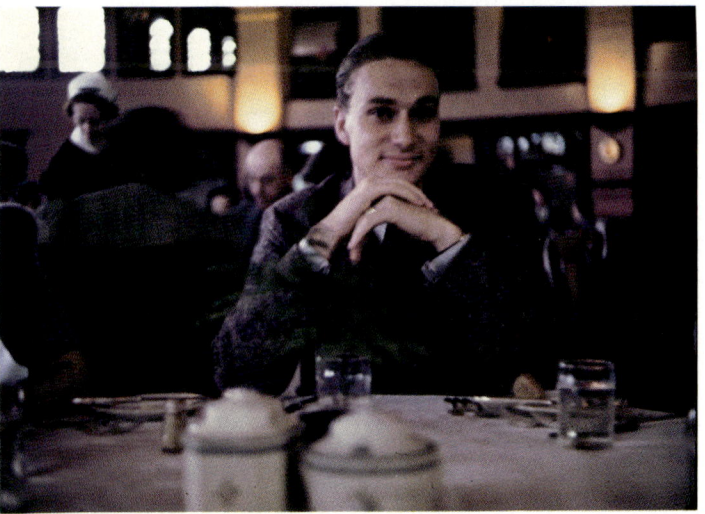
Awaiting sumptuous repasts, Pauline Gill and Carl McLennan sit at C.O. Shaw's private table amid the elegance of the Indian Head Room. The hotel's crested china was imported by Cassidy's Ltd., Toronto, and was supplied from Wood and Sons Ltd., Burslem, England. The resort's dishwashers or "pearl divers" were paid $20 per month for their services, which included inspecting dishes for streaks, blemishes or chips.

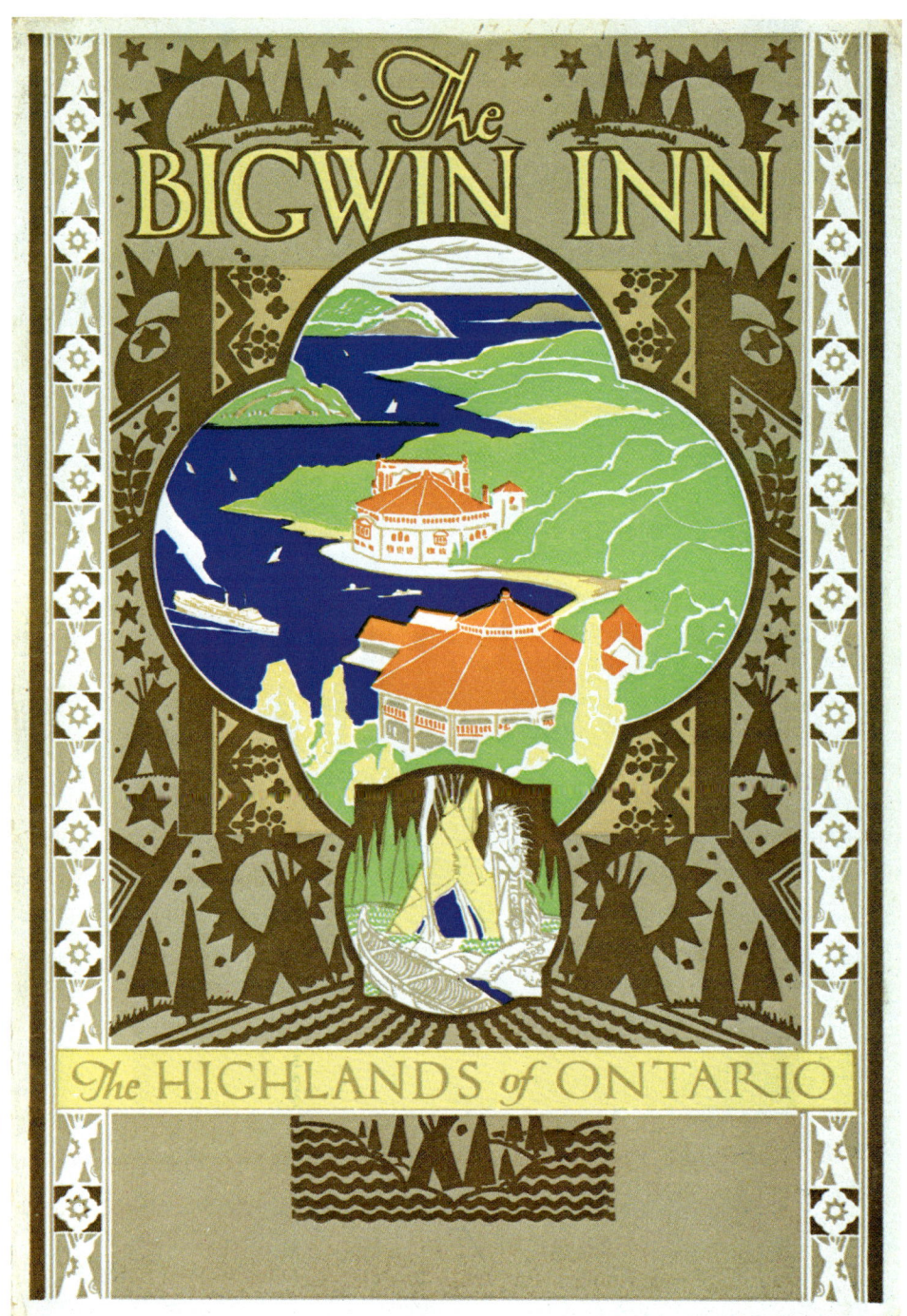

Each autumn, the management at Bigwin produced promotional pamphlets for the following season. The brochure for the 1928 season was designed by Franklin Carmichael of the Group of Seven. The 1941 brochure contained poetry by famous Canadian poet Pauline Johnson.
- *Robert McLennan, Frank Mills Leslie and by kind permission of Mary Mastin*

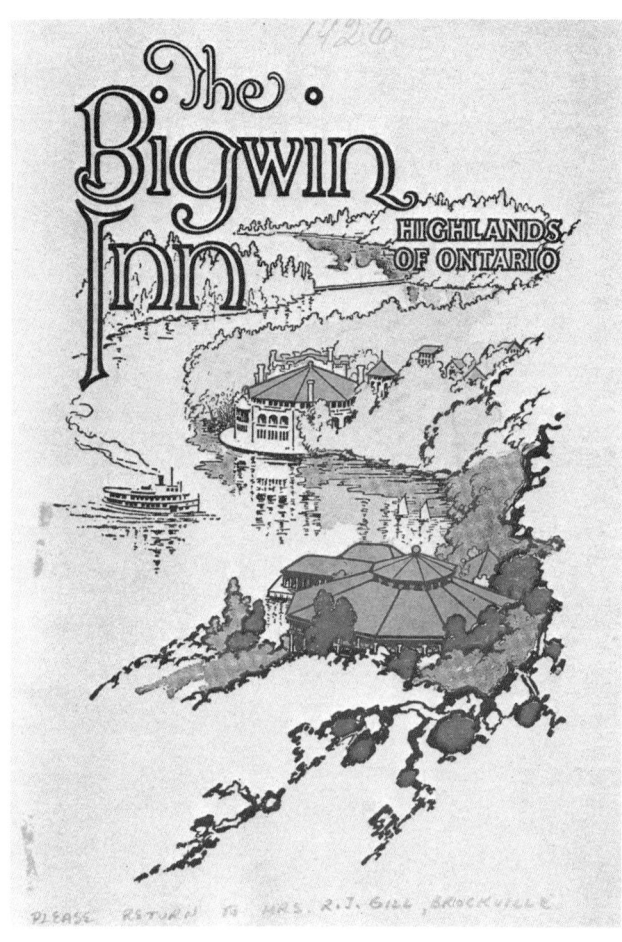
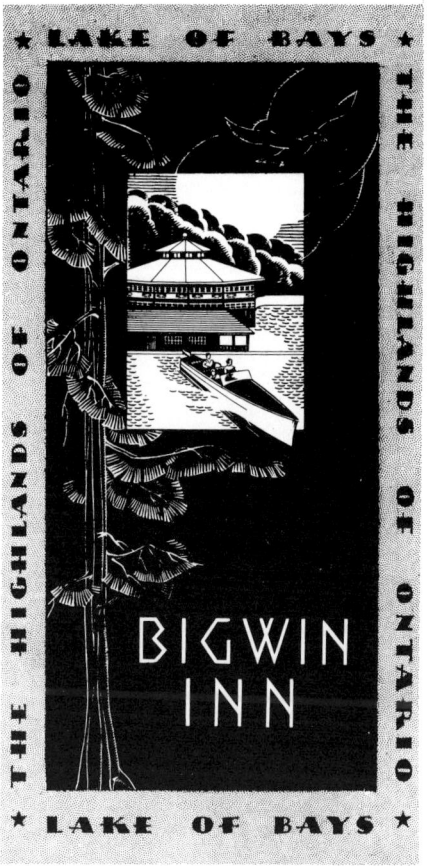
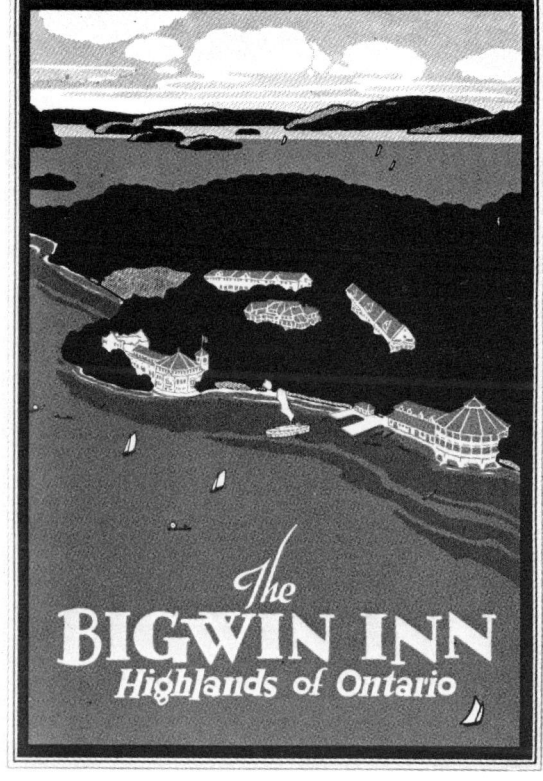

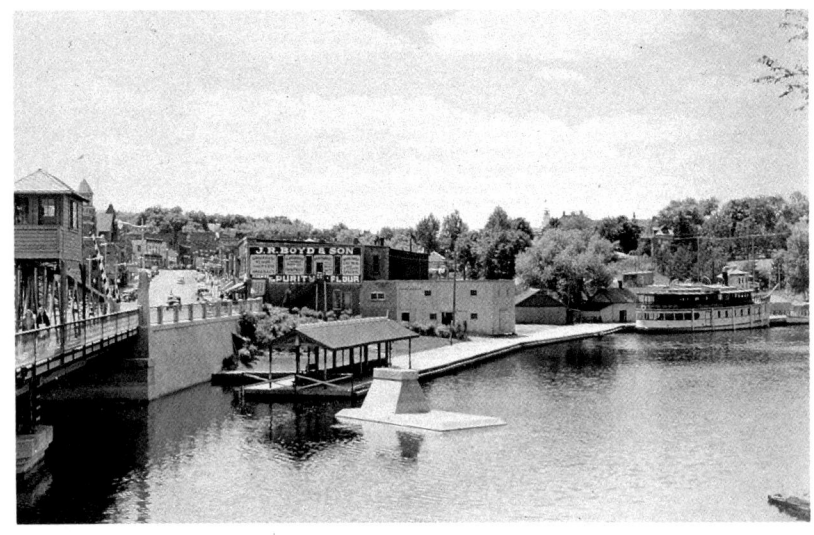
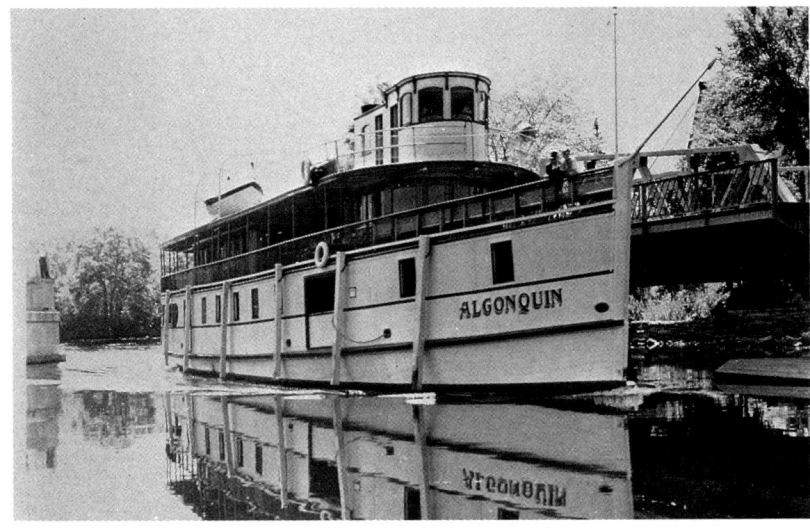
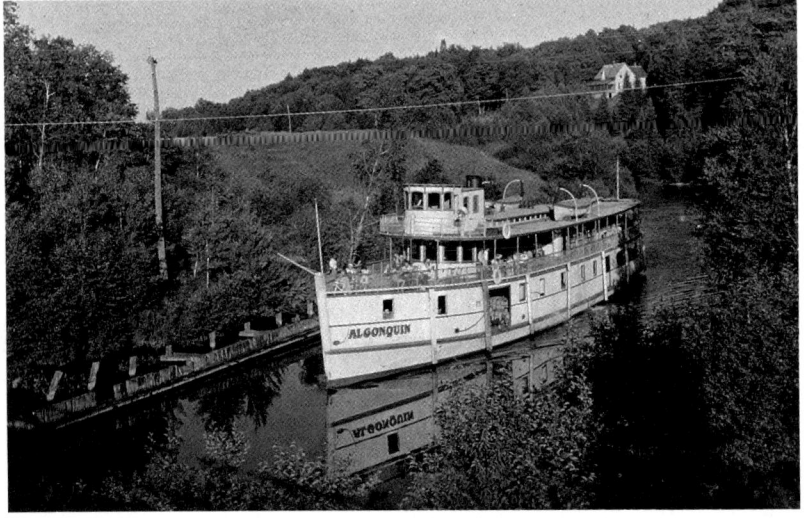

From a wharf in Huntsville, tourists boarded a steamer such as the *Algonquin*, which carried them past the swing bridge, down the canal between Fairy and Peninsula lakes to North Portage.
- *DGM*

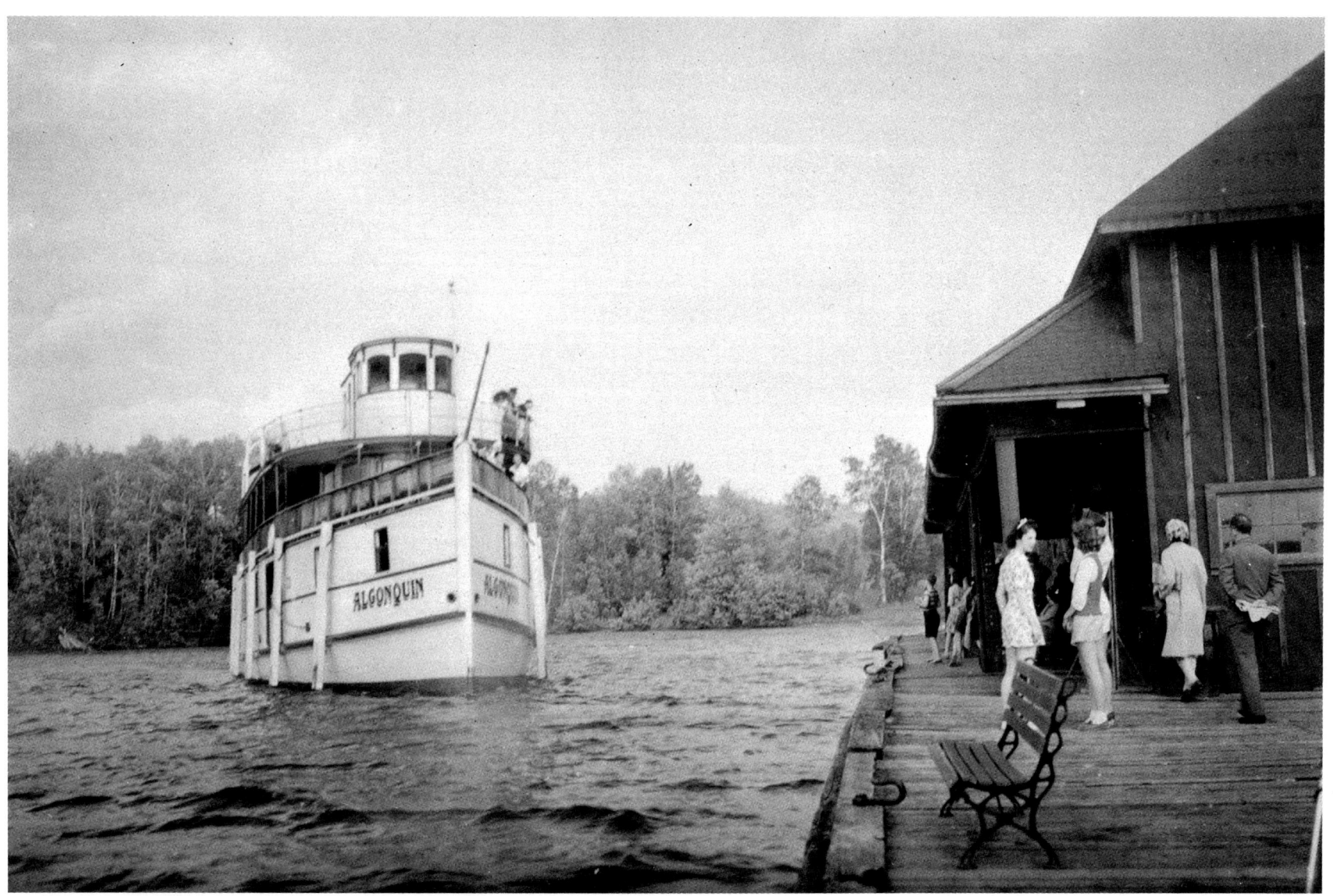

The steamer *Algonquin* approaching the dock at North Portage. - *DGM*

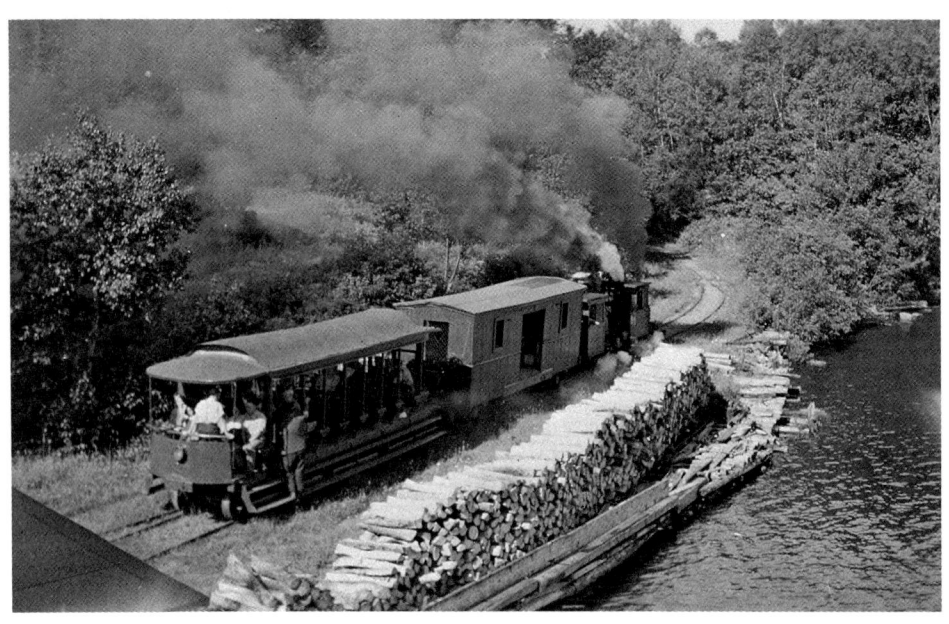

From North Portage, the Portage Railway carried guests to South Portage, where steamers such as the *Mohawk Belle* or *Iroquois* waited to take them down the Lake of Bays to Bigwin Inn.
- *DGM*

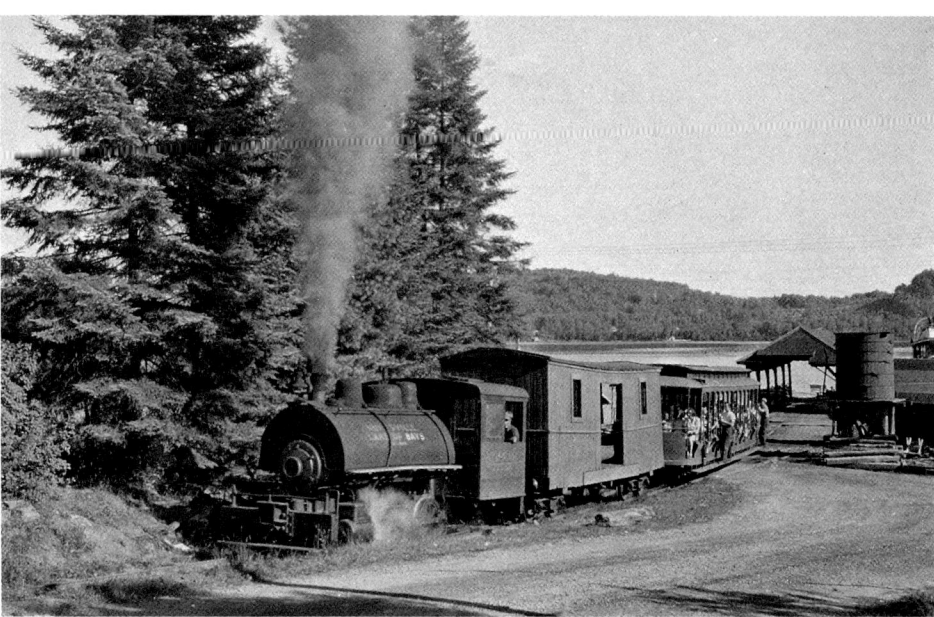

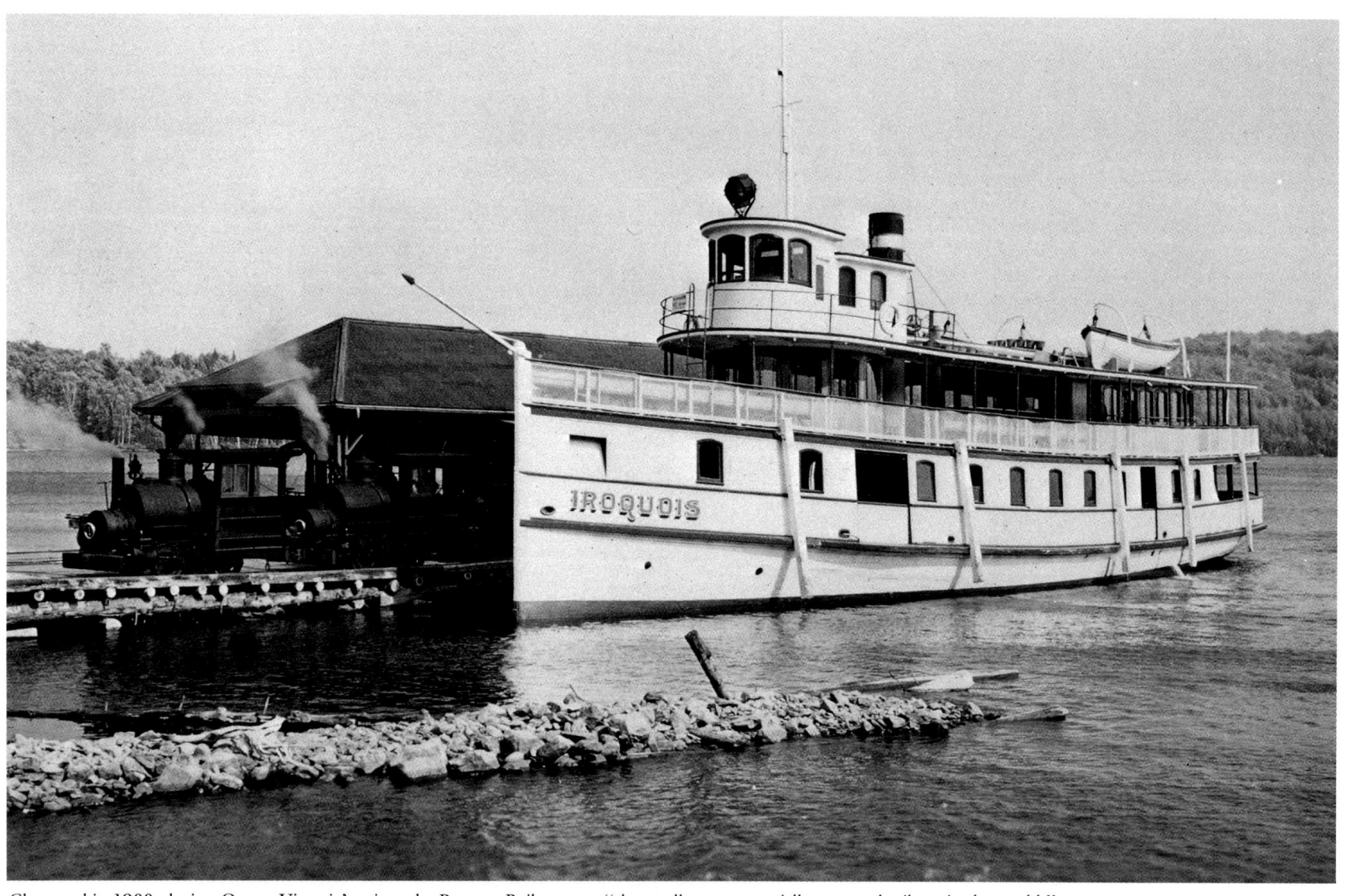
Chartered in 1900, during Queen Victoria's reign, the Portage Railway was "the smallest commercially operated railway in the world." - *DGM*

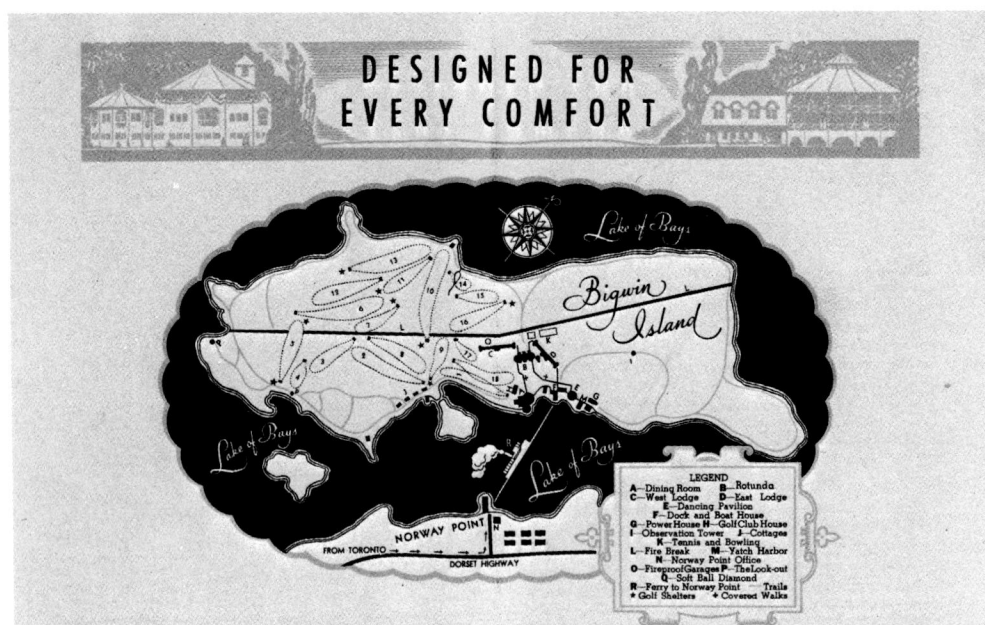

Often parked in one of the fireproof garages at Norway Point was C.O. Shaw's black V16 Cadillac, which he had purchased at the CNE's car show. In the late 1930s, Mario Pesando, an employee of the resort, drove Shaw from Norway Point to Gravenhurst to pick up a guest waiting at the train station. With C.O. never allowing the car's gas gauge to fall below half a tank and always encouraging his chauffeur to keep the car to the far right on the narrow Muskoka roads, the sedan pulled into the town of Gravenhurst without incident. At the train station, Shaw climbed out of the car and sauntered over to an elderly man seated at the far end of the platform. Bending over, he greeted the visitor, a close friend, with a smile and warm embrace. The old man was Chief Bigwin.

- *DGM*

A VERY IMPORTANT THOUGHT
for your 1932 Vacation Plans

In planning your vacation for the Summer of 1932, naturally the question of expense is one to which everyone will have to give serious consideration due to the fact that we are passing through times and facing conditions which force all of us to give careful thought to items of cost.

A vacation spent in Canada is the solution of this important question. At the present time the value of the Canadian Dollar is eighty cents as compared with the value of the U. S. Dollar. If you are a guest at Bigwin Inn next summer, when you come to the Hotel Desk to pay your bill you will be allowed a reduction from the total of your account based on the rate of exchange which may be in effect on the day you make payment,— and based on to-day's relative value of the Canadian Dollar and the United States Dollar, this would be approximately twenty per cent. In other words the Bigwin Inn Company will allow the prevailing rate of premium on American Funds, in effect from day to day.

To ensure the full premium of approximately 20 percent prevailing to-day, those contemplating a vacation at Bigwin Inn can purchase $120.00 Canadian money for every $100.00 American money, now, by buying a Bank Draft payable in Canada; or we shall be glad to recommend Banks in which you can deposit your funds in Canada (with the premium added) until the summer, and obtain 3 percent per annum interest in the meantime. Thus you have assured for yourself a most economical vacation.

This information will be of special interest to Convention Parties who may contemplate holding their meetings in Canada during 1932.

Bigwin Inn will open for the Season of 1932, for Convention Parties, during the latter part of June, and for the regular patrons, after the close of the early Convention Season early in July. The Hotel will close about September 10th

Bigwin Inn,
Bigwin Island,
Via Huntsville,
Lake of Bays, Ontario.

January 5th, 1932.

Reeling from the effects of the Great Depression, potential hotel patrons gave second thought to their summer vacation in Muskoka. The Dirty Thirties, a decade of heightened class consciousness, also brought Shirley Temple, Greta Garbo, W.C. Fields, George Gershwin, Martha Graham, Fred Astaire and Ginger Rogers to the forefront of public acclaim.

- *DGM*

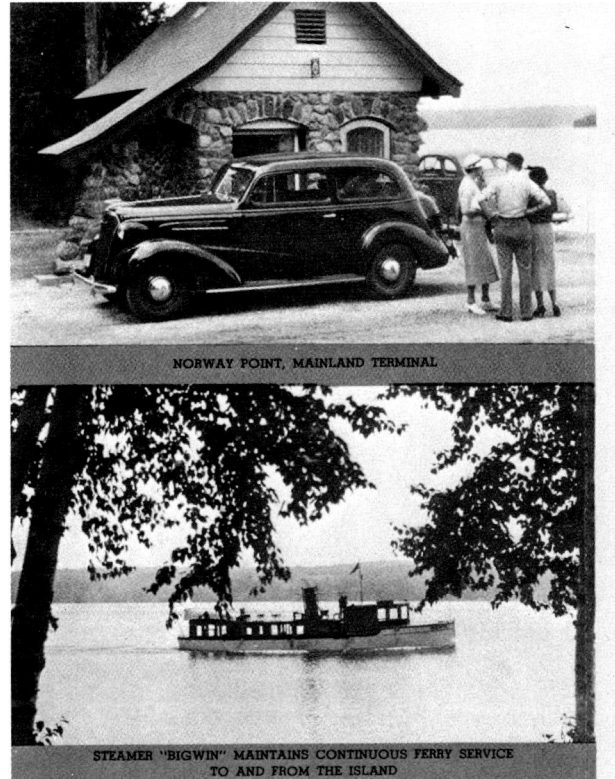

NORWAY POINT, MAINLAND TERMINAL

STEAMER "BIGWIN" MAINTAINS CONTINUOUS FERRY SERVICE TO AND FROM THE ISLAND

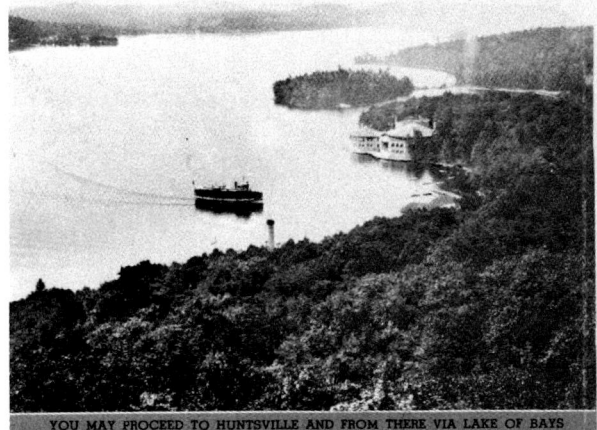

YOU MAY PROCEED TO HUNTSVILLE AND FROM THERE VIA LAKE OF BAYS TO BIGWIN ISLAND

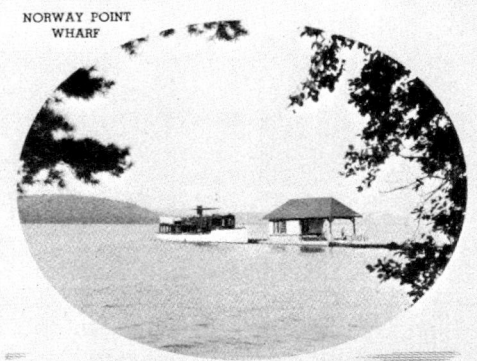

NORWAY POINT WHARF

IDEAL RESORT FOR REST AND RECREATION

Bigwin Inn is noted for the artistic grouping of its buildings. These are arranged with an eye to the convenience of the guests and to give the most effective measure of service. Separate buildings of **FIREPROOF** construction wing out along the waterfront and are connected by covered walks.

The Central Building, around which are broad, open porches and loggias, is the centre of social activity. It contains the rotunda, executive offices, telephone and telegraph offices, post office, writing rooms, library, gift shop and news stand, medical service, barber shop, valet beauty parlor, children's play room, and table tenni

The great lounge, which occupies the whole leng Central Building, is a room of magnificent pro luxuriously furnished. Its nine huge, open firepla masterpieces of natural stone beauty and guests about them in the cool of the evening to listen to th Sunday evening concerts which are a delight to held in the lounge. The smart tea house, which adj boon to the late sleeper who has missed breakfas guests who arrive tired and hungry between m tactful hostess is present to welcome the newcomer arrange bridge and dance partners.

The dining room, built over the water, has a capacity for 700 and is quiet and restful with it decorations and unsurpassed scenic views from windows. The table appointments are of the fin Bigwin Inn is famous for the excellent quality of served. Fresh poultry, fresh vegetables, fresh fr berries are used at all times, and the salads are o outstanding features of every luncheon and dinne Guests may arrange for special diets, when th required. Music is provided at luncheon and dinne is a special dining room for children and nurses accompany them, the use of which is optional.

Sleeping accommodation is in the east and wes These are of **FIREPROOF** construction, three stories i have 280 spacious airy outside rooms, all with run and cold water, private telephone and 230 with bath. They are comfortably furnished and all doub have twin beds. The location of these lodges ensur of quiet rest at all times, as they are removed amusement centres of the hotel.

The dancing pavilion is of generous proportions and has a fully equipped stage. Week-nights a fine orchestra plays for dancing and the colored lighting effects add a touch of glamour to the gay scene.

By 1939, the road from Bracebridge to the Norway Point parking lot was hard-surfaced. During construction of the lot's stone valet cottage, recently minted Canadian pennies were buried in the mortar. Operating from a frame cottage next to the stone building, a resident family offered 24-hour service to guests.
- *DGM and Edith Cardy*

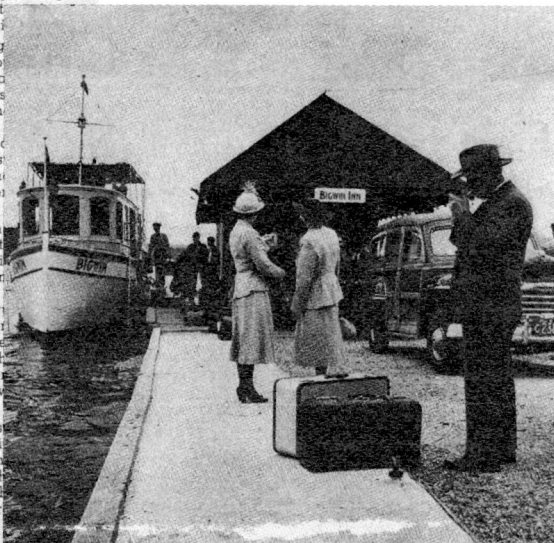

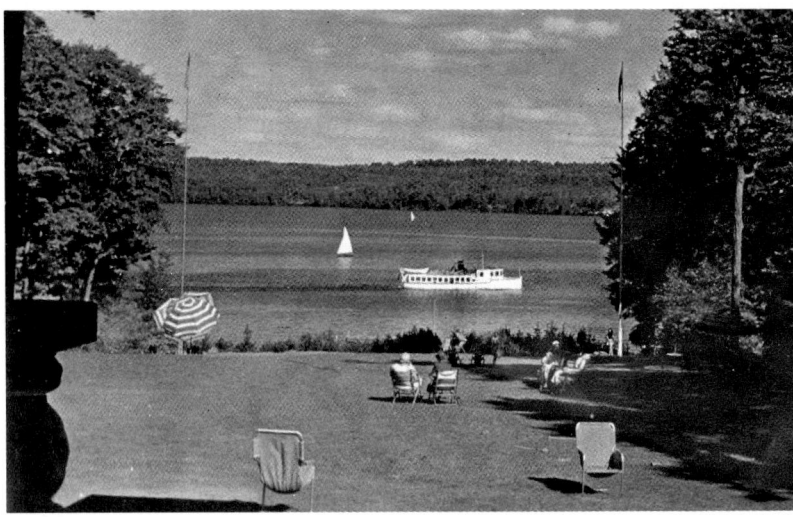

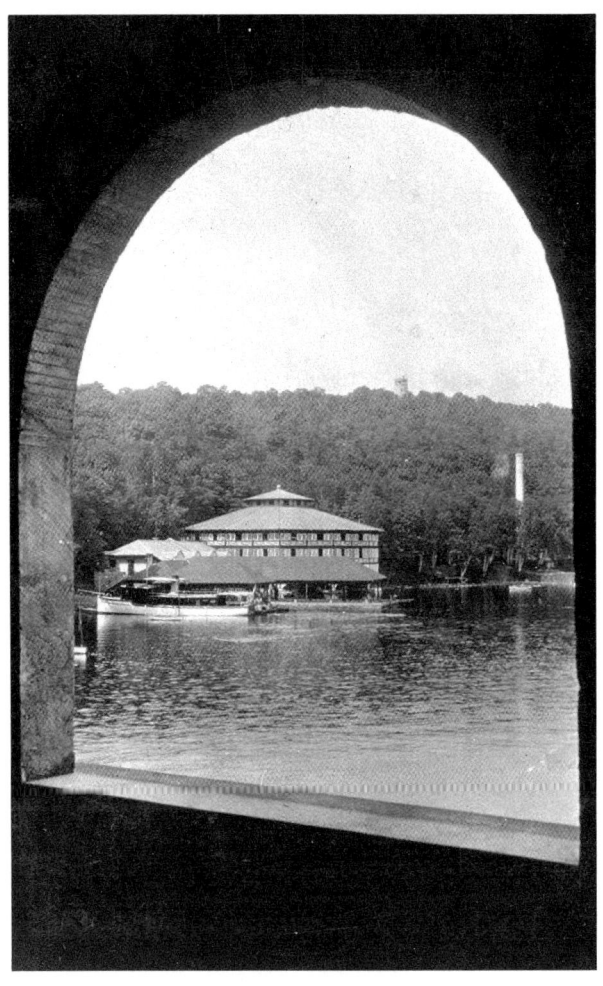

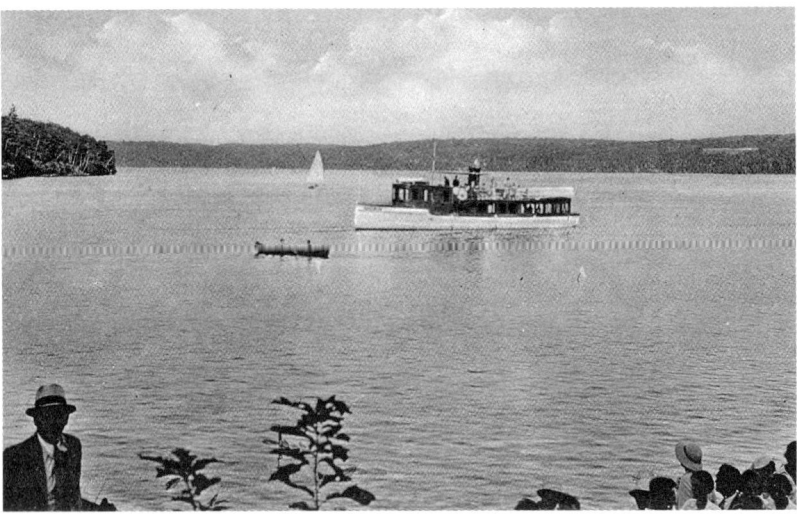

The steamer *Bigwin* maintained continuous ferry service between the mainland dock and the island wharf. An edition of the *Bigwin Banter* dated Saturday, August 26, 1939, noted: "About 1,000 cords of wood will have been used this year in Bigwin's power house, in the kitchen boiler, the steam yacht *Wanda III*, the ferry *Bigwin* and the famous stone fireplaces! Most of it comes from the mainland, brought over on sleighs during the winter and on scows during the summer. The average year burns 800 cords, which would mean a woodpile four feet high and twenty-five miles long if a twenty-year supply were laid in at one time! What a fire!"   - *DGM*

CHAPTER 3

Twilight Of A Dream

On the cold, wintry day of December 3, 1942, eight years after his first wife succumbed to pneumonia, Charles Orlando Shaw suffered a fatal heart attack at the age of 84. With his passing, and changing times, the curtain gradually began to fall on the glorious, golden era of the Bigwin Inn.

Eulogies remembered C.O. Shaw as an outstanding leader in the community and as the hard-driving builder of a business empire, but one who balanced this life with a great love of music and children. C.O. Shaw was interred with his first wife at Mount Pleasant Cemetery in Toronto. He was survived by his second wife, Amanda Paulley of Huntsville, whom he married two years after the death of his first wife and who had worked in the Shaw household for a number of years. Also surviving him were many relatives, including his one son, Charles George Shaw of Omemee, Ontario, and his two daughters, Mrs. C.W. Conway of Huntsville and Mrs. Pauline Gill, wife of Colonel Robert J. Gill of Brockville.

C.O. Shaw's eldest daughter, Pauline Lavinia Gill, took over the Bigwin Inn Company's operation for a number of years and, as the largest stockholder, assumed the position of president. John W. McKee became the new vice-president and James G. Reid returned as manager of the Inn after a 15-year absence. In 1947 Mrs. Gill sold Bigwin Inn to the first in a series of new proprietors, each of whom brought a distinctive style of management to the resort.

The first to acquire the resort was Cardy-Bigwin Limited. At the time, the Cardy hotel conglomeration controlled the largest group of privately owned hotels in Canada, including Toronto's King Edward, the Royal Connaught in Hamilton, the Prince Edward in Windsor, the General Brock in Niagara Falls, the Leonard in St. Catharines, the Alpine Inn in Ste. Marguerite, and the Mount Royal in Montreal.

Vernon G. Cardy, of the hotel chain, was also involved with many hotel, tourist, publicity and business associations, including Colonial Airways and Guarantee Trust Company of Canada Limited. In 1916, at 27 years of age, Vernon Cardy married his first wife, Hilda Bouvier of Toronto. They had one son, Bruce. Cardy later married Miss Edith Ferguson. Having prolific membership in various clubs, the Cardys were well known in both Montreal and Toronto societies. They enjoyed golf, motoring, hunting, yachting, and were also recognized for their great interest in horses, showing them on many occasions at leading North American horse shows. With such prominent business and social profiles, the Cardys brought a more flamboyant pace to the Bigwin resort.

Under new ownership, attempts were made to operate Bigwin Inn in a streamlined corporate style. At the time, Cardy announced to the press, "We plan even greater development of the island and estate. We have had a constant growing demand for fine summer resort accommodation from countless numbers of guests at our hotels. Bigwin has a glorious setting and an excellent physical set up." Cardy continued to suggest that "the improvements and extensions will mean the enhancement of property values and increased public interest in the tourist facilities throughout the whole Lake of Bays." The general manager of Cardy Hotels, H. Alexander MacLennan, added that renovations and improvements were to begin immediately.

The first of Cardy-Bigwin Limited's modifications included the lengthening of the operating season by one month in order to capture international convention business in June and September. As a means to offset the cost of this extension, Cardy trimmed the number of staff at the Inn to approximately 250 people. Bigwin also enjoyed many added conveniences and received an extensive facelift in the attempt to attract a new generation of visitors.

Before long, the stately touring sedans of Bigwin's venerable guests were outnumbered by new sports cars, which often sped into the parking lot, stirring up clouds of dust. For those demanding even quicker transportation, the Cardys established a new convenience. The inauguration of regular air-taxi service from Toronto's Island Airport allowed tourists to experience all the joys of Muskoka after only a 30-minute flight aboard a float plane. Visitors were also offered a new agenda of activities, including horse shows.

Huntsville and Lake of Bays Line
SUMMER TIME TABLE 1946
IN EFFECT JUNE 27th AND UNTIL FURTHER NOTICE AND UNLESS OTHERWISE NOTED.

Huntsville - Portage - Dorset

FROM HUNTSVILLE READ DOWN				EASTERN STANDARD TIME		FROM DORSET READ UP			
				RAILWAY SERVICE					
x	11.30 p.m.	D	11.05 a.m.	Lve.	Toronto via C. N. Rlys.	Arr.	D	3.45 p.m.	x	7.05 a.m.
		D	3.22 p.m.	Arr.	Huntsville Station Wharf	Lve.	D	10.50 a.m.		
x	4.43 a.m.	D	3.32 p.m.	Arr.	Huntsville Station	Lve.	D	10.39 a.m.	x	1.45 a.m.
	June 28th to Sept. 2nd		June 27th to Aug. 31st					June 28th to Sept. 2nd		June 28th Sept. 2nd
				STEAMER SERVICE					
D	6.50 a.m.	D	3.30 p.m.	Lve.	Huntsville Station Wharf	Arr.	D	10.45 a.m.	D	6.45 p.m.
D	7.30 a.m.	D	3.00 p.m.	Lve.	Huntsville Town Wharf	Arr.	D	10.30 a.m.	D	6.30 p.m.
A	7.35 a.m.	A	3.45 p.m.	Lve.	(Memorial Park)	Arr.	A	10.20 a.m.	A	6.25 p.m.
A	8.00 a.m.	T		Arr.	Swallowdale	Arr.	A		A	
A	8.05 a.m.	T		Arr.	Grandview (Fairy Lake)	Arr.	A		A	
A		A		Arr.	Canal	Arr.	A		A	
A	8.20 a.m.	T	4.25 p.m.	Arr.	Deerhurst Inn	Arr.	A	9.40 a.m.	A	5.40 p.m.
A	8.25 a.m.	T		Arr.	Pow-Wow Point	Arr.	T		A	
A	8.30 a.m.			Arr.	Grassmere (Tally-Ho)	Arr.			A	
A				Arr.	Winoka	Arr.			A	
A	8.40 a.m.	T		Arr.	Isle Dunelg	Arr.	T		A	
A		T		Arr.	Sekani	Arr.	A		A	
A	8.45 a.m.			Arr.	Springsyde	Arr.			A	
D	8.50 a.m.	D	4.45 p.m.	Arr.	North Portage	Lve.	D	9.25 a.m.	D	5.00 p.m.
D	9.35 a.m.	D	5.20 p.m.	Lve.	South Portage	Lve.	D	9.00 a.m.	D	4.20 p.m.
D	9.50 a.m.	D	5.40 p.m.	Arr.	Britannia	Lve.	D	8.45 a.m.	D	3.50 p.m.
A	10.10 a.m.	A	6.00 p.m.	Arr.	Bona Vista	Lve.	A	8.25 a.m.	A	
A	10.20 a.m.	A	6.15 p.m.	Arr.	Point Ideal	Lve.	A	8.15 a.m.	A	
A		A		Arr.	Robinsdale	Lve.	A		A	
A		A		Arr.	Clovelly	Lve.	A		A	
A	10.30 a.m.	A	6.30 p.m.	Arr.	Glenmount	Lve.	A	7.20 a.m.	A	2.55 p.m.
D	10.50 a.m.	D	6.50 p.m.	Arr.	Bigwin Island (Bigwin Inn)	Lve.	D	8.00 a.m.	D	2.45 p.m.
A	11.00 a.m.	A	p.m.	Arr.	Port Cunnington	Lve.	A	a.m.	A	
A	a.m.	A	p.m.	Arr.	Grove Park Lodge	Lve.	A	a.m.	A	
A	a.m.	A	p.m.	Arr.	Chevaliers	Lve.	A		A	
A	a.m.	A	p.m.	Arr.	Cliffdene	Lve.	A		A	
A	a.m.	A	p.m.	Arr.	Raymur Pines	Lve.	A		A	
D	12.30 (noon)	D	8.00 p.m.	Arr.	Dorset	Lve.	D	6.00 a.m.	D	1.15 p.m.

Explanation of Signs

X—Daily. D—Daily except Sunday.

T—Call will only be made to take on or deliver passengers to or from connecting trains.

A—Steamers will stop to land any passengers, and will pick up on previous arrangement.

NOTE: Dwight and Glen Cove service handled by Private Ownership Launch from and to South Portage. —Ticket and check baggage to SOUTH PORTAGE only.

Flag Signals—The Company will not under any circumstances accept responsibility for failure to stop on flag call. Where steamers are required to call at wharves (designated A) for outgoing passengers, General Office must be notified 24 hours previous or the Captain of the steamer 12 hours previous in writing.

Time table shows the time steamers should arrive at and leave different ports, at their departure, arrival or connection at time stated is not guaranteed nor does the Company hold itself responsible for any delays or any consequences arising therefrom or for failure on the part of our steamers to call by appointment or notice, either verbal or written, at any regular stopping place. All times subject to fluctuation from stress of weather, etc., and change with or without notice.

Mrs. Pauline L. Gill,
President.

Huntsville, Ontario, May 14, 1946

W. J. Moore,
Gnr. Mgr. and Sec'y.

- Robert McLennan

Like a small town in its heyday, Bigwin Inn catered to thousands of discerning guests. Regular patrons of the resort received top priority and were usually booked into the same rooms as in previous years. — *DGM*

Joseph E. Atkinson, a man of exacting standards, operated *The Toronto Star* for over half a century, transforming it into the nation's largest and most powerful newspaper. The 1947 season was his last at Bigwin Inn, as he passed away in May of the following year. He is remembered not only for his accomplishments in the publishing industry, but also for his unwavering commitment to charitable causes. Many of Bigwin Inn's musical concerts were held in aid of the *Star* Fresh Air Fund. (Chief Bigwin himself visited the CNE as a guest of *The Toronto Star* during the 1940s, where he was seen wearing his eagle head-dress, trimmed with weasel, which denoted his position as tribal head of Ontario's Ojibway tribe.) Today, the Atkinson Charitable Foundation continues to support many worthy causes. — *DGM*

Summer jobs at Bigwin Inn were much sought after, regardless of how uncomfortable uniforms may have been during the warm summer months. — *DGM*

At the recommendation of top interior designers and promotion experts, many of the buildings were reshingled, repainted and redecorated in a flurry of activity before the start of the tourist season. Dial telephones and electric heaters were installed in all guest rooms (at a cost of well over $250,000) and a raft was added to the harbourfront facilities. However, the most noticeable change was that Bigwin Inn was no longer officially "dry."

Two cocktail lounges were quickly added to the resort. The management had doors installed in one of the exterior walls below the Marine Dining Room and the vast room behind, the Casino, was remodelled as a lounge. Known as the "Round Room," this quickly became one of the most popular gathering spots on the Lake of Bays and in all of Muskoka. Here, the sedate music of Victorian chamber trios gave way to the new, energetic sound of big band swing. Frequently, musicians from New York City set up instruments beside the grand fireplace and serenaded dozens of visitors until the early hours of the morning, performing such selections as "In The Mood," "Marie" and "String of Pearls." The audience of guests was offered built-in seating around the perimeter of the room, as well as large, comfortable wooden chairs and tables, with waiters in white or scarlet jackets to cater to their needs. Other entertainment could be found in the Rotunda, where the west end of the main lobby had been enclosed as a separate room. In the "Fireplace Lounge" selections of piano music could be enjoyed while sitting in one of the fireplace's massive stone armchairs or lounging in one of the many pieces of cane furniture arranged in front of the immense hearth and throughout the room.

While the extensive renovations made by Cardy-Bigwin Limited were much welcomed by visitors to the Inn, they failed to generate a satisfactory return. Shortly after the end of the 1948 summer season, the ownership of the hotel passed into new hands.

In January 1949, the resort was sold to 54-year-old stockbroker and hotelier Frank Shepard Leslie. Frank Leslie began his career at 20 years of age at the Bank of Ottawa. He later entered the stock brokerage business and eventually gained a seat on the Mining Exchange of Toronto. Shortly thereafter, Frank S. Leslie and Company established brokerage offices at 210 Bay Street, near the intersection of Bay and Wellington streets in Toronto. Leslie lived with his wife, Audrey Correen (nee Mills), and their three children, Ruth Eleanor, George Ross and Frank Mills, at 62 Old Forest Hill Road, Toronto.

Shortly after he acquired ownership, Leslie effected various improvements to the island resort. In 1956 the ferry *Bigwin* was refitted with a diesel motor, the smokestack relocated, the hull reinforced with steel ribbing, and finally, the vessel ballasted with fieldstone and cement. The Marine Dining Room had new awnings installed over its windows, and a huge green marquee designed by Simpson's Special Contract Division was built over the marine and sundeck. A new soda bar was installed in the Pavilion, a ski jump added to the harbourfront facilities, and financial services made available in the Rotunda.

Leslie had admired Bigwin since his first stay as a guest in the late '20s, and as owner he took great pride in maintaining a presence at the Inn. Frequently, he would stand by the reception desk in the Rotunda and warmly greet newly arrived guests or cottagers, who often enjoyed his hospitality in the Fireplace Lounge or in the Round Room. Leslie already owned the Glenmount Hotel and Tea House on the Lake of Bays and belonged to the National, Granite and Saint George clubs in Toronto, thus he was a familiar face to many island visitors. During ownership of the island Inn, he also acquired Miami's popular Golden Strand Hotel.

Leslie's fondness for popular music was instrumental in attracting many entertainers to Bigwin. One of the great talents who came to the island resort during the Leslie ownership was Cuban-born Chicho Valle. Leslie had retained Valle for summer engagements at the Inn after meeting him in Toronto's "Cork Room." Upon his arrival at the Island's steamer dock, Valle was escorted by a young bellboy, through the pines and birches, to the far side of the island. As they approached a building, Valle inquired about its use and was promptly informed that the modest structure was the musician's accommodation. Well accustomed to modern comforts, he politely retorted, "This may be where *you* stay, but it is not where *I* stay. Bring the bags, I am leaving." Before Valle could board the ferry, however, special arrangements were made for him to stay in the hotel. Chicho Valle and his orchestra continued to perform at Bigwin each summer for more than a decade and established a great following with island visitors and resort personnel.

During the summer season, staff of the Inn often enjoyed parties at the Glenmount Hotel or in the island powerhouse, where a separate band played regularly. Frequently, resort personnel and the bands from the Tea House (or Canadiana Room), Pavilion, Round Room and powerhouse were invited by Leslie to participate in late night jam sessions in the Round Room. Other, more traditional festivities took place at the end of the season, with many of the hotel staff members participating in the annual masquerade in the Pavilion. During those evenings, Leslie would often sing one of his favourite songs, such as "Love is Sweeping the Country" or "There'll be a Change in the Weather."

As such soirées would sometimes keep Leslie at the resort until the early hours of morning, a plaque was affixed to the door of one of the rooms in the West Lodge, assuring him that accommodation would be available at any time. However, he primarily stayed in the magnificent private stone cottage at Norway Point, built where the WaWa Hotel's bowling greens had been. Constructed in the mid-thirties, the family cottage was reminiscent of the WaWa Hotel in its architectural plan and of Bigwin's Tea House in its elaborate masonry. The building was

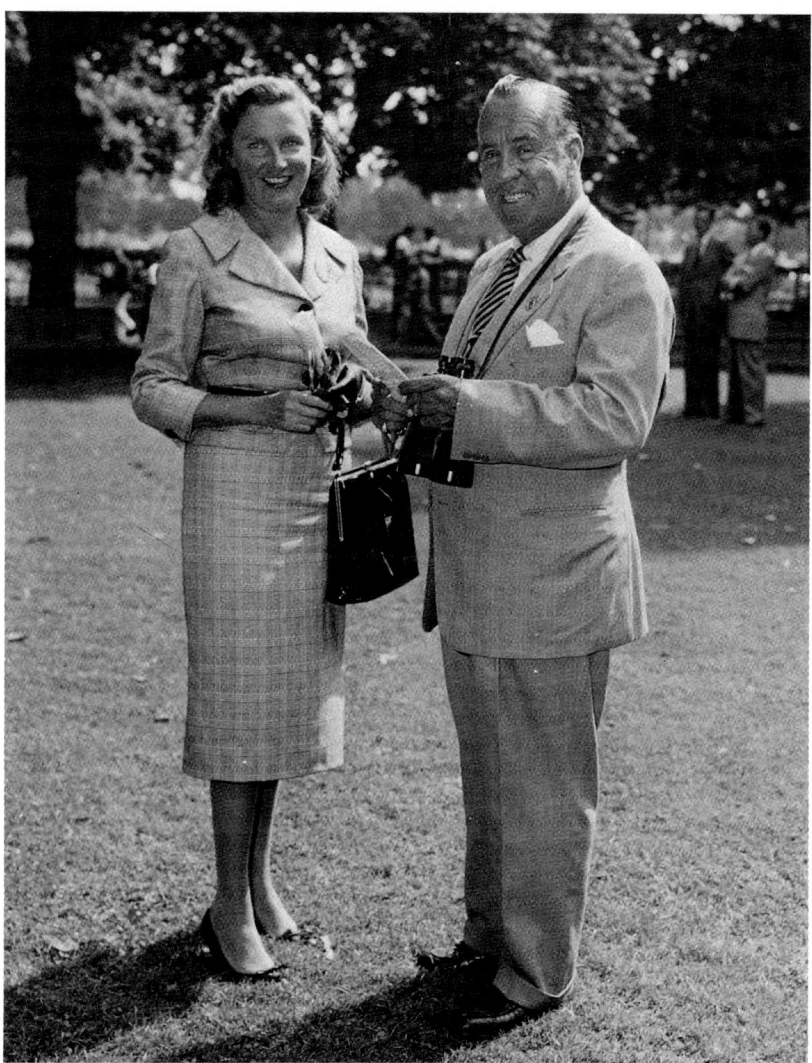

A newspaper headline in the 1940s read: "Latest and Most Glamorous Addition to the Cardy Hotel Chain, Largest Group of Privately-Owned Hotels in Canada, is the Ultra-Swank Bigwin Inn." With the Cardy takeover came a steady stream of limousines through the town of Baysville en route to the Norway Point wharf. Pictured are Mr. and Mrs. Vernon Cardy.   - *Edith Cardy*

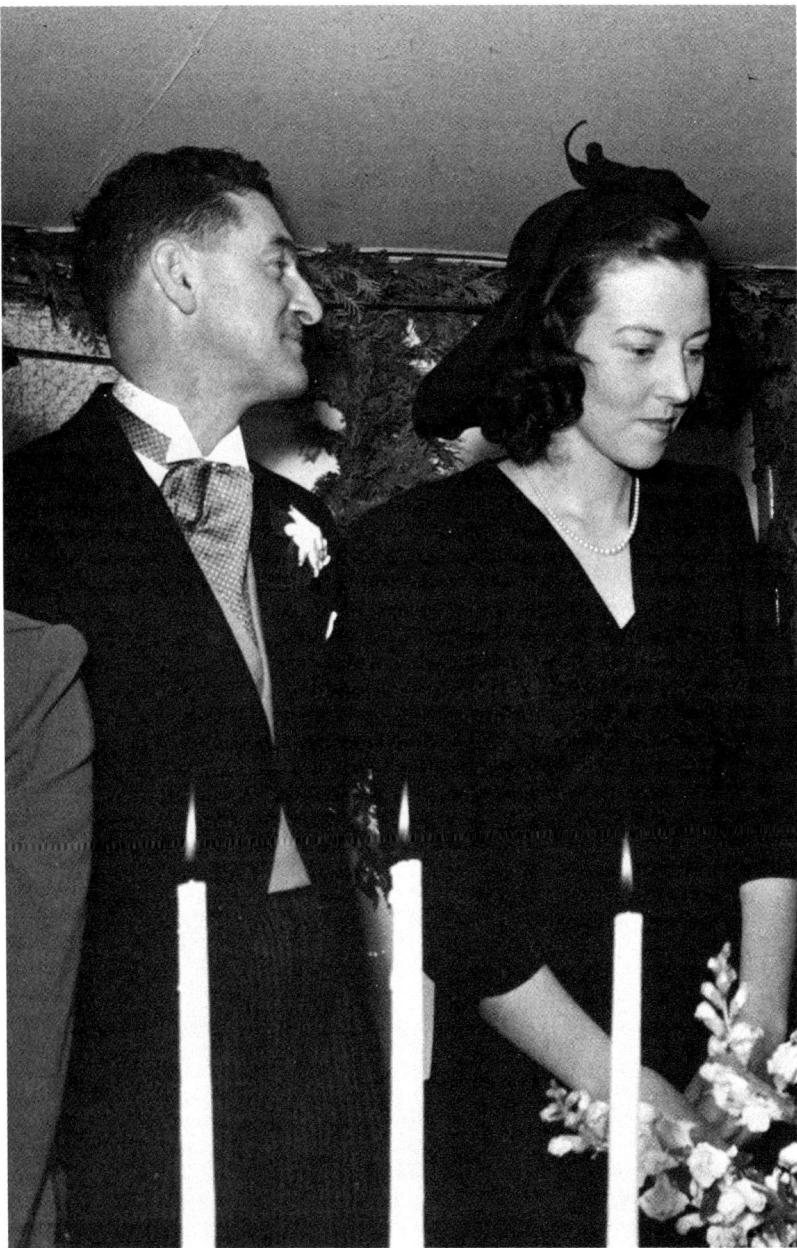

Frank Shepard Leslie. — *Frank Mills Leslie*

Bigwin Inn
LAKE OF BAYS, ONTARIO

OFFICE OF THE MANAGER

Tuesday June 3 rd 1952.

Dear Buddy:-

    Tell Ruth that I received her letter the other day and have not been able to run down to Toronto. There is so much to do and so little time. Our Post Office opens to-morrow and I must be here to receive the equipment. The first guests (the advance guard of a convention will arrive on Thursday and by Sunday they will total 250.

    The 'Wanda III' was put in the water on Sunday and sailed to Baysville to get her kitchen equipment. The S.S.Bigwin should be in the water by Friday. I have had two meals in the Cafeteria so far. The weather is backward and as Arthur Sprott says (where I was for Saturday dinner and Lester a guest) it is the latest spring in his memory.

    Enclosed is a check for $13.00 an extra person eating this week.

    Tell Ross 'Radio' Leslie that I may get the radio into Huntsville for repairs to-day.   As ever,

A letter from Frank S. Leslie to his son, Frank Mills Leslie. — *Frank Mills Leslie*

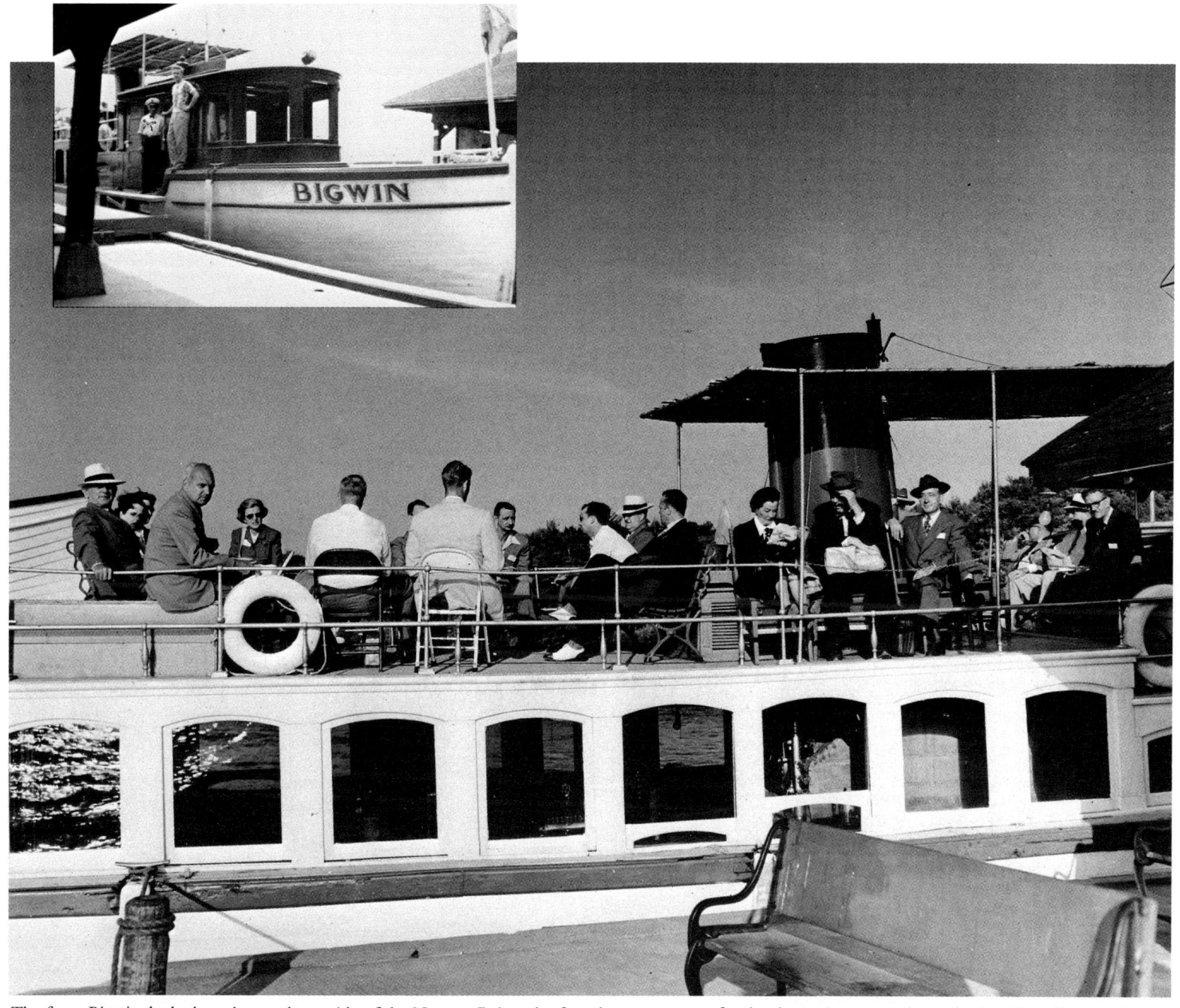

The ferry *Bigwin* docked on the northeast side of the Norway Point wharf, took on passengers for the short trip over to the posh island Inn. Pictured inset, at the resort's steamer wharf in 1949, is Captain William P. Tinkiss.
— *Ontario Archives 10999-2-4-70 and Ruth Tinkiss*

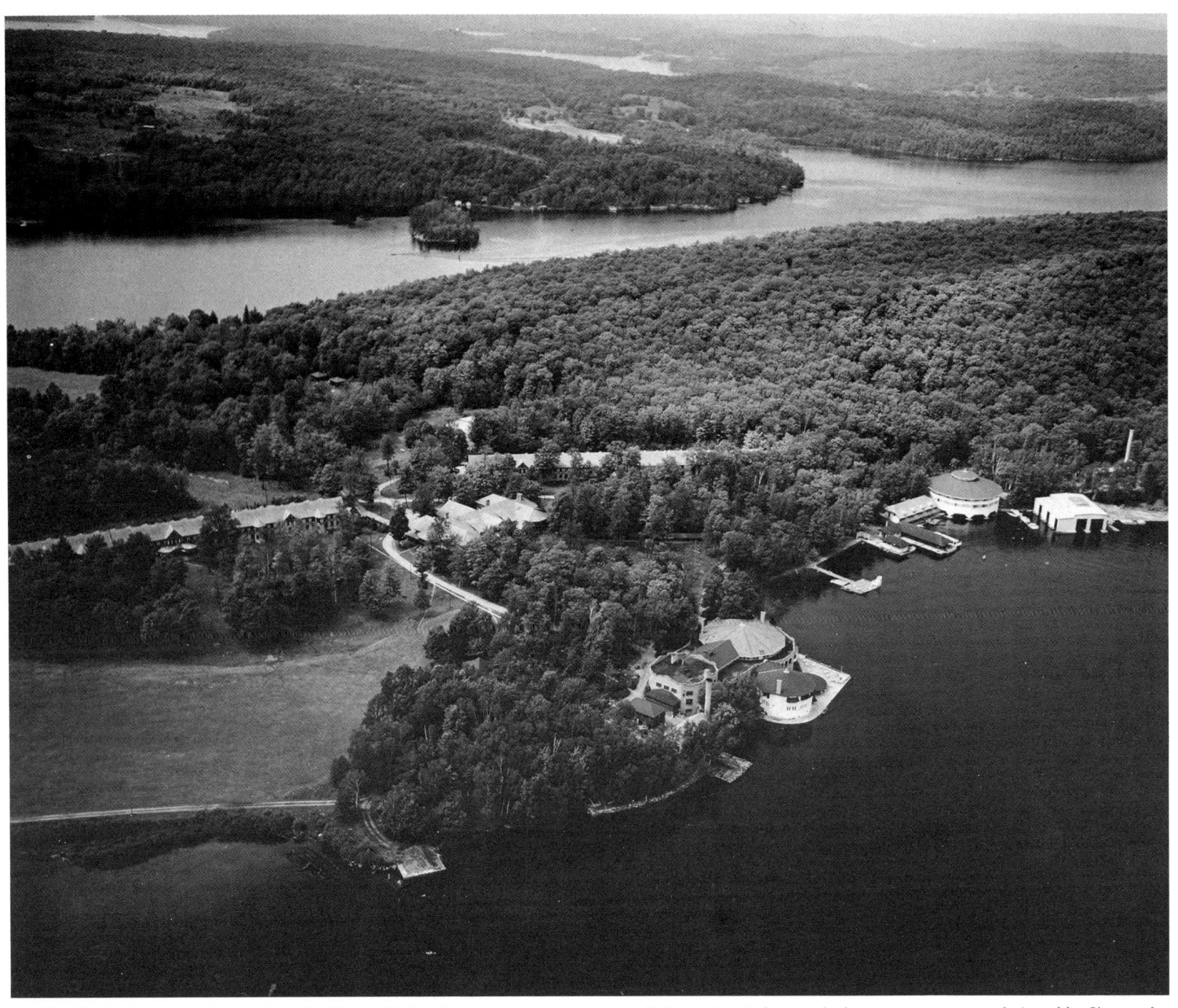
Shortly after Leslie acquired ownership, the Marine Dining Room had new awnings installed over its windows and a huge green marquee designed by Simpson's Special Contract Division built over the enlarged marine and sundeck.
- *DGM*

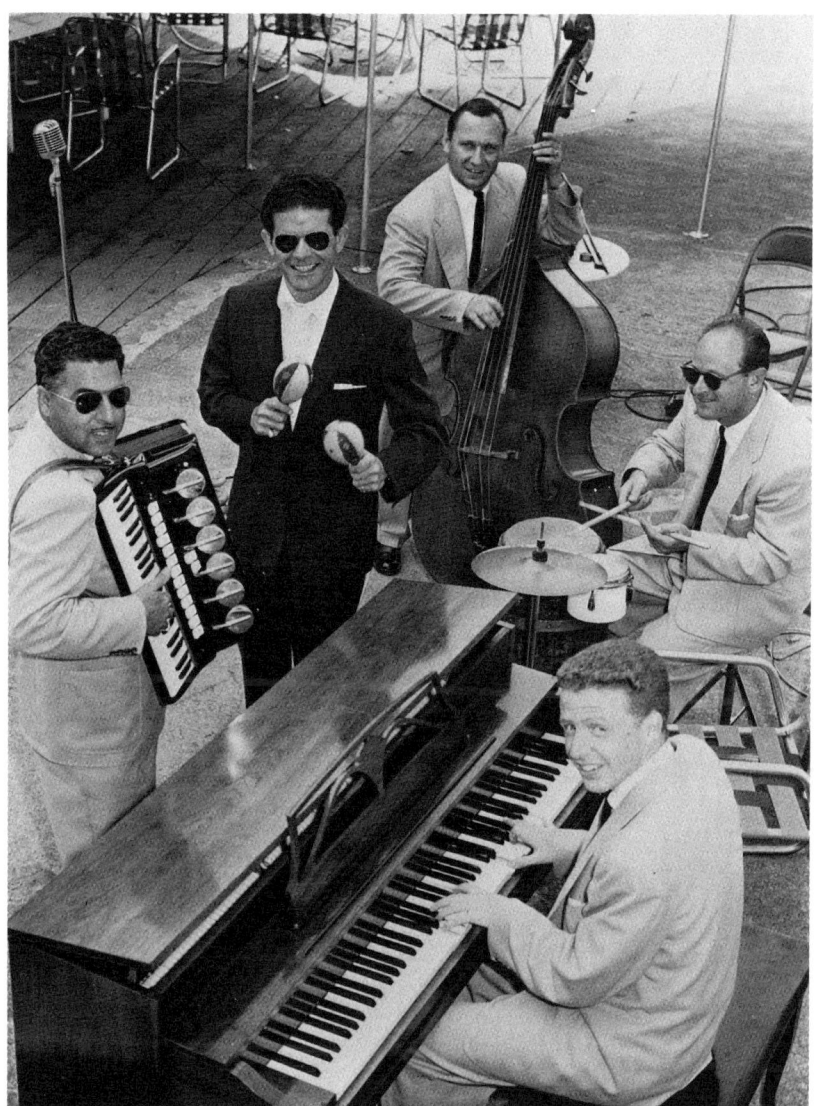

Frank Leslie contracted some of Canada's most renowned musicians to perform at his resorts. Chicho Valle and his orchestra performed at Bigwin Inn for more than a decade. Valle later recorded with Capital Records. (clockwise: Ernie Capellacci, Chicho Valle, Wally Ewanski, Bob Reinhart, Red Mitchell).
- *Margaret Tolton*

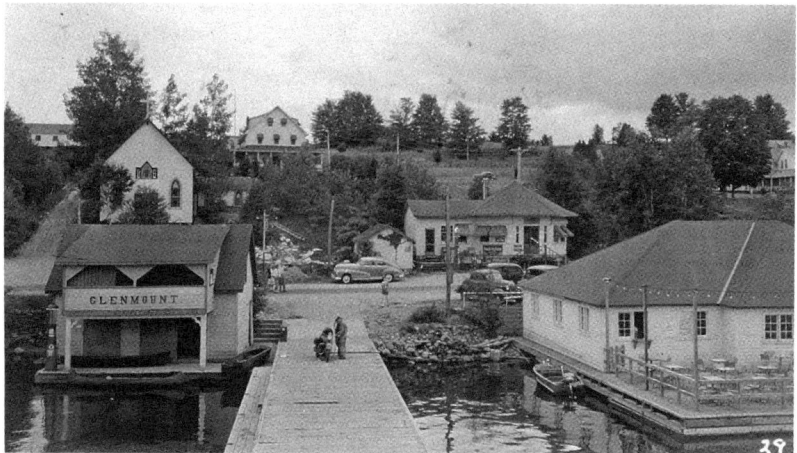

Gisele LaFleche MacKenzie, one of Canada's internationally renowned singers, worked at Glenmount during the summer and visited Bigwin frequently. On one occasion, she and a friend, Hillel Diamond, attempted to paddle from Glenmount to Bigwin. As a storm began to brew, they hailed a passing launch and were towed into the safety of the Bigwin harbour. Pictured here in the 1950s are the Glenmount Hotel, church, tuck shop, boathouse and teahouse.
- *DGM*

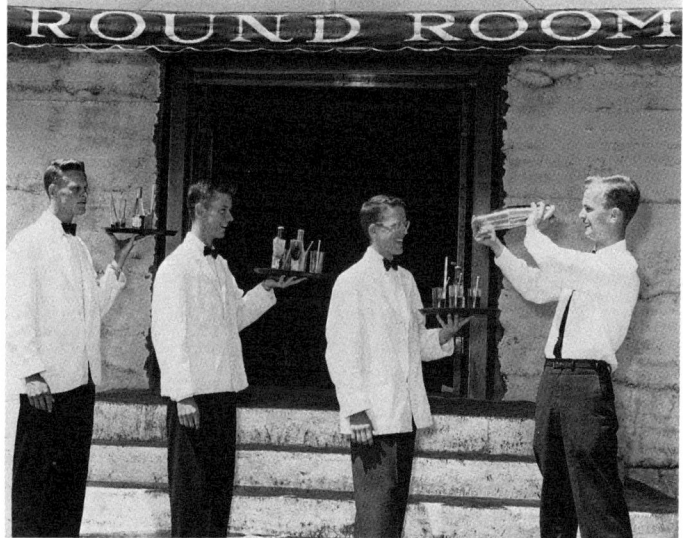

During the late 1940s and 1950s, many staff members came from the American south. Through those decades, the sounds of "the big bands and society music" could be heard from the Round Room, one of the most popular gathering spots in Muskoka.
- *Margaret Tolton*

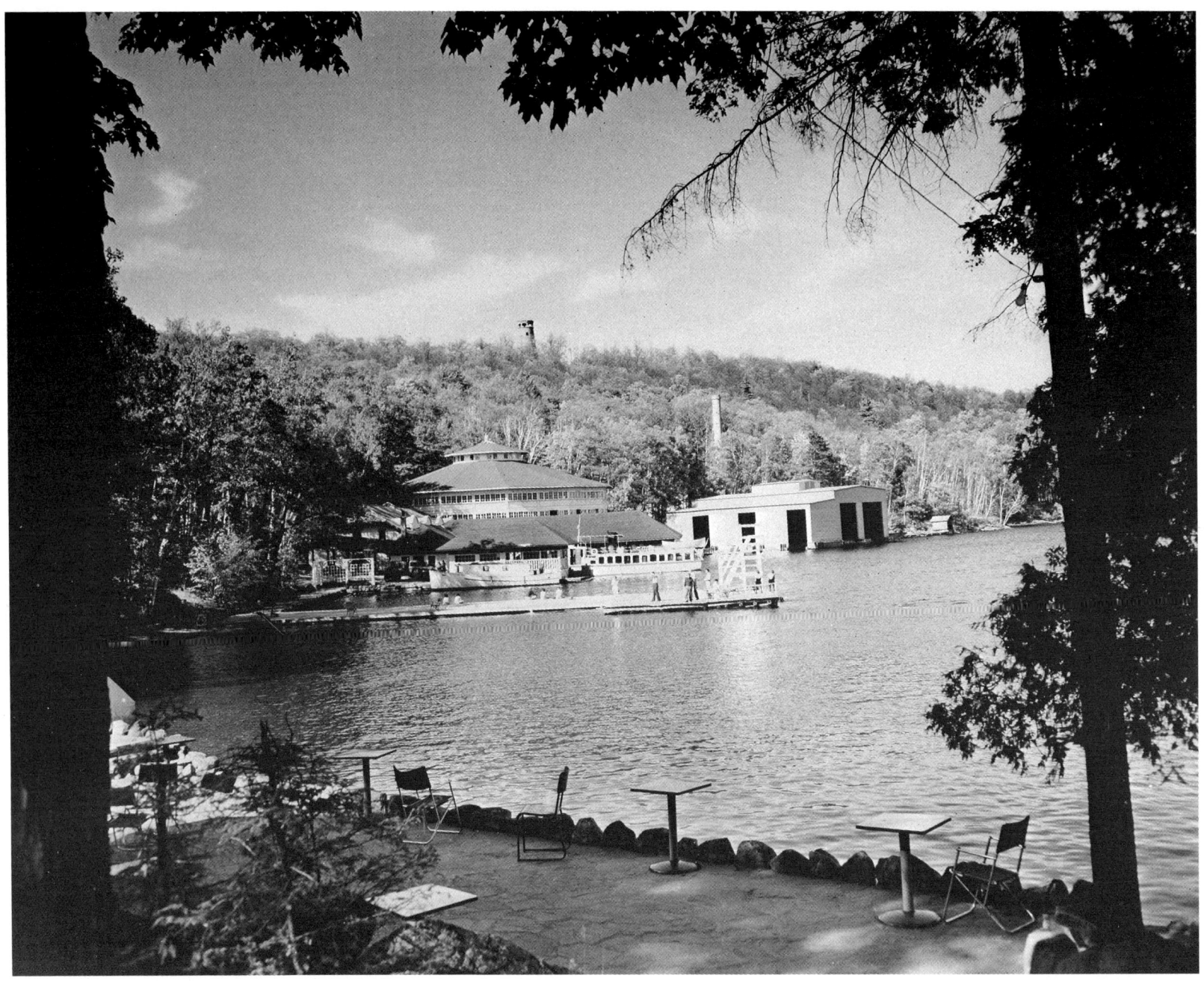
Listening to radio hits like Bobby Darin's "Beyond the Sea" or Tommy Edwards' "It's All in the Game" was how many enjoyed a place in the sun during the late 1950s and early 1960s.
- *Ontario Archives 18999-6-F-171*

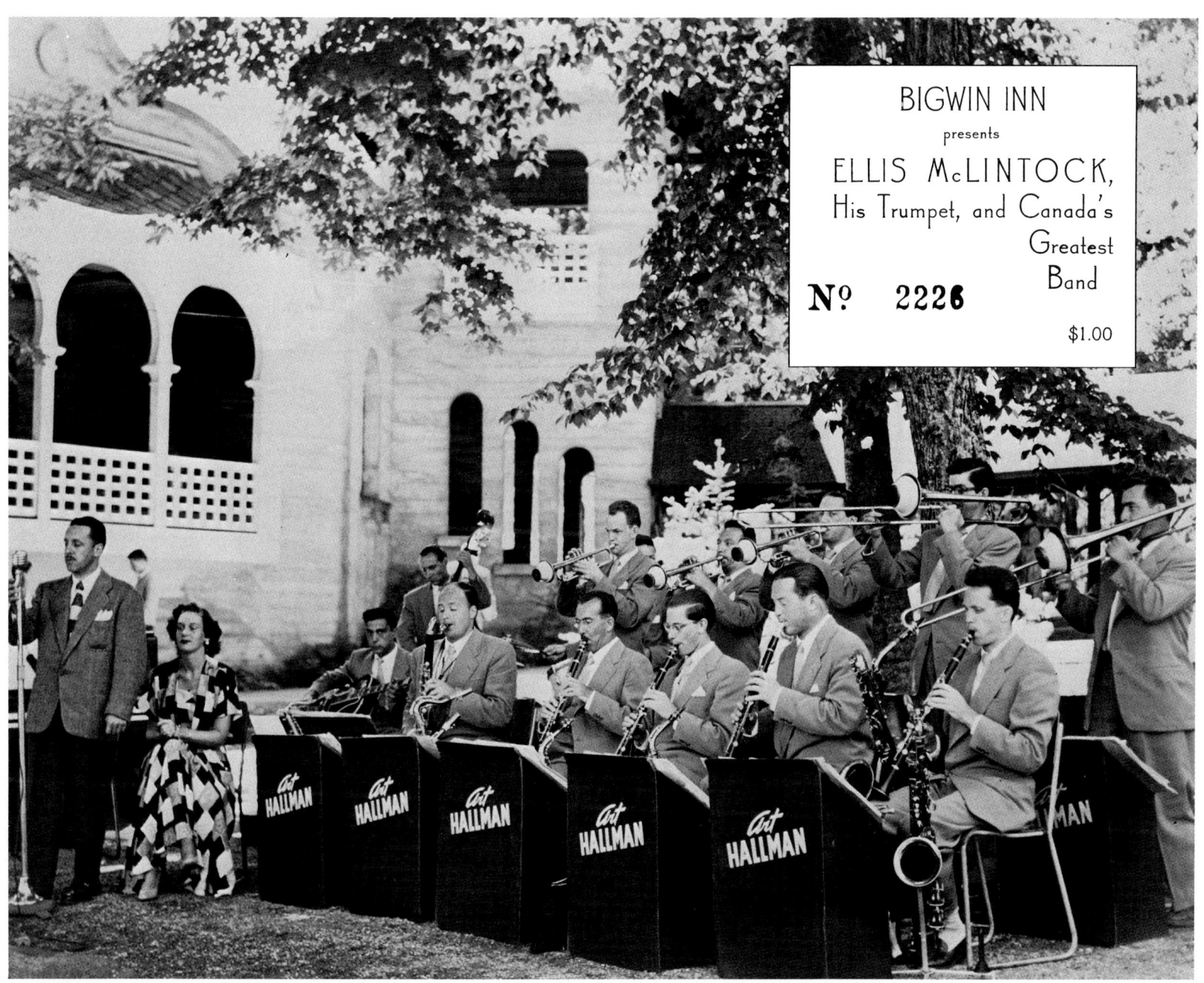

In 1949, the Art Hallman Orchestra performed at Bigwin Inn. (Brass: Graham Topping, Solly Sherman, Harry Hamilton, Don Humble, Ron Hughes. Saxes: Hart Wheeler, Jack Heath, Don Pierre, Marc Mortimer, Shadow Jackson. Guitar: Greg Antonacci. Bass: Wally Ewanski. Vocal: Terry Dale.)   - *Hart Wheeler*

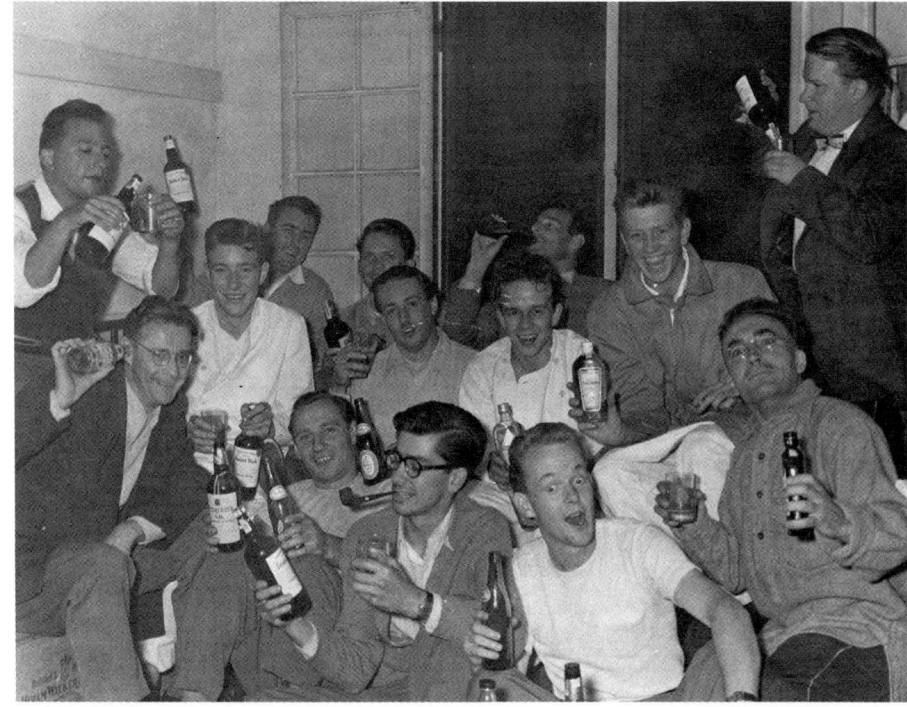

Musicians and resort personnel played on long after guests had retired. An evening in the Clubhouse in 1949 was a memorable event for many. Seen here are Solly Sherman, Gordy Brown, Ronny Hughes, Wally Ewanski, Shadow Jackson, Harry Hamilton, Don Humble, Graham Topping and Rolly Rowlandson.
- *Hart Wheeler*

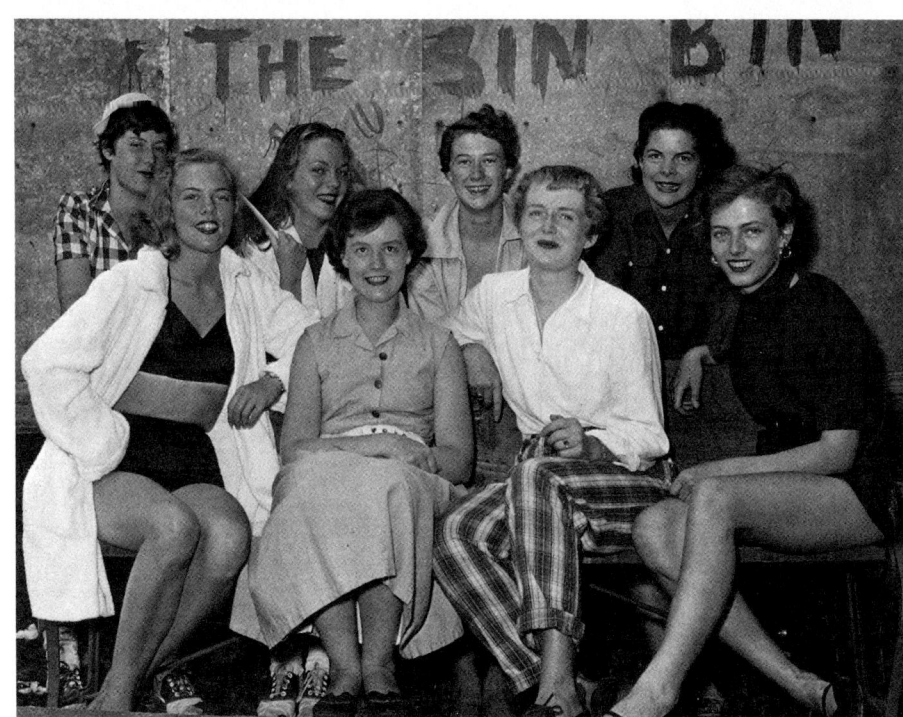

The 1950s brought in T-Birds, rock and roll, and Sandra Dee. For those lucky enough to land a waitressing job at Bigwin, still the grande dame of summer resorts, the summer brought great fun and many new friends.
- *Frank Mills Leslie*

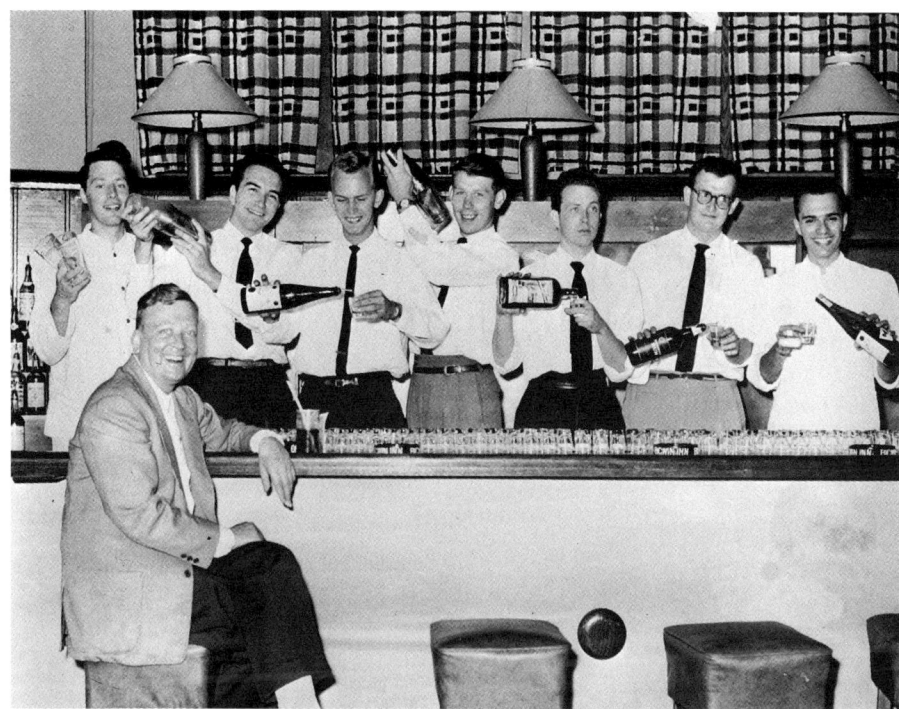

Evening soirées in the Round Room were popular among resort personnel. The black ceramic Bigwin Inn ashtrays on the bar were modelled after ashtrays from Sherman Billingsley's Stork Club in New York.
- *Donald J. Donahue*

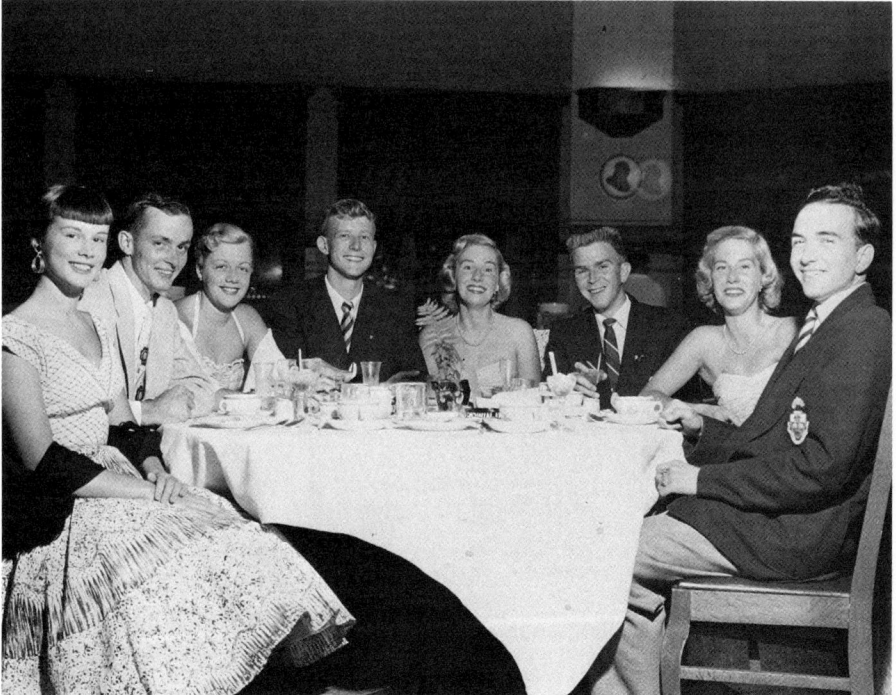

On special occasions, Frank Leslie permitted staff to dine in the Indian Head Room. During the winter months, Mr. Leslie hosted an annual staff reunion, often at Simpson's Arcadian Court in Toronto.
- *Donald J. Donahue*

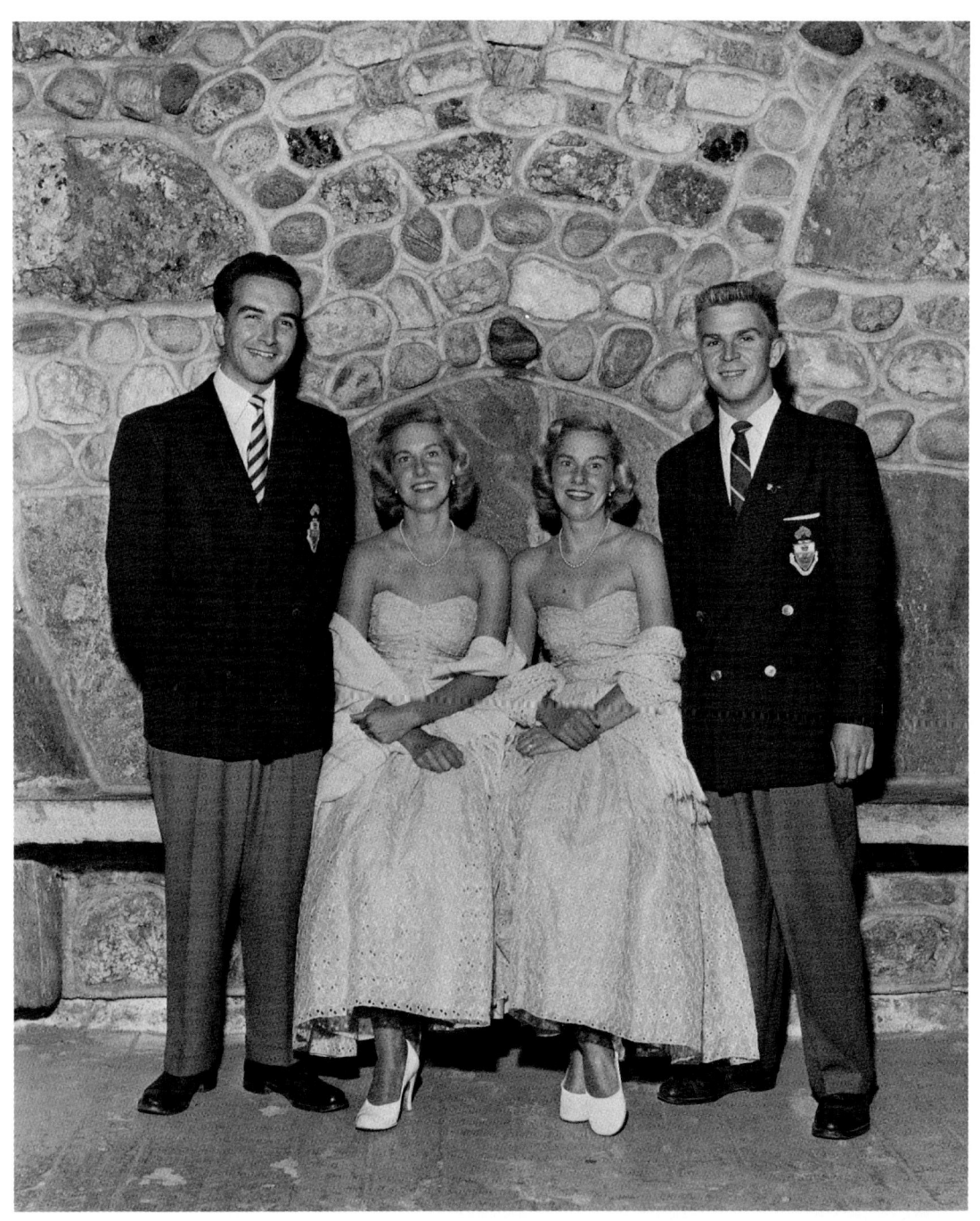

The 1950s, a decade that featured Marilyn Monroe, Audrey Hepburn, Cary Grant, Truman Capote, Billie Holiday, Nat King Cole, Elvis Presley and Ed Sullivan.
 - *Donald J. Donahue*

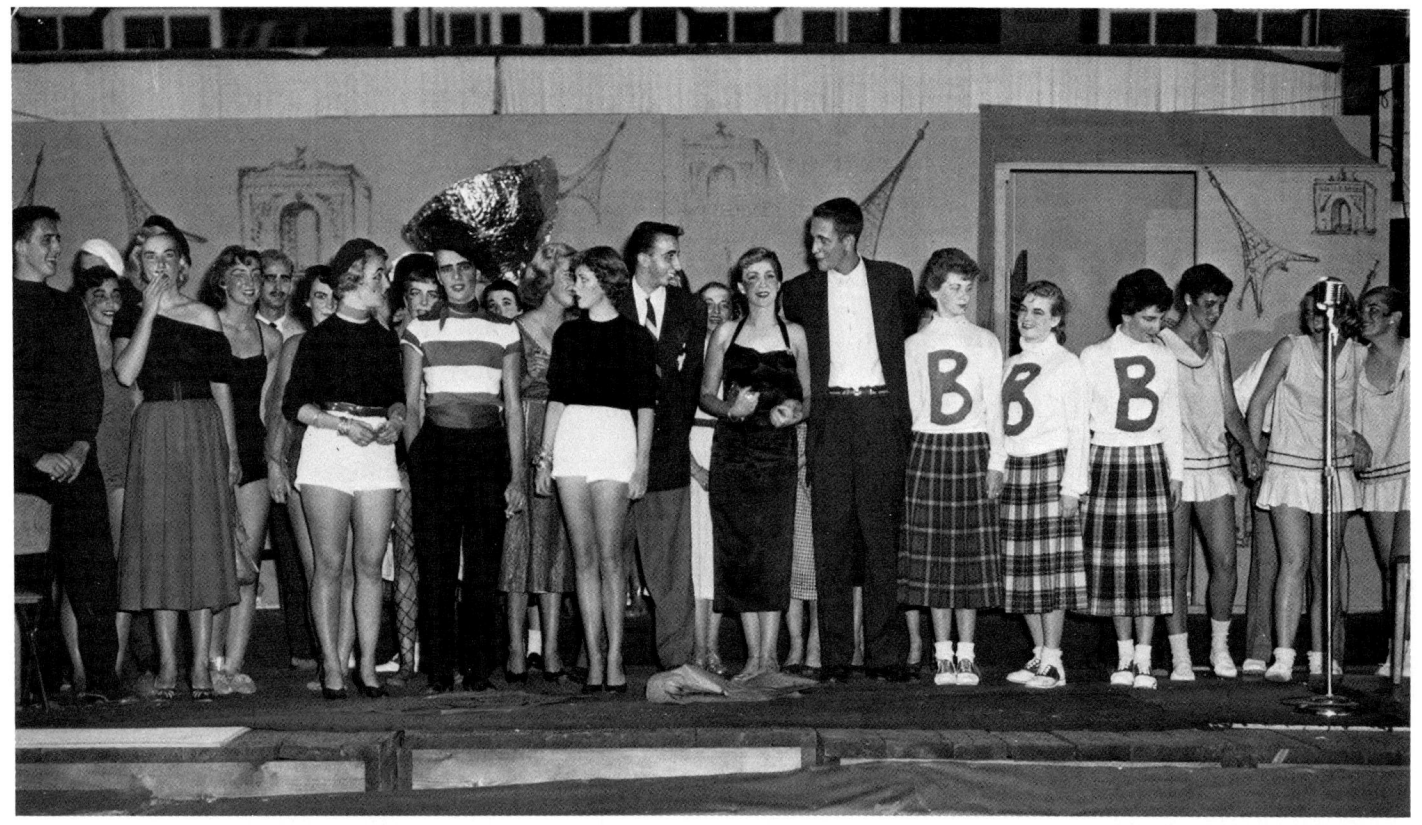

"Sing, sing, sing" – *A Bigwinite In Paris* was performed on the Pavilion's stage at the end of the 1953 season. In many instances, staff at the resort was made up of young members from both the Canadian and American Establishments — future ambassadors, bankers, doctors, film stars, financiers, judges, lawyers, musicians, and entrepreneurial giants.
- *Shirley Ransom and Margaret Tolton*

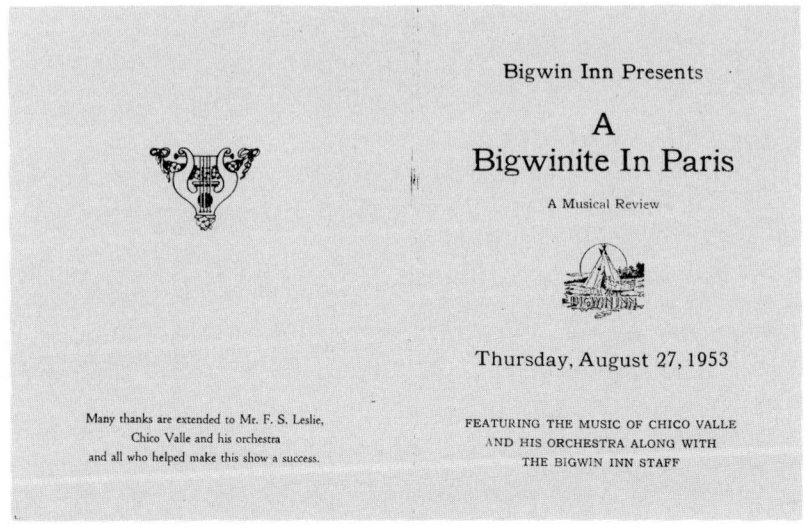

Bigwin Inn Presents

A
Bigwinite In Paris

A Musical Review

Thursday, August 27, 1953

FEATURING THE MUSIC OF CHICO VALLE
AND HIS ORCHESTRA ALONG WITH
THE BIGWIN INN STAFF

Many thanks are extended to Mr. F. S. Leslie, Chico Valle and his orchestra and all who helped make this show a success.

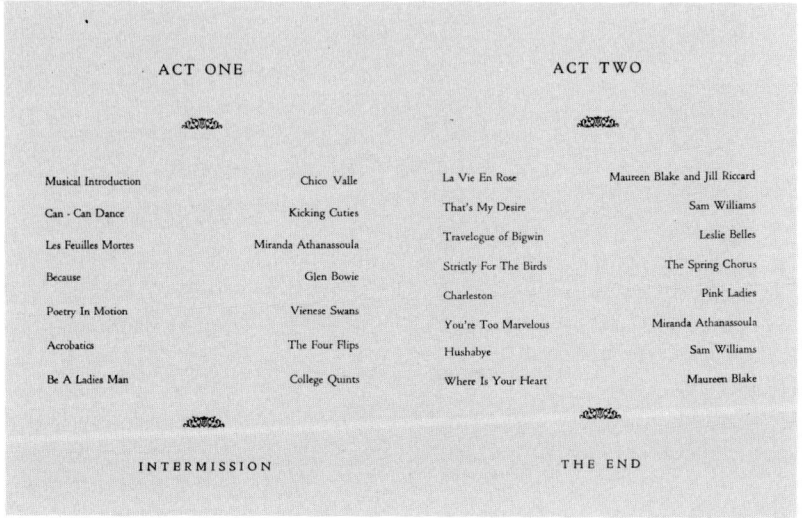

ACT ONE

Musical Introduction	Chico Valle
Can - Can Dance	Kicking Cuties
Les Feuilles Mortes	Miranda Athanassoula
Because	Glen Bowie
Poetry In Motion	Vienese Swans
Acrobatics	The Four Flips
Be A Ladies Man	College Quints

INTERMISSION

ACT TWO

La Vie En Rose	Maureen Blake and Jill Riccard
That's My Desire	Sam Williams
Travelogue of Bigwin	Leslie Belles
Strictly For The Birds	The Spring Chorus
Charleston	Pink Ladies
You're Too Marvelous	Miranda Athanassoula
Hushabye	Sam Williams
Where Is Your Heart	Maureen Blake

THE END

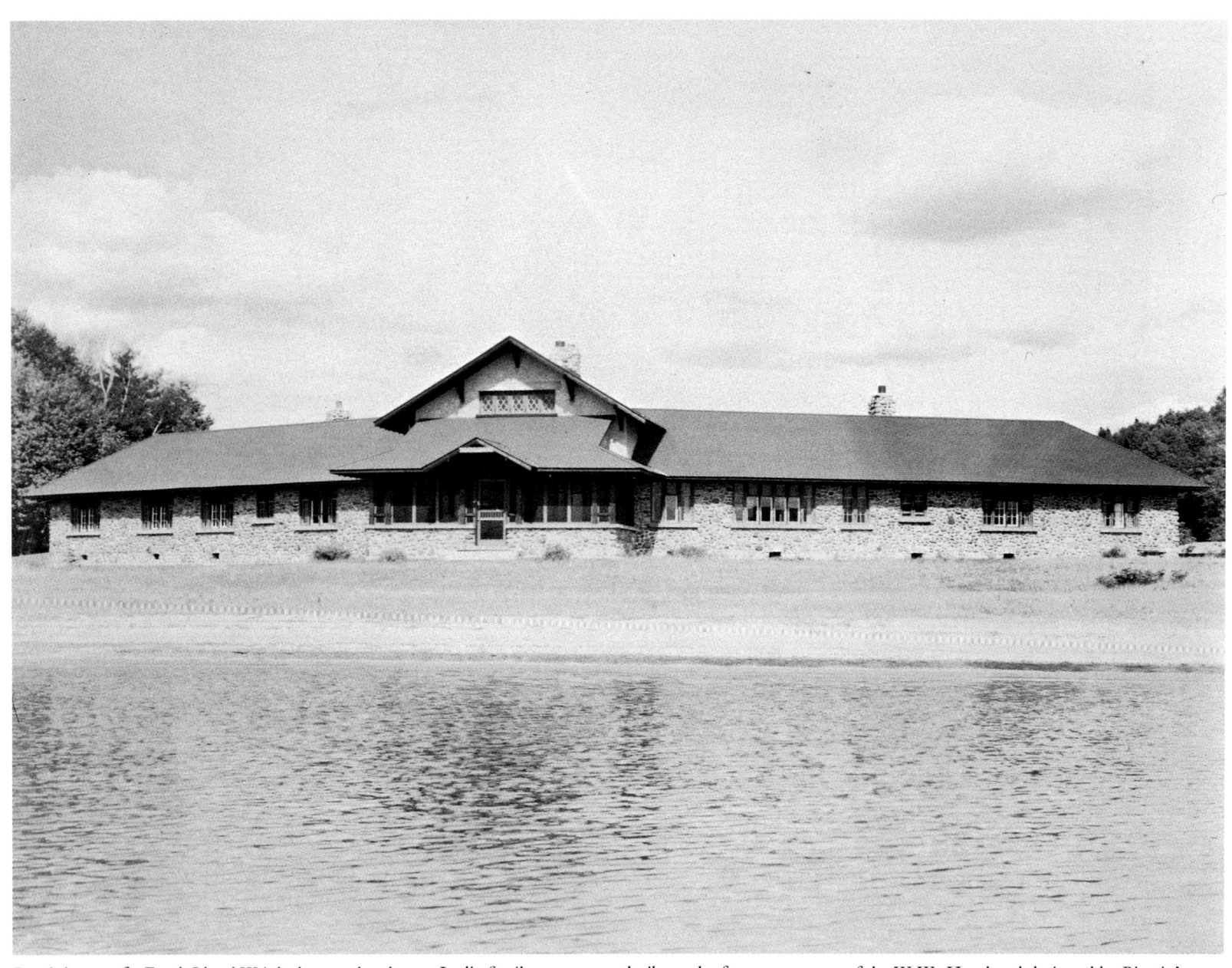

Reminiscent of a Frank Lloyd Wright house, the elegant Leslie family cottage was built on the former property of the WaWa Hotel and designed by Bigwin's architect, John Wilson.
- Frank Mills Leslie

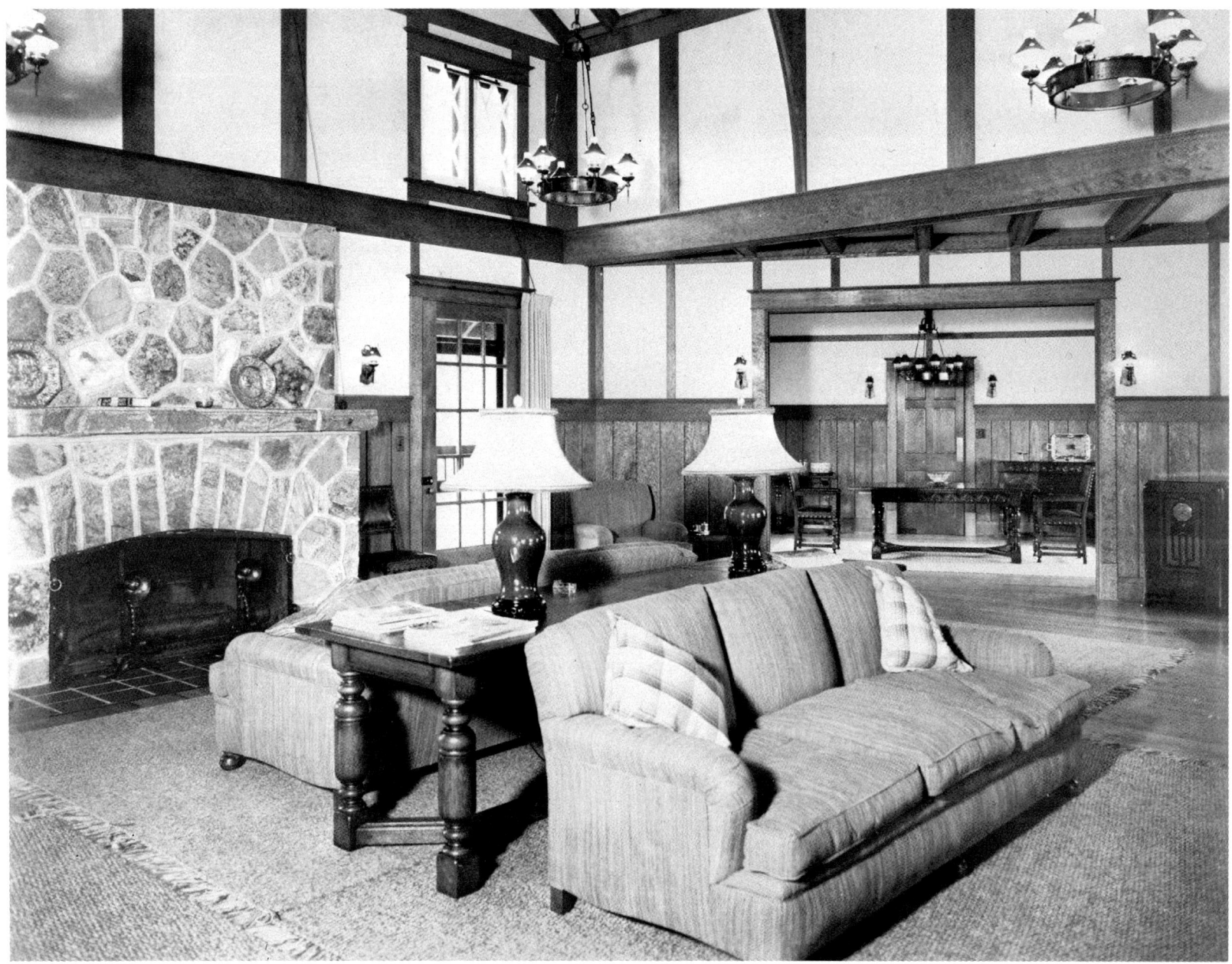
The spacious living room of the Leslie cottage featured many of Wilson's signature elements.   - *Frank Mills Leslie*

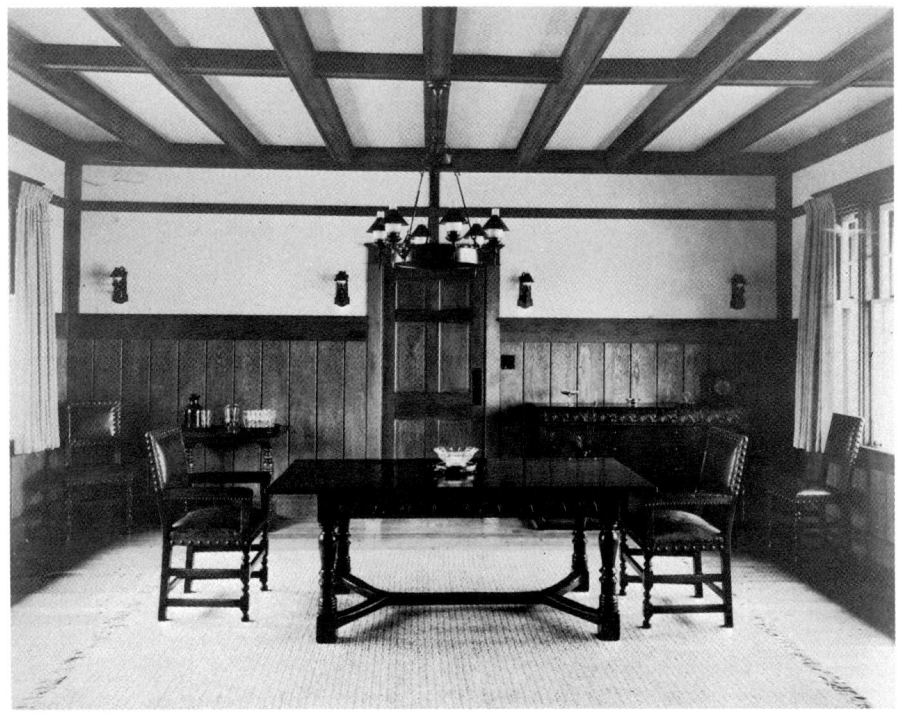

Of generous proportions, the cottage dining room was simple yet elegant and featured Spanish-style furniture.
- *Frank Mills Leslie*

The screened verandah of Leslie's summer residence offered a spectacular view of the Glenmount shoreline and Lake of Bays.
- *Frank Mills Leslie*

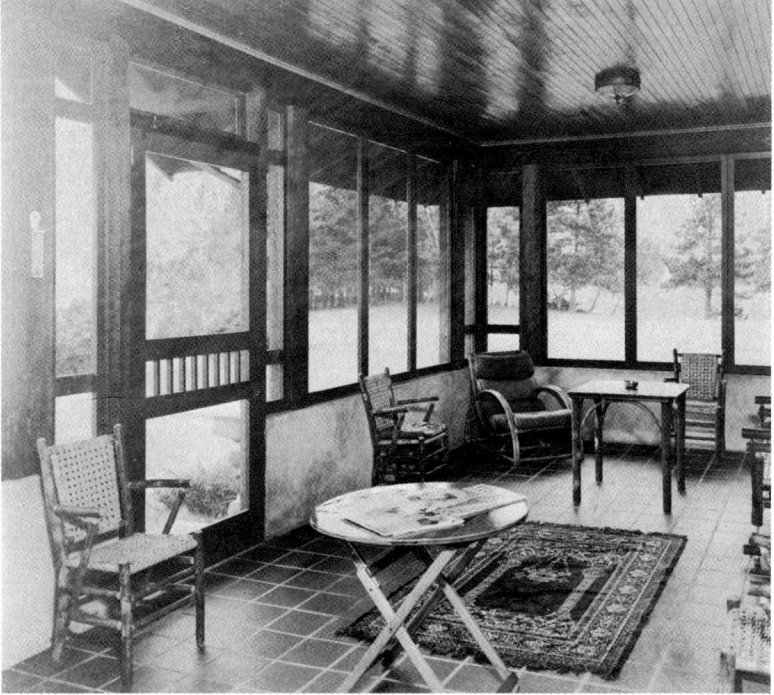

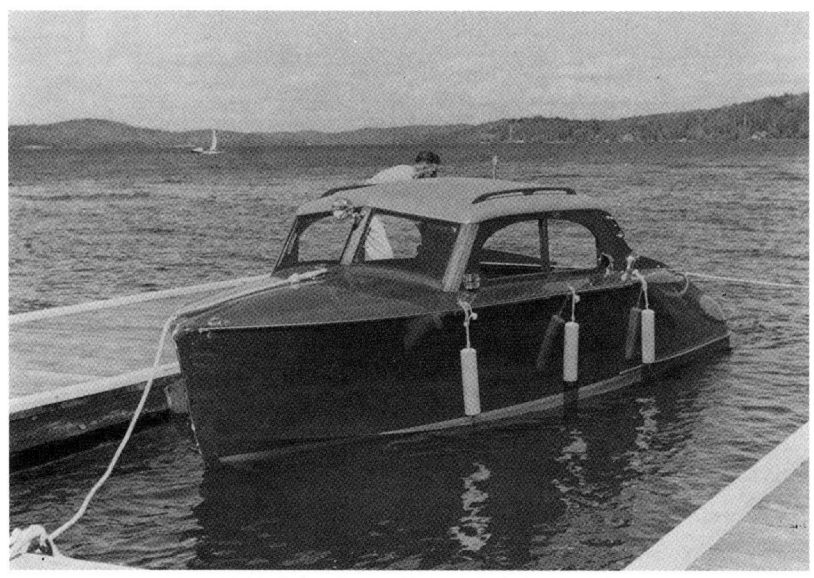

Chamoised to a shine, Leslie's hard-top Shepherd boat *Nor-Les*.
- *Frank Mills Leslie*

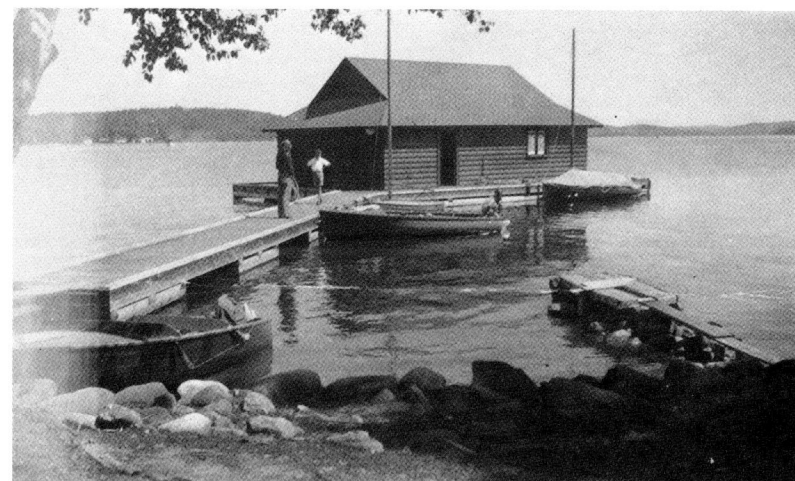

Leslie's boathouse at Norway Point had an extension added by the mid-1940s.
- *Frank Mills Leslie*

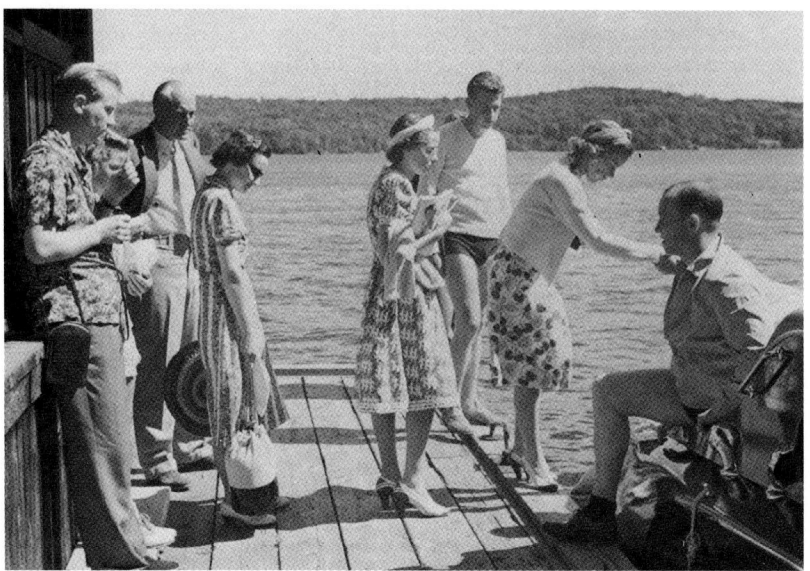

Climbing aboard the *Nor-Les* at Bigwin Inn.
- *Frank Mills Leslie*

designed to Leslie's specifications around a large centre module with cathedral ceilings and a huge stone fireplace. To the front of the module was a verandah overlooking the beach and to either side of it were large wings where the bedrooms, bathrooms, kitchen and library were located. Nicknamed "Norway Lodge," the Leslie cottage was thought by many unsuspecting tourists to be a hotel.

Also erected on the property was a small coach house. Later, a boathouse was built, and by the mid-forties, an extension added. There, Leslie kept a collection of vessels, including the hardtop Shepherd boat *Nor-Les* (named after Norway Point and the family surname), *El-Mar* (named after his parents, George Elmer and Martha Louise) and the *B-4*. In addition to his motorboats, Leslie enjoyed various recreations, including badminton and, in particular, sailing. As commodore of the Lake of Bays Regatta Association, he encouraged sailing among cottagers, who vied annually for the prized Leslie-Byrnes Trophy, the J.N. Dalley Cup, the Norway Point Dinghy Trophy and the Bigwin Sailing Trophy.

Though many people enjoyed Leslie's hospitality at both his residence and the Inn, vacancies at the island hotel grew to an unprecedented number. During this era, Bigwin was still the biggest and most expensive of summer resorts, but its once coveted reputation was overshadowed by senescent facilities and a weakened Ontario tourist industry. Despite a decline in his health, Leslie continued to maintain a presence at the Inn until he broke his hip. This injury, and his failing health in general, eventually led him to sell the resort. Two years after his death in July 1969, the Glenmount Hotel property and the cottage on Norway Point were also sold.

During the 1960s, Bigwin passed into the hands of JAL Corporation the letters being the initials of Joseph Anthony Lobraico, the father of Paul Andre Lobraico. Bigwin had paled considerably from its original 1920 stature, and the new owners faced substantial investments to resuscitate the resort's patronage and to restore financial well-being. Their diligent endeavours to achieve this were typified by the concentration of approximately $350,000 on basic capital improvements to guest facilities. Simultaneously, the staff camps were abandoned and employee housing consolidated on the lodges' seldom-used third floors. In order to facilitate business, in 1964 the newly formed Lake of Bays Sailing Club office was housed in a room of the dining complex. In another attempt to attract people to the Inn, a suggestion was made to build a bridge that would connect the island to the mainland, but fatefully the request was denied.

While every possibility was explored and every effort made to promote business, poor weather, the level of vacancies at many Muskoka resorts, and the enormous operating budget of Bigwin itself took their toll. Worsening the situation was "the maturing of certain short-term mortgage and loan commitments which compounded the working capital shortage, exhausting the book profit with fixed principal payments."

Though the financial picture continued to darken, a bright spot in the twilight was sustained by the Saturday evening supper dances held in the dining room or, as it was coined at the time, the "Sumaro." These dances remained popular and continued to draw large numbers of cottagers from the surrounding areas. Docking facilities at the Inn were often so inundated with watercraft that boats had to be tied side by side, four or five vessels deep.

On one such evening, visiting cottagers borrowed the Lobraicos' beautifully kept Shepherd boat *Rum Runner* for their return home. But disaster awaited the splendid vessel. Just beyond the west shore of Bigwin Island, as the orange glow of lights from the Inn fell from sight, the mahogany vessel ran aground on a shoal of jagged rocks. Fortunately, no lives were lost in the accident. As pitch darkness gave way to a misty dawn, Paul and Sandra Lobraico took the hotel's 41-foot steel tugboat *Big Chief* to the forlorn wreck. Shortly after salvage, the ravaged *Rum Runner* was sold. The hotel soon faced a similar sad fate. In 1966 Bigwin was again for sale, this time for a reported $1,800,000.

Newspaper articles headlined the November 22nd auction of Bigwin Inn, which took place in a salon of the Lord Simcoe Hotel in Toronto. Arthur Roberts, president of Maynards Industries Auctioneers Limited, indicated a reserve bid of $600,000 for the resort, mainland docks, 18-hole golf course, diesel tugboat, ferry, 45-foot barge, and what was left of the island's beautiful waterfront lots. Maurice East, president of Muskoka Sands Resort, gave favourable commentary on the potential for convention trade at Bigwin and of the real estate value of the waterfront lots, which were estimated to be worth $30 a lake frontage foot. General figures made available included Bigwin's "auction value of 1.2 million dollars, replacement value at 3.6 million dollars and present value of 1.8 million dollars." Also available in the dossier were the financial profiles of the Bigwin Inn Company Limited. "In 1964 and 1965, profits were at $21,710 and $56,657 respectively. On October 31, 1965 deficit position of Bigwin was at $216,716. Bigwin's gross sales had hit an all time high in 1948 at $540,000, a low in 1961 at $99,000 and in 1965 were $532,000." From a mixed crowd of about 50 people, only 3 appeared to be serious bidders. With bids falling $250,000 short of the reserve, the auction was closed to the general public. However, various publications stated that negotiations continued with the sellers, Trusco, who were exercising power of sale provisions under the Mortgage Act.

On June 9, 1967, Paul Lobraico formally resigned as postmaster of the Inn, transferring the position to Gregory Lambert, who stayed on as the new president with Bigwin's new owners, Baywin Investments Limited and Baysville Investments Limited. With the change in ownership, the resort also became known as "Bigwin Island Hotel — Bigwin

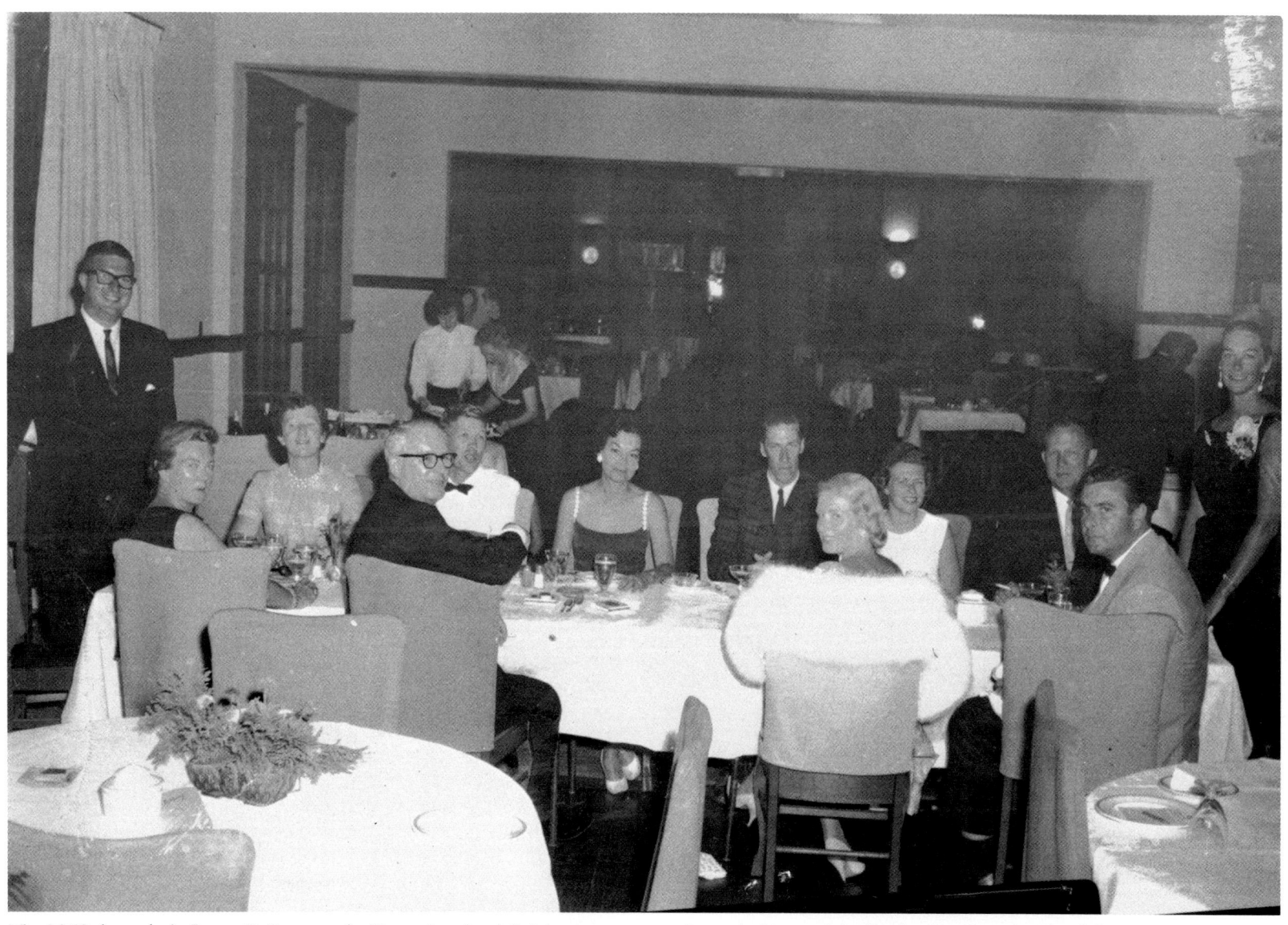

The 1960s brought in Lester B. Pearson, the Kennedys, the civil rights movement, colour television and the Beatles. Despite a decade of change, Saturday-evening supper dances at Bigwin remained a popular tradition in Muskoka. Paul and Sandra Lobraico (far left and far right respectively) host one of their summer dinner parties in the Marine Dining Room.

- *Sandra Horkins*

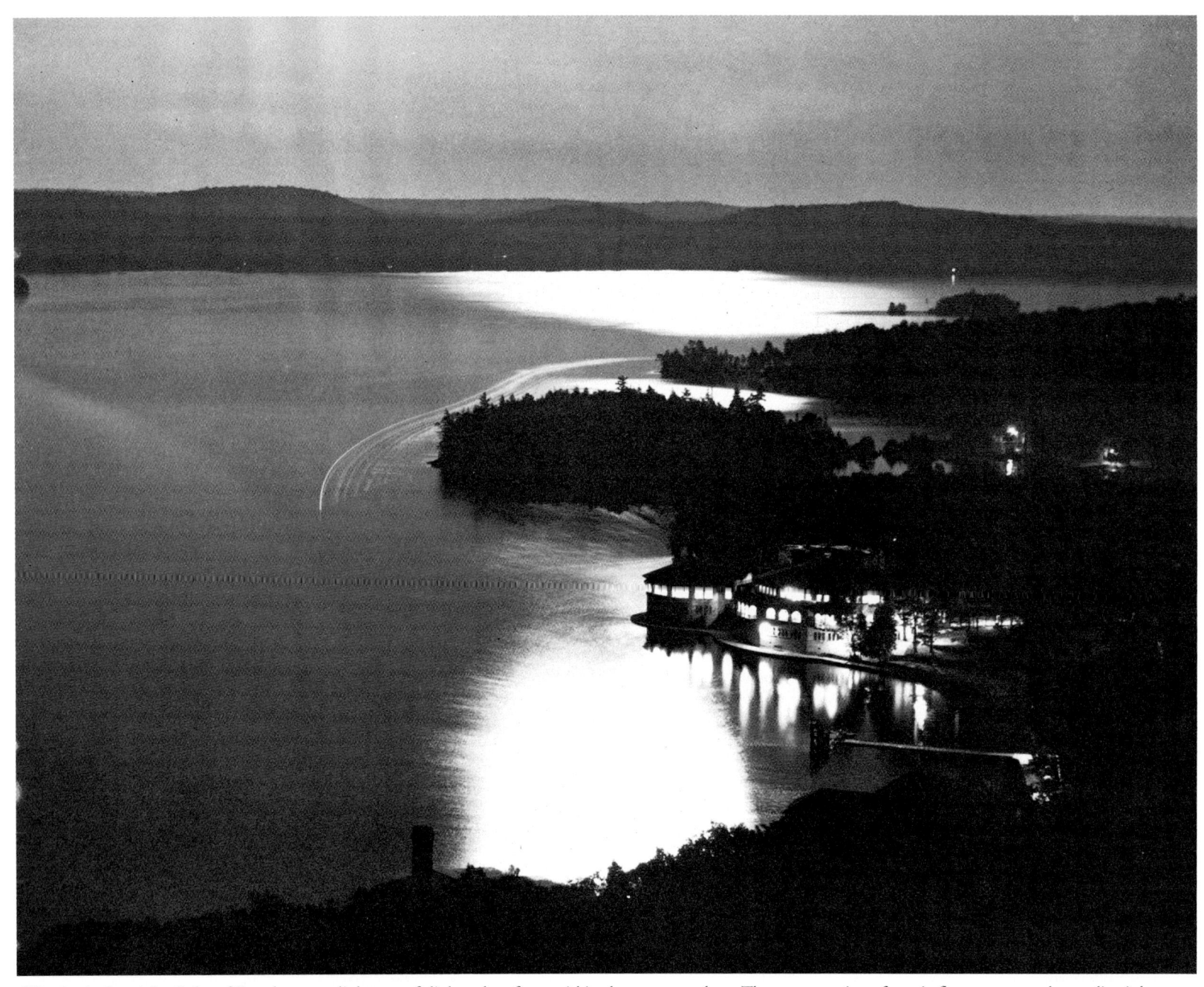

"Tender is the night. Lake of Bays by moonlight — soft lights glow from within the summer place. The sweet strains of music float out over the starlit night, gaiety, happiness and romance abound at Bigwin Inn."
- *Frank Mills Leslie*

Island Golf and Country Club." Because of the poor publicity previously attracted to the resort through the uncertainty of the hotel's continued operation, Bigwin's reputation and loyal patronage suffered an almost fatal blow. In an attempt to restore a reliable clientele, expenditures were made to renovate the facilities which had continued to fade from their original splendour.

In 1968 tons of machinery and dynamite were brought to the island and construction of a 3,000 foot licensed airstrip commenced. Fifteen-dollar shuttle flights from Toronto were to land on the strip after their 135-mile, 30-minute journey. Other features added to the resort included a paging and background music system, new golf course tees and a discotheque in the Rotunda (the first in a Muskoka hotel).

While the renovation project seemed an excellent idea at the time, it ultimately proved to be financially overwhelming. A letter from the hotel's president, Gregory Brian Lambert, dated October 25, 1968, summarized the position of the project and the turn that it would soon take:

"During the past summer the added participation of cottagers in our activities, plus a remarkable upsurge in the number of visiting guests and conventions, resulted in an overall increase in business of 35% over 1967. This is truly encouraging and extremely satisfying to the senior staff responsible for the operation.

"Of major concern, however, is the vast size of the complex, and the continual expenditures required to keep the facilities acceptable to both potential guests and lake visitors. In 1967, approximately $50,000 was invested towards capital improvements, the majority of which are not visible to visitors. In 1968, we once again expended a large amount of capital on improvements of observable types. This figure, yet to be finalized, is approximately $65,000. Operationally the resort is profitable, and certainly an increased number of pleased guests and lake visitors commented on their general satisfaction.

"It is with regret, however, that we have decided — due to the lack of sufficient capital to continue the renovation programme — to discontinue the operation of the hotel. It has been decided to sell the buildings and their contents if possible, and we feel that the first opportunity and advice of this pending sale should be given to the residents on the lake. Several satisfied lake residents have suggested the possibility of a syndicate being formed by interested parties on the Lake of Bays. The suggested price for the hotel operation is $200,000 and this amount is realizable if forty people were all to contribute $5,000 apiece. A syndicate of this nature would certainly ensure the continued operation of Bigwin, and avail its facilities to the Lake of Bays residents and the Lake of Bays Association as it has done for so many years in the past. Terms would certainly be made available to provide this syndicate every opportunity to benefit from the participation in this venture." In November 1968, Gregory Lambert resigned from Baysville and Baywin Investments, advising that all company records were to be handled by Roger William Morris, barrister and solicitor of Trusco Investments Limited.

With transfer of ownership to Pontercove Realty and subsequently to Bigisle Enterprises Limited, major changes were made to the resort in accordance with a new business plan and estimated million-dollar renovation budget. Bigisle planned to promote Bigwin as a year-round vacation paradise, and the resort soon became widely known as "Bigwin Estates." Various documents, newspapers and magazines, named 13 individuals linked to the project. *Engineering and Construction* noted: "The resort is being operated by Bigisle Enterprises Limited. Thirteen investors plan to spend $1 million on the resort. They include Aldo Lorenzetti, President of Catkey Construction Limited; H.J. Scheckenberger, Vice-President of Ekistics Consultants Limited; Sidney MacMurray, President of Trend Flooring and Supplies Limited and Angelo Del Zotto, President of Del Zotto Enterprises Limited." *Daily Commercial News* also noted: "Shareholders in the Bigisle group are: . . .Terrence E. O'Neill, member of the law firm O'Neill, Browning and O'Neill. . . other members are: R.P. Bratty, member of the law firm of Gambin, Bratty, Chiappetta, Morassuitti and Caruso; Emilio Valentini, President of Valentine Enterprises contracting; Joseph Zentil, President of Joe Zentil Plumbing and Heating Limited; Louis Sherkin, Restaurateur; Vince Paul, Chartered Accountant; Jack Stott, President of Bulk-Lift Systems Limited; Gregory Lambert, Hotel Manager and James Ponzo, Realtor."

The new owners recognized that times had changed dramatically in the almost 50 years since the resort's grand opening of 1920, and like previous owners, they too made alterations in an attempt to breathe new life into the property. One of the investors, H.J. Scheckenberger, was quoted as saying, "Our plan is to turn the 600-acre island into a year-round resort with a golf course, swimming pool and skiing. One of our aims in this development is to retain the natural character of the area." Given consideration for future development was the rebuilding of the golf course, an 880-foot bridge to the mainland, three ski slopes with T-bars, and snowmobiling facilities.

Under the conditions of the Condominium Act of 1967, renovations began in the East Lodge in the spring of 1969. With over $450,000 earmarked for Muskoka's first condominium project, the hotel rooms of the East Lodge were transformed by a crew of 80 workmen into a series of self-contained units complete with living room, bedroom(s), bathroom and kitchenette. The units were marketed at approximately $7,000 and $17,500 each, depending on size, with all facilities of the hotel being available with the purchase of family membership. The West Lodge was subsequently stripped for transformation into luxurious tri-level condominiums and new facilities for transient hotel guests were discussed. In early August 1969, 21 days after scheduled occupancy, advertisements noted that many of the East Lodge units were still available.

While the condominium concept seemed an excellent one at the time, it failed to come to fruition, with renovations soon grinding to a halt. The East Lodge (set aside as a separate property from the resort property) was completed and eventually occupied by condominium owners, but tragically the beautiful West Lodge was left unfinished and abandoned. Most of the resort's accoutrements were auctioned on July 24, 1970, and the other buildings, swimming pool and golf course were closed, although the Tea House was run privately as a restaurant and open to island visitors as late as the summer of 1976.

The years ahead would prove to be darkly disappointing for what was once North America's finest and most luxurious summer resort. While countless people faithfully awaited its resurrection under new ownership, renovations of the resort property's buildings were never resumed. The doors of the beautiful island Inn remained closed to the public through financial gymnastics in the early 'eighties. In that time Canadian newspapers headlined the controversial happenings behind the Ontario government's takeover of Crown, Greymac and Seaway Trust companies. Caught in the limelight was a man named William Player of Elmvale, Ontario. According to the book *Public Money Private Greed*, Player was alleged to have conspired with individuals at Greymac Credit Corporation and Seaway Trust Company to "flip" 11,000 apartments purchased for approximately $270-million from Cadillac Fairview Corporation Limited. Those apartments were quickly resold to Player's Kilderkin Investments Limited for roughly $312.5-million. Within a few hours, the units were resold for $500-million to 50 numbered companies allegedly controlled by unnamed Arab investors. Partial financing of the deal was said to come from Greymac Trust and Seaway Trust companies. *Public Money Private Greed* noted that of Seaway Trust's 92.7-million in outstanding mortgages in 1981, approximately $25-million to $30-million was believed to be related to Player with roughly $2 million of that amount said to be tied to the stagnated re-development project on Bigwin Island. As the affair came to a boil, Player reportedly pleaded guilty to 35 counts of fraud and was subsequently handed the longest prison term for fraud in Canadian history.

By 1986, the resort property emerged from this affair in the hands of the Public Trustee complete with 191 acres, golf course, hotel buildings, landing strip, swimming pool, tennis courts and docks, and was listed for sale at $495,000 in Canadian funds with seasonal-residential zoning and deferred planning, while the mainland property was zoned tourist-commercial.

The outlook of the hotel property's future was somewhat brightened by new ownership in the late '80s. Local publications raised the profile of Bigwin in 1990, suggesting the possibility of new development around the perimeter of the island, interior lots, as well as potential rehabilitation of only a few of the historic buildings and the golf course. With a glimmer of optimism, they noted that development was restricted to existing uses by an interim by-law and that only limited expansion of those uses was permitted until various assessments (including engineering, biophysical, limnological, landscape, visual, land use and financial studies) were completed by Bigwin Resort and Development Corporation, R.A.P. Trading Corporation, the township and other interested parties.

CHAPTER 4

A Summer Place Revisited

In its glory days Bigwin Inn was the quintessence of elegance in Canadian summer places, attracting the greatest of entertainers and most glamorous of guests. While many of the country's grand hotels are now gone and forgotten, Bigwin valiantly stands as a rare microcosm of Canada's architectural, cultural and social heritage.

Today the hotel's monumental structures evoke great ambivalence. While the garages were dismantled long ago and the dilapidated clubhouse and staff camps only remotely resemble their former stature, most of the resort property's other buildings, the steamer *Bigwin*, the airstrip, the 18-hole golf course and the WaWa Hotel's waiting room miraculously survive like rare vestiges of a lost civilization. Although encrusted with a rich patina and stripped of many of their original appointments, they are in remarkable condition despite 20 years of assault by the relentless forces of nature, a lack of general maintenance and periodic bouts of vandalism. Linking Bigwin's glorious past to a possible restoration in the future is its relatively good condition today, its irreplaceable heritage value and its corresponding economic potential.

If the great legacy of Bigwin is to survive as testimony to an important part of the Canadian identity, the landmark demands immediate heritage designation, structural stabilization and protection against the implications of an ill-defined future.

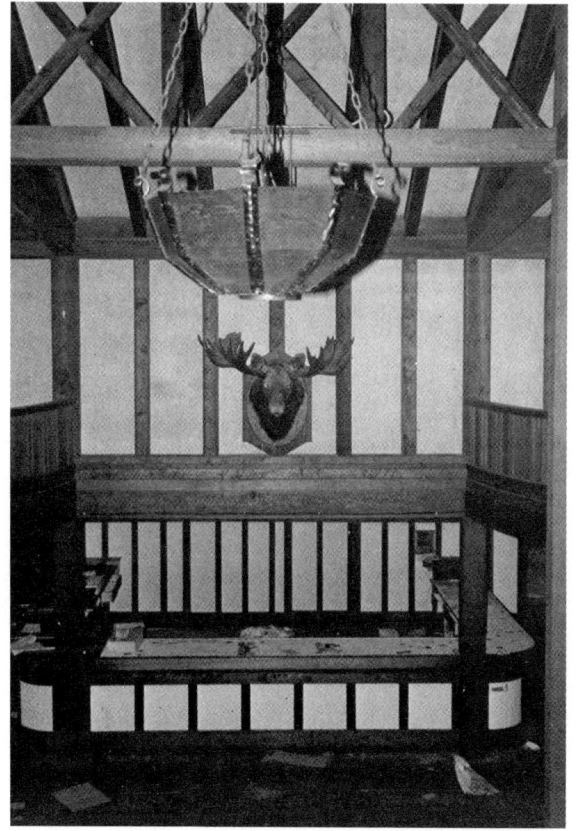

Bigwin Island is a spectacle of haunting beauty, a vestige of another era. The importance of the island's environmental heritage, the archaeological heritage of its First Nation burial grounds, the nautical heritage of the *Bigwin*, and the architectural heritage of the entire Bigwin Inn complex are undeniable.
- *DGM*

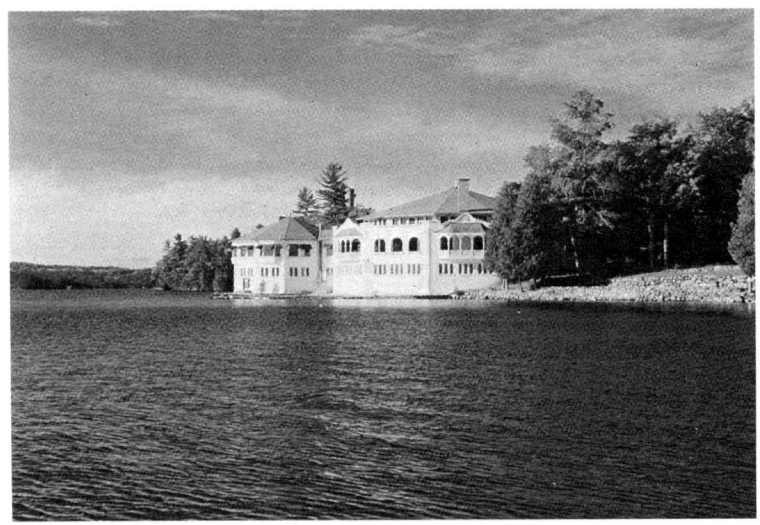
The solemn stillness of the Indian Head Room, Venetian Terrace, Marine Dining Room, Round Room, Canteen and Sun Deck.   *- DGM*

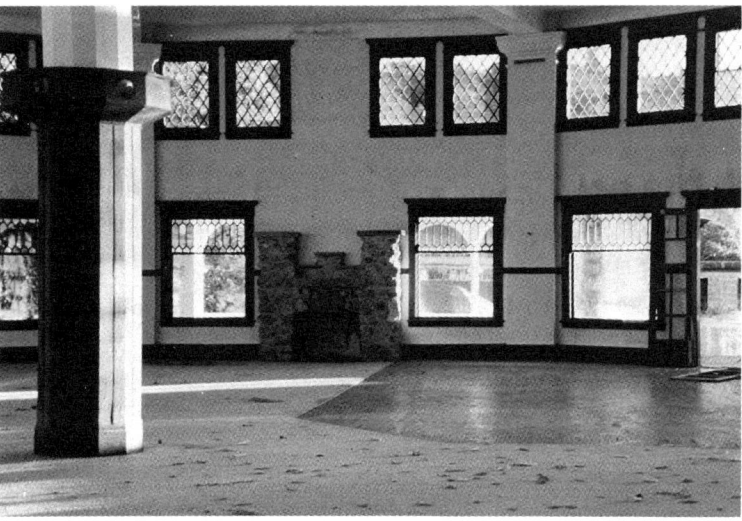
Sunlight still splashes across the Indian Head Room.   *- DGM*

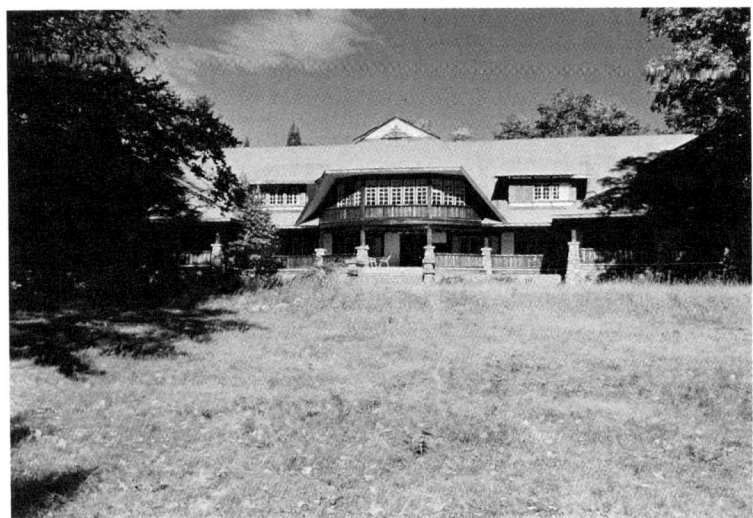
The Rotunda's lakeside façade and front lawn.   *- DGM*

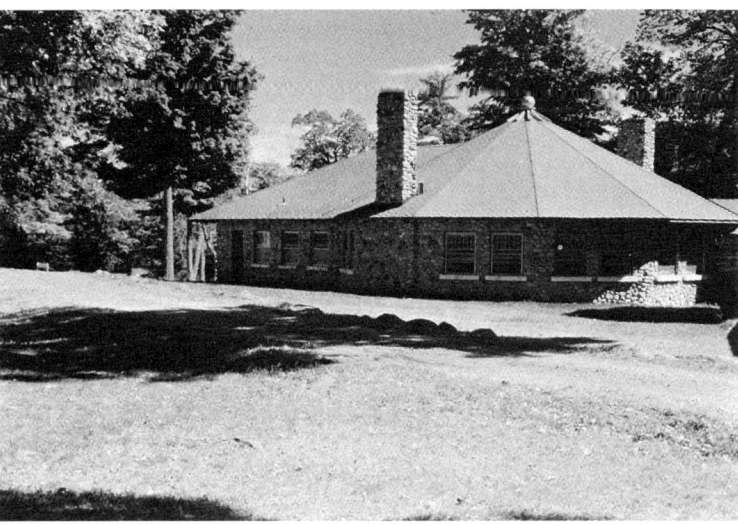
The northwest façade of the Tea House, a vestige of a bygone era.   *- DGM*

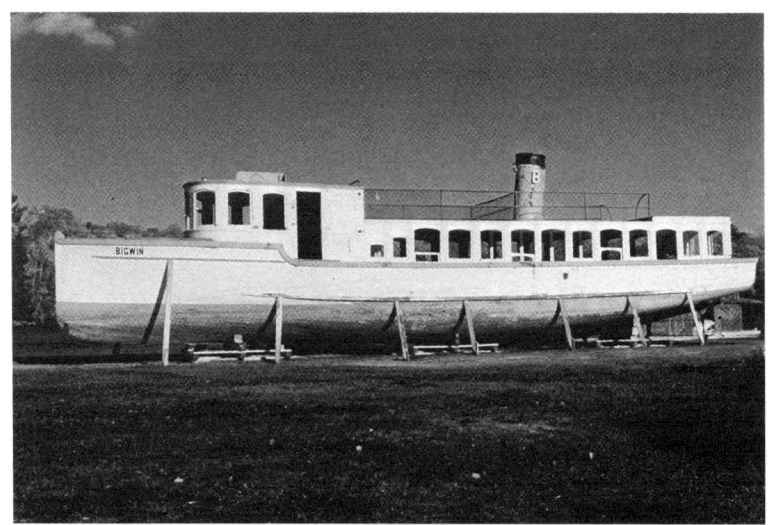

In a rare state of preservation, the ferry *Bigwin*, is an important part of Canada's nautical heritage. *- DGM*

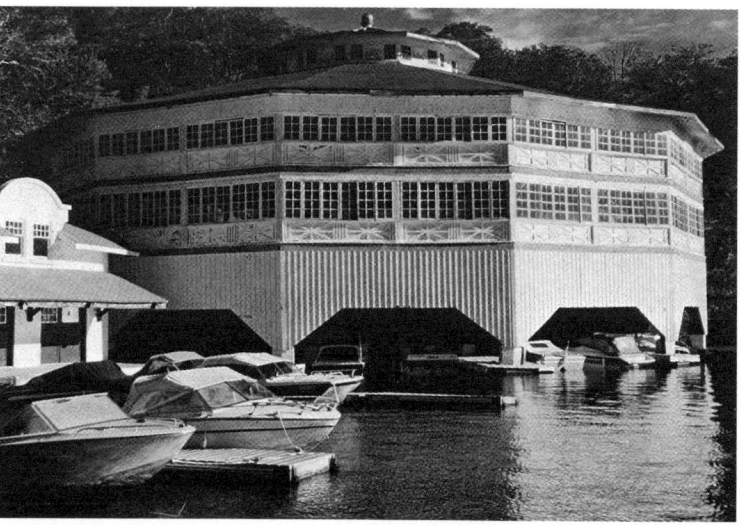

The Bigwin Boat Livery and Pavilion, important threads in the tapestry of Canada's architectural heritage. *- DGM*

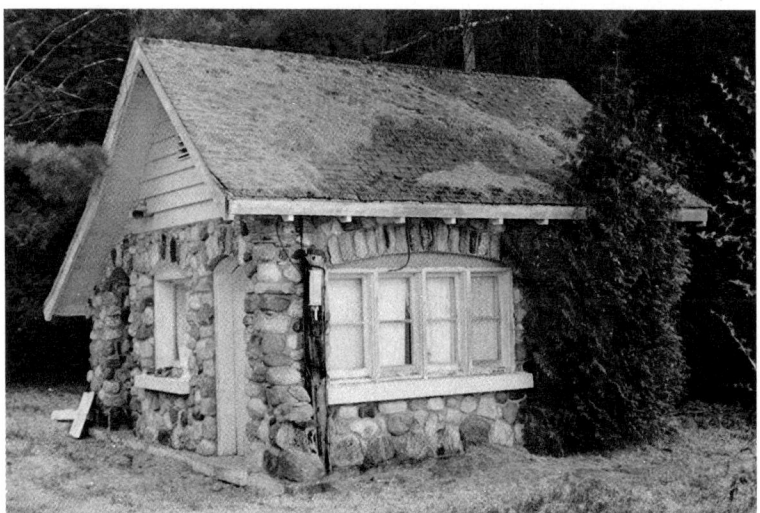

The Valet Cottage at the Norway Point wharf embodies the grace and charm of another era. *- DGM*

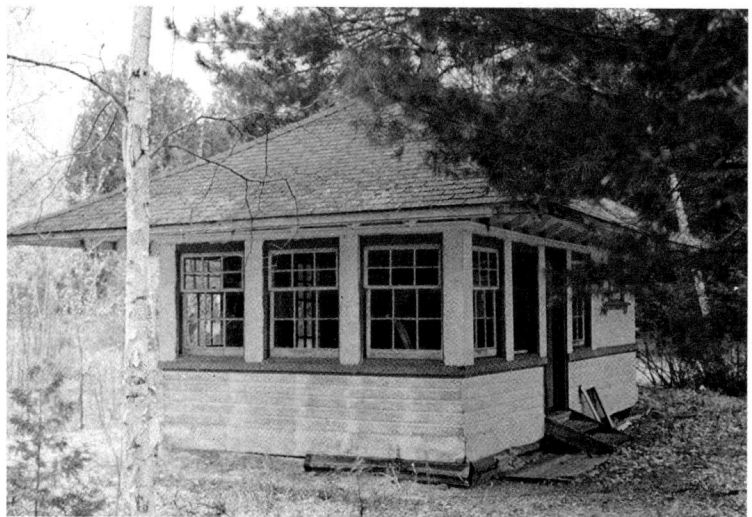

At Norway Point, the Waiting Room of the WaWa Hotel survives as a remnant of Muskoka's grand frame hotels. *- DGM*

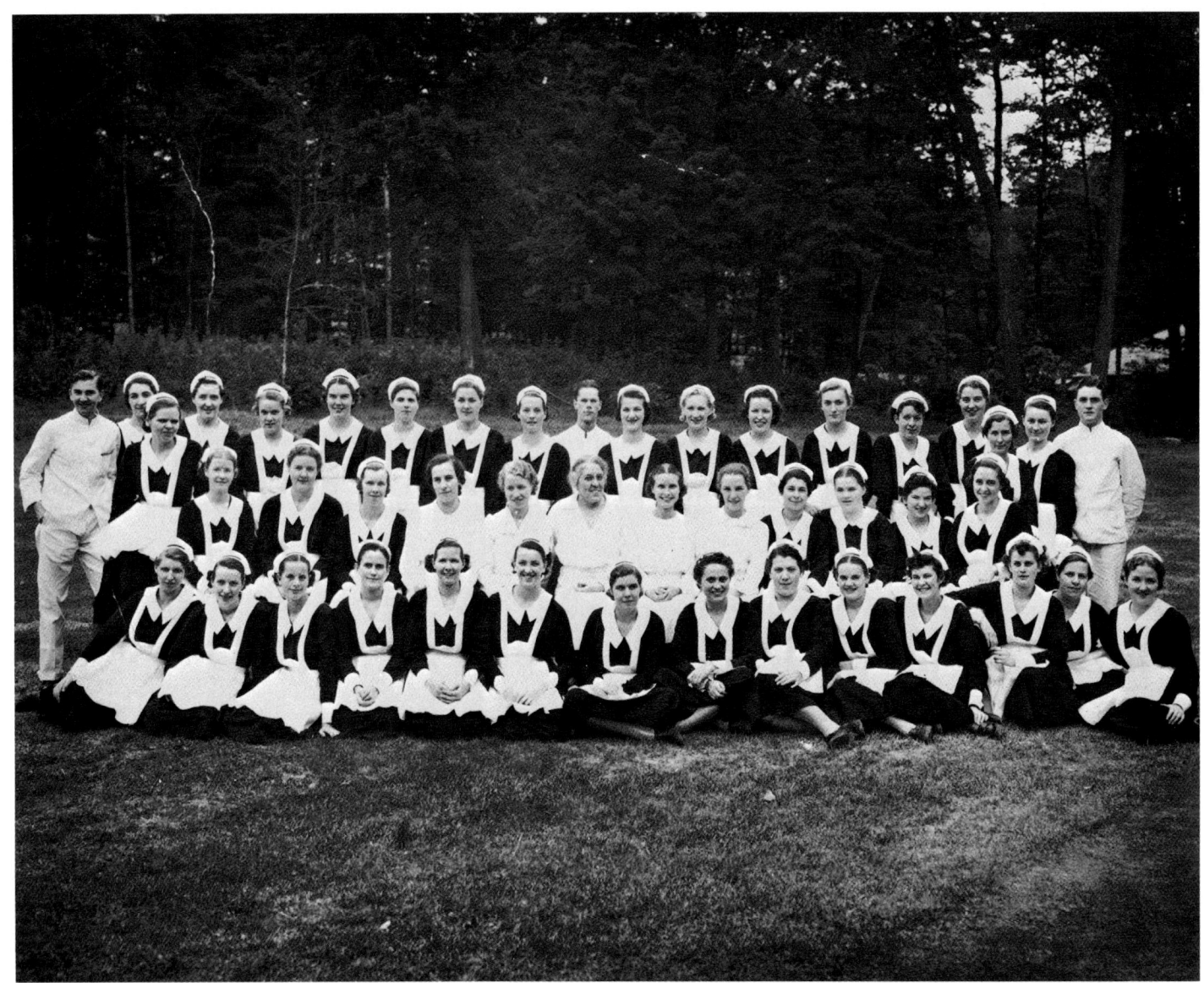

Pictured are some of the dining-room staff from the Shaw era. Cecilia Kieswetter (seated in the middle row, sixth from the left) was the dining-room hostess for many years and is well remembered among former resort personnel. Having the summer off from study at Lawrence Park Collegiate, Lois Maxwell waitressed at Bigwin. While serving the table of a family from New Jersey, she struck up a friendship with the family's young girl. During the family's stay, Ms. Maxwell often spent the afternoons swimming with her new friend. As a token of their friendship, the American girl gave Ms. Maxwell a pair of maroon moccasins. Uncomfortable with the notion of a waitress socializing with a guest, Ms. Kieswetter disciplined Ms. Maxwell, but Ms. Maxwell and the young American girl continued their friendship. Ms. Maxwell later went on to join the Canadian Women's Army Corps. She is well known to many for her recurring role as Miss Moneypenny in the series of James Bond film classics. Today, she is a columnist for the Toronto *Sun*.

- *Marye G. Sefl*

Staff Lists

In the decades of its operation, Bigwin Inn accommodated thousands of guests and countless employees served the resort. Because hundreds of people staffed the hotel each season for 50 years, it is impossible to list all the names of former employees, for few records survive. Many of the existing documents are badly damaged or barely legible. In assembling this staff list, names were included only if direct reference to them was found. Unfortunately, this method may exclude some from the compilation of names and may generalize the working periods of others. However, it is hoped that this incomplete list will serve to acknowledge many of the special people who brought Bigwin Inn to life.

THE 1920s
E.B. Ambrose
Al Baker
Alice B. Baker
A.H. Ballard
Charles Bandoux
Sidney Bates
J. Herbert Batten
K.R. Baxter
Gus Braido
T.E. Brennand
Harold Briggs
Nellie Bruce
D. Budreau
Edith B. Caan
W. Newcomb Calyer
J. Cameron
R.H.S. Cameron
Mrs. R.M. Campbell
Edwin J. Carter Jr.
H. Chisolm
Winnifred Coker
C.W. Colledge
Ada M. Collins
Isaac B. Collins
J.V. Cooper
Mary Cullon
Jean Dale
Walter E. Dauk
Marsh Davidson
Edward Devon
Jackson Allen Dinsmore
G.N. Doble
E. Harvey Doney
Violet Douglas
Frank L. Dow
Catherine Duncan
Evelyn Dyer
Helen Ellis
Charlie Evans
J.C. Evans
K.M. Farlenger
Joseph Del Ferrio
Dr. E.M. Fisher
Elmer H. Forbes
Mrs. Elmer Hart Forbes
Frank Ford
Lorraine Ford
Samuel Forsythe
Mae Fraser
Bruce Frelton
Howard Friedriche
Eva C. Gale
Helen Gibson
Rose Gibson
Dorothy Gilbert
"Gertie" Graham
W. Graham
Murray Gris
Bertran Haigh
Kathleen Halloway
Alice Hambly
John P. Hanna
Flora Harding
Eleanor Harkness
Mrs. Jess M. Harris
Edna A. Harvie
J.K. Hawes
Jack Herald
Robert Horton
Mary S. Howard
Bess Hubbell
Grace Hubbeth
May Ireland
Helen M. Irwin
William Keating
Chris Kellock
James Kellock
Cecilia Kieswetter
C. Krieger
R.W. Krusern
Margaret Laidman
Deny Lesenko
W. Lockwood
George J. Lomas
Mrs. J.S. Lomas
J.E. Long
Alvin E. Luck
Frances H. MacCallum
J. Lorne MacDougall
Harry Mahony
Walter E. Mann
Eunice Louise Marhause
Frances Marr
L.W. McConkey
Richard A. McConnel
George McCracken
W.A. McFairsh
A. McInerney
Bob McIntyre
Martha W. McKee
Ralph D. McNally
Jerome McNamee
Joseph McNamee
John McNance
Norman McNeely
W.A. McTavish
Gertrude Milliken
Olea M. Montgomery
Fred C. Moore
Eunice Moorhouse
Ross Murison
Ed Murphy
Ted Musgrave
James Nichols
Frances Noble
Helen Olmer
Molly Parker
Margaret Peckenaw
Marjorie M. Pinder
Chuck Power
S. Railton
Charlotte Rapley
Duncan M. Reid
James Reid
Al Remley
William Rennand
Maisie Renshaw
Iona M. Richardson
Henry Richmond
Robert C. Riley
William Robinson
William Rodger
Robert Roley
Max Schellner
Mildred Schultz
Jack Scott
J. Allan Scott
Marge Scott
R.E. Clark Scott
George Simmons
Hunter Singer
Flora Slater
Dorothy M. Smale
J. Kenneth Smale
R. Blake Smale
C. Smith
Phyllis Smith
W.J. Smith
Fellman Snell
Ida Southall
Franklin Spearn
Roy C. Spooner
Marg Strachan
Ruth Suggitt
V. Suggitt
Dorothy S. Sullivan
Elizabeth Sullivan
Eric Tattersall
Arthur Thomas
F.E. Thomas
Margaret Tough
Donald Tow
Clarence Trimble
Gordon Tutty

Jack Tutty
G.S. Varcoe
Stewart Vincent
Mary Watson
Ruth E. Watson
Walter Welsman
A. Whel
C.A. "Doc" White
Eileen R. White
Glad E. Wiggins
Lorena Wiggins
John Wilson
M. Wilson
Roger A. Wilson
Jean Woods
Margery E. Woods
Alfred E. Wright
Isadore P. Young

The 1930s
Isobel Anderson
Margaret Anderson
Mary Beattie
Norma Bidwell
Louis Braida
Robert Brennand
Cliff Burnet
Betty Burnt
Tom Burry
R. Cameron
Reg Cameron
Ted Cameron
Dorothy Chapman
Charles Cherrier
Wes Clare
Dot Coulter
Bob Cowan
Bill Cowhue
Bill Cross
Frank Cross
Harry Culley
C.H. Curter
Jack Dawkins
Mary Dean
Harry R. Donald

Jack W. Donald
Bob Dorsey
Frank Dracup
Onie Dupre
Wm.H. Elder
Buck Evans
J. Douglas Ferguson
Ed Field
Grace File
Gordon Foster
Campbell Graham
William Carroll Grant
L.M. Gray
Ernest Griffith
Harold Guilfoyle
Ben Guyatt
Jean Hall
W. Gordon Hanna
Del Harwood
Esme Houghton
Helen Irvine
Dorothy Jobbins
Bert J. Jones
Fred Keb
Betty Kettles
John Kettles
Betty Keys
George Kiash
Florence King
Robert King
William Lake
Harry Landon
Ted Lawson
Frank Lobraico
Gladys M. Loets
F. Long
Beth Mader
H.L. Main
Jessie Marlia
Jack Martin
Elizabeth Massie
Molly Maw
Dick McCallum
Johan McInnes
Dinny McKay

John McKee
Alma McKenna
Ross McNiece
Dorothy McTavish
Irene Miller
J. Moogk
W.J. Mooney
D.A. Moore
M. Morden
Isabel Morris
W. Morris
H. Mount
George Munroe
Frank Murray
Elizabeth Myers
Arthur Neve
Henry Orb
Marion J. Orr
R.D. Oxford
William Paul
Harold Percival
John Perouds
John "Jocko" Pesando
Joyce Plumtree
Hilda Pratt
Fred Preston
Margaret Reid
R. Richardson
Charles Rober
Bill Rodgers
Robert Rogers
Harry Ross
Therese Ruly
Jack Scott
Marie Shannion
Jack Sim
Roy Skinner
Joe Slatt
Adelaide Smith
W.J. Smith
Helen Soine
Mart Stapleton
Earl W. Stephens
Leola Stephens
Dorothy Sullivan

Marjorie Thompson
H. Tossack
Vivienne Van Huson
Bill Waddell
Michael Wain
Esther Wallace
Ernest Wells
Jack Whitehead
William Whitehouse
John Wilson
R. Wilson
Ralph Young

The 1940s
A. Agnelli
Donald Aldcorn
Harry Blackmore
P.H. Borridale
Don Burke
Catharine Carson
E. Casen
Gregory J. Clark
Dunc Coates
Ada M. Collins
Ruth Conway
Clarence Couston
Angus Crawford
Donald Crawford
Don Currie
Peter Currie
A. Davidson
Connie Dawson
Mrs. Dowell
John Duff
Allan Elhaith
George Elliott
Earl Fairbanks
Hugh Forsythe
Paul W. Fox
Alfred Franchi
Frank Gough
Cameron Gray
Miss Griffith
Miss Guthrie
F.J. Hall

J. Hawkins
S. Hisey
W.L. Hiesey
Morley Hodgins
John Honsberger
James How
David Humphries
Ernie Irvine
Frank J. Irving
Jean E. Jackson
Sam Johnson
Marg Jones
Bill Jordan
Kaspar
Cecilia Kieswetter
Ray Kimble
Jessie King
Pierre Kushnier
Amy Lawson
Mrs. Macintosh
Frank Mastermack
Lois Maxwell
S. Mayor
George McCartney
Dr. McDonald
Mrs. McDonald
Miss McFarline
John McKee
Captain McLean
Dorothy McTavish
Douglas Mills
Miss Parks
John Pesando
Mario Pesando
Jean Phillips
Don Platt
Ed Platt
Hugh Platt
Cecil Preston
Ann Reid
Marie Rose Reid
Peter Ridout
Philip Ryan
Donald Shaw
Peter Simmons

134

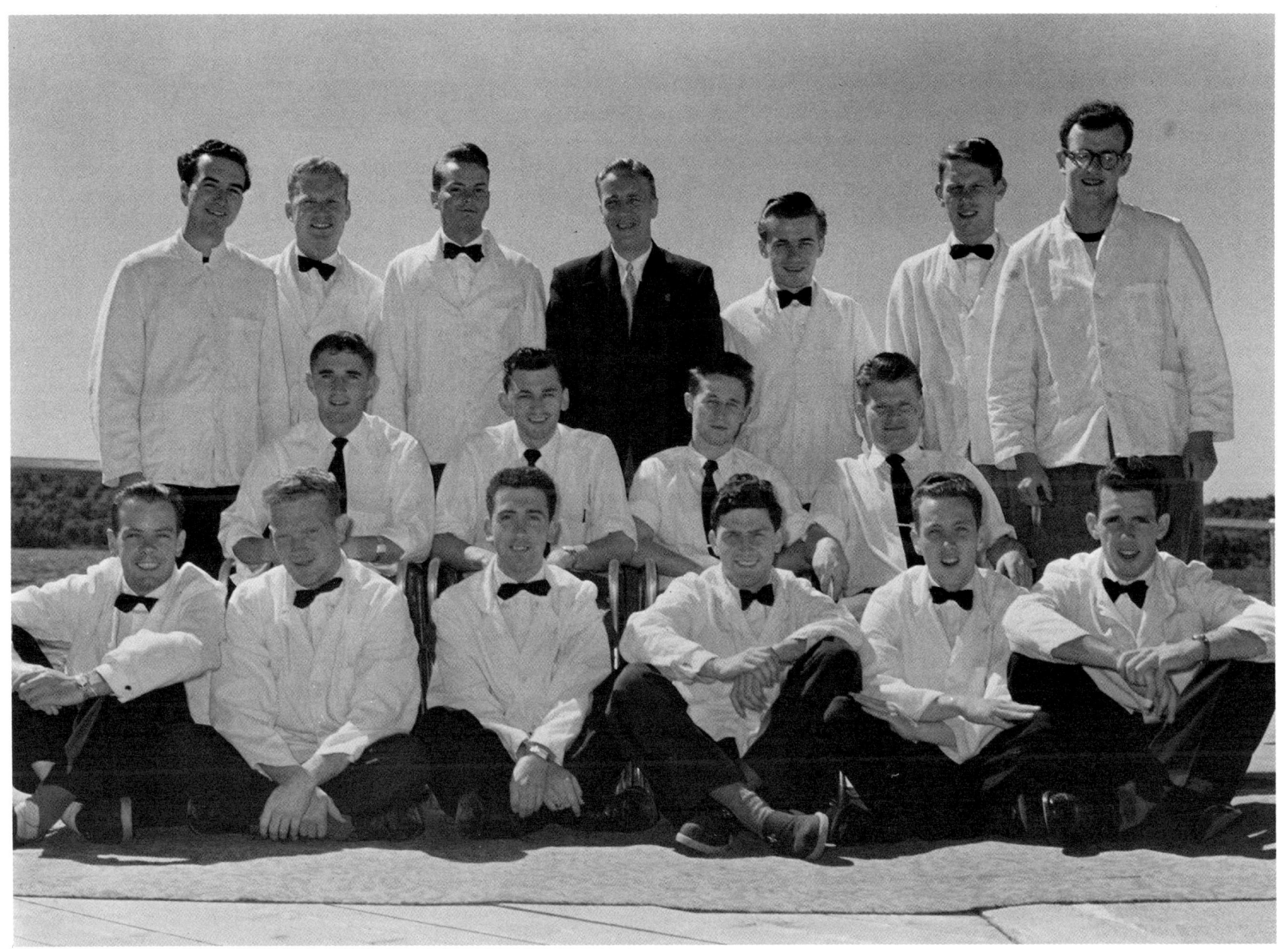

Round Room staff from the 1950s.

- *Donald J. Donahue*

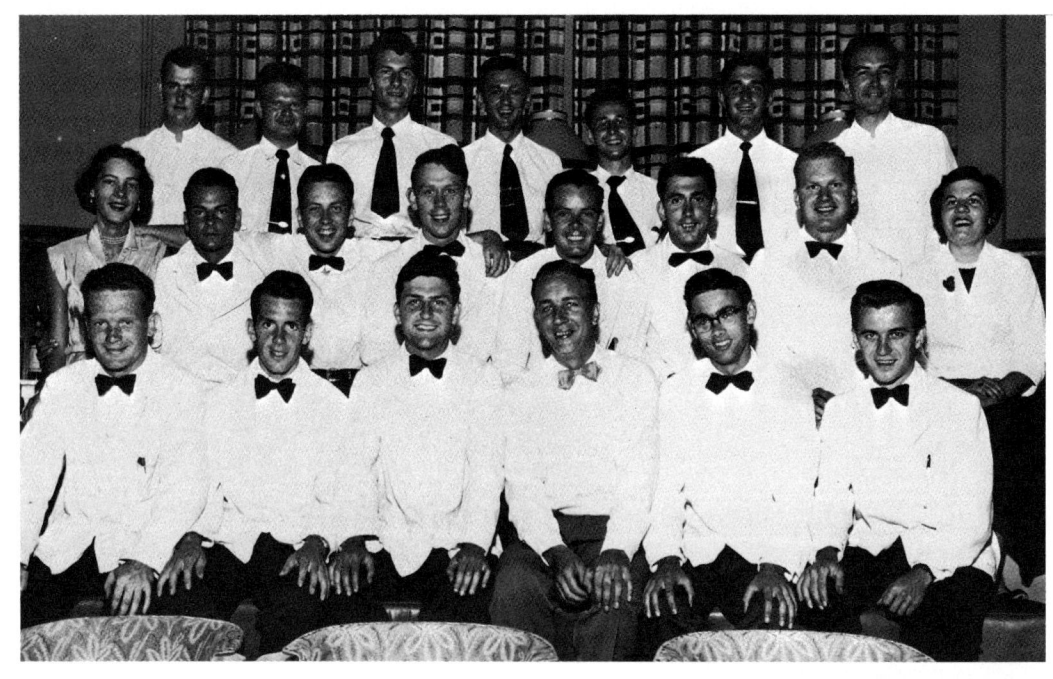

Round Room staff from the 1950s. - *Donald J. Donahue*

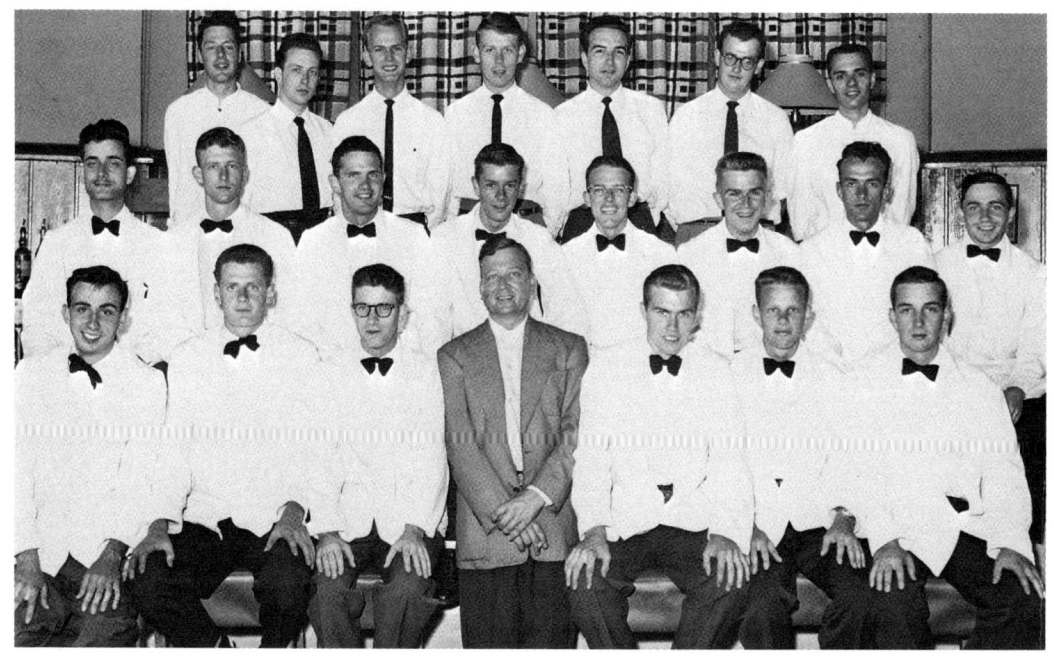

Harry Somers
Reg Stott
Sam Thompson
Frank Tufts
E. Vancleaf
W.R. Vanloon
Mr. Veal
H. Vernon
Steve Voytch
Stuart Waddell
Mike Wain
Allan Webster
Murray Whan
Charlie Winter
Nestor Wookey
Charlotte Wright

The 1950s
Anne Adams
C. Black
Bill Burrows
John R. Campbell
Don Carroll
Hugh B. Croxton
Alex Davidson
Hillel Diamond
Donald J. Donahue
M. Duschene
Roger Earl
John Ellis
Joan Giddings
June Giddings
Bill Gilchrist
David Gilmor
Enid Hampshire
David Harris
Frank Harris
Peter Harris
Charles Helmsing
G. Holloway
Mike Homenylo
Margaret Kirby
Fred Ladley
Gordon B. Langille
Tom Lawson

John Leishman
B. Manion
B. Martin
Jack Martin
N. Merkle
Donald Mooney
Saunders Moore
Robert Murdock
Ross Murray
Douglas Neill
E. Potts
D. Seagram
Bob Smith
Bob Sutherland
Tommy Thomas
Captain William Tinkiss
James Torrence
Norm Wells
Peter Widderington
Bob Woods
Ed Wrodland

The 1960s
Mrs. C. Aitcheson
Norman Allen
Sydney Allen
Ann Armstrong
Richard Auger
Joseph Barrette
Mel Barrick
Henry Bassols
L.P. Beers
Philip Bellavance
Edward Belobaba
Daniel Bluteau
Jean-Guy Bluteau
Nicholas Bodnaruk
Peter Boswell
Peter Bouffard
Bruce Brown
Jack Budd
Robert Buller
Bob Bulloch
Ruth Burgess
Colleen Burk

Claire Callaghan
Faye Campbell
Chuen Chen
Carol Clark
Serge Colekessian
Eric Conroy
Patricia Corcoran
David Courtney
H. Dafoe
Louise Daigle
Yvonne Daigle
Heather Daynard
Anna Di Cienzo
David Dime
Jamie Dorian
Denis Dumont
Allan Eddy
Patricia Elliott
Carole Fischer
Ms. Ford
Richard Fournier
John Francis
D. Frieschlag
Jacques Gaudreau
Rene Gauthier
Judith Goodhue
I. Hailwood
L. Hall
Francis Harkness
Ms. Hart
John Herold
Robert Heyes
Clive Hobson
Elaine Hope
Barry Howard
Michael Howard
Anthony Hui
Louise Irvine
Awadh Jaggernath
Thomas Jordan
Peter Kalman
Andrew Kandel
Gabor Kandel
David Kirsh
Margaret Kramer

Brian Laflamme
Beth Lalonde
Greg Lambert
Alexander Lee
Albert Li
Raymond Liu
Franz Loesgen
Jasmin Lovric
Ross MacFarlane
Carol Macleod
Patricia Mackie
Helen Mak
R. Mason
Deborah McBride
L. McBride
Michael McCarthy
Phil McCloy
James McCormick
Lynne McCrum
Paula McFarland
Mary McLaren
Linda Mickelson
Leo Mok
M. Munn
Georgina Murphy
Timothy Murphy
Jocelyne Murray
Keven Ng
William Osborne
Timothy Parker
Marc Paupe
Denis Paquin
T. Peters
Sandra Pollock
Lucy Richardson
Peter Roche
Bob Rogers
Brenda Roles
Ethel Royle
James Saar
Susan Sandford
Peter Saunders
Alison Scott
John Scott
Martha Scott

Eric Sellors
Donald Sheldon
Phil Shepherd
Leslie Sheppard
Wayne Sisson
Mr. Slater
James Slimmon
Neil Smith
Christine Snider
Gary Snider
Dane Sommerville
J. Stafford
Bob Stevens
Ann Stewart
Lindsay Strachan
Norma Sullivan
Che-Soo Tang
Douglas Tate
Robin Thomson
John Tollady
Jacquie Toop
J. Turner
Paul Uphill
Scott Wagner
Bill Walker
Deborah Watson
Donna-Lee Weber
Harry Weber
Henry Williams
Steve Williams
Joanne Wilson
Rick Wink
Barry Wood
Joshua Wu
Patricia Wylie
Thomas Yang

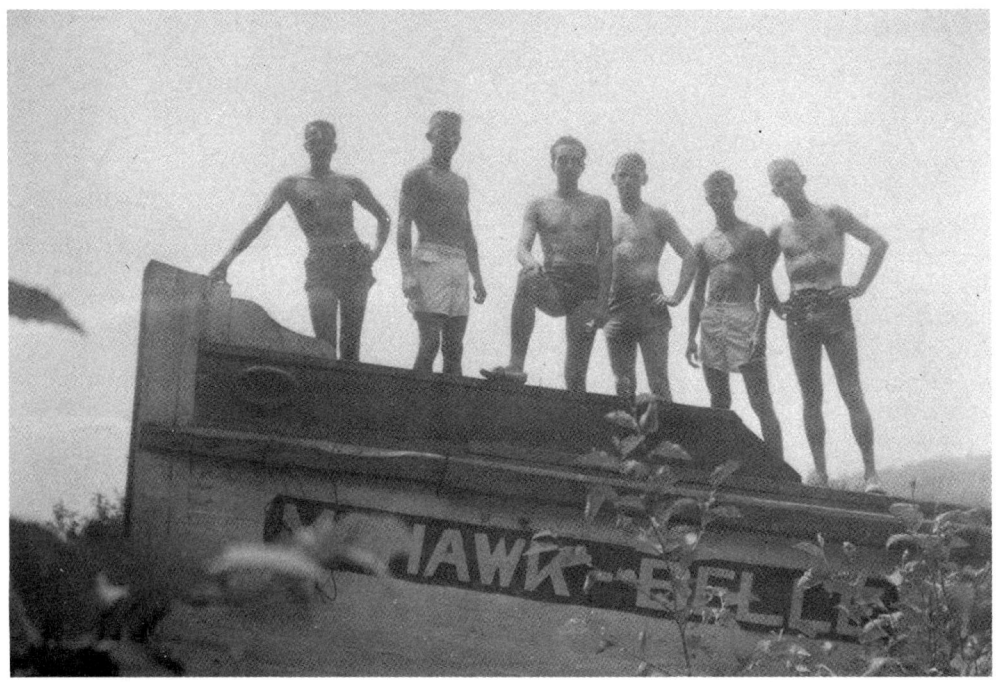

Between shifts, staff of the resort could often be found at the island's drydock, swimming off the wreck of the *Mohawk Belle*, circa 1953. — *Donald J. Donahue*

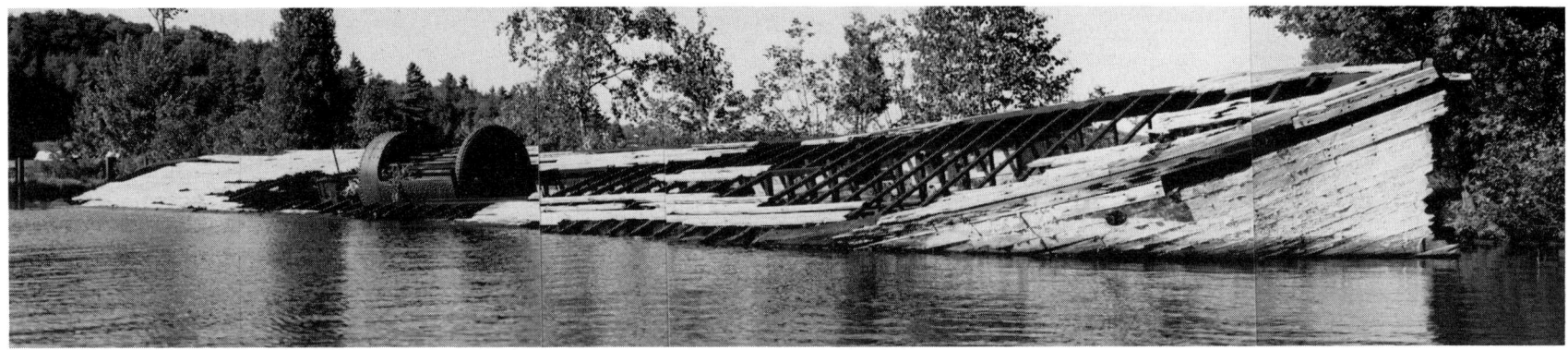

The wreck of the *Mohawk Belle*, 1991. — *DGM*

Bibliography

Audio and/or Visual Sources

Os-Ke-Non-Ton. Taped Recordings of "Happy Song," "Mohawk's Lullaby," "Tribal Prayer," "Every-Day Song" and "War Song."

Sparling, Gordon. *Pleasure Island*. Associated Screen News, 1936.

Wilson, John. Taped Conversations about Bigwin Inn. Brampton, 1990.

Newspapers

Bracebridge: The *Muskoka Sun*.

Huntsville: The *Huntsville Forester*.

Toronto: *Daily Commercial News*.

Toronto: The *Globe and Mail*.

Toronto: The *Toronto Star*.

Secondary Sources

Avery, Sydney. *Reflections, Muskoka and Lake of Bays Yesteryears*. Bracebridge: Herald Gazette Press, 1974.

Boyer, Barbaranne. *Muskoka's Grand Hotels*. Erin: The Boston Mills Press, 1987.

Conway, Abbott. *A History of Beardmore and Company Limited and Anglo Canadian Leather Company Limited*. Canada Packers Incorporated, 1990.

Corcoran, Terence, and Laura Reid. *Public Money Private Greed*. Toronto: Collins Publishers, 1984.

Findlay, Mary-Lynn. *Lures and Legends of the Lake of Bays*. Bracebridge: Herald-Gazette Press, 1973.

Fraser, Captain Levi R. *History of Muskoka*. Bracebridge, 1946.

MacKay, Niall. *By Steam Boat and Steam Train: The Huntsville and Lake of Bays Railway and Navigation Companies*. Erin: The Boston Mills Press, 1982.

Tatley, Richard. *The Steamboating Era in the Muskokas, Volume II — The Golden Years To Present*. Erin: The Boston Mills Press, 1984.

Terziano, Ed. *The "Little Town Band" That Grew and Grew*. Huntsville: Forester Press Limited, 1986.

Periodicals and Brochures

Engineering and Construction: Construction News. June 1969.

Lake of Bays: Highlands of Ontario. Grand Trunk Railway System, 1913.

Ontario Hydro News. "Bold New Beginning For Bigwin." July-August 1970.

Silver Anniversary: Bigwin Inn, Lake of Bays. Muskoka, 1944.

The Bigwin Inn. Brochures 1920-1970 inclusive.

Unpublished Documents

Bigwin Inn. Title Search. December 1990.

Bigwin Inn. Inventory of Eighty-Five Architectural Plans.

Index

Abbott, Fred **90**
Abbott, Imogene **82**, **90**
Astaire, Fred **102**
Atkinson, Joseph E. **90**, **93**, **107**
Beatrix, Princess 67
Beer, Mrs. Walter 30
Bernard, Prince of Lippe-Biesterfield 67
Big Wind, Chief Joseph 9, 11
Bigwin, Bill 11
Bigwin, Chief John 11, **12**, 20, **85**, **102**
Blakely, Mrs. Olive Barlow 4
Boothby, Edward 9
Bowker, Margaret 78
Bratti, R.P. 127
Bridgland, Clark Benton 9, **12**
Bridgland, Henry Hugh 9
Briscoe, Lieut. Henry 9
Cadman, Charles 60
Cameron, Ross **73**
Capellacci, Ernie **113**
Cardy, Bruce 105
Cardy, Hilda Bouvier 105, **109**
Cardy, Vernon G. 105, **109**
Carmichael, Franklin **96**
Carnegie, Andrew 60
Carswell, Bill 30
Clark, Greg **73**, **93**
Clarke, Herbert L. **19**, 20, 52
Conway, Mrs. C.W. 105
Dee, Sandra **116**
Defoe-McTaggart, Hazel **44**
Deer, Louie (Os-Ke-Non-Ton) 52
Del Zotto, Angelo 127
Deyell, Betty **82**
Diamond, Hillel **113**
Diefenbaker, Prime Minister John 70

Dwight, Harvey Prentiss 9
Eaton, John David 52
Ehrenfeld, Nick 124
Elder, Captain 4, 79, **85**
Ensign, Frank G. 52
Ewanski, Wally **113**
Ferguson, Miss Edith 105
Fields, W.C. **102**
Fleming, Miss Amy 4, **56**
Forsythe, Samuel 42, **73**
Gable, Clark **85**
Garbo, Greta **102**
Gershwin, George **102**
Gibson, Charles J. 79
Gill, Pauline **90**, **95**, 105
Gill, Colonel Robert J. 105
Goffat, Thomas 9
Gouldie, Edmund James 9
Graham, Martha **102**
Grewar, Sid **58**
Grosso, Vincent 17
H.R.H. Princess Juliana 67
Hague-Defoe, Annie **44**
Hallman, Art (and orchestra) **115**
Hanley, Margot 30
Hemingway, Ernest **93**
Hill "Nipper" 79
Hodgson, Fred T. 30
Holden, John 52
Hosking, Roxie Joy 67
Hughes, Bob **58**
Irene, Princess 67
Irvine, Miss Helen **43**
James-Kennedy, Leonora 52, 60
Johnson, Pauline **96**
Kieswetter, Cecilia **132**

Lackner, Mrs. Graham 4
Lambert, Gregory 124, 127
Lambert, Gregory Brian 127
Leeder, Reg 79
Leslie, Audrey Correen Mills 108
Leslie, Frank Mills 108, **110**
Leslie, Frank Shepard 108, 109, **110**, **113**, **117**
Leslie, George Elmer 124
Leslie, George Ross 108
Leslie, Martha Louise 124
Leslie, Ruth Eleanor 108
Lobraico, Joseph Anthony 124
Lobraico, Paul Andre 124, **125**
Lobraico, Sandra 124, **125**
Lombard, Carole **85**
Lorenzetti, Aldo 127
Margriet, Princess 67
Marsh, Captain George Francis **84**
Marshall, Harvey **56**
Martin, Jack **58**
Maxwell, Lois **132**
May, Captain 79
Meighen, Prime Minister Arthur **70**
Miller, Miss Irene **43**
Mitchell, Red **113**
Morden, Malcolm **63**
Morris, Roger William 127
Murray, Alexander 9
MacKenzie, Gisele LaFleche **113**
MacLennan, H. Alexander 105
MacMillan, H.R. 52
MacMurray, Sidney 127
McConnell, J.W. 52
McFarlane, James 67
McKee, John W. 20, 60, 67, 105
McLean, J.S. 52

140

McLennan, Carl **95**
McNally, Mrs. James 78
McTaggart, Douglas **44**
McTaggart, Paul **44**
O'Connell, Christine **82**, **83**
O'Neill, Terence E. 127
Paul, Vince 127
Pechin, Ernest 52
Peck, Cameron 87
Pesando, Signor Jocko 73
Pesando, Mario **88**, **94**, **102**
Player, William 128
Ponzo, James 127
Pratt, John 10
Rayfield, Lorne **58**
Reid, James G. **19**, 62, **64**, 105
Reid, Mr. and Mrs. 42, **90**
Reinhart, Bob **113**
Roberts, Arthur 124
Roell, Madame 67
Rogers, Ginger **102**
Roy, Mr. **92**
Rutherford, George 20, **94**
Scheckenberger, H.J. 127
Scollard, Bill 79
Shaw, Allan Thaxter 4

Shaw, Amanda Paulley 105
Shaw, Anne 90
Shaw, Brackley **83**, **90**
Shaw, Brackley II 10
Shaw, Mrs. C.G. **82**, **89**, **90**
Shaw, Mrs. C.O. 4, 60
Shaw, Charles Orlando 10, **16**, 17 **19**, 20, 27, **32**, 35, 39, 52, **54**, **59**, 62, 67, 71, 74, 78, 79, 80, **81**, **95**, **102**, 105
Shaw, Charles 17, 67, **82**
Shaw, Charles George 42, 79, **80**, **83**, 105
Shaw, F. 10
Shaw, Jennie Lavinia **16**, 17, 39
Shaw, Pauline and Jennifer 17
Shaw, Ralph **82**
Shaw, Rena **82**
Shaw, Walter Brackley **88**
Shay, Allan 10
Sherkin, Louis 127
Shuttleworth, Miss Edythe 85
Simmons, George R, 17
Sinclair, Gordon 78
Sparling, Gordon **75**
Stott, Jack 127
Temple, Shirley **102**
Terziano, Ed **58**

Thompson, David 9
Tinkiss, Captain and Mrs. William P. **21**, 67, 79, **111**
Valentine, Emilio 127
Valle, Chicho 109, **113**
Van Horne, William Cornelius 20
Wall, E.A. Sr. 20
Wells, H.G. **93**
Weston, Garfield 52
White, E.B. **73**
White, Thomas J. 27
Wiggins, James 56
Wilson, Ann McAllister 30, 74
Wilson, Daniel 30
Wilson, J. Donald 30
Wilson, John 27, 30, **32**, 35, 42, 62, **66**, 67, 74, **120**
Wilson, John McAllister 30, 74
Wilson, Mary J. 30
Wilson, Robert 30
Wilson, Walter A. (Bill) 30
Wilson, Walter C. 30
Wiman, Erastus 9
Wright, Frank Lloyd **66**, **120**
Young, Jack **58**
Zentil, Joseph 127